From Boys to *Men of Heart*

...Advance Reviews of

Randall Eaton's

From Boys to Men of Heart

Hunting As Rite of Passage

"In depth exploration of the Hunter's world, philosophically, culturally, spiritually. The book talks to the philosopher, psychologist, conservationist, wildlife manager, the clergy and the Hunter. A major contribution to literature,"

Bob Norton, Ph.D., Professor Emeritus of Psychology, U. of Wisconsin, author of *The Hunter: Developmental Stages And Ethics*

"In his new book...he argues that to understand hunting is to understand a great deal about men that has heretofore remained hidden...I find this argument quite persuasive. *From Boys to Men of Heart* is a penetrating and masterful piece of scholarship that interweaves at least a dozen disciplines into a profound theory of male development. Eaton shows us how embattled our culture has become, and how dangerous. He provides an intriguing formula for recovery, one that harmonizes nature with male spiritual development...his scientific background is uniquely qualified both to expose our culture's weaknesses and provide clues to our better survival. This book ...will become a major title in the future."

Michael Gurian, best-selling author of *The Wonder of Boys, A Fine Young Man* and *The Purpose of Boys*

Randall Eaton offers a compelling account of how the sacred act of hunting can help realign our culture and consciousness with the rhythms, patterns, and laws of nature. In this comprehensive treatise, Eaton chronicles hunting as an ancient and timeless right of passage; one that can provide boys with an opportunity to participate fully in nature's complex dance of life and death. Randall's keen observations and deep understanding of this process clearly comes from a lifelong practice and passion for the sacred hunt. His message is critical for anyone concerned about the health and well being of the Earth.

Matt Kolan, Lecturer, Rubenstein School of Environment and Natural Resources, University of Vermont

"In a world where disrespect and violence prevail, it may seem an irony to call for hunting as a way to regain a sense of balance in our world. However, Randy has synthesized the wisdom of the ages in this book in an engaging argument that makes this very point. Whether you are a hunter or are anti-hunting, the material in this book will reveal some ancient truths and ways of knowing that can stop the downward spiral that modern humanity has created on this planet."

Four Arrows, aka Don Trent Jacobs, Ph.D., Ed.D., author of *Primal Awareness, Unlearning the Language of Conquest, Teaching Virtues, and Social Neuroscience* and *Indigenous Wisdom.*

"Nothing less than brilliant....some of Randy Eaton's writings in this book are among the most quotable I have read since Aldo Leopold's. His belief in the importance of hunting and the outdoor experience to mankind is a great but unrecognized truth in our urbanized and cyberized world."

Larry Marchinton, Ph.D., Professor Emeritus of Wildlife Biology, University of Georgia

"Very interesting, provocative and timely....wonderful."

Valerius Geist, Ph.D., Professor Emeritus of Environmental Design, University of Calgary and internationally recognized wildlife authority

"Brilliant!...Dr. Eaton has elevated the subject of hunting to the heights of true philosophical inquiry and (his book) ranks...with Ortega's *Meditations On Hunting*.

Tom Dolph, author of *Book of the Hunt: Initiation to a Life of Honor*

"Dr. Eaton is a fearless writer...where others have...taken a feeble undisciplined stab at description and/or explanation of why man hunts, Eaton's writing puts a fine point on the relevant questions and attacks them with uncommon scholarship...drawn from numerous discipline...he argues that hunting is a psycho-spiritual necessity in the development of boys and men...His points are well made and his arguments convincing...Eaton's writings are important, long over due and most welcome....broad reaching implications not only for the hunting community but to society at large...stands to make a positive contribution to rearing children in modern society. His work deserves our attention and support."

Craig Dougherty, Ph.D., Chairman of the Board, Quality Deer Management Association

"As an outdoorsman, and a teacher, I spend equal amounts of time surrounded by those who love, and despise, the act of the hunt. If ever there were a book that could foster true understanding and respect between Hunters and non Hunters ...this is it."

Elias Putney, Waldorf Teacher and Screen Writer

"*From Boys to Men of Heart* is a fascinating and comprehensive defense of hunting, looking primarily at how the practice of hunting in cultures all over the world serves to enhance the senses and sensibilities of boys as they develop into young men. Dr. Eaton uses a variety of means to present a compelling argument, ranging from scientific evidence and first-hand interviews to legends, stories and personal experience. This book is sure to open people's eyes to the significance of hunting as central to the human experience."

Richard Kyte, Ph.D., Director,
Reinhart Institute for Ethics in Leadership,
Viterbo University

"I love the way this book has us look more deeply into 'hunting', avoiding the usual black-white quick answer that stops fertile consideration. In our world today most of us can too easily detach ourselves from the truth that we must kill in order to live. Eaton returns us to the sacred nature of this relationship, the 'giveaway' that it is and that was deeply honored by indigenous peoples, and to the natural and sacred ceremony of killing, and of death itself."

Meredith Little, Co-founder of
The School of Lost Borders,
co-author, *Book of the Vision Quest*

Randall Eaton, Ph.D., a wildlife biologist, is part Aldo Leopold and part tribal Shaman. His intellectual curiosity allows him to explore the world of science as well as the primitive world of spiritualism. By morphing science and spiritualism together Randall has created an unsurpassed depth of understanding of the world of hunting, land management and ethics. I recommend his work to all who are curious about our natural world.

Rob Arnaud, Wildlife Manager
and Big Game Outfitter.

ALSO BY RANDALL L. EATON:

The Sacred Home: A Guide to Sustainability

The Sacred Hunt: Hunting as a Sacred Path – An Anthology

The Orca Project – A Meeting of Nations

The Human/Animal Connection (Editor)

My Animals, My Teachers

Zen and the Art of Hunting

Marine Shoreland Fauna of Washington (Editor)

Evolutionism or n+1 (poetry)

The Status and Conservation of the Leopard in Sub-Saharan Africa

The World's Cats: Volumes I, II and III (Editor)

The Cheetah: Nature's Fastest Racer

The Cheetah: The Biology, Ecology and Behavior of an Endangered Species

From Boys to *Men of Heart*
Hunting As Rite of Passage

by Randall L. Eaton

With Interviews of
Michael Gurian
Jon Young
Don Four Arrows Jacobs
Wade Brackenbury
and James D. Rose

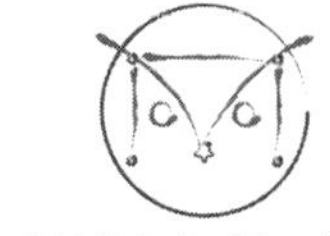

OWLink Media

210 SE Cedar Hill Lane
Shelton, Washington 98584

~ 2 0 0 9 ~

From Boys to Men of Heart
Hunting as Rite of Passage
by Randall L. Eaton, Ph.D.

ISBN: 978-1-57994-026-3

FIRST PRINTING ~ 2009

OWLink Media, 210 SE Cedar Hill Lane,
Shelton, Washington 98584.

For information about other titles please visit
www.owlinkmedia.com.

For information about other work by
Dr. Randall L. Eaton, please visit
www.randalleaton.com

Cover Art:
Jodi Bergsma

Cover & Book Design:
Paul Cirac
White Sage Studios
Drawer G, Virginia City, NV 89440

~ Printed in the United States of America ~

To the significant mentors in my life:

Ray Carpenter, Dan Eaton, Bill Lyons Sr.,
Clarence Garbolino, Bill Shad,
Jack Hills, Udell Meyers, Dave Casteel,
Gordon Orians, Bill York, Walter Gassaway,
Charles Cameron Stephen Barr, Milton Freeman
and Jon Young.

To my sons, Robb and Drake.

To Men of Heart *everywhere.*

To the Animals.

Contents

Acknowledgements

Thanks to Jon Young and OWLink Media for publishing this book, Peter Schlenzka for funding it, and Deb Winters for facilitating the process. Thanks to Jon Young, Wade Brackenbury, Don Four Arrows Jacobs, Michael Gurian and Jim Rose for permission to use the interviews I did of them in the Sacred Hunt video series. Thanks to Marty Stouffer for allowing me to use portions of his interview of Peter John, Athabascan elder. Thanks also to Michael Meade, Jon Young and John LaFountain for inspiration and ideas about rites of passage. Joe Pearce has inspired me for years and also has generously granted permission to quote him often. Thanks go to Erich Klinghammer for provocative discussions about animal behavior, imprinting and human development. Gary Snyder has been exemplary in thinking about our relationship to food and animals, and he, Paul Shepard, Dick Nelson and Jon Young have looked wisely to indigenous societies for answers we need today. Special thanks go to my grandfather, Ray Carpenter, who demonstrated in a profound life crisis a deep personal transformation to a man of heart who then became the most important mentor in my life.

For constructive comments on the manuscript I give special thanks to Jon Young, Matt Kolan, Josh Lane, Rick Kyte, Rob Arnaud, Larry Marchinton, Elias "Tuna" Kolsun, Chris Reynolds and my son, Drake Eaton, who also contributed some of his poetry. Thanks to Cathy Eaton and Dan Eaton for all their help. Thanks go to Jodi Bergsma for the lovely cover art and to Paul Cirac for his excellent design. Thanks to Barry Moses for contributing his story, and to Charles Cameron for his insights.

Preface

There has been much study and speculation in the last hundred years about the different modes of perception and understanding that human beings can experience. The range spans everything from the rational, calculated knowledge of the sciences to the kinesthetic-emotional knowing of the intuition that is the foundation of the arts. To look at a subject from just one of these perspectives seems incomplete at best. Although we may benefit from diving fully into one approach or the other at times, in the end there are many approaches, and "the Way is not the Way."

Indeed the last quarter century has seen a significant movement towards integrated fields of study that bridge the different realms of experience. Through this synthesis, an even more powerful era of discovery and understanding has been entered.

This book gives us a deep look at both the heart and mind of a hunter. Dr. Eaton explores through powerful first-hand experiences the ways that hunting as a rite of passage can enhance a person's life and serve as a bridge between the intellect and emotion, leading to the deep empathetic connections and understandings that create lasting stewards of the land and animals. The archetypal hunter relies on both skill and a deeper sense of trust and reciprocity in the larger field of life for a successful hunt. The mind must be in accord.

To read this book fully requires an opening of the heart – a willingness to let a poetic vision of the mystery of the hunt to arise and complement the rational. There is poetry even in mathematics, if we care to look for it, and how much more so in this most ancient of human rites. It is up to each of us whether our "hunt" – whatever it is in our life that we are hunting for – is a sacred one. For this reason, Randall's book leads us on a trail of discovery that can offer perspective on all of our journeys.

~ Josh Lane, Mentoring Specialist,
Shikari Tracking Guild,
Santa Cruz, CA

The hunter is older than the hills,
younger than the morning.

Interviews of
Michael Gurian
Jon Young
Don Four Arrows Jacobs
Wade Brackenbury
and James D. Rose

JON YOUNG, author of *Animal Tracking Basics* and *Coyote's Guide to Connecting with Nature*;

DON FOUR ARROWS JACOBS, Ph.D., Ed.D., author of *Primal Awareness* and *Teaching Virtues: Building Character Across the Curriculum*;

WADE BRACKENBURY, D.C., Former Field Supervisor, School for Urban and Wilderness Studies, author of *Yak Butter, Black Tea*;

MICHAEL GURIAN, best-selling author of *The Wonder of Boys, The Good Son* and *The Purpose of Boys*; and

JIM ROSE, Ph.D., Professor Emeritus, Departments of Psychology and Zoology, University of Wyoming.

Why Hunting Is Good Medicine for Kids

"The way of knowledge is like our old way of hunting. You begin with a mere trail – a footprint. If you follow that faithfully it may lead you to a clearer trail – a track – a road. Later on there will be many tracks, crossing and diverging one from the other. Then you must be careful, for success lies in the choice of the right road."

~ Many Lightenings Eastman, *Santee Sioux*

Native Americans view education as a process that includes difficulty, risks and hardship, and much time with the help of an elder. For primal people, learning is not achieved by creating an artificial environment, such as a school. Learning is not pursued for its own sake, but rather is about life itself.

Gail Keffer, with whom I dined last night, told me about his experience in the public schools. He taught an outdoor education program for a number of years in the schools of Springfield, Oregon, and when he took out the boys who were doing poor in school and causing problems for their teachers he launched them into playful discovery: getting on hands and knees crawling through brush or marshes looking for scats, droppings, or tracking animals and figuring out what they were doing.

In every case, the boys lives were turned around and parents were immensely grateful, but Keffer told them he didn't do anything but let them follow their own natural instincts to learn about nature and animals. He sees institutional education as unnatural and artificial, ultimately counter-productive. He says that young people can learn to read and write and do math in the outdoors, too, and cited one case where a failing fourth grade student came to him with a turtle he had been given by his father. Keffer was not sure what to feed it nor did he know what species it was so he suggested to the boy that he go to the local library, ask the librarian for help finding books on reptiles and find out what he could. The boy did so and in the process not only learned about the turtle and how to care for it but also about other reptiles and wild animals.

He became an outstanding student because his natural proclivity was aligned with education, i.e., made relevant.

My own story is much the same. From my teenage passion for hunting ducks came a fascination for the natural history of waterfowl. To this day my eyes still scan the sky looking for flights of ducks and geese. Not unlike my first year in graduate school in Seattle when I was walking to the campus and heard Canada geese. Right there in the middle of the university district was a flock of geese flying low over the buildings and honking. I pointed to the sky with my left arm and yelled out "Geese!." On that busy street no one heard the geese overhead or responded to my shout or gesture. And that is the difference between a person who grew up with animals and nature as his teachers and people who succumbed to the illusion that learning is its own reward. Though I have lived in their world, for me nature is different, more interesting and alive, and unlike so many I never feel alone.

Philosopher Jose Ortega y Gasset would agree with the Lakota that learning is about life. The sooner we restructure education in light of what is natural for us the better. Moreover, we must escape the prison of pious idealism and intellectualism and reset learning on the authentic fact of life as interdependent relationship between us and our circumstances, giving nature the status of school room. An organization in Tennessee, Kids in the Outdoors, has worked with educators to develop a K12 curriculum taught completely in the outdoors.

Tracking, Mentoring and Nature Education:

An Interview of Jon Young

JON YOUNG is the founder of an international movement based on mentoring nature connection. He currently works with the Regenerative Design Institute as a master teacher, and travels internationally helping communities develop effective nature education systems. He founded the 8 Shields Institute to support this work, as well as OWLink Media, and is the founder and former director of the Wilderness Awareness School with headquarters in Duvall, Washington. Jon was the first person to be mentored by Tom Brown Jr., who was mentored for years by Stalking Wolf, an Apache medicine man. Stalking Wolf had told Tom Brown that he would recognize his first learner "by the sign he carried." Tom kept a vigilant watch for years before he met Jon Young, who was standing on a street corner with a large snapping turtle on a string. Tom saw this as "Mother Earth on a string" and realized this might be the sign. Later, Stalking Wolf confirmed that Jon was the right choice.

After decades of learning about cultural mentoring from traditional communities around the world, Jon has become a global leader in mentoring people to nature and is promoting sustainable, self-replicating communities and regenerative design. He is the author of *Exploring Natural Mysteries, The Kamana Naturalist Training Program*, and the *Shikari Tracker Training Program*, and co-author of *Animal Tracking Basics* and *Coyote's Guide to Connecting with Nature*. Additionally, Jon has produced many audio programs for training and listening enjoyment.

The following interview is derived from my video production, "Respect and Responsibility: The Truth About Kids Who Hunt." I am convinced that the kind of mentoring Jon and his associates offer is the ideal way to connect young people to nature, and prepare them for a lifetime of hunting, fishing and responsible stewardship of the earth.

RE: What is the mission of Nature Connection Mentoring? Why do you do it?

JY: The reason we focus on Nature Connection Mentoring is to take people on a journey. Their senses are dulled, their experiences are artificial, they don't really have access to their hearts. Not to say that everybody who comes from the Western world is in that state, but a great many of them are. I think I can sum it up with what my friend, Gary, says, "When I look at all the experts I know, the Ph.D.s, the sports heroes in the NBA, and I think about the folks whom you have mentored in tracking, I'd much rather spend the holidays with your trackers than any of these fancy people who are experts." He's talking about all the people he has to rub elbows with in the Bay Area in California. He's the founder of an organization called the Riekes Center for Human Enhancement, so he was just observing that there's some quality of spirit of gentleness, of goodness, in people who come from our programs, and he's seen it consistently, and he asks, "Can you bring that spirit to the Riekes Center? We need to overcome some of the things that people are suffering from."

He sees it as a kind of suffering, and I agree. I feel it is truly a type of suffering, I think it is also a form of poverty. The spirit of the nature connection mentoring movement is to provide a healing journey, a healing path. The vision brings people on a journey through their senses for more than reading or writing, as you utilize your senses for reading the stop sign or walking into your door or doing the things that become rote or a rut for us in our modern life. You develop a patterning experience. I know that this gear, this brain, these eyes, these ears, this nose, this body, was designed for its three million-year history, which is interaction with and connection with nature. It's not really designed for what modern people try to apply it for, and so doing they get off course, they can't follow their instructions, so to speak, so the DNA is saying one thing and the lifestyle is saying something else, and there's a confusion that results from that – people don't know who they are.

Our mission is simply this: Connect people to nature, themselves and the other people in their lives… let's get people back to what they were designed for. Let's get them out of the idea that this is about philosophy or religion or ideology. It's not. It's simply about neuro-muscular patterning in the natural world.

RE: Give me an example of the kinds of experience a young person can get in one of your programs that is likely to be transformative.

JY: We use a whole collection of teachings that we work with. The Art of Mentoring is a body of teachings. There's hundreds of techniques in there that are drawn from things we see universally in native tribes around the world. This material is now represented in *Coyote's Guide to Connecting with Nature.* We researched tribes in North America, and not only through anthropology and anthropological sources, but also directly from the elders themselves, in Hawaii and other parts of the world, Australia, Africa. We have direct descendents from native tribes in these areas who have consulted with us, and we see again and again a tool box of things that are done for children. Essentially that tool box is built on the hunter-gatherer lifestyle and the cultural framework in which a person grows. You can draw on and model these experiences without hunting or gathering. What you end up hunting is knowledge. You hunt information about tracks, or you gather plants with kids, but liability issues being what they are some parents don't even want you to gather with their children, to eat berries or pick leaves.

People may experience a variety of things from that setting, and it's very flexible and we tailor it to each group and to each location. The most powerful tool that people like most is the sense of adventure. When we're going out on a wander, a lot of times we'll feign the sense that we're lost. The instructor will say, "I'm not sure how to get back, do any of you know?" To give them that sense, "Oh, my God, I haven't been paying attention," just to wake them up. Or we go on adventures to look for something, it's the treasure hunt, whatever form it ends up taking.

Often there's a group going in one direction and another instructor out there with folks over here, and an instructor will stop and say, "Shhh, do you hear that? I think the other group's trying to sneak us," and all these kids' light switches go on. We have what we call the child passion's toolbox. What does that mean?

The things that you and I did when we were little, that no one had to tell us, the things that we spontaneously enjoyed, that caused us to feel alive and electric, and Mom had to come out and hunt for us in the station wagon to get us to come home for dinner because we're having so much fun we forgot ourselves, those are the tools that we're drawing from because that's the source of energy that is in all of us, not just children, because every one of us is still a child inside. When you connect those kinds of activities to real learning experiences where you'll able to say, "OK, building on this adventure and the exciting time these kids are experiencing in the field, we're going to draw in knowledge of plants, animals, tracks, the old skills, and build on them in a way that people don't notice that they're learning anything."

The kind of programming we facilitate in the nature connection movement, at our trainings at the Regenerative Design Institute, and throughout our affiliated network of programs is really very different from what people currently expect when they attend an educational program or school. In a way Wilderness Awareness School (the program Jon founded in 1983) is a misnomer because the kids don't perceive it as school. They perceive it as a bunch of instructors who are misguided but fun, hapless but with a sparkle in their eyes, mischievous and, "Hey, you know, he doesn't know much but he sure is cool." But the truth of the matter is that the instructors know a real lot, and they sometimes play dumb, and when they're in a situation they always ask questions and help folks develop their own inquiry skills, and develop their own creative expression, "Hey, I think I know the way back. I think we ought to go that way." "Oh yeah, why do you say it's that way?"

We let people express what they sense and what they feel, and in that way we're constantly profiling people's interaction with their own sensory experience, their own sense of confidence or courage or whatever it is that's within them that they can express. We read their body language, and from the peoples' point of view it's an adventure, it's fun, it's mischievous, but from an instructor's point of view, it's an art, it's a science, they're watching everyone carefully. Though instructors appear somewhat in the moment, they all have goals for the participants learning and experience, and of course we might reach them in a week-long program because we throw so many of those child's passion tools at the children in our summer camp that they go home and their parents say, "What did you do to our child?" Because he's talking so fast when he gets home, and the mom says, "My child never talks. What did you do? She wouldn't shut up all the way home." Or, "When I got home she was hopping around the garden like a rabbit, and I can't get her to stop imitating animals. What have you been doing with these people?"

From the participant's point of view—whether young, middle-aged, or elders, they don't even know what it is. They have mixed feelings even inside – they can't describe it, because we're hitting on so many of those old (genetic) memories within them that they want to turn on.

RE: How do these experiences influence the rest of their lives? Do they have life-long consequences?

JY: They are life skills. There is no more life skill than what we are talking about right here because this is all about knowing life, about what it means to be alive, and so everything they do has a transference value. For instance, they learn that when they first walk into the forest off the city streets that they have a very big ripple effect on the forest. Their presence is known not only by the sounds they make, by the clumping of their boots and their loud Gortex jackets, but their unconscious awareness even of their own bodies and how they're relating to their bodies, but they also have this loud mind – it's the only way to explain it – they come with it into the forest and they send a ripple out there.

The birds know they're coming as they're getting out of the car, and the birds are already moving to different positions in the trees, and they're sending out alarms, and the deer are getting up and moving out of the way, just a little bit away because they know they don't have to be Houdinis to hide from these guys, they're not going to be very aware anyway. The fox takes a new position, the bobcat slips away. I explain that to them, "You guys, when I'm in the woods by myself, it's a totally different world. I and these other trackers here, this young lady, this young man to my right and left, we don't have that impact on things. As a matter of fact, kids, we know you're coming ten minutes before you get here." So we can hide and pull stunts on them, and a lot of times we prove that to them.

The impact of that is profound. We basically say, "Look, what you need to do is get your awareness bigger than it is right now. Your awareness is so small that you hold it close to your body like a garment. You're not even aware of the loudness of your feet, you're not even listening to the impact of your body on the ground around you, so your awareness is small, your ripple is huge, and what we're asking you to do is to pull your ripple in and push your awareness out then you're going to start to see the animals because at some point in this journey they have that need to see the animals. There is a longing that these kids express and that is, "I'm in the woods," and this applies to adults, too, "but I don't feel part of it. I'm walking through these woods and know somehow I'm related to it, but I can't make the connection. I go hiking all the time, I go bird watching, I go out in the woods, but I always feel like an intruder, and that breaks my heart. I have a longing to heal that somehow."

This journey that I'm talking about when the ripple and the awareness switch heals that longing to feel connected with nature. It's very hard to put your finger on it in terms of when and where it happens. It's a cumulative effect of a lot of mind-brain repatterning experience in nature, and spiritual connections develop and all kinds of things happen that are nothing less than miraculous, really, and as a result when they walk into a room they sense themselves as though walking into a forest, and they act differently. They don't bulldoze their way into a crowd, energetically. They look carefully at whose in front of them, and they consider them carefully before they speak to them, and choose their words carefully.

As my friend Gary says, they become kind and gentle people, who really know how to reach out and be empathetic and sincere because they're authentically in their being. I can't think of a field in life in which you would not do better if you were authentically in your body, if you were fully present in each moment. The only place that would not work would be if you were in a situation where you had to do something cold-hearted because there's no way that trackers don't feel. Trackers become better people. Tracking has wide transference: pattern recognition; learning to see beyond the surface; learning to question; not taking things at face value. These are things that help them in any setting whether it's in the wilderness or the modern world. But maybe the most important thing is that they get to know themselves, they begin to hear their own voice, they know that even their thoughts send concentric rings or ripples through their own being and they create mischief in their own body just in the same way that their thoughts create mischief in the forest. So the microcosm within the macrocosm keeps repeating itself.

RE: How is your program like or different than hunting in terms of initiation to adulthood?

JY: These tools that we work with in this program are drawn from hunter-gatherer societies, so it has many parallels to hunting, to fishing. I grew up with a fishing pole in my hand and did a lot of hunting when I was younger, and I see the total correspondence to what we do. Some of our strongest supporters are hunters. They see it right away, "Yeah, we see in your kids what my grandfather did for me."

Even in Hawaii a woman was asking me about the art of mentoring, and I said, "Tell me about how you grew up?" She's a native traditional healer, though she denied it, "Oh no, I'm not, they say that about me, but I'm just a regular person just like you." I said, "That's what they all say." She said, "My mother would bring me down to the river and we'd catch these little shrimp, you know. She'd go and take a stick and beat on the bushes and we'd catch these little tiny shrimp. Then we'd put them on a hook and catch that fish in the river," a species she used an Hawaiian name for, "I still do that now, I still go down to that river now," she's a woman in her 50s, "and I hit those bushes, and people come over to me and ask what I'm doing, and I tell them I'm catching those little shrimp, and people ask me why and I say because that is what my mother taught me."

So I said, "Well those are the things that the art of mentoring focuses on. It's not just the Hula and the language that are important, it's all these little things that you never thought of that were taught to you by your mother or your grandmother when you were a kid that prepared you to be a hunter-gatherer."

They had hunting and fishing traditions all over the world, and there's a tool box that goes with it. I might say this: not only is hunting parallel to tracking, our program augments hunting. When our program ends, hunting begins. There's a practical side to what we do, and hunting may not be appropriate for some of the audiences that we reach, but everything we do dovetails perfectly with hunting. Everybody who is on the path in these programs comes to a point where they feel the need to hunt, and they hunt, and they hunt in a sacred manner, they need to approach it that way. It's not about the firearm or archery experience; for them it's about harvesting in a sacred way because that's been emphasized again and again in our program because the things we eat, even berries, are treated with that kind of respect. But it all sneaks up on them slowly because at first they're not ready to hear that. Through continuous patterning in nature they are prepared.

RE: What are the consequences of mentoring young people in tracking and/or hunting for society and the environment? What are the benefits?

JY: I don't want to be another person jumping on a bandwagon, but the World Trade Center experience is a poignant thing that keeps coming back and recycling through my mind. I know this intuitively: if the people on any of those jets had been trackers, the terrorists never would have gotten away with it. Because the pre-incident indicators that trackers experience are so strong that they know a deer's going to step out in front of them a minute before it happens. Because of a lack of training of human instinct, we've lost much of our abilities. There's a lot of people who know this, who study this, in law enforcement, who investigate people who have experienced crises. They say that in every situation, people have had indicators that something was going to happen, but more than that, as a tracker, I know this: a person comes into a room – I don't have to look at them, I don't have to make eye contact with them to sense their intent. I know what they're thinking, in a sense, I know what they're up to, and I can see what they're going to do before they do it. It's there; it's there for the reading. I learn this from the animals, I learn this from the sensitive nature that I have to develop to be a tracker, and it is the gift of bird language, the gift of tracking in a deep and long-term way that can't be taken from a human being, but which empowers them to be stronger as human beings. I consider tracking to be a domestic national security measure. Can we awaken our sleeping public? Can we awaken them out of the dream they exist in, which exists in some commercial, and bring them back to the sacredness of what it means to be alive?

RE: Are you suggesting that we'd have a different military today if they had been mentored in tracking and hunting?

JY: We may be dependent on high-tech gear, but we would kick some ass! Much of what I'm describing about tracking is from a hunter tradition, but it's also from a warrior tradition, and I draw heavily on my own ancestry now. On both the Polish and the Irish sides there were great warriors. The Hussars from Poland had their connection with the animals. They gained their power from awareness and from hunting and gathering, and they honored a kind of sacredness of life. No one messed with them. When the Hussars rode out it was time to hit the road, and the same thing was true of the Irish tradition. In times of peace, the Red Branch Knights were the bards, the singers and story-tellers, they were the ones who mentored the children and taught the ways of the forest, and in time of war you didn't want to be on the wrong side of them, and that's the spirit that's missing today. I don't think our youth have that; I don't think our country has that anymore – the honorable warrior.

I love the story from Tony Ten Fingers, whose from the lineage of Crazy Horse. He says that Crazy Horse would not bring warriors into his war party who couldn't cry. He wouldn't ride with men who had grown cold and sharp in their life or who were hateful or prejudiced. He only took men who cried from the sensitiveness they felt because they knew the value of life and they saw the sacredness in all things. Our warriors would be like that if they grew up tracking and hunting, and I think that's what warriors need to be.

RE: What lies ahead for Western civilization if it does not heed the call to recover tribal values, aboriginal values?

JY: Microcosm repeats in the macrocosm. I watch people destroy themselves and their lives. I watch them destroy themselves through workaholic tendencies, through drug addictions, you pick it, whatever demon it is that they obsess on. They pick it and they follow that road, and they destroy themselves and all that's around them. The same thing is going to be true if our population continues in the same direction. There's no question; the writing is on the wall, it's been there for a long time. We can see it. The ecologists know the extrapolation of current trends. It was written on the wall for me in 1983 by learned men of science and internationally acclaimed ecologists, the global presidential reports and everything else. And as a tracker, I watch the tide of life recede. As a young man there were so many life forms that mentored me, and in my short time growing up the forest diminished. The number of frogs, birds, turtles, it's there for me to see: how it goes in our forests is how it's going to go on our planet because it all adds up (tears from JY here).

There's going to be a time when we can't take another debit on that account and we're going to be bankrupt. And it's going to happen either from war, it's going to happen from disease, it's going to happen in some way or another, but it's going to happen. It's already happening in other parts of the world right now, as we sit here enjoying the peace of this moment, of this time. There's other people dying as we speak, in terrible, inhumane ways, and it's all a greater reflection of choices that we made. The Western people have tremendous influence on this planet. We are a small percentage of the planet, but we are huge on the resource consumption side – we're off the charts. If the rest of the world is a little angry at us, I can understand. But we can't go on this way. There's a thousand prophecies that you can quote, and they're all probably potentially true. We need to wake up.

RE: Many of us grieved over the death of many people (9-11 incident), but I have orca friends in Puget Sound who are dying from pollution, and no one's grieving over them. Can we extend our circle of caring beyond humanity?

JY: There is a principle that my uncle, Gilbert Walking Bull, taught me, which translates as, "those that we carry in our hearts." Every human was born with a network that we are connected to, that we are meant to caretake. That network includes our blood family by default, and it includes the ones we love deeply with our hearts, our spiritual friends, our lovers, that we end up marrying and having family with, and it includes a mysterious connection with the natural world. The Creator put all of us here on this earth together with an already preprogrammed network of sorts with which we connect.

I am so connected to the frogs and because of that I am connected to water. As a little boy I sought the frogs. It was an obsession, like a knight on the quest. I had to go to the pond, I had to go to the creek. I had to catch the frogs. It was an impulse.

Each of us is drawn to something, and something in nature is drawn to each of us. When we are living in the modern world we pattern our brain on so many things that insulate us from those feelings, those connections, and we drop our network. We forget about it. We do not only forget about the natural world, we forget the other people around us, but we also forget about ourselves. We lose our love for ourselves, in the sacred way, not the vain way.

When we take kids out in the forest we work with them on a continuous basis, and that caretaker network, that principle, that attribute, awakens naturally, and they awaken in this caretaker network. They might take the cause of the wolf or the forest or they might take up the cause of hunting or fishing, but they will follow the cause of something all by themselves. There will be no need to think about it. It's in the simple act of reconnecting our senses, reconnecting people, in routine ways. Not in one-day workshops as is proposed by environmental education standards, but by having a continuous on-going mentoring relationship between people and nature, that they automatically claim their sacred responsibility to caretake this place that we share. It happens automatically. There is no way to impose that on anyone. No laws, no ideologies, there is nothing that can cause a person to take up that lance of stewardship except through mentoring, whether it is through hunting or fishing or wandering, or in a more conscious way as we do in our programs. We see the results. I'm looking at thousands of people who've been through the program, all of whom have become highly effective in caretaking the rest of the world, including nature.

RE: Do you see proper mentoring in hunting producing that same result?

JY: Proper mentoring in hunting is a continuum of what mentoring people do in tracking. Western people are so far gone that they need some intermediate steps so they can appreciate hunting as more than killing, because they don't see it: "You're just killing!" Yet they themselves don't think about the impact of their lifestyle on their natural world around them, and if they were able to view the impact of their lifestyle they would be horrified. As a matter of fact, when people get through this journey of tracking, they have an ideal of what they think reality is, and one day they wake up and they see the impact of their lifestyle on everything else, and they go into a tailspin. So I think we need to build hunting back into what we're doing here. There will always be those kids who aren't called to the hunt. And there's always been men who have not been called to the hunt, and through time some of these have become the sacred people of their community.

A lot of times hunters have been hunting for many years and one day they awaken and have a spiritual moment when they can no longer take a life, and they become very sort of gentle, sacred teachers in a way. Nonetheless, I think hunting has its place, it has its role in our community... The kinds of mentoring that I'm currently involved in really help the hunting movement, and really bring people to a sense of the sacred harvest. Heck, it brings them into gardening, it brings them into every aspect of interacting with the land that there is, they take up all different lifestyles after taking a journey through the mentoring of tracking. Whether they are men or women, young or old, it strikes that place. They're likely to pick up the hunt at that point and take it all the way. Not only that but then turn around and mentor it backwards, and that's very important, too.

I think the short answer to that question is, "Hunting and nature education are absolutely interdependent."

RE: Does it come down to Western civilization thinking with intellect compared to aboriginal peoples feeling with their hearts?

JY: I think that aboriginal people, especially those that I've been fortunate enough to work with, think with their mind, their heart, their spirit, their soul and their body. They think with the whole package. They think with all they've been given, and the way they look at life is this: "We belong to the Great Spirit, we belong to God, we belong to the Creator, we belong to whatever you want to call that power. We were placed here with sacred instructions, and we listen to our Creator and we live according to the ways of our grandmothers and grandfathers. And we raise whole people, we raise them as whole members of their community with good values and good feelings and connections and caretaking spirits."

I think the modern world says it uses its intellect, but my experience is that native trackers use their intelligence in a far superior way than we do. Intellect does not stand alone. It is not an island unto itself, and when it is an island unto itself, it chases its own tail and builds its own destruction. It's a trickster. It creates it's own mischief. People say that they've got it together when I push them and ask questions when they're out there in the field with me, but these people with long qualifications after their name are not functioning with all of their facilities. I really don't think that they ever use their intellects. Personally, I think it's a myth. I don't think the Western world has got much going at all upstairs. I look at what's going on within our own society. We have no common sense, our children are killing each other. We are our own best example of what we are not accomplishing, or what we are failing to do. They can wave their flags of intelligence all they want, but I still haven't seen any real hard evidence of intelligence, to tell you the truth.

When it comes down to individuals, this nature connection path is healing them all the time, it's working them through their walls, helping them find themselves, helping to put their lives back together. Where do they come from? It's not my fault that they're in that state, but the children are coming to us and they are wounded. That's our Western world. What kind of intelligence did that? That's not intelligence, it's a partially functioning machine. It's not working (tears).

RE: I once wrote that the earth is crying out for more young people to fall in love with it. What's going to happen if civilization does collapse by whatever mischief it created? What significance does the kind of work you're doing have in a post-collapse world?

JY: I had a board of trustees a few years ago that told me I had to grow up and work with a business model if I wanted the WAS to affect the world. "Frankly, John, the world is a business world, you've got to adapt to the times," and all that sort of thing. And I said respectfully to all of them, "I highly value your willingness to help me and I respect you deeply, but make no mistake, what I do is not a business. What I do is a sacred vision."

If the whole business world goes up in smoke tomorrow, you know what I'm going to do? I'm going to continue doing what I do everyday because it's really about living in this world in a responsible manner as a human being. It's not about pleasing any imaginary system that was created in the minds of human beings for a world of commerce or any other thing that's artificial. It matters not. Authentic living heeds not the will of man. It heeds the will of God and this creation. I almost can predict that those who survive through any kind of earth changes that may come will be graduates of a program like this one. They'll be the ones who carry on and carry the knowledge forward because I've been told so. I see it. That's the way it's going to be. The people who live in the cities now, who have no connection with nature whatsoever, it's going to be a dangerous place if that collapse ever happens. It'll be a very dangerous place to be, and I don't imagine that they'll be the ones who survive. I can't imagine it, but I can see the ones who have the hunting, the fishing, the trapping, the ability to build shelter and make fire, the skills of tracking and all that are going to be the ones who know how to be in the right place at the right time and how to make it count when they need to, so it's an insurance policy one way or the other, though I hate to think of it that way. But I also know they have the gifts to be able to do that and to pass on what it means to be a human on this earth regardless of what the Western world does or does not do. If it collapses, life will go on unless all human life is destroyed.

RE: What would you say to parents who are concerned about a child taking up hunting or fishing?

JY: I know a lot of parents are going to be afraid. There are a lot of parents today who shelter their children from anything that could be perceived as dirty, harmful or scarey. I don't think that they want their children to experience the fleshly reality of what death really is. And in many cases, I don't think the parents themselves are ready to face that. Because of that I can only appeal to the parents to take all this in consideration. Maybe they also need to go out in the forest and examine themselves, take time to sit in the stillness and allow birdsong to penetrate their hearts again and get through the agendas that are on their lists. And to look at the goodness that their children receive from the earth directly, and ask the children frankly, "Do you love the earth? Do you like nature? Do you want to be part of it?" Let the children decide what they are drawn to by their hearts, because, in the end, they are not our children. They belong to the next generation. We are their mentors. We're the ones who are supposed to give them all the tools they need to make it, and have health and happiness in the next generation. It's their world, give them a chance, let them experience it, and don't put so many pressures on them to fulfill and reach, all these obligations that children have piled on them that are so unrealistic and so painful. Let them be kids. Let them be barefoot and feel mother earth in their toes, and let the children decide.

Is Hunting Good for Bad Kids?

ESKIMO TEENAGERS who got themselves in trouble in the city have been ostracized to wilderness islands where they had to fend for themselves or die. Some other native peoples have done the same with their youth, with good results. That hunting is good medicine for bad kids also is indicated by the unparalleled success of a wilderness survival program in southern Idaho in which the boys had to gather or kill whatever they ate for two weeks. At the School for Urban and Wilderness Studies (S.U.W.S.), delinquent teenage boys went into the wilderness with nothing but their clothes, a sleeping bag and a pocket knife.

Field Supervisor of S.U.W.S. for 13 years, Dr. Wade Brackenbury, had this to say in "The Sacred Hunt II: Rite of Passage" about the role of hunting in the transformation of the meanest boy he'd taken into the wilderness:

"There was this one boy who was 15 years old, and he was a neo-Nazi. He was in a gang that believed in white supremacy. He was just filled with hatred. I've never known anyone so filled with hate. He came to us because he had taken a shotgun and beat another boy, a little black boy, half to death. We brought him out to the desert where we had him and other boys for about two weeks, and he didn't show any signs whatsoever of changing.

"One of the integral aspects of our program was that we were hunter-gatherers, but we also were hungry most of the time, just as the Indians probably were while they were out there. I remember when we had gone two days without eating anything, and this boy was starving – all he could talk about was food.

"We were trying to get a marmot – a marmot is a large rodent-like animal that lives in the Great Basin Desert…This marmot we were particularly interested in trying to get would come down out of his hole in the morning, we'd watch him over the ridge and just as he'd come to the water we'd get up and run after him and try to chase him and catch up to him before he got back to the hole. And one day finally it got far enough away from the hole that we were able to catch up to it, and that boy chased it underneath a rock. It wasn't able to escape to its hole. He took his hunting knife and bound it to the end of a stick and reached up under there and stabbed the marmot and wounded it. And then we pulled that marmot out.

"I've never forgotten the look on that boy's face as he looked into the marmot's eyes – it wasn't dead yet. It looked up at him and there was this light of understanding or of mutual empathy, then the light went out of the eyes of the marmot and it died. And that boy started crying, just broke down and wept, and the reason he was able to feel that was that he watched that marmot for several days. He'd almost gotten to the point to where he understood who that marmot was, how that marmot lived. I think he almost got inside that marmot and could see the world through the marmot's eyes, and in that way when he hunted down and killed it he had some empathy for it, and I think... that he was able to feel the things the marmot felt.

"Now as the marmot was dying, that boy looked into its eyes and I can remember his face just kind of falling and it became very solemn. And then he started crying, and he tried to resist that because I guess it wasn't manly to cry and then he just broke down and cried and then he wailed. To me it was like a huge abcess inside him had opened up and all this hate and all these terrible things he had done came to the surface and came out through his crying. In fact, he was quite upset for several days and cried for at least two or three days after the incident, and afterward he was a very different boy, a very different young man. In fact, several years later he came back to become a counselor in the program, and I think directly from this one experience which transformed him.

"You've got to understand that this was a boy who'd beaten another boy half to death and had done many violent things in his life but never shown any remorse. You'd think that maybe the act of hunting would bring out more violence in somebody – would bring out more aggression – but in his case and in most of the children I worked with, it was just the opposite. Through the act of hunting and actually killing an animal, they developed a profound respect for life which wasn't available to them in the concrete jungle where they came from.

"In the world we live in, cause and effect have really been separated. You go to school and you study but you don't see meaningful results, but in the wilderness, in that survival situation, if we hunted very diligently we might have something to eat – there was a direct cause and effect relationship. If we didn't succeed we obviously were going to starve. If we worked hard to build a fire with the primitive means we used (no matches or lighter), we were warm and if we didn't we were cold. There's a tremendous amount of empowerment in having that kind of effect over your own destiny, being able to do something directly, physically, and to see something manifest as a result of your effort.

"Those kind of experiences are gone from our life today. Hunting is empowering because food is a basic need right up there with warmth and shelter. The boys had never had to provide for themselves and when they were out in the desert it was suddenly totally on their shoulders to provide food, and the best food we got was meat.

"The most calorie-intensive food we got was meat. We had yampa, we had roots we ate and a few other vegetables, but there's not many calories in these plants so when we got an animal, primarily snakes, lizards and small rodents, and cut it up and cooked it we were full, and we were able to feel good about that.

"We used to do follow-up surveys on the children. The program would send out a questionnaire to the parents a year after the children had gotten back to their homes. About 85% of the families said they had had a significant turn-around in the boy's behavior, that the boy had not gotten into trouble again during that year, and that he had acquired a significantly different outlook on life because of the wilderness survival experience.

"Now, interestingly enough and sad to say, because of the pressures of society we had to change the program around quite a bit in the years that followed. They took out hunting as part of the program. We couldn't hunt by primitive means. We used to hunt by bows and arrows we made and also used to make primitive traps to catch animals.

And they felt it wasn't safe and wasn't right for children to go out and kill animals, and the State considered it cruel for the boys to go without food.

"In my experience – I worked there for 13 years – I was able to see a significant drop in the efficacy of the program that correlated with this removal of the real survival experiences, especially hunting and gathering food, and ever since it's been very, very sad for me.

"I think it's tremendously important for children to have these kinds of experiences, to go out into the wilderness and have this rite of passage. In the concrete jungle of the cities it's very much absent. The boys try to make up for it by forming gangs and going out and doing other things that are terribly detrimental to society, detrimental to themselves, perhaps taking drugs and hurting others. I think they need more of these real cause and effect experiences.

"Hunting is very basic. When I took them out to the desert or to the mountains there seemed to be this ancient wisdom that came up in them. It was almost like an instinct that they had to do these things, an almost instant fulfillment. I saw changes in their lives that I didn't see in other experiences, in other programs, especially not in counseling or putting them in institutions."

Quite possibly the most successful rehabilitation program ever launched for delinquent boys, S.U.W.S. was forced to cancel the most effective component of its curriculum when a boy was goofing around and fell off a cliff and died, which precipitated "official" inquiry by the State which in turn decreed that it was cruel and inhumane punishment to make the boys go without food. There are risks in life, and risk-taking is one of the fundamental ingredients of rites of passage for young males. What made the program so effective was the necessity of survival.

The boys learned to cooperate with one another to feed themselves. They had to undertake genuine observation and study of nature. They had to be inventive and creative to construct traps and weapons from natural materials. They subordinated their own egos to a shared purpose. They faced real risks and overcame them. They discovered first-hand the mystery of life and death and their own impermanence, which engendered humility. They developed a deep sense of self-reliance and self-esteem, and most important perhaps, an abiding respect for living things which died so they might live.

Brackenbury shared with me encounters he had had years later with some of the graduates of the original program. Several of the young men showed him the skins or other parts of animals they had killed and eaten in the desert. They had saved their "trophies," symbols of their rites of passage and a continual connection with the animals that fed them.

The case of the neo-Nazi boy's transformation speaks to the immense power of the hunt as an initiation to manhood. The marmot not only filled the boy's stomach, it also gave him back his heart. It is a poignant example of what poet Robert Bly terms transmuting wounds into gifts for the community. The death of the marmot precipitated the boy's descent into his wounds, and his grieving healed those wounds so well that he came back at the age of 18 to become a counselor and help heal other boys.

Animals can be better teachers of the heart than other humans precisely because our egos do not stand between us and them. When we interact with other people, desire and fear stand between hearts: Can I trust this person? What do they really want from me? Will she break my heart? Will he give me the job I want? It is true that the hunting instinct provides a strong desire to hunt the animal, but normally the animals hunted are as harmless as the marmot the boy killed, i.e., there is nothing to fear from them. The same principle applies to pets: humans often are more affectionate and caring to a pet cat or dog than they are to their own wives or husbands! The boy who hated a black boy enough to nearly kill him, felt no anger or fear towards the marmot which presented no threat. As a result, the marmot could do for the boy what no human could. The taking of a life that sustains us is transformative: it does convert the food chain to a love chain.

Life lives on lives, mythologist Joseph Campbell said, and many animals die to support the life of each one of us. The least we can do is make it possible for our boys to participate in the food chain and thereby gain valuable experiences for which there are no adequate substitutes. Hunting is good medicine for bad kids because it is good medicine for all kids.

Is Hunting the Ideal Way to Teach Universal Virtues?

An Interview of Four Arrows, aka Don T. Jacobs, Ph.D., Ed.D.

FOUR ARROWS is the author of 20 books, including *Primal Awareness: A True Story of Survival, Awakening and Transformation with the Raramuri Shamans of Mexico*; *Teaching Virtues: Building Character Across the Curriculum; Unlearning the Language of Conquest* and *Social Neuroscience and Indigenous Wisdom* (in press). A leading innovator in education and several fields before that, Four Arrows has worked with troubled youth and studied with and taught Indigenous Peoples on several continents. At one time he directed a wilderness program for delinquent boys. In several interviews excerpted from "The Sacred Hunt" video series, he explains how hunting can be made into an effective rite of passage, and why hunting is the ideal way for young people to learn universal virtues. Although Don now goes by his given Oglala name, Wahinkpe Topa (Four Arrows), since during the interview he went by his Anglo name, Don Jacobs, the initials "DJ" are used below.

RE: Can hunting serve as a rite of passage today?

DJ: It is a kind of rite of passage that is missing today. In my work with troubled youth I find that their anger and their sense of intolerance and animosity that leads to gang behavior and killing human beings comes from a lack of that rite of passage. Maybe their callousness comes from watching people shoot and kill on TV, I don't know, but whatever it is, if they could latch onto the comprehension offered by proper initiation to hunting, I think it would draw them to a reverence for all life. They should not be afraid of hunting or guilty about killing an animal, if indeed, they are going to use the animal for food or clothing, but instead can embrace hunting as a connection to this reverence.

I believe that "sacred hunting" experiences transform angry youth in ways that the reverence for animals can be extended to the people for whom their anger was targeted. Of course that reverence would also be directed to the earth and its creatures. I think it is profoundly important to have an experience like this, which in my own case was quite accidental, but could be developed with intention.

RE: Do you think the hunt as rite of passage is more appropriate for boys?
DJ: I think the young men in our society really need a sacred hunt experience. I say young men because women already bleed, and it's men that need to realize the connection between bleeding and life and the life force. I think that before a young man is allowed to take a rifle or bow out to hunt they should experience a certain amount of sacrifice or suffering on the part of that individual. That could be something as simple as a "little death" in a sweat lodge or something to that effect with some conscious dialogue with an elder or someone he respects about the life force in that deer or that animal they're about to hunt. With that sense of suffering there needs to be articulation through language of the relationship between him and his bullet or his arrow and the prey. From this an awareness that is natural but in our society stifled will come forth, and the hunt could become a rite of passage.

RE: What has your experience with indigenous hunters taught you about what hunting offers our youth today?
DJ: My experience with the Raramuri Simarones of Copper Canyon, the subject of my book on *Primal Awareness*, taught me that there is an innate consciousness, if you will, that relates to a state of concentration I think people of all walks and cultures enter into when they go on a hunt. My experience with the Indians taught me to be aware of four influences represented by F.A.W.N. They stand for fear, authority, word and nature. In a nutshell what I mean by that is when we're on a hunt we must comprehend and interpret the feelings of fear that affect our concentration: the fear of killing, the fear of injury, the fear that the animal may have. We then use the identified fear as a catalyst to practice a virtue like patience or generosity.

Then, we must ask whose authority is really operational. In Indigenous ways of knowing, the only true authority is reflection on personal experience in light of understanding that we are all related. Then we see the authority the animal has to teach us. As for "words," our language and our dialogue about hunting: we've got be aware of what it means and what the words evoke in us, that words are vibrational forces in the universe. Finally, and most importantly, we've got to understand our connection with nature, that we are a part and process, and not above it.

RE: Can you explain the relationship between hunting and character education?
DJ: My belief is that the purpose of education is to make good people and smart people. Yet, for the most part our education is focused on academic content. Many of the things that relate to character are being taken away – art, music, drama, but especially spirituality because of a separation of church and state. It has had political ramifications, but largely it's not being taught. Ironically, it is being graded. On almost every report card for first graders there is a little box to put a grade for "civic responsibility" or "citizenship".

Character education is a big deal in many schools but it is mostly Christian religion based or stems from the notion of conservative ideology. It is about earning gold stars and it is anthropocentric. When we remember that it is the animals who are ultimately the teachers of virtues, and this is why children's books on morality usually are about talking animals, then we can develop character more authentically.

Our teaching college, Oglala Lakota College, a four-year tribal college on the Pine Ridge reservation, is, ironically but not coincidentally, the first university in the U.S. in which the whole faculty has been trained in character education and has made it a priority for teacher certification. In spite of the rhetoric that says character education is what we need to do, many of the programs are add-ons and teachers just don't have time, especially with the new state standards. (ed.note: Four Arrows is no longer Dean of Education at OLC, but works as a professor for Fielding Graduate University.)

RE: What is the difference between values and virtues?

DJ: We need to distinguish between virtues and values. Values are preferences and can be local and different for different people. Virtues are universal. Courage, all cultures know that's important, as they do generosity, patience, fortitude, humility and honesty. These are things that need to be woven into all subjects. Not separately taught, not inculcated, but giving children an opportunity to learn them through their own experience. Now it's not just a product of the school. We need to involve the family, the school and the community.

RE: Is it possible to teach virtues in a classroom?

DJ: In our modern times and in our modern world-view of making money and materialism it's really difficult to do the application part because you can't learn virtues unless you have the opportunities to apply them. When you are separate from nature and separate from strong and deep emotional opportunities, those avenues for really being generous and really showing courage and patience and humility are lacking. In nature and especially in hunting, if someone goes into that endeavor with spirituality, and when I say spirituality I'm talking about the awareness that we're all connected, that each of us is part of something greater than ourselves, when one goes out into a wilderness environment it's a different kind of environment. You know you're out there, you're in a sense a part of the food chain, you could get bit by a rattlesnake, you could fall off a cliff. Then, you're involved in the stalking of a fellow creature. If you've already really thought about it and gone out with the right attitude you already know there's going to be generosity involved because what are you going to do with the meat when you get it? You're going to share it. You're going to be generous in how you take that game and you're going to use the training to kill it properly and to make sure you honor its spirit.

You're going to show fortitude because you may be in the cold and wet climate for a long time or it may take a long time, maybe even many days to actually get to the game. That takes patience, humility. When you go into it the right way even when you take a powerful weapon, you go into it with a sense of humility, and when you see this beautiful animal, whether it be a pheasant, a rabbit or a large animal, if you truly feel that this is my teacher, that this is a creature who is giving me its spirit and body for my use, the hunt is something that will make me a better person, will make me more connected to the whole world. That's an experience of humility and you become a better hunter because you're listening more and you're not superior to the whole thing.

RE: It sounds to me like you agree with Mark Twain that we should not let schooling get in the way of our education.

DJ: I really do think experiences in nature are paramount and crucial to what I envision as ideal virtue teaching. But of course students in inner cities don't have that many opportunities so we do what we can in every classroom situation. But if we're working in and talking about nature, I think it would be a good idea to encourage proper hunting. It would move people into natural areas. It would give young people a chance to understand the power of weapons but also about the spirit in life and death and the responsibility that comes with them.. This does not mean people should hunt for the sake of hunting though. Young people must really understand that today's food is unhealthy and that the food taken from a hunt is healthy. When they understand this, and then have a good reason for hunting, and then make the spiritual connection and offer appreciation and do the dirty work of gutting and skinning, etc., then the hunt can be important for their character development. In my diet I'm very reticent to eat meat that is not wild, because of feedlots, artificial hormones and pesticides.

RE: Recreational hunters talk a lot about kids learning respect and responsibility from hunting. Do you agree?

DJ: I really think that respect and responsibility go together. If you have the respect, you will act responsibly. There is a responsibility to our fellow beasts, the four leggeds, the two-leggeds, the swimmers, and crawlers. We have such a responsibility to them. Now interestingly, hunters for the most part have done a great deal to save and preserve wildlife. If it wasn't for hunters I don't think we'd have as much wilderness as we do. But now I'm talking about the hunters that hunt for the right reasons...

RE: How does the hunting experience change a young person's relationship with other people?

DJ: I think that in every hunter who takes an animal, there is a moment when they realize we are brothers. I think there are a lot of hunters who could benefit from understanding how hunting is a spiritual process. Maybe it could be one of the last rites of passage for our young people many of whom otherwise would be going out and taking life in the city streets. There is no respect there, no understanding of the sacredness of life that comes from the hunt.

RE: How do you think young people should be prepared for the hunt?

DJ: If a group of young people who wanted to hunt came to me I would bring in relevance to social issues, to the social justice issues, environmental issues, and prepare them by talking about why it is economically good to go hunting, to why it is healthier for the diet, why the animals have the wisdom they do and how they can be our teachers and why it is okay to take their life for food and for ceremony.

In a non-Indian culture, where you don't have access to a spiritual tradition of hunting, outdoor education programs like Project Wild of the National Wildlife Federation, really teach people about ecology of animals, how animals live, how each animal is unique. I think students at a young age need to learn about all the different animals; how they live, what great wisdom they have, what things the animals do that we should do to live our lives in more harmony. Once that respect is built, then it's appropriate to introduce the idea of going out and killing it. First you have to do this at an age-relevant stage, but once you start to say, "Now this animal that you've gained all this respect for and that you want to preserve as an environmentalist or as an activist, now we're going to say we want you to go out and take its life."

RE: How do you teach respect for wildlife then encourage someone to hunt it?

DJ: Initially, many young people in the dominant culture see a contradiction here. They think, "how can you go out and shoot a deer you just taught us to preserve and admire?" At this point you begin to talk about the kinds of food that we are growing up eating. We are what we eat in many ways, and how de-spiritualized our food is and how when we eat these foods we become de-spiritualized. The animals are out there and have been for thousands of years to share their life with us so we can live and be healthy. They begin to see a connection when you talk about the animal giving their life as a gift, and the fortitude and patience and humility and the generosity that are really essential to the hunt. You can show this even in the dominant culture, without using an American Indian perspective because it's something that is inherent in all people – this propensity to hunt. All of our ancestors, whatever culture, were hunters. It is fundamental to all people.

When you prepare them with this way of respect, it takes them away from the sense of superiority and dominance. When it is done in this way it can be a powerful transformation.

RE: Do you think that hunting should be incorporated as curriculum in our schools?

DJ: I think the sacred hunt should be taught in city schools, too. There are many wilderness areas, but there is the problem of getting there, who is going to take them, how they will afford a rifle or bow. Yet there is really no energy put into that category. Maybe hunting groups could organize and go into the schools and teach these ideas, and maybe they could fund field trips to take selected groups of students, because I would say that within a hundred miles of any city there is a preserve or wilderness area where legal hunting could be done. It would take them out of their structured schools. It would give relevance to their life in more meaningful ways, especially for young boys who all have a natural tendency to hunt.

There is a widespread perception of hunting as a macho thing, and it can become that when it isn't taught properly. If it is taught properly and you go out into the wilderness and watch something die, you know the animal died for you. When people go out and buy a bologna sandwich they don't know anything about the animal it came from. Not only is there a lack of spiritual health from that food, there is a lack of understanding our role. When it comes from a grocery store wrapped in plastic, what good are animals? We've lost connection with the source.

RE: What do you say to a mother or teacher who can't see how killing an animal will develop virtues in a boy?

DJ: When someone kills an animal, whether it be a rabbit or a deer, and one does it in a sacred way and truly understands he is taking a life, instead of feeling really arrogant and powerful, one would wind up feeling humility if it is done in that way…because it takes courage many times just to be in the wilderness, to face big game, but also it takes a kind of courage to kill in a way that's sacred, because when you are realizing how connected you are to the animal, and that you and the animal are one, it's not like killing an enemy. It's not killing something that you think is worthless and that is there only for you to kill or eat, that it's there for the same reasons that you're here – to live this life in a good way, and when you take that animal with that in mind it takes a lot of courage to do that. In short, to truly have a population that in this country practices the virtues, to teach them in schools is good if we can teach it in the way of weaving into all curricula, but if young people could have fathers or mothers or uncles or grandfathers who could take them into the wild and teach them the respectful way to hunt, teach them that spiritual sacredness, that really is represented in that Lakota phrase, "Mitakuye Oyasin", which means "we are all related." If one goes out into the wilderness with that sense of relatedness then I think it would be almost impossible for them to emerge from the experience without having learned one of these universal virtues if not all of them.

RE: How will hunting as a rite of passage make our boys into better men?

DJ: In the traditional American Indian initiation into manhood, manhood is really represented by living a virtuous life. Even with the Lakota in war it was more honorable to count coup just to be able to show your courage and your generosity than it was actually to kill anyone. So I think that the idea of a rites of passage that emphasizes hunting also has to emphasize that it's not just that you are old enough to carry a weapon and kill an animal. I think it has to emphasize that you have truly embraced what it means to be a man, and that means to live in a virtuous way, to be an adult who has generosity, that has humility, that has courage and fortitude. I think that's what it means to be initiated. So I think that hunting can offer that possibility in these contemporary times.

I think an often overlooked part of hunting is the idea that animals and humans can communicate with one another, and when that is understood, when you see a rabbit or a buck up on the hill and you actually look at it and you communicate with it and there's an understanding that goes back and forth between you, then it's not unusual to understand why the American Indians would ask the animal to give itself to the hunter. The idea that we're all connected, we're all related, and that we communicate with each other is something that you can learn very easily if you go out into the wild when you see the animal, and even before you see him, you know he's there, you tune in almost telepathically. Then that's a way to learn we're all related, and only through that awareness can we practice the virtues.

In my book, *Teaching Virtues Across the Curriculum*, I am careful to avoid the typical problems of what is being called "character education," when teachers sort of inculcate values or they really are more concerned with behavioral issues – making kids be compliant to authority. You really cannot teach virtues that way. The only way to teach virtues is to help the student, the young person, to become aware of how the virtues relate to the subject being taught. The hunt is an ideal format for that. If during the hunt the mentor of the young person helps the young person become aware of how fortitude, patience, courage and humility and even generosity are connected to what happens before, during and after the hunt then it's more likely to be something that carries over into other aspects of the person's life and that's what makes the hunt a rite of passage potentially.

In summary, I would say that hunting is a significant way to teach young people universal virtues including generosity, patience, courage, fortitude and humility.

Does Hunting Make Men More Compassionate and Peaceful?

An Interview of Michael Gurian

THE BOOKS of best-selling author, Michael Gurian, include *The Good Son, The Wonder of Boy* and *The Purpose of Boys*. He is a family therapist who specializes in boys and properly initiating them to manhood. The following interview comes from a TV production I made entitled, "Respect and Responsibility: The Truth About Kids Who Hunt."

RE: What role can hunting play in the proper development of boys?

MG: Well, I think it can play a crucial role, of course, if the family understands what it is about. It plays the role of initiation because there are so many steps to it. It requires the child to use all the appropriate equipment, and it requires focus and concentration to learn to use weapons. It may take a year or more just to learn to use the equipment and then you have to know how to take care of it so you can shoot it. All those stages or steps are inherent in the hunting process. It also should be a completely spiritual experience for the participants. Sometimes it's not if you're a drunk and you teach your kid to hunt and you teach him to drink and hunt at the same time, that's not what we're talking about, obviously. But we're talking about a spiritual experience that includes a submission or surrender of the ego. My sense of it is that the self has to completely merge with the environment in order to understand how to accomplish in the natural environment what is required, and so one has to be instinctual, intuitive, one has to listen really carefully so the senses are really alive. Whatever psychological stuff that one brought into nature needs to dissipate, disappear, and we have to be one with this experience. That's really great for kids, it's just so great for kids to experience themselves being at one with nature, and then there is a didactive element there. I think there's no doubt that people who hunt and hunt consciously are constantly teaching their kids about spirit, about God, about nature, and saying this is how you deal with it, with deer or with the squirrel or if you trap something this is what you say. I think it is great if there actually are rituals, but at least they're taught to have empathy and in someway to be one with the animal through empathy.

Then there is the whole process of cleaning something you killed. Kids have to learn how to skin it or pluck it and going through the process of caring for the animal and getting it ready for use is very maturing. It is so much more maturing than going into a supermarket – nothing wrong with a supermarket, but the maturing process includes the neurological, the heart, brain and soul, and having to go through it all with this animal's body that was hunted grows the soul.

RE: Do you consider hunting to be an integral aspect of male initiation?

MG: Well, I think in this culture it is not. For most males in this culture it's not right because hunting isn't that popular anymore. In parts of the world, as where you and I live in the northwest or the west, there is much more hunting here, but you know for the city kid there's not much hunting and most people live in the city so population-wise, it's not. Could it be? Yeah. The difficulties I see with hunting becoming an integral part, kind of a nature-based initiation of males, is the availability in this culture of guns and all the guns that are really hurting the inner city. It makes it so that people have a visceral fear of guns and have therefore a visceral fear of hunting. It would take tectonic shift that I know you're working for and I would support to get the use of guns that is not healthy moved aside so that guns, also archery and all the other things we hunt with are respected for the nature-based tools they are, and not for entertainment and not drug war, and not all that stuff, but nature-based tools that connect the nature of a human being with the nature of the environment. I'm not optimistic.

Could it be one of the best forms of initiation? Yes. Is hunting proven to be useful in the initiation of young males? Yes, across the spectrum, and, ironically, especially those males we think of as violent, criminal males, having great results in teaching those guys to hunt and getting them reoriented towards empathy, towards things they couldn't get in the inner city, so they even see a gun in a new way by learning to use it to hunt.

RE: Doesn't it strike you as incredibly paradoxical that the same boy who could kill another kid and show no remorse could weep when he kills an animal?

MG: I think about the object a 12-year old boys sees. He looks at a squirrel and the classmate that is bullying him and they are not the same object. There is something pure about the squirrel, and obviously the classmate bullying him has hurt his ego and is part of a whole syndrome in this country that I call character regression syndrome, boys whose character regresses at 15 as they become like 7 or 8, and they use a gun as they do a video game. I don't think the boy sees the squirrel in his video game in the same way he sees this enemy, this person whose hurt him. There's something naturally soulful about the connection that human beings have with animals, like we have with pets, that is different than what we have with someone who is hurting us. The purity is gone now in that – that's all embroiled in our ego problems, but the squirrel is not, the fox is generally not, the deer is not embroiled in our ego. So I think this is why, maybe at a spiritual level, we're having success using hunting at places like Idaho Youth Ranch, places where the boys are hardened criminals, but they'll kill an animal and hold it and weep. I don't think they can put the squirrel in the video game in their minds, but I think these boys are putting their friends into a video game in their minds and they're playing out the video game and "hunting" their friends. We haven't lost the purity of nature yet, thankfully, but we have lost some of the purity of humanity.

RE: Is there an adequate substitute for hunting? People often ask, "Why not sports, why not this, why not that?" Why not go out – a woman just asked me this on TV last week – and take a camera instead of a gun?

MG: I don't think there's one act that would be an adequate substitute. I think that you can put together a process of initiation over a five-year period, from say 10 to 15, that doesn't involve hunting but that can take the youth to the same place. The reason I think that's an important answer to give is because it's not realistic for so many people to use hunting as their (initiation) process. So I see hunting in two ways: I see it as a discrete entity that we should all utilize as it fits us; then, I see it as a model for how to create something for (the future) that fits urban families.

Since it's unrealistic for so many families to use hunting, even though it'd be great if they did, let's look at hunting as a model for an initiation process that everyone can use. If a family organizes an initiation process, let's say of a male from 10 to 15 or 16, from boy to man, hunting is a great model, they don't even have to hunt, but it's a great model. So what they would have to include are all the elements of hunting, have to find a way to do it. Photography is great, that could be a piece of it – you go out and hunt visually. Definitely a lot of time in nature; I don't think you can initiate a male into healthy, sacred manhood, complete holistic manhood without that male spending a lot of his adolescence in nature. I know some people disagree and they say, "You know you're in the city so the city is your initiation." Fair enough, but that's just not the way I look at it. I really think human beings are natural, so nature wants to have an influence on the adolescent male, that that's how the universe set it up.

So going out to hunt something using photography is fine, but it can't be that alone. We also have to spend a lot of time in nature doing a lot of nature-based activities. There has to be group work in nature. Hunting's a group activity as well as an individual activity. There also has to be solo individual time which hunting also gives. Hunting, as we get older, allows us solo time. It allows a 15 year-old to go out for hours and spend solo time. Well, a family that's not going to use hunting still should do that, figure out a vision quest tradition, like in my books, I go into the whole vision quest system that can be used, three days alone in the woods, but let's do that at age 13 as well, with dad a 100 yards away, but then by 16 dad's not really needed. By then the kid should know, he's had five or six years, that he could be solo for maybe a week.

Then there are elements of fending for oneself, which hunting requires. When I'm a kid I can't do it, but by the time I'm 15 or 16 I can – if I'm good at it – I can fend for myself, I can hunt or fish and get the food I need for three days. That's great, that's very maturing if we can incorporate that in the process.

Then there's hunting as a community activity – everyone celebrates the sacred object that is brought home, a deer, a pheasant, whatever it is. Everyone celebrates that so the young male is admired by the community and he has a sacred role in the community which is to feed the community, and he sees the fruits of his labor shared – part of the give away. So all these things have to be part of the initiation experience between 10 and 16, so if he can get all these things together between 10 and 16, does he ever have to pick up a gun? I don't think he has to. Could he get some of it simpler if he learned to use archery or a gun for hunting? Could he get it more purely the way his ancestors did a million years ago? Yeah, but for those families for whom it's not realistic, these other elements can make it happen and they can be an adequate initiation.

RE: If I understand you, you're really saying that if there is a substitute it is built upon the instincts and rewards that hunting offers anyway.

MG: Whenever we start measuring the human being, whether as *Australopithecus* or *Homo erectus*, hunting was the template for male initiation, for males' rites of passage, for male development of a sacred role in life, an important role in life. It was the template. So we've had a few hundred years when it hasn't been, but it still exists as a template, and we just have to now go back to the template and look at it in all its complexity and all its purity and take from it what's in our nature and adjust it to modern life.

There is an incentive to do that – the incentive is that males have to be made into men and females become women. They don't have to be made into women. I write about this in *The Good Son*, a big section on how to develop self-worth. To cut it down to a minute, females have a natural process that initiates them into womanhood, and they can't escape becoming women, but obviously females need rites of passage, we're not saying anything like that, females, girls, do need rites of passage. Since they have an internal rite of passage and they have a cyclical hormonal system that allows them a rite of passage every month – and a series of these every month, a four-cycle series in one month – they're constantly connected to nature and they're constantly connected to their responsibilities as adults.

But every culture on earth has had to connect its males to their responsibilities because a wet dream, masturbating, these things are not like menstruation, they just don't connect us. So it's been the job of cultures, especially during the years of adolescence, which now in our culture is 9 to 21, it is especially important that males get shown a template or path to self-worth, and they follow that path, and the adults are there along the way giving them rites of passage until they get to be men and they know as men what to do… civilized cultures always knew they could kind of screw up with initiation or not complete it, but the males would go to war, and at war they would get initiated. They would either come back broken, or in a box or initiated, for better or worse, however we thought of war, that is part of what it did. Well, that's largely gone, and the extended families are gone, too, to a great extent, so all these possibilities – even the religions are gone, a lot of people don't involve themselves in any kind of religious activity – so we've got these boys who naturally need a sacred role in life, they've got to have something that makes them good men, that makes them men that are of worth to their community, they need that naturally. There's an available template through hunting that is millions of years old that can be adjusted to fit modern life, and since they're not going to get it through war, we hope, and since they're not going to get it through religion and extended family, these boys are hungry for these templates, so hunting, once again, is a very useful template to create five or six years of rite of passage based on it.

RE: The taking of an animal's life? In my own mind I can't find a substitute for that, meaning in terms of the sorrow that I feel, the tragedy of it, the paradox of life and death, all that these words stand for emotionally, I don't know what I can do out there that will make me poignantly aware that something died so I may live.

MG: Yeah, I've really thought about that, and there is no substitute in modern life for the taking of an animal life, and there's no substitute for the taking of an enemy life. Hunting and war provide this incomparable experience, and, ironically, people don't often get this, but paradoxically war makes males more empathic, hunting makes males more empathic, because of the very things you're talking about. Because we take a life we value life, and we understand how to value it, and we feel intensely the need to care for life, and hunting was of course the original way that happened, and about 10,000 years ago population rose and the wars rose. We became agricultural, we didn't hunt as much but we made war, and war also created that empathy, and now, you're right, for taking an animal's life I can't give the substitute. For that, over the next 10 to 20 years, because of wise-thinking like you're thinking, we probably should watch that, we should see, are our young males able to develop empathy in the ways we need them to?

Maybe we'll substitute for it with attachment (meaning bonding, as between child and mother), and the reason I say we need to think along the lines of how we'll substitute for it is just because so many families are never going to be able to hunt, so how do we use it as a template? Caring for pets, obviously watching your pet die, that could help build empathy, especially in the inner city parents might want to give their sons or daughters a pet.

RE: Yeah, but you know what they do? They haul the pet off to kill it behind the kid's back!

MG: When our cat died – the vet's a friend of ours – we took our kids to the vet. Our kids were right there for the death, the injection, a good time to teach them about death, and they cried and I cried and, so yes, thank you, if parents are going to have a pet the child needs to be part of the death and life process with the pet. It's not a substitute, I know, for hunting. You might have the answer to that; I don't have the answer. I don't know how to get that into a boy's life, who'll never hunt. I don't know how to do that.

RE: There is no substitute. You probably touched on this, but is there an optimal age to start initiating a boy using hunting?

MG: I think that in the initiation process, there can be some tool training before nine – tool training, equipment training and some modelling, and nine or ten is about when to start the initiation process so that would be when to go to the next level, beyond tool training.

RE: Do you think hunting engenders self-esteem?

MG: Oh yes, oh yes, in so many ways. Anything that challenges the human being's search for meaning is engendering self-esteem, anything that requires the young human being to face life and death, and to endure is developing self-esteem. Then there's the basic skills – he learns a skill, he utilizes a skill. Then there's the admiration from his culture, "You did this really great. We admire you." So all these things are building self-esteem. Also, at the soulful level of meaning, of facing life and death, of facing a search for meaning, and constantly having to ask why, because when someone hunts they are always unconsciously saying, "Why am I doing this?" And having always to justify this activity, what is not only basically natural, but which is also basically different from just about everyone else in society, so I think people want to make a comparison between hunting and non-hunting activities. Watch a video game in which a kid appears to be hunting. Video games are using male neurology, they're using basic male evolutionary biology, and they're using warring and hunting scenarios – very smart of these people who develop them to get to the male brain. But at the same time watch a kid that plays a video game for two hours, say Mist or Doom or Apocalypse, then take them hunting and watch them hunt for two hours. You know the serenity in the hunting experience, the self-esteem gained and all of those things compared to the basic entertainment and neural stimulation of the video game, they're really different. People can see it themselves. If they want to answer this question, watch the boys who hunt and watch the boys who play video games, and they'll be really impressed with the self-esteem levels of the boys who hunt.

RE: Do you think the youth hunting experience overflows into responsibility?

MG: Hunting requires us to develop these basic moral competencies: responsibility is one of them, but also fairness, a sense of justice. Hunting requires someone to constantly be thinking, "Why am I doing it? How does this fit? What is giving its life for me so therefore what responsibilities do I have to use this correctly, to use this practice in service?" All these things are coming up.

RE: Let's imagine you have parents who come into your practice and say they're really upset, "Our son got ahold of the neighbor boy's BB gun and shot a robin, and we want him to stop it. He wants to hunt, that's all he ever talks about, and we think it's terrible. What are we going to do?"

MG: In one case it was a family whose kid just loved the BB gun, and I had to say to them, it's a hunting instinct, and so don't think it's a bad thing, his hunting instinct is kicking in and he happens to have access to this BB gun, so we started there. You know, I'm nature-based, my therapy practice is nature-based. Let's first figure out what the nature is of the child, what's natural about this, then let's figure out how his culture might be messing with him. So that helped a lot, and they looked at what piece of the extended family is out there that's under-utilized who knows something about hunting, and there was an uncle in Missoula, about 3.5 hours away, and he was very into hunting so the family had to make a decision. The dad leaned toward letting the kid spend more time with the uncle, the mom leaned toward not, and that's very common and I completely understand it because hunting is definitely much more a male instinctive thing, and its hard for females to see it as something other than teaching your son to kill.

So we talked about that. It was really important that the mom's feelings were understood and that she looked at resources so she'd understand – I think I actually had your video, "The Sacred Hunt," at that time and gave it to her to watch. Anyway, the decision was made over several weeks that, yes, they would try this, so, since the kid already had the instinct, the question was how do we train the instinct – do we shut it off or do we try to train it? So the uncle was involved and it worked out great for all of them.

In another case, a mom came in from a divorced family, a divorced couple, the dad was already wanting to teach his 4-year old about equipment, and the mom was really worried, and I can see her point. She was not a hunter. This all seemed like war-making to her or something like that. The mom and the dad came in without the son and we talked and got him to make some agreements that he would not use this as power over her. Like, "Oh, I can get her goat because she's scared of this so I can make her scared." He was doing that and he had to stop, that wasn't sacred activity, but he got that, and she got that there was some incredibly sacred bonding going on between father and son.

This was a pretty stoic father, he didn't talk a lot, but her model was to talk so she wanted him to talk to the son and to bond that way, but that's not the way he was built, so this was one way he could bond, by activity together, which is very male, and hunting activity, and that worked out well. It took a while but it worked out well.

Two single moms had read *The Wonder of Boys*, and in *The Wonder of Boys* I talk about how hunting can be useful and I make some reference to the rite of passage experience. The line I have in there that they were responding to was for single moms, "When your son gets to be as tall as you are it's time to find a man to help you make this boy into a man."

One father lived 3,000 miles away and he wasn't available for these two single moms. The other father was one of those not very good guys. So one of them had this idea, "Uncle Hans in South Africa," this is a true story. So what they did is save their money and planned this all out because their sons had turned 13 and they were getting pretty tall, and they planned it out that by 14 they were going to send these boys to South Africa. And they live in Spokane, Washington, and this is a big investment for them but they really believed that their sons really needed initiation and rite of passage.

So a year later that all worked out. They called me and told me about it and I helped facilitate it a little, but basically this was their thing. They sent the boys, the boys spent six weeks, 14-year old boys, with their uncle in South Africa. One of them – I feel emotional about it because I felt so emotional when she told me – one of them called her on the phone while he had held a liver in his hand of an animal, I'm not remembering the kind of animal now, but they had hunted it and he had Uncle Hans to teach him about what to do, and he held the liver in his hands and he was crying on the phone to his mother, and he said, "I'll never see life the same way after this moment." Well. You know I still know those people; the kids are 18 now. I saw one of the women last year at a social engagement, and she said that whole experience changed their lives, especially her son who was being really belligerent, a lot of the normal stuff that happens in a divorce-family, separation from the mother, trying to psychologically separate from mom, dad's not available, a lot of anger, but that hunting journey changed their lives.

The other boy came home and said, "Mom, I'm going to treat you differently now, I understand you better now, and I haven't respected you and I haven't respected life." That's a true story!

RE: Is there a relationship between hunting and violence? That's one I'm asked a lot. People say you're teaching kids violence by getting them into hunting.

MG: Partly my answer is that I have not done a study, maybe someone has, I don't know if it exists, taking a control group of hunters and a control group of nonhunters and seeing if the sons of nonhunters become more violent than the sons of hunters. I haven't done that study, I don't know if someone has or if they've controlled all the variables.

My instinct – and I think we have four million years of history to support this – is that healthy, sacred hunting creates less violence, and "hunting" by playing video games creates more violence. The reason I say that goes back to nature and how the brain works. My understanding is that the more holistic the experience, the neural experience that the brain has, they lead to future holistic activities of that brain system or that neural web, so if I sit around and play a bunch of video games which are based on hunting scenarios and warring scenarios, and I play those, but I never see the consequences – I never touch the liver of the antelope, I never touch the squirrel – that's not a holistic experience, that's just a hunting-war experience that's going on in my fantasy world, and I don't feel the consequences. I don't develop any kind of respect or justice or decency or fairness from that kind of experience.

But if I'm hunting, that's a holistic neural experience: I not only have to have the skill to acquire the animal, to kill the animal, I skin it, I take care of it, I feel it against my body, I smell it, I have the blood on my hands – that's a holistic neural experience that should lead to future holistic experiences when I'm faced with life and death again.

This we do know from catscans, a kid whose playing Apocalypse or Cardinal Sin, which are violent video games, is getting almost no neural activity in the frontal lobes, almost none – most of the neural activity is in the back of the right hemisphere. It's the frontal lobes and prefrontal cortex where moral decision making, executive decision making occurs. My guess is that if you catscan a guy who is hunting and who touches his dead deer, we'll see a lot of activity in the frontal lobes because he's having to understand this life experience, and a lot of that happens in the frontal lobes. So my guess is that if we use catscans we'll be able to show that experience of hunting builds moral energy, more neural energy where the moral stuff goes on – builds more character.

RE: When you hunt you identify with the animal. You move where it moves, you're listening for it, you imagine what it's perceiving, where it is at this moment. You may end up calling it, imitating it, and I think that the identification process enters into the incredible empathy that comes from taking the animal's life, even though, ostensibly, physically in terms of form, it is very different than you are, you literally crawl inside that animal's skin, but then turn around and take its life.

MG: You have to develop compassion in that experience, you have to. Your body and soul are going to develop compassion. Playing the video game there's no compassion.

RE: I'm curious what your comment will be to the question I asked a Western Shoshone elder, "What kind of country would this be if the majority of men in it had been properly initiated to hunting?"

MG: It would be a more peaceful country. It would be a place in which men would be less concerned with hunting in terms of getting themselves to the top of the corporate ladder and competing for these things, because they would have experienced what it really means to hunt, to reach the object, to acquire the animal, be part of the drama of life, so they wouldn't have to step on everyone to create the drama. So therefore I think it would be a more peaceful world, country. It would be a somewhat less competitive country. I don't think people would be as competitive. There'd be a lot more empathy and compassion, I think, in the culture. I suspect that there would be a little more peace between the sexes because it would be clearer to men who they are and who they should be – and by "should be" I do not mean what I think they should be, but that they would internally sense what they should be to fully be men, and therefore life would be easier for women because they would know who a man was, and men would know how to express who they are. Initiation makes a healthier man and helps him know how to be of service.

We wouldn't have service education in high school or middle schools today if most of the men had been initiated into hunting properly. Service education would just be a part of life – the sense of the give away, the Native American expression for our word, "service." That would become more a part of life, which would bring more peace, so I think it would be a more peaceful country. Especially men would know better who they are.

We'd be closer to nature and we'd definitely take better care of the environment. Definitely.... most hunters know, because they're nature-based, that if they don't take care of the environment they won't have the deer or elk or turkeys. It's as simple as that. So there would be much better care of the environment.

RE: Many men compare hunting to religious experience. How does hunting enhance our spirituality?

MG: I have no doubt that we have peak experiences in hunting. Some people have peak experiences just being in nature. Hunting is so dramatic and so life-and-death that that increases the peak experience. My sense is, as a nature-based person, that the foundation of peak experiences and spiritual experiences is in nature. We can recreate them in a church, beautifully, in a synagogue, in a mosque, they can be created, but I think that if we trail every spiritual ritual back we're going to trace it back to something that was natural initially. So the hunt, I think, is the pure experience, being involved in the life-death drama in nature. It's the same life-death drama I'm involved in if I go to a Christian church or a Catholic church and I'm involved in Jesus' life and death, that's very important, obviously, to me as a Christian, and I'm getting that naturally in hunting. So my sense is that the basis of these peak and religious experiences that people have when they hunt is related to the fact that it's nature-based and that we are in our own nature, and our own nature is spirit. Whenever I talk about nature I'm talking about spirit.

The Neuropsychology of Youth Hunting and Shooting:

An Interview of Jim Rose, Ph.D.

JIM ROSE is a recently retired professor of psychology and zoology at University of Wyoming who specializes in the neuropsychology of adolescent male development. The following interview, excerpted from the video, "Respect and Responsibility: The Truth About Kids Who Hunt," summarizes his perspective on initiation to hunting and what it and shooting do for boys.

RE: Is hunting a legitimate rite of passage for boys?

JR: Initiation to hunting, whether traditional or modern, results in development of restrained, controlled behavior and discretion. The young recreational hunter has to acquire the ability to handle and use weapons safely, adhere to hunting regulations and make ethical decisions. The reality and serious consequences of hunting behavior have unique features unmatched by most other experiences in modern life.

Behavioral inhibition and discretion required of the hunter rely specifically on the operation of a prefrontal cortical brain system, which is late to develop, typically becoming functionally mature during the mid-teens through a combination of processes related to brain growth, puberty-related factors and pertinent life experiences. Therefore, the timing of rites of passage with expectations of mature behavior coincide with and are functionally dependent on this phase of brain development.

RE: In terms of the brain's development, what is the difference between aggression and hunting?

JR: The neurobiological controls underlying hunting are distinctly different from those underlying non-predatory aggressive behavior in humans or non-human predators, such as cats. While there are certain brain diseases that may lead to release of hostile aggression in humans, there are no neuropathological conditions that cause pathological expression of hunting or predatory behavior. Aggression, as exemplified by homicide, is a product of species-typical evolutionary factors such as competition for status or reproductive opportunities, and moment-to-moment factors, especially impulse control.

RE: Are you saying that proper initiation to hunting and shooting teach young men self-control?

JR: The critical role of poor impulse control in human aggression, especially in young males, stands in direct contrast to the cultivation of restrained, controlled behavior associated with becoming a responsible shooter or hunter. The prefrontal cortical system required for controlled, discriminated behavior must be functional to override impulsive behavior. Most hunting, for example, is done in isolated situations far removed from the scrutiny of enforcement agencies, but the deliberate violation of game laws is notably rare.

RE: Why is it important that young men are initiated to hunting and shooting?
JR: Initiation to hunting serves two functions in the development of young men. It provides formalized, systematic training in controlled, non-impulsive behavior, including adult models to emulate, fostering functional development of the prefrontal cortical system. It also places responsibility on the adult model to behave in an appropriate manner. The role of adult men as teachers or mentors, by example, of responsible, mature, socially acceptable behavior would restore hunting as rite of passage to its proper place in the culture.

> *"Take your boy hunting today and you won't be hunting for him tomorrow."*
>
> ~ Herb Parsons

Why Hunters Save the World

"Oh, it is hunters alone
Regret the beastly pain, it is they who love the foe
That quarries out their force, and every arrow
Is feathered soft with wishes to atone;
Even the surest sword in sorrow
Bleeds for its spoiling blow..."

~ RICHARD WILBUR, *"Castles and Distances"*

That humanity may threaten its own survival and the viability of the biosphere is reason enough to question the influence of civilization on sanity. It is imperative that we examine ourselves. With so much science, technology, specialized knowledge and information how could we be at this point? What is wrong with us and what can we do about it? Exactly what are we missing?

Is it possible that the very thing we believe will solve the global crisis is actually the problem? Men and women all around the world are hard at work coming up with myriad ways to alleviate human suffering and environmental degradation. They trust the human ego and intellect to save the day. But is it not the ego-intellect that created the crisis and spawned domestication, civilization, warfare, materialism, unsustainable economy, greed, massive starvation, environmental degradation, disharmony and ultimately the meaningless of life? If the fear that fuels defensive ego-consciousness is ultimately responsible for our suffering and that of the planet, can more of the same serve us well? According to Einstein, no problem can be solved from the same consciousness that created it.

The Spanish philosopher Jose Ortega y Gasset defined reason as an orthopedic device imposed on a broken instinct. By instinct, Ortega means every capacity of knowing outside of reason, from biologically inherited instinct to intuition, which, from mysterious, uncharted depths, gives rise to great scientific ideas and art. Ortega was wise enough to know that intelligence is much more than reason.

Joseph Campbell, the well known mythologist, was fond of saying the world is a mess, but it was not always a mess; moreover, it is a mess now because we are a mess, and we are a mess because we have for too long sided with fear and ego. Presence is the state of being of the "noble savage," who, as wilderness educator, Jon Young says, "thinks with the whole package."

"Absence" is the state of being of most of civilized humanity, which thinks with the ego. When Jesus said that we must be like little children to enter the Kingdom of Heaven, perhaps he meant that we must be present because presence is the state of innocence. The moment we identify with ego we move into fear and lose innocence. Joseph Chilton Pearce is a foremost authority on intelligence and creativity. If he is correct, it is loss of innocence in civilization that breeds egoism and blocks the natural emergence of transcendence.

Ortega's "original man," the hunter, is so extremely alert and keenly present that for him life is sheer transcendence. He identifies with the wild animal he hunts and feels submerged in the environment, every component of which he perceives as being alive. Content with landscape as utilitarian or abstract sightseeing, the civilized man is asleep, absent and egotistical. What is worse, he accepts his dis-ease as normality.

Paul Shepard was the original human ecologist. He said that it was domestication of animals and plants that radically altered the human relationship to the non-human other. He did not identify the fundamental principle behind this shift – defensibility of resources – which changes human society from relatively peaceful and egalitarian to warring and patrilineal. The ecology of pastoralism and farming evoke a psychic shift to what the Buddha termed "defensive ego consciousness," the pathology now threatening humanity and the earth. It is a monumental tragedy that the great monotheistic, pastoral tribes are assembled for war on the pastures of oil where civilization was born.

By a distinctly different route I arrived at the same place as Shepard, through the development of a new theory for social evolution: competition between species for resources, such as between lions and hyenas for carcasses, favors grouping. Humans and their hominid ancestors were right in the thick of this interspecies war, which primed them for warfare with their own species once predator enemies were bested. That led me on a quest to understand precisely what motivated humans to become the dominant species of the planet. I saw in the evolution of trophies from game/food animals to large predators/enemy humans an ecological shift from hunting to pastoralism, agriculture, civilization and warring.

The theory of trophyism, that individuals gained status and reproductive success according to their hunting prowess as indicated by trophies, is supported in mythology. Nearly every culture on earth claims it was founded by a great man who killed an awesome beast, but we end up with the warrior-heroes of civilization, such as Orion and Hercules, in whose shadows we have been living ever since. We forget that Orion raped the women he wanted to wed, and that Hercules killed his own children, finally acquiring psychic composure only after he was forced to live like a woman, which tempered him.

Ortega said that the essence of every contemporary man is Paleolithic. Shepard asserted that we still are adapted to the Pleistocene. Anthropologist Richard Nelson and poet Gary Snyder are right that we very much need the wisdom and humility that they discovered in hunting societies. Like hunting societies, Shepard and Joe Pearce before him, understood that a key factor in "proper relationship" to the "other" is human development, which, properly experienced, strongly bonds humans to nature and society. Among these developmental processes are years of childhood close to nature followed by rites of passage, the oldest and most universal of which has been hunting, the way in which a boy proved himself worthy as a provider and suitable mate.

While the first menses is a girl's rite of passage to adulthood, a woman's greatest initiation to life is birthing a child, which most opens her heart and connects her. Imagine what kind of world this would be if women did not have babies? There would be much less compassion. What kind of world would this be if men had babies? There would be more compassion, and we may be sure that men would be less eager to send their sons off to war.

Hunting and killing are as fundamental to male development as birthing and infant care have been to women. These are in fact the radical polarities on which the matrix of human life inextricably rests. Men take life to support life, and the kill itself is the event that engenders compassion, respect for life and the moral responsibility to protect it. There is no adequate substitute in male moral development for hunting. Life lives on life – vegetarians are just eating something that can't run away – said Joseph Campbell, who was an avid fisherman.

I am convinced that the world is a mess because for too long we have failed to raise boys properly. We have not tempered masculine fire with feminine compassion, the radical function of male rites of passage among pre-pastoral societies. We have not given our young men those rites of passage that transform them into men of heart, men who are profoundly married to nature and society, and who think with the heart and therefore are wise. Heart-intelligence, not ego-intellect, informs us what is appropriate to do. The development of wise men rests not on conceptual knowledge and abstraction but upon transcendent and transformative experiences. The word "education" does not mean to put into, but to draw out of, the function of rites of passage.

Recently I conducted a questionnaire survey in the U.S. and Canada, which examines in depth for the first time how recreational hunters really feel and the role hunting has played in their lifelong development. Contrary to the unfounded assertions of the anti-hunters it reveals that almost all hunters feel sad when they kill an animal, and likewise it shows that nearly all recreational hunters feel admiration, reverence and respect for the animals they hunt. Most have let suitable specimens pass simply because it didn't feel right to take them, quite in contrast with the bloodthirsty image portrayed by the media. Even more surprising, over 80% thank the animals they kill and/or the Creator. Most men feel they have learned universal virtues from hunting, such as inner peace, humility and patience, and most older male hunters rank taking the life of an animal for food highest in those life events that have opened their hearts and engendered compassion in them.

That hunting teaches compassion is a powerful message for a world in conflict and crisis. Michael Gurian, an authority on how to raise boys into fine young men, adolescent neuropsychologist Jim Rose, and Helen Smith, a leading authority on youth violence, recommend hunting because it develops empathic, responsible, respectful, self-restrained, more peaceful men.

Joe Pearce and Paul Shepard may be right when they say that industrial birthing on a large scale has generated pathological materialism, consumerism and unsustainable economy. No bonding with mother, no bonding with Mother Nature or with wife and children. Given proper early development certain critical experiences during adolescence open the male heart and marry males to nature and society. The rites of passage in my formula for men of heart include: subsistence survival/hunting; vision quest; and art. For those who participate directly in it, the taking of an animal life converts the food chain to a love chain.

Among many Native American tribes the ancient traditions of initiating boys to manhood included a vision quest consisting of three to four or more days alone fasting in the wilderness and praying for a vision regarding one's adult purpose in life. As a dynamic form of meditation, the vision quest originates from still hunting and its unparalleled state of alertness. As the exemplary path of self-examination, the vision quest fulfills Lao Tzu's admonition that if you would save the world, look first to yourself. It teaches a young male the difference between the ceaseless traffic of the ego and the quiet intelligence of the heart. It teaches us that there is more to life than this body and the senses. It keeps us humble, receptive to wisdom.

The Native American vision quest is virtually identical to the pagan – and later Christian – rite of passage known as "tending the fire" among northern Europeans, a ritual perpetuated today among chapters of the Orden der Valknut, a llth Century offshoot of the Teutonic Knights, in Europe and North America.

While producing "The Sacred Hunt: Hunting as a Sacred Path," I interviewed Felix Ike of the Western Shoshone tribe, "What kind of country would this be if the majority of men in it had been properly initiated to hunting?" He said, "It would be a totally different world." Ike asserted that, "Anyone can be Indian. Being Indian means having a feeling for the environment." We very much need to recover a life founded on essential tribal wisdom, which includes elders mentoring rites of passage so adolescent males may become men of heart who have a feeling for the environment and take care of their world.

Ortega's philosophy of co-existence (life as interdependence) is necessarily the true psychology, and though Paul Shepard was much influenced by Ortega's book on hunting, he did not embrace the immense importance of Ortega's actual philosophy and its moral complication, a revival of the ancient wisdom of hunting societies. Ortega says that my life consists of my ego AND my circumstances in mutually transcendent interdependence. And since my circumstances are as important to my existence as myself then I must take care of them as much as myself. I am convinced that Ortega's philosophy is the truth we need in this time of social/environmental crisis brought on by the hubris of Western culture. However, it is actual bonding of humans with mother, nature and society that produces humans, who, because they identify with the "other," not merely the ego, are respectful and responsible stewards of society and the environment.

From hunting comes a supreme lesson for environmental conservation: self-interest extends to what we identify with, and we identify with whatever we are emotionally bonded. The spectrum may be as limited as the body or as extensive as the cosmos, which is the case for the Kalahari Bushman who see the stars in the night sky as incarnations of great hunters.The key to greater cooperation among humans and between them and the environment lies in carefully mentored development, from birth through adolescent rites of passage. It follows that the "selfish gene" theory of sociobiology may be in part cultural artifact, a reflection of improper development that engenders fear, egoism and selfishness.

Let me put it this way. Put a 12-year old boy in a duck blind with a shotgun in his hands and a mentor and there is a fair possibility that he will grow up to join Ducks Unlimited and protect wetlands. He is likely to embody Ortega's philosophy, a restatement of the timeless wisdom of hunting peoples everywhere. The power of the hunt to bond males to nature is seen in contemporary hunting. The fact is that hunters were the original environmental conservationists, and they still lead in that field. Ducks Unlimited has conserved over 12 million acres of wetland habitat to the benefit of the entire living community of North America. In less than 20 years, the Rocky Mountain Elk Foundation has conserved over four million acres for elk and other wildlife, not to mention successfully reestablishing elk throughout much of their former range in the northeast and Midwest U.S. Hunters are behind the National Wildlife Federation and The Nature Conservancy. While the rest of the environmental community is engaged in defensive action, the hunting community is on the offensive.

Hunting teaches us that, like all lifeforms, we are dependent upon the integrity and viability of nature. Though the hunt is goal-oriented, it teaches us that all of creation functions by deeply interconnected processes and that we are part of the process. It engenders a "7th generation perspective," making decisions today with future generations in mind. As Athabascan elder, Peter John, said, "The animals you take are important to your grandchildren." Because hunters are motivated to fiercely protect nature, as poet Robert Bly said, they are the leaders in environmental conservation.

Hunting teaches us to be observant and to emulate nature and slow down, to "be here now" in the present moment. It teaches us that inner peace and sanity are possible in a world gone mad. According to Don Jacobs, a leader in educational reform, "Hunting is the ideal way to teach young people universal virtues including patience, generosity, courage, fortitude and humility." He defines humility as knowing you are part of something greater than yourself, an apt definition of spirituality.

The hunt may submerge us in the subtle realities of life. These include the power of prayer, envisioning what we want, tempered by ethical choice. Every hunt is a prayer in motion, and seasoned hunters know that faith in the outcome has much to do with success. Hunting teaches us the significance of attitude, intention and right-mindedness, ingredients of the worldwide reciprocal relationship between indigenous hunting societies and wild animals which offer themselves to worthy hunters who prepare themselves properly.

These are some of the secrets hidden deep in hunting, the original rite of passage for which there is no substitute, a powerful path of initiation that marries men to the "other" that is nature. Those who directly participate in the food chain enter into the Great Mystery of life as life and death.

A major obstacle to the recruitment of youth to hunting is that parents cannot imagine that it promotes compassion. Perhaps it is impossible to comprehend the inner side of hunting without experiencing it directly. However, sex is an appropriate analogy of an instinct that links up with the heart. The young man is propelled towards a sexual encounter, but a surprise awaits him when he falls in love and is transformed by the merger of instinct with heart, eros with agape. Ortega defined sex as the bicep of love, and just as the sex drive may lead a man to love, mating and fatherhood, marrying him to the human community, and finally to wisdom and elderhood in it, the hunting instinct culminates in kinship with the greater family of life, the biotic community. The hunt is the bicep of conservation. It extends the social ethic to the land and sponsors "wise use" of it, i.e., thinking with the heart.

In hunting, the counterpart to falling in love is the death of the animal. In that eternal moment, a young man realizes that his life is as impermanent as the animal he pursued. He is stunned by his power and the necessity of using that power responsibly. He knows that the animal died for his physical and spiritual sustenance and he is grateful. At the deepest level he knows that, despite all appearances to the contrary, he and the animal are essentially the same. He discovers the unity of life.

The death of the animal opens a young man's heart and tempers the fire of his passion with compassion. Aldo Leopold was the father of wildlife biology and the land ethic. His life history is a model for understanding how hunting develops moral responsibility to nature. As a young man, his hunting instinct was strong, and the day he killed a she-wolf and saw the green fire die in her eyes, he married wilderness and began to think like a mountain. I was 13 when I shot my first duck and have worked hard for environmental conservation ever since to be worthy of the gift of that mallard hen's life to me. Her death was for me the death of childhood and the birth of manhood.

A Nez Perce hunter told me that before he shot his first deer his grandfather gestured toward the deer then pointed to his own heart and whispered, "Your good heart." He explained that these words mean that it is important when you take an animal that your heart is good because that keeps the whole thing going. Spiritual ecology means reciprocity and renewal. Hunters feel they are a part of life and that the life they are part of is sacred. Because they know life is sacred, they honor, serve, protect and provide for it. That is why hunting is good medicine for boys, society and the environment, and why older hunter-mentors are there quietly but steadfastly doing the real work for youth and nature.

More than at any time in the history of the world we need men who are deeply wedded to nature, which is to say that we need men who value the viability of the entire biological community above consumerism and the unsustainable economy that feeds it. Hunters are such men. Their unparalleled performance on the front lines of conservation makes them the ideal model for a world in crisis.

I agree with mythologist Michael Meade that Western culture is unraveling. As apocalypse, the process may be gradual instead of dramatic, but surely it has begun. The first teen suicide recorded on earth was in the 20th Century. From 1986 to 1996, the number of children taking psychiatric drugs tripled. Depression is epidemic, and all the while species are disappearing at an alarming rate.

A U. N. global survey compiled every nation's many problems and placed them into four categories. Then they reduced all the problems in each of these categories to a single word, as follows:

CATEGORY	ONE WORD SUMMARY
Culture	rootless
Politics	powerless
Economics	ruthless
Environment	futureless

All these words ending in "less" indicate that modern life is meaning-less, exactly what Laurens Van der Post concluded after spending time with the still wild Kalahari Bushman for whom life was always meaningful.

Meade believes that the deterioration of culture appears first among the youth and the elders. He believes we have forgotten our elders as the source of guidance to help us find our way home. The ancient Greek story of Narcissus makes the point. Narcissus was hunting with his young friends when he left them and went to a pond where he saw his face reflected. He fell in love with himself, but his fate soon followed in the form of suicide, the cost of turning one's back on nature, which is exactly what civilization has done. Like Narcissus, we suffer from undaunted pride, and our failure to rejoin our hunting companions may destroy us.

In the Iron Hans mythology from northern Europe, the boy ends up looking at his own reflection in the proverbial pond, but unlike Narcissus he has the Wild Man standing behind him so he does not get stuck on himself, but instead maintains his connection with nature. The Wild Man helps a boy discover through the hunt the power, beauty and intelligence of nature.

Meade suggests that pursuit of the "normal" is not what we need. After 9-11, President Bush recommended that we resume normal life, like visiting Disneyland or shopping at the mall. Instead, Meade advises us to look to the edge of our culture for answers. To him the edge means art as soulful expression, but for me the edge of culture is nature, which shrinks as our abusive, exploitive culture expands. At the edge of culture are the wild men and women who still communicate with animals, fight to protect wild places and work to pass on the original human culture, hunting, a culture founded squarely on nature and harmonized with human nature. When culture does not harmonize human nature with nature, it is doomed to failure. If the truth be known, the heart of the hunter holds the keys to the future of human life.

Thomas Jefferson, Audubon, Thoreau, Teddy Roosevelt, Leopold, Steinbeck and Joseph Campbell are among the civilized Hunters Hall of Fame, white men with red hearts who called us back to nature-culture. So are Jimmy Carter and Nelson Mandela, contemporary peace-makers both of whom are avid hunters. Proper development may shift our men from ego-intellect dominance to heart-intelligence. Thinking with the heart may forge a North American culture founded on tribal wisdom which marries men to nature and saves the world.

The heart of the hunter agrees with Lao Tzu, the 6th Century B.C. Taoist philosopher, who said that the earth is sacred, we cannot improve it, if we attempt to change it we will ruin it, if we try to own it we will lose it.

The Two Wolves

The elder explained to his grandson that inside each one of us are two wolves.

One is evil. It is anger, envy, sorrow, regret, greed, self-pity, guilt, resentment, lies, false pride, superiority and ego. One is good. It is joy, peace, love, hope, serenity, humility, kindness, benevolence, empathy, generosity, truth, compassion and faith.

The grandson asked which wolf will win.

"The one you feed most."

~ Cherokee

Chapter 1

Zen Cowboys and Native Elders

"In sharing, in loving all and everything, one people naturally found a due portion of the thing they sought, while in fearing, the other found need of conquest."

~ Chief Luther Standing Bear

Zac Reisner is a friend of mine whom I've likened to a Zen cowboy. He lives next to Wyoming's Wind River Range, greatest wilderness in the lower U S. Each fall he works as a hunting guide and takes over-civilized men of means into the backcountry to hunt elk. He demands from his clients the practice of fine hunting art, including tracking and reading sign, and by the time the hunt's over, the men are in top physical, mental and spiritual condition. Physical because they have been led up and down mountains by the Zen cowboy; mental because their alertness has been awakened and honed; and, spiritual because the guide introduces them to the hunting tradition of the Crow with whom he lived for two years. Like them he purifies himself, prays and fasts for several days before hunting, and once an elk has been killed, he and his clients practice the traditional rituals for the animal, and with empathy, the guide helps them express their gratitude to the spirit of the animal and to Creator.

Men who arrived in Wyoming with thoughts of elk-rack trophies for their den walls leave in gentle spirits, speaking softly and warmly with reverence for the Elk Nation and the old ways. They have discovered what it means to be a hunter, and the rest of their days they will be married to the sacred ways of nature.

The modern hunter finds true alertness first by merging with the animals and land, and if he's fortunate this leads him backwards to the inner hunt. No doubt many indigenous hunting cultures understood all this. A young man on the verge of egoic obsession by sex, hunting, competition and warfare was prepared by the elders for a vision quest which would merge him with the mystery that transcends all earthly gains and losses. Long before the Yogic tradition of the East, hunting societies consciously sought the softening of the potentially destructive male ego by integrating and balancing it with the heart. The city men who break down upon killing a Wind River elk are conducting the most ancient of sacrifices: tears of surrender to the Creator. This is the meaning of hunting for civilization.

Civilization is in dire straits. The first teenage suicide recorded in the history of the world occurred in the 20th century, also when the first case of colon cancer was recorded. Teen suicide and colon cancer are now epidemic in civilization. There are many indicators of a social-environmental crisis on earth, but quite a few rural folks are suspicious. The appearance of *A Skeptical Environmentalist* had them saying, "What I'd tell you?"

Having first-hand experience as a leader in the preservation of endangered species, I can speak with some authority on that subject. Yes, there have been abuses by environmental and animal rights groups as well as government agencies that have made false claims about the conservation status of many species, especially the glamorous larger mammals. They have done so to attract funding and to enlarge or protect their personal position, bureaucracies and organizations.

Unfortunately the overall situation is dismal at best. Here is what human ecologist Paul Shepard had to say in his final book, *Coming Home to the Pleistocene*:

> "The world is full of war, terrorism, social disintegration, poisoned air and land. The soil that has been accumulated for centuries is washing into the sea; the earth's forces are being devastated. Virtually all the diseases of the past are with us in more virulent form, and new epidemics of psychic breakdown, dysfunctional families, and organic infection are upon us. The last benefits of the raiding of the earth by the affluent minority still give us an illusion of well-being in the midst of worldwide calamity..."

Shepard asks how we may recover the experience of a world in which we are surrounded by a multitude of conscious, powerful and natural beings. His answer is that we need to recover the Pleistocene human within ourselves. Anthropologist Carleton Coon says of the human species that when he becomes coldly practical, discards his beliefs and rituals, begins measuring and counting everything accurately, building efficient machines, inventing weapons of mass destruction, sending men into space, and burning up more of the earth's oxygen than its plant life can replace, he also has begun warming up the wax that will seal his own fate.

Coon describes the human being who is prisoner to the ego with its rational and analytical functions. The global crisis has one, ultimate cause, the ego's domination of the civilized psyche.

Harvey Kleckley's *The Mask of Sanity* proposes that psychopaths hide behind a mask of normalcy in the routines of daily life. Could pathology be epidemic in a culture but remain hidden from itself? Erich Fromm asked if a society can be sick. He concluded that consensual validation has no bearing on mental health, that just because millions of people have in common the same forms of mental pathology does not make them sane. The famous teacher, Jidu Krishnamurti, once said that it is no measure of health to be well adjusted to a profoundly sick society. For years I have told my students, "There are two kinds of people in the civilized world: those who are crazy and those who know they are crazy." There are few of the latter.

Child-rearing practices are much more than another item in a list of cultural traits. They are the actual condition for the transmission and development of all other cultural elements. DeMause documents the extensive abuse of children over the last millennium in the West. Surely he is right that the psychic foundation of modern society is severely dislocated, but he makes no comparison to the healthy archetypes among primal human societies.

The fact is that especially among hunting-gathering societies, "a demonstrable affection for children is manifest, in loving concern and a benign strategy of appropriate, age-graded care that fosters their growth toward maturity and the capacity for wisdom and mentorship," Shepard says in *Nature and Madness*.

What happened to humans who left the sanity of a foraging lifestyle? Stalking Wolf was an Apache medicine man who mentored Tom Brown Jr, the famous tracker. He had a vision in his youth of a barren landscape occupied by sick and starving children. He asked the Spirit that revealed this possible future to him about the meaning of the vision. The Spirit explained that what Stalking Wolf saw was the consequence of agriculture, which led humans to live beyond the carrying capacity of the earth and thus pay the consequences. In essence, the Spirit said that the Creator intended humans to live close to the earth, dependent on it, and not in a way that calls for control of nature or the environment.

If Stalking Wolf's prophesy is true, and at least some of it has come to pass in the form of "holes in the sky," meaning holes in the ozone layer, which he envisioned decades in advance, then perhaps our reliance on agriculture which we see as the foundation and blessing of civilization will prove disastrous, not only regionally as in the Sahel in recent years, but globally. You don't have to be a rocket scientist to see that if human activity is causing a warming of the planet then there could be serious repercussions on the climate and weather and therefore food production, which could mean massive starvation.

All it would take on a cosmic scale is a period of prolonged solar activity slightly higher and hotter than normal to bring us to our knees. And for all we know, the Native American philosophers are right when they account for major earth events, such as the explosion of Mt. St. Helens, as an expression of the Earth's anger at us. Angry, they say, because we show no respect for the earth and the nature spirits who make our life possible. The educated in the West don't even think they exist, and the Gaia hypothesis may be given left-brain acknowledgement, but it is not something we feel deeply to be true. In short, for most of us today, the idea of a living earth is just that, an idea, an abstraction, hardly what we feel toward our mother.

Likewise regarding the sun, which after all is the Great Life Giver for us, and like us and the earth, an extension of the Creator. That does not make of us nature-worshippers as some Christian churches fear so much, but it does mean that we see Creation in a horizontal expression permeating all things equally. A horizontal organization of the universe has no room for arrogance.

In this period of crisis, explanations abound, and one of them sees the contemporary plight as an expression of the imperialism of Rome, which, though it died in a political sense, has continued to prosper ideologically in Europe and America.

The Romans put power into the hands of government, and the key was control of nature, which originated with the Greco-Roman heritage of subjecting nature to rationality, which is another way of saying that western civilization placed itself above nature. In so doing, as singer Leonard Cohen said, we sank beneath our wisdom like a stone.

Physicist Fred Wolf wonders why we chose the alternative of centralized government and centralized religion? He proposes that it was for survival, but one might argue that it was for enhanced reproductive success, i.e., it was a more successful strategy. But at what cost? Wolf suggests that we may gain a stronger economy at the price of losing our souls, and that on a global scale, we are losing our planetary soul.

In wondering why modern humans persist in destroying their habitat, Paul Shepard suggests that either our species is intent on suicide or the problem is simply greed. However, greed is an expression of emotional insufficiency, of low self-esteem, insecurity, inadequacy and fear; in another word, it is the disease of an egotistical culture in which proper child development including rites of passage to adulthood have been long lost, replaced by doctrines of individualism, competition, social Darwinism and all the rest of it.

Among tribal peoples who are at peace with their world rather than striving to dominate it, the development of the individual has a characteristic pattern, a standard from which we have deviated. The ontogeny of their children is an adaptive sequence that fosters a sequence of mental growth, cooperation and service, and continual study of the mystery and beauty of the world in which the clues to the meaning of life were found in nature, where everyday life carried spiritual significance, and the members of the group celebrated passages as ritual.

Shepard believes that the seed of normal development is still present in all of us. In early development nature is a lexicon where words first have the solidity of real things. Real creatures are watched and playfully mimicked. Each species has gifts of behavior, gestures, and proclivities that reflect some aspect of the child's own inner zoology of emotion. Their forms come to life in stories which train the imagination. The natural play space of the child is another prototype of a dependable world. In this world there is nothing wild, nothing tame. Any power that humans have over nature is limited to the exercise of simple tools and by the generosity of animals. As Shepard says, when the young person goes out with adults to dig roots or stalk an antelope he understands that success depends on the readiness of the tuber or prey as much as the forager's skill. In this sense, predation is cooperation.

When a boy reaches puberty he finds himself on the edge of a miracle of transformation. His childhood experiences will be seen as joyful language, and the rites and myths he faces will not indicate that his passage to adulthood means that he must leave behind his love of nature. He will not graduate from a world of otherness to a world of humanness, but will begin a life of study of the natural world limited solely by the extent of his creative thought. Already he has discovered kinship: "likeness but difference." As he imitates adult hunters, he will observe a lack of anxiety and the presence of enduring patience and trust. The world he encounters is full of clues, and his new curriculum is devoted to the art of learning to decipher them.

As civilization becomes the primary mode of living, people lose their connection with the land and with it those sacred values that bond man to man, family to family and humans to the divine. We've lost family life because we've lost community, real society. We've lost community because we no longer share a direct link to the earth.

Contrary to the assertions of historians, most civilizations have died from abuse of their environments. City people take for granted the earth and creatures that sustain their life. When they no longer find themselves in a community that respects the earth and sees it and life itself as sacred, disintegration is inevitable, which is where we find ourselves today.

In his book, *The Biology of Transcendence,* Joe Pearce describes peaceful human societies such as the Senoi and Kalahari Bushman, in which youth develop naturally into caring, healthy adults without hearing "no" and "don't" every nine minutes, on average, of their childhood. He identifies enculturation as the process that pollutes human potential. He defines culture as the body of knowledge and belief regarding survival in a hostile world passed on from one generation to the next; however, culture encompasses much more than survival. Primal human societies do not view the world as hostile nor do they live in a perpetual state of fear. Pearce agrees with the English poet William Blake that all evil consists of self restraint or restraint of others, meaning that, "Accusation, in any of its forms, is a negative judgment, and a negative judgment in any form ruptures relationship – the classical definition of sin…When we accuse or judge another, it has the same effect on us as being judged ourselves. Any judgment we make, no matter of whom, registers in the heart as a disruption of relationship, and the heart dutifully responds on behalf of our defense, shifting neural, hormonal, and electromagnetic systems, from relational to defensive."

Essentially, it is the use of judgmental language and signals to change behavior that are the very core of egoism. They trigger our ancient survival instincts and promote the rank and fearful influence of ego. "Though shalt not" is the foundation of law and religion, the cement holding civilization together, the origin of all legal systems, prisons, war and our downfall. More about this in Chapter 5.

For the present round of civilization, the industrial revolution was the final blow as it pulled the vast majority of people from the farms to the cities. Boys began growing up without men and nature in their lives and it's been downhill ever since for society and the environment.

Robert Bly is a poet and a leader of the men's movement. If he's right then the deterioration of society and the destruction of the environment have a common origin: the lack of initiation of young men into adulthood. Considering the fragmentation of the family, teenage violence and the disastrous state of the environment, it is imperative that we rethink the kinds of experience young men need.

In Bly's book, *Iron John,* three aspects of the male initiation process are identified; one of these is the discovery of the intelligence and power of nature. The young man also learns at a deep emotional level his inseparable relationship with nature as well as his responsibility to protect it. Bly says,

> "We sometimes assume that contemporary initiation is accomplished by being confirmed or receiving the Barmitzvah ceremony or getting a driver's license. To receive initiation truly means to expand sideways into the glory of oaks, mountains, glaciers, horses, lions, grasses, waterfalls, deer. We need wilderness and extravagance. Whatever shuts a human being away from the waterfall and tiger will kill him."

Without rites of passage during adolescence that affirm the mystery and metaphoric quality of nature, the world can become empty and lifeless.

There are only a few paths a young man can walk that allow him to link up the instinctive with the spiritual. In 1975, I was mysteriously drawn to Mary's Lake outside Fall City east of Seattle in the foothills of the Cascades, where I was inspired to undertake a vision quest for three days which included fasting. My first evening consisted of a series of dreams that seemed more like feature films: their themes were sex, war, hunting and sports, the primary biosocial themes of adult male life.

In every case, the instinctive may link up with the spiritual. Falling in love, for instance, connects the sexual instinct with spiritual love. The result of initiation on the path of love changes our life irreversibly. Music never sounds the same as it did, we move with a new form and grace, and our life is changed forever after falling in love. Henceforth we shall know the meaning of authentic love experienced with the fullness of our being. We are saying that when we fall in love, the instinctive or primal self (eros) merges with the spiritual (agape). It is a vertical convergence of subconscious with superconscious, lower to higher.

Sport and war are like romantic love in the sense that they involve a vertical expansion of spirit, and each expands us laterally: the athlete to teammates and opponents; the lover to his beloved; and, before war descended to barbarism, warrior to enemy, who also was beloved. But only hunting with its full awareness and sensitivity expands us sideways into nature, and that is why it is unique and so very important to the psychic development of young men and to the salvation of the earth.

If sex is the bicep of love, as Ortega asserted, then it is the sexual instinct that launches us into a qualitatively new and unexpected arena where we fall in love and bond powerfully with another person. That marriage is consummated by sexual union, which, in a sense, is the death of the ego-self and the birth of the lover who discovers his spiritual self, the life of the heart and divinity. The hunting instinct also launches us into a new territory where, quite unexpectedly, we fall in love with nature. The kill itself consummates a young male's marriage to nature because it opens his heart. Those who have had the experience know what I say is true, even if their only experience was a raw, instinctive impulse as a boy. Even if that original experience meant subsequent denial of hunting, nonetheless it opened their hearts to animals.

Lack of male initiation in the modern world is among the most recent insults of civilization against humanity and the earth. This book proposes that the global crisis is the consequence of rampant egoism that generates fear and insecurity, which in turn promote greed and obsessive materialism as well as anger and distrust toward other humans, creatures and the earth. The medicine prescribed for the dis-ease of defensive ego-consciousness includes proper bonding during a sequence of critical stages of human development culminating in adolescence with mentored rites of passage that engender responsible men of heart.

The ideal formula proposed for initiation of boys to adulthood consists of properly mentored subsistence survival, vision quest and artistic expression. Of these, subsistence survival in the wilderness is the archetypal ideal precisely because, lacking the necessary experience and training, a young man is forced to surrender to spiritual power if he is to survive. Which is to say that ego-intellect is given up for heart-intelligence. Since it is difficult today for most adolescent boys to undertake wilderness survival as rite of passage, I recommend hunting, the original, universal rite of passage that proved a boy to be an able provider. A critical aspect of subsistence survival is the taking of animal life for food which does open a young man's heart and tempers his instinctive passion with compassion. Properly mentored hunting sponsors the fierce protection of nature, as Bly said. Hunters were the original environmental conservationists and they remain the leaders in that field today. The hunting experience and the vision quest hold powerful keys to solving the abuse of the environment as well as social disintegration.

There was a time when I was convinced, as my professors still are, that evolutionary theory contained all the explanations and answers for humanity, and I became proficient at reducing virtually everything from cosmic evolution, mathematics and why women go to restrooms together (but men don't) to natural selection. I was a reductionist on the rampage, a successful strategy in science.

Recently I phoned up my first graduate professor, one of the foremost ecologists and evolutionary thinkers on earth, a man I much admire as a human being whose intentions are the highest. Like Joseph Chilton Pearce, he perceives culture as a sorry set of prohibitions on what is natural or biological. I agree with both that negative enculturation promotes ego-defensiveness, but the fact remains that without cultural mentoring that promotes cooperation and transcendence humanity is apt to succumb to separation and selfishness. We are not merely biological but also cultural, and culture can enhance our biology as well as our spiritual life. The transcendent life of the Kalahari Bushman rests in part on an extensive cultural inheritance. The stories of many hunting societies are instructive about place, resources and creatures, but also are intended to help individuals cope with potentially harmful negative impulses. Among many North American native tribes, for example, it helps to deal with the potentially destructive bear inside by knowing the bear outside and the stories about bear – and bear-people – who sometimes go "berserk". Animals are our teachers, but their medicine is embedded in stories - culture.

In our age, culture has bifurcated and we stand at a crossroads. On the one hand there is more neo-Darwinism reducing human behavior and life to selfish gene-machines, on the other is the new physics, which, despite all appearances to the contrary and its complicated experimental procedure and technique, recovers the aboriginal and ancient wisdom of interdependence and the unity of life. If we retreat further into mechanistic science we will suffer further egoism, because mechanism is the perspective of the ego. But if we recover the transcendent awareness offered by the humility of quantum physics there is hope for the human spirit as well as our animal kin.

Einstein said that there is no place any longer for both field and matter in a physics text, that there is only field, which is to say there is a common ground or essence for everything. "Thou art that" means that the belief in separation and limitation is not real, but only in our own minds. Which is why Joseph Campbell's first love was the American Indian to whom every part of creation is sacred.

A possible paradigm shift in biology started more than 20 years ago with an unexpected outcome of an experiment in which bacteria without lactase, the enzyme needed to digest lactose, milk sugar, mutated and were able to consume the lactose medium. That may seem trivial, but it decidedly is not because it means that genetic change, mutation, is not a random event at all, but an adaptive response by the individual to its environment. In short, Darwinian evolution is no longer the only game in town, and the really good news is that our DNA even may be influenced and altered by our thoughts and feelings, i.e., our beliefs. Bruce Lipton's *The Biology of Belief* affirms that the Newtonian view of reality - that our bodies are mere machines subject to physical laws of cause and effect – may be abandoned in favor of a much more empowering perspective, that we are cause, not merely effect.

Robert Bly wrote a book about *The Sibling Society.* That book and others have wondered why we seem to hold onto the dreams of childhood. Why is it there no longer seem to be any grownups home? It seems to me that Bly answered this question in his earlier book, *Iron John*, which addresses the critical importance of proper initiation of young people into adulthood. It also seems to me that Joseph Chilton Pearce and Paul Shepard are right, that human development from the age of three to twelve, is best spent interacting with nature and animals from which we learn who we are. Ultimately the process results in our identification with all of life, even the cosmos. We become as connected as the Bushman mother who lifts her newborn baby to the night sky to be blessed by starlight.

But there is a related reason why we hold onto childhood and resist adulthood, and that is, as Michael Meade suggested, that perhaps the rest of life appears empty and meaningless. Life without initiation is meaningless because it is terribly one-sided: masculine, competitive, intellectual and egotistical, nearly devoid of the feminine aspects of heart and soul.

I wonder if the straw that broke the back of the modern age was the Second World War. Meade was born during the darkest night of that war and so was I. Our mothers were terrified about the world we were entering. What we saw as adolescents was what our mothers saw and felt but did not express: a world wrecked by the dark side of the masculine – destruction, greed and possessiveness. The women's movement was born along with us as were the seeds of discontent of the hippy generation, a generation whose mission, and the mission of all the generations since, is still unsettled. Perhaps there will be no settlement until industrial civilization dies and we resume the lifestyle the hippies embraced: small forager-farmer societies living peacefully close to nature.

In this book I say that the great corruption begins with the separation from and domination of nature represented by domestication of plants and animals, which ultimately erodes civilization from the inside out. That erosion is not only of topsoil but also of the mythological landscape and fertility of the soul. As western civilization became a scientific culture, rampant male egoism culminated in severe psychic fragmentation and sheer madness.

While proper initiation could help heal the modern soul, it may not revive without a collapse of civilization and recovery of the earth ways and the deep sense of connectedness they evoke. We stand at the edge of that precipice now, and I feel that the most important contribution of my generation will be gifts we offer as elders who took on the sins of the fathers. The protests we made then as overgrown, angry adolescents may yet come to meaningful fruition in the ashes of a self-consumptive world.

Meade says it well,

"As we draw near the threshold of change, we face the question asked at the end of each age or stage: is this the end of reality, or is it a metaphorical ending that is occurring? Is it the shedding, breaking down, and falling off of old forms so that the threshold can be crossed into another stage of culture, another age of life? Or is this the final curtain?"

In adolescence, each one of us discovers the awesome biological power within us and each one of us is faced with the challenge of tempering that power. Culture consists of keeping those symbols alive that help individuals and generations find their way to the top of the mountain. An old Zen proverb teaches that "If you want to know the way to the top of the mountain it helps to talk to the man whose been there." Submission and acceptance are those qualities that allow us to make that inevitable descent into the waters of the soul, transmute our wounds and reemerge as tempered men and women able to climb the mountain and mentor others on the journey.

I am not alone in my conviction that we very much need a totally different world, a world in which humans recover the respect, humility and psychological composure that comes from proper relationship with one another, the creatures and the earth. I am not promoting earth worship so feared by some Christian fundamentalists, but a recovery of the sense of sacredness in all dimensions, human and nonhuman, life and death, that comes from the direct participation in the most fundamental processes of life including our food. A great teacher once implored me to, "Go out and teach your brothers and sisters that life is sacred and to honor it."

To comprehend the depth of meaning in these words and the primary role that hunting may serve in the initiation of boys into manhood, we'll need to search for what is real in the original hunting-gathering lifestyle of humanity and what we retain from it today that will guide us in the recovery of proper relationship.

"Civilization is the limitless multiplication of unnecessary necessities."

~MARK TWAIN

Chapter 2

The Failure of Civilization

> *"You can't say civilization don't advance...in every war they kill you in a new way."*
>
> ~ Will Rogers

The Great Mystery Of The Illinois Wolfen

Wilder than the wolf, bear and cougar suffocated from this land more than a hundred years ago, a yet-to-be catalogued life form makes its way through bottomland forests. Hidden by day in the dense growth of hardwoods along the Illinois and its tributaries, the Sangamon and Spoon, they wait for dark. Even now I shudder to think they might know I've broken a solemn pact. Perhaps this breach will come to naught. After all, who would believe there are wolfen in Illinois?

The passion of the hunt found me standing among cottonwoods on the river bank waiting for sunrise when I heard their peculiar, muffled cries. Not the bark of dogs nor the howl of the coyote or wolf but more like the finely orchestrated chorus of jackals keeping their ranks intact while scouring the savannas for gazelle fawns hidden in clumps of grass.

Through the dim magenta light, a white-tail buck ran out of the willows along the levee into the field and stopped directly in front of me, its chest heaving and tongue draping. The buck caught my eye for a moment before they rushed into the field, and then he bounded into the next stand of forest surrounded by an inverted phalanx of wolfen.

Coal-black, sleek and uniform, they have long legs and thin bodies, and weigh about forty pounds each. Conformed like the Cape hunting dogs of Africa, they are perfectly designed to hunt deer. Some wildlife biologists would say that they are domestic dogs gone wild for generations, filling a void left by the hand of European man on less wary hunters of this once most productive watershed of Turtle Island. I know better.

They course deer with precision far beyond the faculty of Illinois dogs, and in the heat of the chase they call back and forth to one another so softly that no farmer could ever hear them. More intelligent than the wolf, they never attack livestock, and they always kill deer in the dense bottomlands where no one may see their ceremonial feasts. The wolfen's bite-the-lip courage goes so far as to tolerate the clumsy intrusions of farmers' dogs pretending to hunt deer, and looking back on all the times I stalked deer with a bow before sunrise where they must have been lurking I wonder if other men were treated as mercifully.

That morning when eight of them ran by me, for a split-second my instinctive urge was to shoot the deer, then to intervene on behalf of it, but these archaic impulses yielded to the profound realization that I was witness to a Great Mystery. No doubt the wolfen could have killed me. They not only spared me that day, but also initiated me into the Brotherhood of the River. The wolfen and I agreed to hold out for another time yet to come in this Sacred Place. Until then, our duty is to hunt silently in the dark. Known only to me among the two-leggeds, the Illinois wolfen are my special totem, my other spirit-self sitting even now beneath a pecan tree on that far away river.

~ Randall L. Eaton, *The Sacred Hunt*

It seems clear that civilization is a failed experiment, that like earlier civilizations, we are abusing the environment that supports us, and that like them collapse is inevitable. In any case change is certain and it could be for the better. During the 1980s there was a global awakening of awareness about the futility of industrialism and with it a growing restlessness caused by a lack of meaning in life. The myth of the grandeur of civilization began to yield to revisions on every front. Not only does techno-industrial life endanger the survival of the biosphere, civilization itself is dehumanizing precisely because it is fueled by fear and egoism.

There are some who think that we can design humanity's next great adventure. In *Beyond Civilization*, Daniel Quinn, author of *Ishmael*, proposes recovery of tribal life using the circus as a model; however, his solution does not lie beyond civilization, but rather how to live better within it.

He's right that humans function best in small groups of truly interdependent individuals, but he is wrong that genuine society is achieved merely by working together. Individuals in real human societies conduct interdependent lives intimately linked to the earth around the clock from birth to death. What we have gained in terms of individual freedom we have given up in terms of meaningful relationships, nature connection and social security, and of course peace and joy.

Quinn is convinced that civilization persists and returns because it is the best lifestyle, but is it best only for the top 1% for whom the rest of us are dispensable worker bees? His revision of civilization to allow tribalism is not a viable paradigm shift because the real difference between civilization and tribal life is not theoretical as much as it is mythical. The shift we are looking for is from ego to heart, from fear to love. The sanity of our minds, the openness of our hearts and the health of our bodies, society and the environment ultimately rest upon our ecology, the way in which we derive sustenance from the earth and perceive our relationship to it.

A Hopi Sun Chief raised in a mission said that he had learned to sleep on a bed, eat with a fork, use a toilet, read the Bible and recite most of the Ten Commandments. He also learned that a man thinks with his head and not his heart.

Kammer and Gold wrote *Call to Connection: Bringing Sacred Tribal Values into Modern Life*. They build an impressive case for our tribal nature and needs, but their solution is weaker than Quinn's circus model because it is completely lacking in social continuity. They would have us form and reform tribes fluidly throughout the day with no regard to constancy of membership, roles or actual interdependence. While they grasp our tribal needs, they fail to embrace the fact that humans seem adapted, apparently by millions of years of hunting life, to function optimally in small, interdependent groups, i.e., true societies.

In terms of our bio-social matrix, it is difficult for all but the most enlightened humans to form meaningful affiliations willy nilly as they move through the crowded landscape. The cost of crowding to our mental and physical health and to the maintenance of meaningful social relationships must be enormous. To expect humans to create tribal affiliations as they move from crowd to crowd and place to place in an overly urbanized world is as short-sighted as expecting mating bonds to hold up under sexual free-for-all or families to accept and nurture equally any children irrespective of genetic relatedness. New Age tribalism will not get off the ground for the same reasons that hippy communes failed. Forming tribes was the right impulse, but expecting mating and familial ties to be open-ended is an insult to the bio-fabric of the human species.

Humans inherit a genome, a set of genes configured by millions of years of adaptation to foraging economy and to the social life of foraging bands. If we have learned anything from behavioral science it is that human behavior is not infinitely malleable or flexible. We are born into this world with a genetic blueprint that "expects" to encounter and interact with a fairly narrow range of social and environmental circumstances, especially during infancy and youth.

Humans inherit the propensity to speak. Language is genetically programmed in our developmental blueprint, but the particular language we end up speaking is culturally determined. On the other hand we do not learn to walk: even blind children end up walking after proceeding through the same stages of development and on the same schedule as normal children. The complex coordination of perception, muscles and limbs is hard-wired. Practice may be important to perfection of walking, but even the determination to keep getting up and trying is inherited. To those people who want to pretend that inheritance is unimportant in human development and life, my professor used to ask, "If children imitate adults walking then who taught them how to crawl?"

The majority of learned opinion is that we cannot go back to the nobler lifeway of our Pleistocene ancestors nor their contemporary counterparts, the dwindling societies of foragers. Paul Shepard's response is that we cannot go back to what we never left, meaning that the adaptations of the Pleistocene are carried within us despite the alteration of external environments. Despite our appearance of sophistication (which means unnatural), we are nonetheless wild men and women adapted to develop and live in nature.

It is an appealing hypothesis, but the fact remains that we also have adapted to civilization, which is to say we have been domesticated. We are rather like dogs, whose ancestors were wolves, and much of our behavior still indicates that wild, ancestral life. Most feral dogs do not survive, though there may be a completely wild breed throughout parts of the Midwest which has fully recovered the niche of a medium-size canine predator which, while silently coursing a deer behind my duck blind at sunrise, I had the good fortune to encounter at close range, and to whom I later composed this poetic tribute:

Illinois Wolfen

There was a time when this land was harrowed by cloven hooves
When wolves corrupted the great silence and put frantic grunts on the lips of bison
On that once trackless plain, a lapping freight howls a wolf-song to bovids whose only prayer is eternal rumination
Asleep in a dream that whimpers for prairie flowers awash their bellies
Illinois dogs are haunted by ancestral memories of tearing flesh and drinking blood
At first light the last untamed forests of river bottoms come alive with packs of coal-black dogs gone wild for generations
Celebrating feasts without voice, they chase and kill white-tail deer who dare to keep their secret

Without wolf ancestry, the Illinois wolfen could not now exist as a feral species. By the same token, because our ancestors were wild living predators we too have the potential of recovering their lifestyle. But perhaps more important we must grapple with what we lost by being domesticated, i.e., from developing apart from nature. More important than what we lost in genetic potential have been entire dimensions of perception, ways of knowing, creative imagination and spiritual power, which we falsely believe have been superceded by intellectual prowess and technological wizardry.

So it is to primal societies that we'll need turn to gain an understanding of how we have failed to meet and nurture human needs. Moreover, reflection on their social life, values and relationship to the environment is a primary source of guidance for how to recover our psychic composure, what in the words of Laurens Van der Post, we are missing. The social/environmental crisis on planet earth demands a search for what we are missing. It is an admission that ego-intellect has failed us and that we are in urgent need of intelligence or wisdom – knowing what to do, how better to live. Conscious mentoring of youth and adults can help recover the relationships necessary to unleash our internal wildness. The foundation of awareness coupled with the ritual of the vision quest and the sacred hunt is the map we need to recover balance.

Not What We Think but What Thinks Us

In the 1950s, when my mother had resumed higher education, I read a poem in one of her texts that went something like this: A man looked up at the stars and said/ Universe, I exist!/ The Universe replied/That fact in me creates no obligation.

What an austere perspective we have come to from three centuries of reason, science and technology. But the new physics changed all that by presenting reality as paradoxical in nature.

Zen Masters teach with "koans," riddles that cannot be solved with the logical mind. A well-known example is, "What is the sound of one hand clapping?" In the early 1980's, this koan was solved, perhaps for the first time in centuries, by an 18-year-old student in a humanities course I taught entitled, "Science for Humanists." His nickname was Fuzon. He always wore tiny Mickey Mouse earrings and a black silk coat, and sat frowning in the back left corner of the room.

Our discussion that morning was about the paradoxical behavior of atomic particles. In some experimental situations, particles act like particles, but in others they act like waves. So what are they, really? The Heisenberg Principle of Uncertainty marked the beginning of the fall of Newtonian-mechanical physics and with it the hubris of the western ego. Until physics discovered that the behavior of atomic particles was dependent upon the experiment – and therefore the experimenter – it and Western life had floated upon a great wave of certainty. It was totally certain about itself and its assumptions about the nature of reality. Physics was the cornerstone, the Queen, of science, and science was our culture.

But when physics was forced to confront its own koan, it tumbled from its lofty position and with it all of Western Civilization. At the start of a new millennium, we are still groping for a way out of the chaos of the collapse of the certainty of scientific knowledge.

We are, as Ortega said, in a state of philosophical crisis. The very thing we thought we could rely on is no longer reliable. We thought we could rely on science, but science has failed us. We could well ask how we failed ourselves because science was nothing more, nothing less than our most basic belief about reality, and if the truth be known, mechanistic science is the paradigm of the human ego.

Ortega defined science as the great myth of western man. He could not have been more accurate. Interest in mythology has been reborn precisely because we are in need of it. Gary Snyder is a Zen Buddhist who won the Pulitzer Prize for poetry. He told my students once that if you want to understand a culture's mythology, ask the people where their children come from, which I have done since to dozens of university audiences across North America. The people in our culture offer a scientific answer about sperm and egg, zygote and embryo. Yet not one of them has seen a human sperm unite with an egg and then develop into a child. But they are as convinced about the process as they are that water consists of two hydrogen atoms and one of oxygen. It's been called the atomic age, but no one ever has seen an atom. Mythology indeed.

Science is a mythology that gave us great power over the world and unparalleled confidence in human destiny. With it we penetrated matter and used it to our advantage. And in that journey of 300 years we developed our intellect only to find that we had threatened our very survival. The uncertainty of scientific knowledge in the early twentieth century was followed by uncertainties of every kind. Despite technological "advance" on every front, the world is daily becoming a more dangerous place to live. Is deterioration of the biosphere reason enough to abandon scientific mythology?

Fuzon solved the Zen koan in that classroom in Reno twenty-five years ago when he sat clapping his right hand against his forehead. He made one hand clap all right, but at the same time he gestured in a way that communicates that we don't know the answer. What he really communicated that morning was that the answer is not in our head. In one brilliant moment of humor, Fuzon told us we were on the wrong path.

Science was simply the right hand of idealistic philosophy, which we identify with Rene Descartes. He asked the question, "What is the least deniable reality in the universe? My own consciousness." *Cogito ergo sum* which, in Latin, means "I think, therefore I am." The very existence of my thoughts is ample proof that I exist. Descartes was right, though we'll show later that he was half-right.

Descartes' philosophy went on to propose that the existence of consciousness implies the existence of God. The existence of the consciousness of other humans is less certain. Animals and all other things in the universe are not endowed with consciousness but are simply mechanical in nature. What a self-centered view of reality! I and God exist, other humans may or may not exist as God and I do, and the animals, plants, stones and stars all are unconscious, unknowing machines placed here by God for my convenience and amusement.

Cartesian idealism affirms my own ego, but in so doing separates me from other humans and reduces non-humans to simple machines. It is the philosophy of separation, undaunted egoism. Let there be no mistake about the nature of the ego. It is the part of the mind whose function is the protection, survival, and reproduction of the body. And as sociobiology revealed, sometimes the body will be sacrificed to enhance reproduction – surviving kin – but the motivation is nonetheless selfish in a reproductive sense.

From idealism's view that the universe is a great mechanism with the precision of a Swiss clock came mechanistic science, devoid of God and soul, as the tool of the ego. The power of science over other humans, the body, animals, plants and things reinforced mechanism to the degree that humans came to see themselves, even their minds and ideas, as mechanical. Thinking of ourselves as mechanical is more than paradoxical, it is contradictory. At least Descartes recognized thought as spiritual in nature. Ideas are spiritual phenomena, and since the heart of science is theories, ideas, it, too, is fundamentally spiritual. That its ideas may be about the nature of physical reality doesn't make science any less spiritual. Science finds itself with a system of knowledge that is not complete but dependent and contingent upon the thinker. Scientific theory does not encompass the scientific thinker, the origin of ideas. In short, science does not encompass us. Where it ends, we do not end. Where it begins, we already have been.

The whole problem is that we no longer think science as a legitimate way of solving problems about the material world. It thinks us. Which is why the paradoxical behavior of atomic particles and Einstein's discovery that time is not absolute, but relative to space, generated a crisis.

Scientific thinking has disempowered humanity. The cause and effect model of the mechanistic universe, like so many balls on a billiard table, is the way we humans have come to see our lives. The mechanistic view of reality had us believing that we are helpless, that we are simply effects of so many different causes. Our absolute belief in that view generated a self-fulfilling prophesy. We believed we are effects or victims, and our beliefs were powerful enough to create victim reality thus perpetuating the myth. The mechanistic mythology has held us in fear, destroyed our health, spawned materialism and greed, and reinforced separatism and egoism to the brink of global annihilation. Beliefs are powerful causes.

Just listen to radio talk shows or watch "reality" TV. My husband made me angry. My parents raised me in a way that caused me to behave as I do. PMS made me do it. We all believe we are effects not causes. We are at the mercy of the laws of the universe. We are victims of other people, the government, genes, hormones and events.

It is a credit to physics that it recognized its own deficiency and reduced its dominion. Unfortunately, most of biology, medicine and psychology have continued to impose the imperialism of Newtonian mechanics. They, too, have their own principle of uncertainty, even if they have failed to grasp it fully. It is known as the placebo effect. Clearly the placebo effect contradicts mechanical theories and threatens materialism. If my belief in the power of a pill is the only thing that gives that pill the power to heal my body, then it is my belief that gives the pill its power. In other words, my mind has power over my body. Which means that I am cause, not effect. The placebo effect restricts science to its limited domain while it empowers humanity. To say we are cause, not effect, is to say that we create our own reality. Those who believe they are effects will experience victimization without ever knowing that their beliefs are the cause of their reality. So powerful is the mind.

To take it further, the placebo effect means that our experience of reality is dictated by our beliefs in reality. If we are convinced that cancer is deadly and a doctor tells us we have it, there is a very high probability that we will die. And I am convinced that is why many people do die. They kill themselves with their beliefs, which also could heal them.

Does that bring us back to idealistic philosophy? Back to consciousness as reality? Yes and no. Yes, because Descartes was half-right. With the precision of a bullfighter, Ortega asks us to examine consciousness. When we do, we discover that the least deniable reality is that living is problematical at the core. Which implies that my life consists of the ego ***and*** my circumstances in mutually transcendent interdependence. The content of consciousness itself is our problematic relationship to the world: Where will I go? What will I say? When should I come back? What should I wear? And so on, ad infinitum. Neither the ego nor the world have the luxury of existing without the other. **Life is co-existence of ego and world.** Not I think therefore I am, but because living is problematical, I think. Thought serves life, not thought for the sake of thought, as Descartes and countless intellectuals would have it. The new philosophy is interdependence, embodied by hunting societies all along.

Hunting is a model of life itself, according to the philosophy of Ortega, who died in 1955. Ortega is of the same generation as Aldo Leopold, Carl Jung and Albert Einstein, and I don't know of four individuals in recent history whose vision is more significant to our present global crisis. In their respective fields, they share a common vision: interdependence. Einstein said that time and space are not absolute but interdependent, a blow to the arrogance of Newtonian man and his God-like belief in his power to control nature; Jung said that the conscious mind is interdependent with the unconscious which communicates to us via dream, symbol and myth, a blow to the superiority of the modern ego; Leopold restated ancient wisdom when he advocated a land ethic that rests upon the fundamental facts of ecology – all life including human life is interdependent.

But it was Ortega's philosophy that underscored the vision of his cohorts. Ortega's philosophy of ratio-vitalism or co-existence put an end to the idealistic trajectory of Judeo-Christian-Cartesian perception. His philosophy places ego in its proper relationship to life and environment; moreover, it complies a moral obligation to care for our circumstances/world. **Since we depend upon our world as much as ego we are obligated to care for it as much as ourself.**

Ortega's philosophy provides the foundation for Leopold's land ethic. Ortega and Leopold were hunters. As prophets of nature-culture, they recapitulated the hunter's spirit and sought an end to the fragmentation of the unlovely civilized mind. For them the hunter is the truly alert man.

Recent discoveries suggest that Fuzon was right when he clapped his forehead but found no answer there. The activities of the body are entrained to the brain, but to what is the brain entrained? The heart is hard-wired to the limbic system and it secretes neurohomones that regulate the brain. Half or more of the heart's cells are neurons, nerve cells, which means in effect that it, too, is a brain. As Ted Nugent said when I shared these discoveries with him, "There you go. The physics of spirituality."

Though our beliefs are powerful causes, our life is also dependent upon our environmental circumstances, and in this regard there is much legitimate reason for us to correct the failure of society to meet our most fundamental, inborn human needs, especially in terms of development from childbirth to adulthood. This failure during respective critical stages of human development has enormous consequences for individual fulfillment, society and the environment, and it has its origins in our false assumptions about human nature as a *tabula rosa*, a blank slate, on which anything may be inscribed. We humans require bonding, cultural mentoring and rites of passage to embody interdependence as a fact of life. We can create teams who are competent at mentoring young men to nature through hunting and ritual vision quest.

"There is a wolf in me ...fangs pointed for tearing gashes...
a red tongue

for raw meat...and the hot lapping of blood – I keep the wolf because the
wilderness gave it to me and the wilderness will not let it go....

O, I got a zoo, I got a menagerie, inside my ribs, under my bony head,

under my red-valve heart – and I got something else: it is a
man-child heart, a woman

child-heart: it is a father and mother and lover: it came from
God-Knows-Where:

It is going to God-Knows-Where – For I am the keeper of the zoo:
I say yes and no:

I sing and kill and work: I am a pal of the world: I came from
the wilderness."

~ CARL SANDBURG, "Wilderness"

Chapter 3

Certainty, Uncertainty and the Sacred

The Old Man Who Said Thank You to the Gulls

It happens nearly every Friday evening when the sun starts to dip into the blue ocean. Old Ed strolls along the beach to the pier, a bucket of shrimp clutched in his bony hand. Ed walks out to the end of the pier. Everybody's gone, save a few joggers on the beach. Ed stands on the end of the pier, alone with his thoughts and a bucket of shrimp.

Before long a thousand white dots come screeching, winging their way toward his lanky frame at the end of the pier. Soon dozens of seagulls surround him, their wings flapping wildly. Ed stands there throwing shrimp to the birds, and with a smile says, "Thank you. Thank you."

In a few short minutes the bucket is empty. But Ed doesn't leave. Invariably, one of the gulls lands on his weather-beaten hat he's been wearing for years.

When he finally turns around and starts walking back toward the beach, a few of the gulls hop along the pier alongside him until he reaches the stairs, and then they fly away. Ed makes his way down the beach and on home. Ed may seem like "a harmless old duck," as my dad used to say. To most onlookers, he's just another old codger, lost in his own world, feeding the seagulls a bucket of shrimp. Rituals can look either strange or empty, altogether unimportant or a lot of nonsense. Most folks down in Florida would probably write off Old Ed.

They'd do well to know him better. His full name is Eddie Rickenbacker, a famous hero in World War I. On a flying mission across the Pacific in World War II, Eddie and his seven crew members went down, but all of them survived and climbed into a life raft. Rickenbacker and the crew floated for days on the Pacific. By the eighth day their rations were gone: no more food or water. Lost at sea, hundreds of miles from land, they needed a miracle.

That afternoon they held a simple devotional service, prayed for help and tried to nap. Eddie leaned back and pulled his military cap over his nose and listened to the slap of the waves against the raft. Eddie felt something land on his cap. It was a seagull! Ed would later describe how he sat still, planning his move. With a flash of his hand and a squawk from the bird, he was able to grab it and wring its neck. He and his starving crew made a slight meal for eight men, and then using the intestines for bait they caught fish, which gave them food and more bait to catch more fish. They were able to endure until they were rescued after 24 days at sea.

Eddie Rickenbacker started Eastern Airlines and lived many years after the ordeal at sea, but never did he forget the sacrifice of that first seagull, and he never stopped saying, "Thank you." That's why most Friday nights he walked to the end of the pier with a bucket filled with shrimp and gratitude in his heart.

~ adapted from Max Lucado, *The Eye of the Storm*

The primal man has no word for the Sabbath; neither does he construct a single place of worship. To him life is divine, worthy of continual prayer, and his temple is the world. Though he has been accused of reducing God to the mundane that is not quite true; rather, he sees all that is as a sacred expression of the Creator. Civilized man sees God and himself as divine, everything else as outside sacredness, and many men are not too sure about God. To refer to what lies outside civilization, men invented words like savage, wild and wilderness, but the primal man makes no such distinctions, as Chief Luther Standing Bear said,

"We did not think of the great open plains, the beautiful rolling hills, and winding streams with tangled growth as 'wild.' Only to the white man was nature a 'wilderness' and only to him was the land 'infested' with 'wild' animals and 'savage' people. To us it was tame. Earth was bountiful and we were surrounded with the blessings of the Great Mystery."

Every pygmy male who proves himself sufficiently adept at hunting to receive initiation takes into his scored flesh the ash made from the plants of the forest, thus uniting his flesh with it. The forest is the pygmy's whole world, but he does not think of himself as its ruler even though for all practical purposes he is the dominant lifeform in it. Hunters may be dominant in their world yet fully dependent upon it; moreover, fully conscious of their dependence. The pygmy of the Congo knows all about uncertainty, but unlike civilized humanity's tormented desire for power and control, the pygmy accepts the limits of his power and his reciprocal relationship with nature.

Moke of the Forest People told anthropologist Colin Turnbull that the forest is a father and mother to the pygmy, and like a parent gives them everything they need – food, shelter, warmth, even affection.

Because the pygmies worship the forest in which they live, they have been branded as heathens by the one-God missionaries. Not so. Moke explained to Turnbull that pygmies have different names for their God (so do Christians and Jews) but that it is really the same one. Just what God is they don't know and that is why the particular name doesn't matter much. Moke told Turnbull that the pygmies can't see Him, that perhaps only when they die will they know, but then they can't tell anyone so they cannot say what He is or what is His name. Moke added that God must be good to give them so many things.

Moke does not believe that the forest is God, nor that God is of the forest, even though these are his words; rather, he means that the forest is of God, His manifestation. In any case, the pygmy God is like their forest – good. Even what seems not to be good is comprehended as goodness. The pygmy has not lost touch with the original wisdom. He still lives in an unfragmented world with an unfragmented heart. His song to the forest attests that though there may be darkness all around, if the darkness is of the forest then it must be good. Negative judgements by the Forest People are rare, usually reserved for egoism.

Like the pygmies, the San Bushman say that God is unknown, a stranger; God created himself and no one can command him, according to the Bushman and all the world's great religions. He created the water, earth, air, and bush-food, and generally is regarded by the Bushman as a supreme good being. The religions of many pre-literate peoples "seem to…be characterized by fear, intimidation or haunting. This does not apply to the !ko religion nor to any other Bushman religion," says Heinz. Preliterate includes foraging and agricultural societies, but on closer scrutiny, hunter-gathering religions are less fearful than those of agrarians which are highly superstitious.

About this Heinz adds,

> "He fears things he knows to be dangerous and with which he is well acquainted, such as snakes, certain lizards…leopards, lions and large animals such as elephants…He fears to walk from his village at night…not because there are spirits or demons about, but because this is the hunting time of snakes. He does not reject a camp site because it may be haunted…(but) because he observes some bones lying about indicating that some animal died of a sickness which may still linger in the ground…bacterial contamination."

Which is not to say that the Bushman do not believe in the spiritual. They do, and what the Bushman cannot explain by employing his uncanny powers of observation and deduction, many of which have proven equal to or even superior to contemporary science, he readily attributes to God's will.

> "Indeed, even understandable behavior comes about because 'Gu/e made the creature act that way.' No mortal man can, on his own, affect the life of a person, unless sent by Gu/e to do so…Animals do not harm man, not even a lion or leopard, unless willed to do so. None the less, one does not step on a puff adder through carelessness, for has he not trained eyes to see it?"

Even more remarkable than the accuracy of the Bushman's natural history and his impressive proto-scientific method is his complete and utter honesty. They "unabashedly lay bare their own limitations and ignorance of things in this world. Thereby they exhibit their humility, that quality venerated by thinkers and philosophers of many cultures and societies." Honesty characterizes hunting societies simply because in them it does not pay to deceive others as to one's knowledge, capabilities or achievements. In a truly interdependent group, in which members are usually closely related, each individual stands more to lose than gain by deception. In larger societies in which interdependence is less important and individuals are either distantly related or unrelated altogether, deception and cheating pay for individuals. Except for warring, civilizations become less efficient with size, mostly because of deception, lying and cheating for gain of wealth, status and power. "Small is beautiful" for this reason.

When the Bushman kill a large animal they pray to its soul knowing that they have removed an important part of their world, thus creating a vacuum, which in no way discredits or invalidates their morality. The killing of a large animal also may constitute a risk of danger, as from lions.

Moral philosopher, Tom Regan has argued that fear of reprisal from nature is merely self-serving and thus immoral, but Regan's morality separates man from nature, a disguised form of Cartesianism, representative of the hubris of civilized man which lies behind the global community's sickness. Wise is the human who recognizes that his relationship with nature is something he cannot escape: to transgress natural, moral law is to pay the price in the end. Hunters are first and foremost spiritual ecologists.

It is common among the pygmies and Bushman for society members to actively inhibit or discourage a hunter's egoism, and though hunters are occasionally egotistical, they are much less so than the heroic warriors of pastoral and civilized societies (below). The true interdependence in the hunting society demands control of egoism, from which everyone benefits, in contrast with civilized societies that promote male egoism for its singular value in warring.

The awareness and holistic lifestyle typical of hunters may account for their ethical attunement. A Bushman comparing the better attributes of animals and men said,

> "Animals can hear better than we do because they have big ears and can move them. Men cannot do this. We think with our heart, for when we know we are doing wrong we say, 'n/n chue' (in the middle of my heart) I know this is wrong."

Hunting as Ecological and Spiritual Interdependence

We humans are what we are as a result of adaptation to hunting animals, defending ourselves against them and competing with them. That is the "meat" of how we acquired the "lion's share." Our relationship with animals literally made us what we are, and it set the stage for the crisis we have made for ourselves. The hunting life gave rise to animal and plant husbandry, agriculture and civilization. Waging a long, bloody war with big predators primed us for warfare with our own species and the accelerating technology that warfare favors. But it was not hunting, as a way of living, that brought on the modern crisis. Humankind arrived full-blown upon civilized life, with nothing to indicate any superiority in faculties or capability over the hunter, so we must give serious consideration to how these two ways of living influence the human psyche.

The hunter depends on nature and her animals for his survival and reproductive success. For him interdependence is a fact of life. The hunter's success depends not only on his own devices, his inherited and developed abilities and skills, but on the knowledge of the formidable skills and abilities of his prey to escape or avoid him. Like the ancestors of Europeans, most contemporary hunting cultures firmly believe that their success also depends upon the cooperation and generosity of animals which in turn depend upon the respect given them by hunters according to elaborate ritual and rules of conduct.

It is customary among American hunting cultures for a hunter to ask the Creator for permission to take an animal, and to promise that he will honor the animal with a thanking ceremonial feast to which people are invited and in which the hunter recounts the story of the hunt. The hunter's preparation may include a vision quest, fasting, or purification by a sweat lodge. He may ask the spirit of the deer nation to present an animal to him of its own volition. In many tribes the hunter seeks the counsel of an intercessor, a person who represents the species he intends to hunt. The intercessor is connected to that species and communicates with it, but does not himself hunt it. The intercessor tells the hunter whether or not it is appropriate to hunt the animal, and if it is appropriate also may tell him where and how.

When the hunter takes the animal he apologizes to its spirit and thanks it for its generosity. If a hunter is not successful then it is assumed that he has fallen short of proper relationship with the animals and corrective steps must be taken. He may not have fulfilled his promise to honor an animal he killed, or bad intentions or negative attitudes toward himself or other people may be obstructing his connection with the animals. Whatever the cause, a forgiveness ceremony is essential, and sometimes grieving is appropriate.

The whereabouts of the animal often is unknown, and the outcome of a hunt varies according to a multitude of factors such as terrain, cover, wind and weather, and there is the specter of competition, direct or indirect, from other hunters, animal and human. The hunter's life is one of relentless uncertainty; he does not possess the animal or nature – they possess him. A player in a game in which nature and the animals make the rules, the hunter is forced necessarily by virtue of his niche into a stance of authentic humility.

The fact that preparation and thanking rituals are similar and widespread among hunting cultures suggests that they may be important to hunting success. Like biological adaptations, cultural traditions survive because they are beneficial.

To hunt is to experience extreme oneness with nature. The hunter is not on the earth but in it: he listens with the ears of the deer, sees with the eyes of the crow, and every plant, each sound and movement live for him. Not only awake to himself, the hunter expands outward into nature and is absorbed by it. He transcends himself, assumes the posture of dynamic meditation, complete awareness and attunement… perfect poise. Submerged wholly in nature with an attention best described as a kind of universal concentration, the hunter imitates his prey to the point of identity. The hunter is, as Ortega y Gasset mused in *Meditations On Hunting*, the alert man. All this is due, Ortega adds, to the fact that the hunter, while he stalks or waits, feels connected through the earth to the animal he pursues whether the animal is hidden, in view or absent.

The "Great Dance" is a brilliant documentary about the Kalahari Bushman hunters. After running down a kudu antelope for six hours in the hot desert a hunter says that while he was running he was kudu, that when the kudu moved he felt it in his own body and that the kudu was in his mind.

The meaning of the hunter's existence is that of a killer; paradoxically, hunting connects a man with the earth more deeply and profoundly than any other human enterprise. Surprising as it might appear at first glimpse, the hunter's feeling for his prey is one of deep passion, ecstacy and respect. The Eskimo who sits in freezing cold for 24 hours or more in silence and stillness, holding a spear and waiting for a seal to emerge at a breathing hole in the ice loves that seal. The hunter loves the animal he kills. Ortega said he who is not a hunter may think these last words are merely a manner of speaking. But the hunters will not. They know it is literally true that when they are in the field the axis of the whole situation is that mystical connection with the animal, an awareness and presentiment of it that spontaneously leads the hunter to perceive his environment from the point of view of the animal, with its particular attention to detail…light, wind, temperature, contour, vegetation, all have a role; they are not simply there, as they are for the scientist or tourist, but rather they perform a function.

Ortega says that they do not function as they do in agriculture, in the sense of their utility for the harvest, but rather each participates in the drama of the hunt from within itself, with its concrete and full being. The tourist views broadly the great expanses, but his gaze glides, seizing nothing, it does not perceive the role of each ingredient in the dynamic architecture of the landscape. It is only the hunter who imitates the alertness of the wild animal, for whom everything is possible danger, sees everything as a facility or difficulty, as protection and risk.

Although Ortega refers to the modern recreational hunter, what he says is true and meaningful precisely because the modern hunter recapitulates from his own being the primal hunter whose instincts he inherits. Those who have studied Buddhism or read Krishnamurti will recognize in Ortega's writing what spiritual masters say about the path to enlightenment, which is, after all, alertness. It is in this radical sense that the hunter, who seems from the outside to be an egotist, is on the inside a transcendentalist.

The Kalahari Bushman hunters compare tracking animals to dancing, which for them is a spiritual practice. They say they are talking with God when they track and dance.

About recreational hunting and religion, Ortega said that the essence of hunting is not raising the animal to the level of the human, but something far more spiritual, a conscious and nearly religious humbling of the hunter which limits his superiority. Ortega sees a fascinating mystery of nature manifested in the universal fact of hunting: the inexorable hierarchy among living beings. Every animal is in a relationship of superiority or inferiority with regard to each other. He views life as a terrible conflict, a grand and atrocious confluence. The hunt submerges man deliberately in that formidable mystery, and therefore it contains something of a religious rite in which homage is paid to what is divine, transcendent, in the laws of nature.

Among subsistence hunting societies, however, it is not man who is superior and who lowers himself toward the animal, but the animals who are superior and who, as an act of grace, lower themselves to humans if they are deserving. (The origin of civilized humanity's belief in its superiority is discussed below.)

In lowering himself toward the animal the civilized hunter does voluntarily surrender his anthropocentric arrogance to be on the same level as the animal, and that movement speaks profoundly to the power of the hunt to erase the artificial and recover what is natural: the hunter's identity with the animal and his agreement to participate with his animal kin in the never ending "game" of life and death. If the hunt teaches us anything it is that who eats today also will be eaten. Fuzon reminded us that everyone is somebody's dinner.

In his book, *Virgin Forest*, Eric Zencey acknowledges the transcendence,

> "when the hunter confronts the hunted and each becomes, in the instant, a part of the other – a psychic erasure of boundaries....a union of self and not-self that is ritually and literally mimicked in the act of eating that comes later, when flesh becomes flesh... when two unite as one....we struggle to recognize in the self's incorporation of the other through eating a spiritual meaning and importance. That moment of recognition, that grace, is not impossible to achieve. I think the hunter is well placed to achieve it."

It is true that re-creational hunting in North America is not based upon a cultural tradition that honors the spirit of the animal, as it is in Europe, and few re-creational hunters have adopted the sacred traditions of the aboriginal hunters of this continent. Yet, the timeless state of being that emerges when we hunt evokes common experience across cultural boundaries, not unlike the fundamentally identical experiences shared universally by humans who make love, give birth, raise children, tell jokes or make music.

There is a surprising portion of re-creational hunters who consider hunting to be their religion and many more for whom it is a well of profound spiritual experience. Here is what Erik Fritzell, former chairman of wildlife at Oregon State University had to say,

> "When I hunt I am immersed mentally, physically and even spiritually in an age-old predatory relationship among animals. I am participating in a common ecological process – just as a fox seeks her prey. I do not need to kill to eat – although I enjoy and appreciate eating game meat immensely. I kill in order to have hunted. To me, hunting is a very personal relationship between myself, the prey, and the environment in which the chase occurs. When I take my annual pilgrimage to the North Dakota pothole country, I take great pleasure in spending the vast majority of my time seeking just the right place to attempt to kill some ducks. In a sense, I am hunting for an ecosystem in which to participate. This participation, to me, is a form of ecological worship."

Author of *The Sacred Art of Hunting*, Jim Swan has this to say about hunting as religious instinct,

> "Taking the life of graceful, awesome animals stirs the deepest waters of the psyche. Sadness, Awe, Respect comes as naturally as the next sunrise as these sentiments find their way into the heart, leading to deeper and deeper feelings of reverence for nature, feelings which ultimately become love."

The phenomenology of the hunt has been largely overlooked for three reasons: a) most re-creational hunters do not openly communicate their deepest feelings; b) surveys have overlooked or ignored the deepest feelings and psycho-spiritual experiences of hunters; and, c) after being ridiculed and shamed by Christian missionaries and outsiders, aboriginal hunters are reluctant to share their innermost experiences with ethnographers. The combination of all these has had serious consequences. Re-creational hunters are not aware that at the deepest level their hunting experience is basically the same as it for aboriginal hunters, and that in turn has meant that modern humanity is ignorant of the underlying psycho-spiritual nature of hunting among men everywhere. Piaget once said that disciplinary lines are a disaster, and nowhere is this more obvious than in the study of hunting. Wildlife biologists have not searched for the "cultural universals" of hunting, and with very few exceptions, anthropologists have not examined re-creational hunting.

After being interviewed on a midwest TV program about the sacredness of the hunt, the interviewer pulled me aside and said, "I don't know why I am telling you this – I've never told anyone this – but something strange happened when I shot my first deer. For years I had had this urge to hunt deer, but no one in my family hunted and I had never been hunting so by the time I got a tag and went deer hunting I was already over 20. Well, I shot this deer and when I kneeled over it..." He paused and was visibly embarrassed, but then went on, "Well, the strangest thing happened. I smeared the deer's blood on my face and said a prayer for it!"

It is not uncommon for hunters, both subsistence and re-creational, to undergo rituals with the blood of animals they kill. The blooding ceremony is practiced regularly in Europe by hunters making their first kill. The smearing of blood on the face is a conspicuous acknowledgement of a critical transition in a hunter's life, often initiation to manhood and qualification for marriage.

On a psychic level the blood of the animal is more than a trophy. The Nez Perce natives near my home practice a ritual after killing a deer or elk in which they put some of the animal's fresh blood in their mouth. They believe that the blood carries the spirit of the animal, and by ingesting it they unite with that animal's spirit.

Jim Swan describes blood as the fountain of life and the cloak of death. To spill blood is to immerse oneself in the drama of life and death. Not unlike the Eucharist, the communion of the deer's blood with our body ritually honors the mystery of life and acceptance of our own mortality.

George Mann killed his first deer at the age of ten in Alabama. That evening at the lodge, he stood up before everyone and had the deer's blood smeared over his face, initiating him into the society of hunters. Mann was much influenced by his initiatory experience and became an avid hunter and conservationist. Later in life he successfully reintroduced deer to his land and nurtured them and the habitat until he had a sizable herd. He set aside a private reserve of several hundred acres specifically devoted to people hunting their first deer. As of 1999, he had personally conducted blooding ceremonies for 224 hunters who had killed their first deer on his property.

In conducting interviews for three documentaries about hunting, I almost always asked the person if they felt sad when they killed an animal. Almost all said yes and many sobbed or held back tears. One man described his first deer hunt as a teenager, but he was so excited to take the deer that he ran up and kissed it! The forked horn buck is the smallest deer the man ever killed and the only head he had mounted. After twenty-five years he said with pride that it still hangs on the wall above his desk. That trophy deer is not merely an ego statement, but an honoring of the animal who gave up its life so a boy could be initiated to manhood. That deer and man are spiritually married.

Gross misperceptions about hunting are prevalent in the civilized world. From the outside hunters are commonly viewed as egotists who ruthlessly impose their will on innocent nature. Hunting is seen as an act of domination. It may be for a very small percentage of re-creational hunters who are perverted. Ortega reminded us that there are rogues in hunting as there are in all walks of life; we find them on highways and ski slopes, in banks, fitness centers and basketball courts. They are rare among hunters. According to a study conducted by the National Shooting Sports Foundation, they may be one in a thousand. After decades of hunting and fishing experience I have yet to encounter one, though I have heard reliable accounts of them, among native hunters, too.

When I was presenting a lecture in Toronto at the annual convention of the Ontario Federation of Anglers and Hunters, I paused to ask how many of the 450 hunters in attendance had a hunting experience when everything was suitable and acceptable, the animal they sought was in their sights, but for some inexplicable reason they did not shoot it. Three out of four of the hunters raised their hands. Why did they let the animal go? Because it did not **feel** right to kill it. The same phenomenon occurs among aboriginal hunters who are hunting for their food.

Personal anecdotes such as these and reports from aboriginal hunters converge to indicate that at the deepest level the hunt constitutes a unified field of human experience that includes the following components. Prior to the hunt recreational hunters invest in prayer or its equivalent including vivid imagination of the animal(s) appearing in range, energized by the hunter's emotion, which amounts to practice of the law of attraction. Aboriginal hunters may ask the Creator for permission and then address the oversoul of that species or their ancestors for assistance.

- a hyper state of sensory alertness and inner awareness resulting in transcendence of ego;
- identification with and imitation of the animal;
- extreme awareness of one's self in the environment;
- a moment of truth in which the hunter decides whether or not to take a particular animal;

- exhiliration if a lethal wound/kill has been made;
- sadness at the animal's death, a sense of remorse and/or the need to seek forgiveness (from the animal, its Spirit Nation – oversoul - or the Creator);
- especially among young or inexperienced hunters, reflection on the impermanence of life;
- a sense of completion accompanied by a deep feeling of gratitude and the necessity of paying respect to the animal, nature and/or Creator, which may be expressed in a personal or culturally acquired ritual; and,
- a deep sense of pride and accomplishment upon presentation of the animal to hunting associates, family or society, which normally includes detailed recounting of the hunt (and sharing the meat in hunter-gatherer societies).

There is a subtle realm of experience in hunting as well as in war, that many men encounter and even actively engage, but which to my knowledge has not been articulated - except possibly by some advanced trackers who intentionally practice awareness - perhaps because it is so much a part of the male constitution that it is largely transparent. I became aware of it first when I was a young hunter stalking squirrels in a black oak forest in central Illinois and came upon a pair of whitetail deer, unaware of me only forty yards away. For several minutes I stood there watching them, holding my "energy" close to my body. Then, when I decided I needed to continue hunting squirrels, I relaxed and it seemed to me that the energy field which had been contracted around me instantly expanded, whereupon the deer suddenly turned their heads sharply in my direction and looked directly at me before bounding away. Since then I have had the same experience on many occasions, not only while hunting but also in the course of studying the behavior of wild animals I stalked in the field…and which stalked me.

The concept of an aura, energy field or subtle body around organisms is ancient and widespread, and even may have been corroborated via measurement (visit www.heartmath.org for research reports). Does it serve as sensory modality as well as communication, though largely at the unconscious level, among civilized people save hunters, warriors and practicioners of meditation, awareness and certain healing arts?

Among both recreational and aboriginal hunters rituals or ceremonies may be public, such as the well established dance for the eland among the Kalahari Bushman, or private. A Western Shoshone hunter told me that following the kill of a deer, making peace with the deer is strictly private, between the hunter, the deer and the Creator.

Before, during and following the hunt, a hunter may intentionally or unintentionally enter into the spiritual realm to receive guidance or communicate with the animal.

A few years ago I took the father of one of my son's school friends hunting for Canada geese on a farm pond near Wallowa, Oregon. It was a favorite daytime resting area and evening roost for geese, and everytime I had come in early a flock flushed off the pond. But not this day. We put out decoys at one end of the pond where I had built a blind from willow limbs, then hid and waited. By 10:00 AM there had not been a goose seen or heard. It was the longest spell ever at the pond without geese at least flying by.

I decided to pray and closed my eyes. The guy next to me could not see my face as I prayed silently in earnest, "Spirit of the Goose Nation, please bless us with geese this morning. My life is devoted to teaching humans to respect all the creatures. We will honor your gifts." As I opened my eyes I was astonished to see a giant goose in mid-air, right in front of me, its beak only inches from my forehead, its outstretched wings still. Its apparent size was about six feet in length with a wing span of perhaps ten feet. And then it vanished.

I wondered if this was what some Native American hunters experienced when they reported seeing the spirit representative of a species? Had I just witnessed the Spirit of the Goose Nation?

A few minutes later a flock of about forty geese appeared on the horizon and flew straight toward us. I told the man that the geese would circle the pond several times before coming in to our decoys. They always had before, but this time the geese flew straight to our blind and at about 35 yards out turned sharp and passed over the decoys at perfect range. In awe that my prayer had been answered so quickly I just watched them fly by and gave thanks.

While it is common for aboriginal hunters to pray for permission to hunt and kill an animal, it is fairly rare for recreational hunters to do so, though many pray for their hunt to be blessed with safety and success. Nonetheless, it is as though the hunter's heart evokes powerful intuitions, including the whereabouts of animals, even in advance of entering the field. Recreational hunters describe feelings that have directed them to prey or to a location where prey then appeared.

Some hunters report that certain animals seemed to be meant for them. Speaking often at their conventions, I have asked thousands of hunters if they believed that certain animals had come to them. From 30-50% normally raise their hands, most of whom had hunted for twenty or more years.

There is a meta-lesson that few recreational hunters discuss but which most learn: attitude and intention have real consequences in the hunt, which is the foundation of reciprocity between subsistence hunters and wild animals.

Spirit Tracking?

Many tracking schools in North America and Europe originated from Tom Brown Jr., who wrote *The Tracker*. His teacher was Apache medicine man, Stalking Wolf, and his first initiate was Jon Young whom I interviewed below. Jon and those he mentors practice and teach "spirit tracking," which they recovered from the great tracking cultures including the Akamba of Kenya, the Apache, the Kalahari Bushman and the aboriginal foragers of Australia. Spirit tracking does not consist of using the usual five senses and analytical thinking, but rather "peripheral" vision which glimpses trails of energy left by an animal or human. In many cases, the ability to access "spirit lines" is connected to an altered state induced by trance dancing, ritual sweat baths, extended running and other activities that tend to sensitive practicioners in similar ways.

The Kahunas of Polynesia call these trails of energy "aka cords," etheric energy trails left by us throughout our lives and also established via eye-to-eye contact. They believe that everything we have ever touched is still connected to us via aka cords, which may be why we save and cherish the jewelry of dead kin. It is commonly believed among indigenous cultures that the spirits of ancestors may be contacted by holding objects they once wore or used. Native Americans have explained to me that the feather of a golden eagle is not merely a trophy, that it connects them with the Spirit of the Eagle Nation. The famous taxidermist, Mike Boyce of Reno, said something similar about the mounted bear in his den connecting him with the "essence" of the bear.

Using spirit trails, a skilled indigenous hunter can literally run while tracking animals. Jon Young has conducted experiments on adults with no background in tracking and discovered that merely by holding their hand close to an animal's track nearly all can accurately describe where the animal is and what it is doing at the time. Conversely, some Native Americans of several tribes say it is not a good idea to step on the track of a bear because doing so may communicate your location to it!

Wildlife professors, some of them avid hunters, have a difficult time with "spirit tracking" because it pushes their envelope of mechanistic thinking. For example, today I received a letter from a former colleague in wildlife biology who stated that this book's combination of science with explicit mysticism including "tracking aura" was hard for him to handle. Isn't it good science to test an idea before discounting it simply because it lies outside the box? Anyone can undertake some simple tests at home to discover perception by peripheral vision. On my own I began doing it about the age of ten by going into my sister's room when the house was empty and sitting in front of her full-length mirror. By focusing my vision on my eyes in the mirror within seconds I could see a shimmering energy field around my head and upper body, but the moment I focused on it the aura was gone. I learned to hold my focus on the eyes and observe the aura peripherally.

Years later while living in Ashland, Oregon, I answered the challenge given repeatedly by the Eastern teacher, Jidu Krishnamurti, who had been groomed by the Theosophical Society as a new world teacher in the tradition of Buddha and Jesus. At the age of 21, Krishnamurti was introduced to the world, but much to everyone's surprise he encouraged the people in attendance not to worship him, and instead to become their own guru. In the fashion of an authentic mentor, he asked far more questions than he gave answers, and his favorite was, "Can you see a tree?" I went out into the gold rush cemetery across the street and sat looking at a tree for a few minutes before the silver aura dancing on the trunk and limbs appeared in my peripheral field of vision.

You may think it easy to see a tree, but when I asked students in an environmental awareness class at Shasta College where I was teaching for a week to go out alone to see a tree they all came back with reports of all kinds: what kind it was; a poem or a passage in a book about trees; memories of climbing trees. All of it memory files, but no tree. Which is why it is so important to practice being present, alert and aware, attentive to other beings, the world and ourselves, a proven path to enlightenment. Attention, Krishnamurti often said, requires affection. The hunter meets all these conditions. Is he the original mystic whose right-mindedness entitles him to miracles?

The Lakota Elder, Gilbert Walking Bull, grew up with little influence from the Western world, unlike most members of his tribe. Having been excused from school by the B.I.A., Gilbert and his cousins were raised in the traditional way by their grandparents, both of whom were practicing spiritual elders. They followed traditional ceremonies, lived off the land by hunting and gathering, and learned from elder hunters, scouts, warriors and medicine people.

Gilbert spent many years mentoring tracker Jon Young and his community of initiates. Often he explained that he and his people believed that animals left a residue which a hunter or tracker could learn over time to absorb and follow. He further explained that there were lines connecting everything in the universe including the animals. He said that his people could see the tracks glowing, like a bluish light. The word for this phenomenon in Lakota is "wakan," which, he said, means "the arteries." He believed that the word described how energy moved through the Creation. He added that the people living on the reservations had adopted a different understanding of the meaning of these old words.

The implications of spirit tracking could be immense. The Bushman of the Kalahari only recently revealed their spiritual life to psychotherapist Bradford Keeney who wrote *Ropes to God* and *Bushman Shaman*. Though the Bushman have been inundated for decades by anthropologists, only Keeney has been honored as a Bushman shaman. The only culture known to dance every night, the Bushman revealed for the first time to Keeney what they actually do when they dance and enter a trance state. They send healing energy across what they call ropes or chains from their bodies to friends or relatives. Bad energy can also be sent the same way, but those ropes are red and can be avoided. They also leave their bodies and travel up the ropes into a spiritual dimension where they meet with deceased relatives to receive their counsel.

Bushman track animals by following spirit trails or ropes. And they communicate with one another on a regular basis using the same cords. In the context of daily survival, hunters follow the ropes that go to the animals. This circle of union with animals and other Bushman amounts to a shift in relation from "I am separate from the other" to "I am inseparable from the other." The relational shift is from egoism to spiritual connectedness. Once again hunting is a model for transcendent living.

Laurens Van der Post, the Afrikaaner who was first to defend the Bushman and produce documentaries about them in the 1950s, was also the first person to write about their "tapping in the heart" system of long-distance communication.

Laurens and his film crew were following a small band of Bushman hunters who had wounded a bull eland with a poison arrow. The crew was in a Land Rover and could barely keep up with the Bushman who were chasing the bull and its harem. When the bull was finally killed and the Bushman had done their ritual ceremony for the eland, it was butchered and loaded into the Land Rover for the journey back to the Bushman camp. Laurens noticed a hunter bent over with his eyes closed, concentrating, and asked his Bushman interpreter what the man was doing. He replied that he was sending a wire to the camp that they had killed an eland and were heading back.

Laurens didn't think much about what the interpreter had said until hours later as they approached the camp and saw a huge bonfire with the women and kids all dancing and singing. The interpreter pointed out to Laurens that they were singing the eland song. The "wire" had been received.

The same phenomenon was filmed in "The Great Dance" when the hunters arrived back at their village where the women and children were dancing and singing the kudu song.

If the Polynesians and great tracking societies are right, each of us has an enormous web of connection with other people, creatures, places and things, even the spirits of the dead. Across this energetic web it may be possible to communicate and transmit energy for good or ill, in which case imagine how much we may continually influence one another with our thoughts and feelings. Imagine how keen self-awareness could elevate the messages we are transmitting. Imagine how responsibility for our thoughts and feelings might change the world. Imagine the awareness we may have lost, but which might be possible to regain.

Keeney says, "In the spirit, all places and living beings are woven together by the lines of light, spinning a web of infinite interconnectivity," which allows the soul to experience any aspect of life. "The lines of relationship are the arcs of the greater circles of life. They comprise the Mind of Nature." It is somehow fitting that the people with the most primitive lifestyle on earth also would exhibit the most spiritual life, and that they would be more successful using spirit tracking than we are using ego and analysis. The same etheric energy system is used by Bushman to heal one another, and it is worth noting that years of study by the Harvard research team revealed that the still wild Bushman were as healthy as Americans, though they have no vaccinations, drugs, doctors or hospitals.

Now perhaps you may fathom why I say that the next kid in the woods better be a hunter.

Spirit tracking brings a new level of awareness to the admonition of Chinese philosopher Lao Tzu who said if you would save the world look first to yourself. The future for us lies in recovering first things.

"Modern civilization has no understanding of sacred matters. Everything is backwards. Modern civilization says, don't pray in school, don't pray at work; only go to church on Sunday. If you don't believe what I believe you'll go to hell. Deviancy is normal. Our role models cheat, drink and run around; these are the people in the news. The news sells bad news; no one wants to hear good news. Kids are killing kids. Violence is normal. Leaders cheat and lie. Everything is backwards. We need to pray for spiritual intervention. We need to have Guidance from the Creator to help us rebuild our families, our communities and ourselves."

~ THOMAS YELLOWTAIL, Crow

Chapter 4

Ways of Knowing

"The heart has its reasons that reason knows not of."

~ Pascal

Face to Face with a Wild Lion

I was driving the Land Rover around Nairobi National Park in search of cheetahs when I came across a small group of lions lying at the edge of shrubs on the shelf above the Athi River Plains. The male was a young adult, perhaps three years old, and he was accompanied by several lionesses. Though his mane was not especially full, he was an attractive specimen and I wanted to photograph him.

That particular day I was driving an open-top Land Rover, better for photography. As I drove close the lions withdrew further into the bush. But I kept getting in just a little closer to get a better shot: the young male became agitated and snarled at me as he crawled another couple of feet into the brush.

I had raised the windshield so I could shoot over the hood of the car. Because I needed to jockey around to take the best pictures, I was using the hand throttle rather than the pedal. When I was about ten feet away from the lion I stopped and started focusing the Zeiss lens.

Suddenly the lion charged out with a loud huffing roar. "Oh, shit," came out of my mouth as I fell back in the seat, popped the gear into reverse and slammed the hand throttle as far as it would go, all the time keeping my eyes straight ahead on the lion who was still charging, taking swipes with his paws at the front of the Land Rover. Though I was accelerating backwards, he was keeping up with me, and then I realized that I was in dire straits: what if he came over the hood? And then I wondered what was behind me: if I hit a large rock or tree or warthog hole I'd be thrown from the vehicle completely vulnerable to attack. There was no one else around. I was on my own.

As the car kept moving backwards at top speed, the lion began to slow down so I figured that I was going to make it through if I didn't collide with something behind me. I got some of my favorite lion photos that day, but nearly at the cost of my life. Such are the risks taken by the ego in its quest for fame and fortune.

Back at the college in Nairobi I didn't tell anyone about the near mishap, and a few days later I was back in the park this time following cheetahs on foot. The mother had four nearly adult offspring that were beginning to fend for themselves. The mother stayed back as one of the young adults led the hunts. As the family headed off towards a bluff above the river I decided to park the vehicle and follow them on foot. The terrain was rocky and I didn't want to lose visual contact. Grabbing my camera and notebook I started out after them.

As I went around the point of a long row of brush I felt strange, as though something were behind me, and I turned to look. There under the bush ten feet away which I had just walked by was an adult male lion – the very lion that had charged my vehicle several days ago. "Oh my God, not you!" went through my mind, followed by "What the hell am I going to do?" I had no weapon and there was no one else in the vicinity. All of a sudden, fear vanished and I was overcome by perfect calm and inner peace. He stared straight into my eyes, not a good sign since that signaled he was not at all afraid. I knew that it was important for me to stare right back at him and never to waiver. Somehow, I also knew that turning to run was not an option.

Do not mistake me. I did not stand there and reason all this out the way you would a chess move. No, I was in an altered state of consciousness, fearless and devoid of reasoning altogether. There was instead instantaneous knowing of what was most appropriate and essential. Considering that I had never pondered the situation, nor read accounts of people in similar circumstances nor talked it over nor had any comparable experience in my life, it is utterly remarkable that I knew what to do. After holding my stare for about one minute I began to very slowly and carefully take tiny steps backwards. Each step must have been an inch or two in length, lasting ten to twenty seconds. Talk about focus!

At a distance of ten yards I began to think that the lion may not attack, though I knew I wasn't out of the woods yet so I kept backing up slowly, still holding the stare until I was about 40 yards away. The lion seemed at that point to lose interest as he glanced to his right when a Bobo bird landed in an Acacia next to him and sounded off. I walked steadily backwards now with bigger steps until about 80 yards away then I turned and walked as fast as I could towards the nearest trees of any size, intending to climb them to safety. The lion didn't pursue me so I headed off after the cheetah family, only to be stalked by one of the young adult males, but that's another story.

How did I know exactly what to do? There simply is no logical explanation, even if upon reflection one's actions seemed quite reasonable. Reason was not at work, at least not initially, though it did click in once I was far enough away to begin thinking about escape strategies and routes.

Was instinct at work? Initially, in the first second or two, fear was the ruling emotion, and it may have called upon inherited information conducive to survival. Do we know instinctively when confronted with a dangerous predator to be quite still and appear unfrightened, which direct staring ought to communicate? Or are these notions simply conformations with evolutionary theory, in which I was thoroughly indoctrinated?

Looking back on it all it is easy to imagine that I believed I was in "clear and present danger, " and ego bailed me out, "It's a damn good thing you let me be in charge that day. If you hadn't been afraid you'd now be dead."

The real truth is that while fear and ego responded initially, very quickly I found myself in an extreme state of transcendent alertness accompanied by total emotional calm. My mind was completely clear, still and empty, the state known as Zen mind or beginner's mind in Japan. I was no longer "me," identified with my body, but I was me and the lion and our shared circumstances.

I wonder if absolute fearlessness would mean a far more wonderful world? Who knows that I even might have befriended that lion? Impossible you say? Counter to the "laws" of nature? I propose that that is the ego talking, and the ego wants to be in charge always and will go to any length to be the chairman of our psychic board. It climbs to prominence through the force of fear.

In those days I did not know about sanyasans, holy men, who befriended adult, wild bears high in the Himalayas. Clearly, they are functioning on another level with a distinctly different set of beliefs. For example, when Guru Dev was located in the forest after decades of solitude, meditation and silence, to be placed as head of the Hindu religion, a tiger lay at his feet, a cobra in his lap. One of his "rescuers" asked if he were afraid. Guru Dev responded that he sees only God.

Deepak Chopra explains the influence of our beliefs. He says, for example, that a person who sees a cobra on the path in India may jump back in fear, and his increased heartbeat and panting are visible signs that the hormone adrenalin has kicked in, secreted by the adrenal cortex stimulated by ACTH secreted by the pituitary. But if a biochemist could track down every molecule involved in his fear reaction, he would miss the invisible decision maker that decided to have the reaction, for even though the person reacted in a split second, his body didn't jump back mindlessly. Someone else with different programming would exhibit a different reaction. My friend, Ron Dupont, a herpetologist, might make every effort to catch it. A Hindu who perceives snakes as a form of Shiva, might kneel in prayer.

Any of a number of possible reactions might have occurred - panic, reverence, paralysis, apathy, curiosity, delight. It all depends on the meaning that a cobra has for a person. There is truth in a saying from Aldous Huxley that the experience is not what happens to us; it is what we do with what happens to us.

~ RANDALL L. EATON,
The Greatest Things I Never Did (in progress)

Ken Wilber is touted by a well-known authority as the leading writer on consciousness today. His *Up From Eden* presents a typical humanistic perspective of progress over time, civilization's myth of history with an expectation of a grand synthesis of scientific reason and religion that will transfigure our lives any day now. Vehemently, I have debated this and other points with Wilber who places faith in reason while I remain convinced that astute erudition has not and likely will not open hearts or bring peace to the world.

What does David Bohm, the great physicist, have in common with Jidu Krishnamurti, the spiritual teacher? What do they have in common with Joseph Pearce, an authority on human development, intelligence and creativity, and with healer Deepak Chopra? And what have they all in common with anthropologist Richard Nelson and the elders of numerous tribes of North America? In their respective ways, each of them discriminates between two radically different ways of knowing. Chopra, for instance, advises us to sit quietly at a table to receive insight. Lakota holy man Wallace Black Elk refers to the normal every day chatter of the ego as "traffic." Krishnamurti and Bohm differentiate normal intellect from true intelligence, and Joseph Chilton Pearce terms these "ego-intellect" and "intelligence," which I prefer to label "heart-intelligence."

We live in a world that worships ego-intellect; behind our great myth of science is an even greater myth of reason or intellectualism. We suffer from what Ortega calls "pious idealism," another way of saying we are extremely egotistical. He defined reason as an orthopedic device imposed on a broken instinct. We are so stuck on the importance of what we and others already "know," that we seldom create a space to allow the unknown to move into awareness. It comes through by no conscious effort on our part in the form of dreams, sudden insights and unexpected intuitions, those "Aha!" experiences that have given birth to scientific and creative breakthroughs. In short, we do not trust higher reason, the intelligence of the heart. Trusting in ego-intellect is exactly what has brought our life and world to the verge of collapse. What we require is a change of heart.

Anyone who has spent much time with the natives of this continent soon discovers that they often think in a different way. Conversation moves quite slowly as medicine people or elders seem to be wasting valuable time and waiting forever to speak. At first, the snail pace of dialogue is downright frustrating. But something valuable is happening; these people do trust more than ego-consciousness and they turn to it for guidance. While it is customary for many modern people to say, "I think...," more traditional folks often say, "I feel in my heart..." Because indigenous peoples tend to surrender to an intelligence beyond ego, they are able to tap into wisdom.

Anthropologist turned hunter, Richard Nelson says, "Over the past 500 years, we have concentrated on promoting Western secular and religious education in Native American communities and have almost completely ignored what they could teach us in return. As a result we've lost the opportunity for a balanced exchange and coalescence of our two great intellectual traditions..." The great traditions of the Western ego and the hunter's heart come together in the hunt, as Nelson himself discovered.

Nelson continues,

> "In my opinion, the ethnographic record supports the existence of a widespread and well-developed tradition of conservation, land stewardship, and religiously-based environmental ethics among Native Americans. I believe that Aldo Leopold's eloquent and insightful formulation of a land ethic is a fascinating example of convergence with Native American thought....Is it possible that wisdom has been more important than knowledge as a basis for the long and successful habitation of North America by indigenous people? Could it be wisdom that explains why the first European travelers found here a vast and untrammeled beauty, an extraordinary wealth and diversity of wild species, an area of intact natural communities?"

In the final analysis, it is the wisdom of humility and respect for nature characteristic of native hunter-gatherer societies that we must adopt if we are to forge a viable culture.

These qualities stem from the hunting lifeway, but they also emerge from the lives of recreational hunters such as Aldo Leopold who recapitulated the ancient wisdom of hunting peoples. Not so long ago Richard Nelson was opposed to recreational hunting, and he disapproved of my promotion of it as a principle way to connect with nature and discover animals as teachers. Perhaps it was the years spent with subsistence hunters of the far north that finally awakened the spirit of the wild in him, and now he is a model for the virtues of recreational hunting. His personal transformation is an endorsement of the theme of this book: that hunting can be a cardinal component in the initiation of boys to men who will think with their hearts, not just their heads.

As Shepard said in *Tender Carnivore and Sacred Game,* "Man is part a carnivore: the male of the species is genetically programmed to pursue, attack and kill for food. To the extent that men do not do so they are not fully human."

Speaking to delegates from 70 nations about a common ground for subsistence and recreational hunting, I was accused by wildlife biologist, Shane Mahoney, of promoting the noble savage. I think Rousseau was right to identify what is artificial for civilized humanity and what we might recover from primal societies that is natural and healthy. I know quite well that foraging peoples are not perfect. For example, they feud and divorce, but they also are anything but primitive in their knowledge of nature, which has been shown to rival the best of our science, or in their mythology, cosmology and spiritual life. War is uncommon; they have no professional soldiers or standing armies. There is more personal choice and freedom in their ranks than among ours. Anthropologist Elman Service said that individual adults participate far more fully in every aspect of their culture than do people of more complex societies. According to sociologist Murray Bookchin, among Ituri pygmies there are outrageously boastful men and extremely shrewd women and those who exhibit humor and gaiety, contradicting the conventional image of preliterate peoples as divested of personality. So does the superb writing of Bradford Keeney about the Kalahari Bushman.

Problems among individuals and between the sexes are resolved in the context of daily life. Colin Turnbull said that in terms of a deliberate dedication to human relationships, both affective and effective, the primitive is way ahead of us. Anthropologist Richard Lee says there is no evidence of exploitation on the basis of sex or age. Except for sex, sharing is a way of life. According to Lee, there is an ongoing struggle against one's own selfish, anti-social and arrogant impulses, which indicates that despite all appearances to the contrary and idyllic social conditions for raising children, nonetheless adults actively contend with negative impulses, and positive cultural traditions help. The good wolf wins over the evil wolf when we feed it most.

Paul Shepard adds that ecological influences of the foraging lifestyle are non-polluting and stable.

Are we on the wrong path? Will science, technology, computers and TV give us what we want? Is belief in a punishing God a projection of the patriarchy, which breeds fear, doubt and murder, not love? The mission of Jesus, Joseph Chilton Pearce insists, was to teach us that, like him, we are divine – "ye shall do these things and greater still" - that the Kingdom of Heaven is within us, and that except as little children we shall not discover the Kingdom through transcendence, our right. Pearce claims that Paul corrupted the teachings of Jesus by deifying and separating him from us, and by infusing the punishing God of the Hebrews into Christianity, and as a consequence the heart is still at war with the ego, and transcendence has not become our way of life. He is convinced that Jesus is the exemplary model for civilized humanity, and that if we do not recover innocence there is little hope for us. His recipe for recovery of transcendence in human life includes endless play for children and for adults, which is common among foraging cultures.

When humanity left hunting as a lifeway in the "wilderness," it started the several thousand year process of dehumanization. Savagery, brutality and barbarity have only increased exponentially since we crossed that threshold. Time was when the world was a temple, every bird, rock and leaf were divine gifts, each animal was souled and life was whole and full, pregnant with its own dimensions. No need for Jungianism among some aboriginal Americans who saw in each person a boy, an old man, a girl and a woman. Like Leopold, Jung's contributions to the modern world amount to wisdom that is ancient among hunting societies.

The lack of balance within and between humans and between them and their world is the tragic outcome of the loss of innocence incumbent to primal living. With civilization defense of resources became practical, and war became the new theme of human life. Civilization means domination and subjugation of that which had been elusive (hunted): primal living necessarily involves at its core acceptance of the "principle of uncertainty" in exploitation of resources, but civilized life is a progressive pretension towards certainty of resources. Big game were converted to livestock which are "managed" instead of pursued at risk of failure and danger; wild plant foods put under the hoe and plow in fields prepared and watered close to home rather than being sought when and wherever local conditions might prove favorable to their production, and, these and their concomitant circumstances rapidly remove humanity from nature and interdependence with her to progressively immodest domination. Humanity reduces to possession what before could never be possessed, and in so doing insulates itself from nature and the compassionate power of the heart. Could it be that as men dominated wild animals they also subjugated women? As competition for clumped food resources became paramount to human success, was the value of women correspondingly diminished except as breeding stock?

Possession of wealth favors warring to defend and steal wealth, so maleness and the Father God rise to prominence until male egoism brings civilized life to collapse – or, in our age, the specter of destroying humanity and its life-support systems altogether.

Without the recovery of the ancient wisdom in the earliest myths of civilization, when people were still consciously aware of what they were giving up in the transition from foraging, there may be no dynamic equilibrium between male and female, nor the inner masculine and feminine of the psyche. Is psychic fragmentation the real origin of a global crisis?

William Irwin Thompson's proposal for solution of the human crisis is that human ignorance of timeless myth is on the verge of recovery as we stand at the edge of the "age of chaos or heroes" glimpsing the recycle of "the age of gods." The last age of myth amply forewarned men of the dangers they were bringing upon themselves with civilization, but it was only in the latter part of the 20th century that humans started taking the ancient myths seriously.

Gilgamesh and the Destruction of Nature

The oldest story recorded on earth comes from the Sumerian city of Uruk (Erek) built to honor the gods Anu and Ishtar. Gilgamesh was the ruler of Uruk, his mother was a goddess, his father a man. Described as tyrannical, Gilgamesh was said to be beautiful in manliness, his whole body adorned with voluptuous grace. Powerful in physique, Gilgamesh had no equal among men or gods.

Gilgamesh had a dream of an axe. His mother, Ninsun, explained to him that the axe in his dream is a man, and that Gilgamesh shall love him. Ninsun tells Gilgamesh that she created the man to rival with him, that mighty in the land is his strength.

When a hunter comes to Gilgamesh and tells him about the wild man who has come from the mountain, whose strength is mighty, and who grazes with the wild cattle, Gilgamesh sends a harlot with the hunter to the wild man's waterhole where she can entice him with her sexual favors.

After three days, Enkidu the wild man comes to the waterhole with the cattle, and the harlot bares her bosom and takes of his lust. For six days and seven nights Enkidu stayed with the whore, but when he tried to rejoin his cattle and sheep they did not recognize him and ran away. Enkidu was weak and could not catch them, so he returned to the woman, sat at her feet and listened as she begged him to return to Uruk and meet the mighty Gilgamesh who sees visions of Enkidu in his dreams.

Enkidu puts on clothing and accompanies the harlot to Uruk where he learned to eat food and drink beer, seven pots at one sitting. He annointed his body and seized a weapon, and attacked lions which preyed upon shepherds at night. Finally the day came when he wrestled with Gilgamesh to a draw and they became the best of friends.

Gilgamesh proposes to slay the monster Humbaba in the cedar forest. Humbaba is the god of the forest, perhaps all things wild and untamed. Having lived in the mountains when he wandered with the cattle, Enkidu respects and fears Humbaba. He says to Gilgamesh, "The roar of Humbaba is as a hurricane, his mouth is fire; his breath is death. Why hast though desired to do this thing, a battle without precedent, the conquest of Humbaba?"

Again Enkidu implores Gilgamesh to refrain as he warns him of the difficult journey and of Humbaba who sleeplessly guards the forest. The commander of the gods, Enlil, decreed for Humbaba sevenfold terror to keep safely the forest. Furthermore, Enkidu advises Gilgamesh that anyone who goes there is seized by disease.

The response of Gilgamesh to his wild-man friend epitomizes the hubris of civilized humanity, "If I fail I shall establish my fame, 'Gilgamesh fell by Humbaba the powerful,' it shall be said."

Gilgamesh vows to conquer the cedar forest, to cut the cedars down with his own hand, and make for himself an everlasting name. Though the elders of the city attempt to dissuade Gilgamesh for all the same reasons given by Enkidu, Gilgamesh proceeded to have the weapons made as he prayed to Ninsun and Shamash for protection.

When Gilgamesh and Enkidu finally reach the far away cedar forest, and Gilgamesh proceeds to clear cut the forest, Humbaba in rage cries out, "Who has come and cut down the cedars which are held precious in my mountains?" Now Shamash comes to the aid of Gilgamesh and Enkidu, and urges them on. There is a fight with disastrous results. But

Shamash inflicts Humbaba with mighty winds, eight in all, which blind him.

Humbaba submits and begs Gilgamesh for mercy, saying he would serve him well by supplying cedars to build houses for him. Strangely, Enkidu protests and tells him not to spare Humbaba. Enkidu decapitates the god of the forest, and for this act the council of the gods decreed that he should die, though Gilgamesh was spared. Gilgamesh mourns a lifetime for his friend Enkidu. Ironically, Gilgamesh gains possession of the plant of life that would have prolonged his mortal existence, but he lost it on his journey home.

The German poet, Goethe, said, "There are two hearts beating in my breast," and in every man among us there is a Gilgamesh, refined, civilized, knowing and prideful. And there is an Enkidu, discheveled, hairy, at home with the animals and nature. Had it not been for the temptation of the city and his love for Gilgamesh, Enkidu never would have dreamed of harming Humbaba. For his transgression against Nature, Enkidu paid with his life.

It is an ominous tragedy: everyone loses. The world loses the cedar forest; the god of Nature is given no mercy even when he offers to serve humanity. Enkidu the wild man dies, and Gilgamesh mourns a lifetime, all because a mighty, civilized man aimed to make an everlasting name for himself! Had Gilgamesh listened to the wild man and respected his wishes, everyone would have been better for it. Here we have in the oldest story from civilization a warning about the dangers of vaulted pride, and the question it raises is whether we will listen to the wild man within or follow the tragic route of Gilgamesh.

It is said that you can take the boy out of the country, but not the country out of the boy. The Epic of Gilgamesh suggests that in fact the country can be taken out of the boy as it was from Enkidu. We cannot afford to overly civilize the wild man.

In the anthology, *A Testament to Wilderness*, Laurens Van der Post confronts wilderness as a way of truth, "...we all know what wilderness really is, because we have it inside ourselves. We know it is a world in which every bit of nature counts...and we know when it is not there....human beings...who live in industrialized environments are...therefore estranged in a sense from their natural selves." Laurens recounts a story of three problem boys of different nationalities from wealthy families which had sought his assistance. He sent them to Zululand where they went on a wilderness trek with Ian Player who said nothing to them about themselves, though they found something of themselves and the wilderness within and went on to distinguish themselves. Laurens says, "Wilderness is an instrument for enabling us to recover our lost capacity for religious experience.... Through wilderness we remember, and are brought home again."

Van der Post's many years of contact with Bushman brought him to realize that in destroying wilderness we have destroyed "wilderness man," which he considers the greatest loss of all because this person could have been our bridge to knowing wilderness and nature in the way it is known by the Creator. The Bushman committed themselves to nature, and nature was kinder to them by far than any civilization ever was. Laurens added that wherever the Bushman went they felt they were known, unlike the staggering loss of identity and meaning in the modern world which has banished the wilderness persons in ourselves and the wilderness that sustained them. He says we are all know-italls, but the feeling that our knowing is no longer contained in a greater form of being known.

Van der Post believes we can recover the "wilderness man" because he exists in us, and he is the foundation in spirit or psyche on which we build, and we are not complete until we have fully recovered him.

> "And before we can live properly, before we can face the future, we have got to remember...the needs and hunger of our instinctive, intuitive, natural self...What we need to do now...is to make the first the last, and to bring what was left behind up to where we are. We still carry around with us the world of nature within. We need to match that to the world without, to make the world without more and more an expression of the world within....Our greed and aggression and corruption by power comes from cheating that first person within ourselves out of his natural inheritance."

Finally Laurens concludes, and I emphasize, "**Somewhere, beyond the walls of our awareness...the wilderness side, the hunter side, the seeking side of ourselves, is waiting to return.**"

Loss of Innocence

Concerning the city man's corruption of the wild man and his loss of innocence let's turn to an ancient civilization, China, and repeat what the *I Ching* or book of wisdom (changes) says. Under the hexagram for innocence are ideas corresponding with the mystical interpretations of the legends of paradise and the fall of man.

> "Innocence frees itself of mistakes, so that no misfortune of internal origin can overtake it. When misfortune comes unexpectedly, it has external origin, therefore, it will pass again...this fact suggests movement in harmony with heaven, which is man's true and original nature...If someone is not as he should be, he has misfortune, and it does not further him to undertake anything...When innocence is gone, where can one go? When the will of heaven does not protect one, can one do anything?
>
> "(Innocence) shows man in the proper relationship to the divine, without ulterior designs and in primal innocence. Thus man is in harmony with heavenly fate... But where the natural state is not this state of innocence, where desires and ideas are astir, misfortune follows of inner necessity."

The wisdom of hunting peoples is echoed among the religions of the world: the human crisis is a result of humanity's desires and fears being astir with ulterior designs in disagreement with the divine plan. In harmonious, innocent living man has heaven to help him against external misfortunes, but when his egoism prevails, which hunting cultures actively guard against, misfortune is inevitable, the price of being untrue to one's heart or deepest self, the same as turning one's back on the divine. This almost all civilizations have done regardless of their beginnings or intentions: civilized humanity becomes top-heavy with self-infatuation, and the foundation its built crumbles. Exceptions to the rule among pastoral and farmer cultures are the Tibetan Buddhists and their New World relatives, the Hopi, both of which have kept alive the humility, wisdom and respect associated with hunting cultures. It would be wise to explore with them the cultural forces underlying their humility.

That the animal was a totally significant being to subsistence hunters seems irrefutable; the animal's importance to civilized man was merely as a stepping stone for his purposes, as indicated in the I Ching's history of civilization. Legend points to the hunter as founder, "The name of the mythical founder of civilization is written in various ways; its meaning seems to point to a hunter…"

After the passing of the first human clan, which seems to represent the passing of the primal or original human lifestyle of hunting, "there sprang up the clan of the Divine Husbandman…which is said to have taught the people agriculture."

Not surprisingly, the I Ching connects agriculture with the trigram for Increase - increase of food, wealth and people. At this stage draft animals could be used and part of the work of farming shifted to oxen.

The next stage in development of civilization is the replacement of the clan of the Divine Husbandman by the clan of the Yellow Emperor who brought continuity through alterations. Agriculture has succeeded so well that social order requires hierarchy of power, centralized government, taxation, bureaucracy. The horse was yoked so that distant regions could be reached, undoubtedly by "all the King's men."

"They introduced double gates and night watch-men with clappers (warning devices), in order to deal with robbers…They strung a piece of wood for a bow and hardened pieces of wood in the fire for arrows. The use of the bow and arrow is to keep the world in fear." Keeping the world in fear is keeping people in a state of defensive ego-consciousness, the origin of identification with the body, materialism and greed… and spiritual disempowerment.

Here we see the great hoax of civilization in the making. Humans living not with greater security as they imagine, but with more fear of being invaded, robbed and killed. Not more security, material or psychological, but just the opposite, not to mention a shift from what ethnographers have documented is, relatively, a life of creative leisure among hunters to one of toil for the farmer and city people.

The last step in civilization was the introduction of written documents as a means of governing officials and supervising the people. Though the ancient Chinese had tied knots to keep records, writing became the last decisive blow in the dehumanization process. Now, no one, not even officials, can be trusted, and the fate of humanity rests not upon human to human communication, but on the cold, hard word.

May civilized man recover the wholeness and peace he knew as a hunter? The I Ching offers this hope,

> "One must draw on the strength of the inner attitude to compensate for what is lacking in externals, then the power of the content makes up for the simplicity of form. There is no need of presenting false appearances to God. Even with slender means, the sentiment of the heart can be expressed." Hunter wisdom.

On our journey from civilized values that emphasize externals, ownership of property and materialism, to the way of innocence, simplicity and the heart it will profit us much to further inspect the pervasive mythology of human societies as a mirror of their economy and ecology.

Romancing the Cow

Civilization rests upon domestication of plants and animals. Farming and pastoralism are made possible by converting wild plants and animals into domestic forms more productive and manageable. Farming succeeds because humans subjugate nature, bend it to their will and control it. Wild animals and pests are risks to crop production; farmers live in opposition to nature, unlike their hunting ancestors.

My neighbor is a grain farmer whose life is drudgery from morning till night. When I asked him for permission to hunt geese on his land, he said, "You can kill every damn goose and deer in the county for all I care." He goes to church every Sunday and prays, convinced that God wants him to subdue the earth, that perhaps geese and deer were put here by mistake. (He's not a hunter, and those farming and ranching families that maintain a hunting tradition truly respect the land and wildlife. I know Native Americans who feel that the members of the non-native culture who are closest to them in feeling and respect for the earth are cowboys!).

Pastoralism is the turning point in human perception away from nature and to the sky God. Herding succeeds only if herders are able to defend herds against dangerous predators and other humans who would steal them. Moreover, herders have to keep their livestock moving to new range or water which means confrontations with farmers or other pastoralists, i.e., war.

The oldest war was not with other human groups but with the large carnivores, and it was waged for meat. In the same way that spotted hyenas, wild dogs and lions contend for carcasses of large animals, even killing one another in the process, our ancestors fought their way up the predatory ladder to become the dominant species of the planet, surely the most impressive achievement – and perhaps greatest curse – of the human race.

It was great men like Hercules who changed human destiny and gave us the lion's share. His first and greatest feat, killing the Nemean lion, was heralded by wearing the lion's mane over his shoulders, a trophy for all to see that advertised his exceptional accomplishment. The trophy communicates prowess, and it was trophy hunting that motivated ego-driven men to risk their lives and kill awesome beasts to gain status and power within society. (Many trophies carry sacred meaning, i.e., there is a time and place for trophies in our lives, as discussed below.)

The herders moved from being hunters dependent upon nature to trophy hunters who dominated nature. That movement gave birth to the mythologies that characterize civilization and which account for its mad rush to annihilation. Essentially, we now endanger ourselves and world because of our adherence to a set of myths which proved successful heretofore, but which now is failing us.

The pastoral myth arose with domestication of animals over which we became dominant. Not only did we take on a new relationship to domestic animals, unlike the interdependent relationship characteristic of hunters with wild animals, we also dominated enemy predators and humans. Herding life is sheer domination. In the same ways that herders shifted from a reciprocal relationship with wild animals to one of domination of domestic animals and enemies, herders shifted their cosmology from a diffuse theology to monotheism. The great one-god religions have their origins in pastoral life. Hunting societies do believe in a supreme creator, but they also believe that all of creation embodies divinity, and that humans and animals are created more or less equally (or that the animals are superior in certain respects).

Just as herding men dominate animals and their enemies, their God becomes all powerful. With the formation of armies required to defend livestock and their forage, human societies shifted from small, more-or-less egalitarian communities governed largely by concensus, to larger, hierarchically structured, patriarchal societies. The new emphasis was on warring ability, masculinity, control of nature, competition for status and rank, and of course wealth.

From the pastoral mythology is born the myth of history, life as time and progress, in contrast to the hunter's mythology of repeating renewal of cycles, seasons and life and death, in which humans and animals participate gratefully in the same on-going banquet. The herders live in a perpetual state of identification with and competition for material possessions. Their heroes, like their gods, are ruthless. A life of restless conquest for fame and fortune besets humanity. So is born the mythos of heroism, rampant male egoism, upon the planet earth.

Science exists in a presumptive state among hunters, who, faced with the problem of hunger, deduce hypotheses, make predictions and then test those predictions in living experiments we call hunts. Einstein envisaged proto-science among hunting peoples. Their ability to observe, deduce and predict the behavior of animals and weapons to intercept them requires complex computation, simulation and space/time reckoning of the highest order, the blueprints and processes for which have been programmed in the human brain. However, the trajectory of idealism and intellectualism that led to science and technology in the West has its origin in the pastoral mythology of domination, which is founded on egoism. It is identity with material wealth that has meant a descent from the Edenic life of hunters for whom universal spiritualism prevails. Cartesian philosophy and science are merely restatements of the pastoral mythology of domination of nature which threatens our very survival.

The combination of monoculture agriculture, diminishing resources, poisoning of ecosystems and our bodies/minds, reduction in biodiversity leading to instability of ecosystems, growing human population and all the rest of it presents a frightening future. Will our children survive? Will they live in a sterile world devoid of otherness save a few domestic species? What will become of the human spirit in a world deprived of wild animals and places?

In essence, the problem we face is how to convert the prevailing mythology of civilization to the harmonious mythology of hunting peoples for whom sustainable economy, cooperation and sharing with one another and nature, humility, gratitude and spiritual values are the way of life?

The starting point for recovery of Pleistocene values is recognizing the fundamental needs of human development, i.e., how to raise children so they are profoundly connected to other humans, the creatures, the earth and the divine. To make that leap, it is necessary to establish that what we perceive as normal actually may be pathology.

We must achieve in the realm of the development of human behavior, the brain and the heart what Rousseau sought for human society: to discover what is natural and what is artificial.

Commentary On Wild at Heart

The day I was confirmed in the church I argued with the pastor about Darwin's theory of evolution. Maybe the local librarian's refusal to let me check out *The Origin of Species* because she thought it was evil had set me on the wrong path early in life. As a child and even as a teenager I always felt the presence of God in nature and that is where I sought solace and peace and composed poetry. In college I discovered a mysterious ability to mesmerize an audience when I entered an oral interpretation contest and read Carl Sandburg's poem, "To a contemporary bunkshooter." The poem starts out, "You come along tearing your shirt yelling about Jesus/Where do you get that stuff?/What do you know about Jesus?"

Carl Sandburg felt as I and Joe Pearce do, that fear, guilt and damnation have nothing to do with Jesus, God or the Holy Spirit. They are instead expressions of the human ego. To this day I still don't see why creationism and evolution are necessarily mutually exclusive, but of one thing I am absolutely sure: if we have free will then we, not God, have authored our own curse. In another word, while I believe that God and the Holy Spirit are there to assist us – and not only Christians – we have to stop blaming God for our mistakes. Here begins my argument with John Eldredge's well known book, *Wild at Heart.*

He is right that as a result of having abandoned masculine rites of passage we have a world of unfinished, uninitiated men, and I could not agree more that we must rediscover and honor the stages of male development. And I agree with him that most messages males receive about what they ought to be or do ultimately fail, however well intended, because they ignore male passions, i.e., what males need to experience to develop well. They do not need to sit at desks in school all day. They do not need to be in Sunday School on Sunday morning. They do not want to be good little boys, like Tom Sawyer, they want to play hookey, go fishing or catch frogs, like Huck Fin. Doesn't it seem intelligent to design their education accordingly?

Eldredge believes that we men need permission to be what we are, made in God's image, living from the heart. That men need adventure and "battles" and, oh yes, a Beauty to rescue. For that is how God made us all, he claims. Boys and men definitely need adventure, to take risks and become fearless, and throughout almost all of human life that came from nature and the hunt, which had its share of danger including lions and bears, but battles with men? Rescuing Beauty? Is this the way God made us? Is it like the song says, the same old story, a fight for love and glory, do or die? Or are these the tragic outcomes of civilization, egoism and the myth of power?

If Beauty has to be rescued perhaps it is because someone stole her, in which case she has the status of livestock. Primal hunting societies do not steal women. Their men respect women too much to own them.

Joseph Campbell's exhaustive inquiries led him to conclude that women are, but men do, meaning that woman creates life, that man is her provider and protector. He recognized among hunting cultures the unifying influence of respect for woman, and he also observed that where male power is dominant there is separation.

If women today long to be "rescued" by a knight in shining armour, perhaps it is because they do not feel genuinely appreciated, which has been the case for women since the onset of civilization and the rise of the dark side of the masculine. Is any of this the handiwork of God? Or is it the folly of men? If God wants anything for us it is peace and with peace come joy and love. It strikes me as sad that the egotistical values of civilization, rather than the spiritual virtues of the hunting life, permeate Eldredge's book, which sold two million copies.

"You can't just sit down and talk about the truth. It doesn't work that way. You have to live it and be part of it and you might get to know it."

~ Rolling Thunder, Cherokee

Chapter 5

The Story of Human Development

"Unless you become as little children ye shall not enter the Kingdom of Heaven"

~ Jesus Christ

Of Raccoons and Boys, Sit Spots and Guardian Angels

One of the core routines recommended by wilderness/tracking mentor, Jon Young, in *Coyote's Guide to Connecting People to Nature*, is "sit-spot," which refers to finding a place in nature to daily go and sit alone to practice being alert and aware of the surroundings and one's self. It is something I began doing spontaneously in my youth and later when still-hunting waterfowl or deer.

Owing to a family illness I found myself living in Cincinnati, the first city I'd inhabited in 30 years, and soon I found a sit-spot at a local park. I went there alone and sat and observed, also to pray and sometimes read or write. It was not long before the birds and gray squirrels recognized me and accepted my presence. The first time I prayed there the top half of a dead maple fell off; the only time I saw a tree break without a strong wind. Was it a sign?

A few days later at about 8 in the morning I looked up at the trunk of the maple that had broken off and saw a raccoon about ten feet off the ground grasping the tree in its claws and looking at me. I have great affection for raccoons which I've raised as pets and also studied so I was thrilled to see it. I let out the raccoon trill and then spoke to it and thanked it. Soon it climbed up another four feet to a natural cavity below where the trunk had broken off and crawled inside.

That day I finished reading Rudolf Steiner's little book on guardian angels in which he advises that when falling asleep we ask our guardian angel to plan our day, which I did that night. I awoke feeling superb, better than I had felt since the birth of my son, Drake, 14 years earlier. My heart was wide open and I was radiating energy. When I arrived at my sit spot in the park the birds flew in from all directions singing as they came. It was almost as if I had been feeding birds in the cold of winter, but I had never fed these birds and it was summer. I knew they were responding to my exalted state of being.

Sitting there feeling joyful and thankful, I saw a black boy walking down a dirt path toward me. He looked about ten years old and was walking in a slumped posture with his eyes pointed down. I wondered for a moment what I could do to make a difference in his life. When he came by me I pointed to the broken maple and said, "You see that tree there? The one with the top broken off? A raccoon lives there." He looked at the tree and asked, "How do you know?" "Well, yesterday morning when I was here he climbed up that tree and crawled into that hole there."

"Don't raccoons usually sleep in the daytime?" he asked.

"Yeah, they usually do, but this one must have stayed out late."

"Gee, I wonder what he was doing?"

"I don't know."

We walked over to the tree and I pointed again to the cavity, and while I was looking up at it, the boy who had shown keen interest up to that point suddenly turned and started walking back down the same dirt path without saying a word. No thanks, no goodbye, nothing. As I watched him walk away with his hands in his pocket, eyes looking down at the ground again, I was overcome with extreme grief. I wondered if this boy had a man in his life. I wondered how many boys in Cincinnati and other cities would never have anyone teach them about raccoons, take them fishing or tell them stories. How many millions of boys out there would never connect with nature? With older men? I wept hard and long and then came back to my place to go to work doing what I can to help.

For several days I was depressed and sought Guidance on the meaning of that morning in the park. If my guardian angel had planned that day, what did it want me to learn? Was my true self, my spiritual nature, and the true nature of all humanity being revealed to me: unlimited, joyous, certain, powerful? Was the boy a mirror of my false self, my ego, and the defensive consciousness of civilized humanity with its disconnection from nature, other humans and the divine? I wondered, too, if what had been revealed to me was the immeasurable tragedy of humanity's fall from spiritual grace into physical form and the pain and suffering that accompany it.

When I felt up to it again, I repeated the prayer and got up in the morning to drive to the park. En route I asked myself, "I wonder what Spirit has in store for me today?" As I approached the entrance to the park I saw a dead raccoon in the gutter of the street, about 100 yards from the broken maple. I slowed down and could see that it was half-grown, the same size as the raccoon I had seen, and when I saw it had the exact same pattern of missing hair on its tail, my heart sank. Normally I would have stopped my car and moved the raccoon's body off the road or buried it, but there was heavy traffic behind me and I was upset. I went to my sit spot and prayed for understanding, but after a few minutes returned to my car and started the drive home.

As I approached the location of the raccoon I noticed that the head and front-end of the body had moved slightly closer to the curb. I pulled off at the first road, parked and ran back. Though barely able to move, the raccoon was alive! I picked it up and put it in my car and drove back home, then placed it in a ferret cage in the basement with water and cat food. It lay there motionless for hours, but in the morning I found blood in the water bowl which meant the raccoon had at least tried to drink in the night. That second day was no different, and again the following morning there was blood in the water bowl.

I did a lot of prayer these two days for the raccoon's recovery, and on the third morning there was no more blood in the bowl, which was turned over, and all the food was gone. The inside of the cage was a mess, a good sign that the raccoon was much improved. On the fourth day it was spry, even eating and drinking in front of me. When it sat back on its haunches looking at me and put its paws through the wire I petted them softly with my fingertips for several seconds, but the raccoon did not withdraw them, something unexpected from a wild animal that had not been raised by humans from an early age. The raccoon had made a full recovery.

That same day I went to my sit spot, and who shows up smiling with three of his friends? Proudly announcing that, "He's the guy I told you about. The one who saw the raccoon that lives in that tree over there." He had brought his playmates to show them the raccoon tree. They were attentive as I told them the story of what had happened to the raccoon. This time when they left, they thanked me, and all the way down the path the boy who brought them could be heard talking about raccoons.

That day I cried happy tears and my faith was renewed, and every night since I have asked my guardian angel to plan my day.

~RANDALL L. EATON

The critical question is what experiences are conducive to development of a sane man who lives in proper relationship with society, nature and the divine? My hypothesis is that the hunt is one as is the mid-teen yearning for spiritual connection that the vision quest offers and which art expresses and maintains.

I have argued since 1985 that we all are victims of the patriarchal, pastoral mythology of male dominance and the subjugation of nature, which tore us away from a relationship of respect and admiration for the animals, the earth and one another. "Medicine men" tried to improve on nature by industrializing childbirth and early development, effectively robbing generations of confidence and trust and propagating massive paranoia, by locking millions of people into ego rather than the heart and higher intelligence, the natural outcome of healthy human development.

We do face the very real possibility of extinction by our own hands, which could be positive if the threat wakes us up to how we have gone astray. In the midst of the global crisis scientists are busy cooking up ways of colonizing space or extending life, perhaps indefinitely. In principle, they believe that the secret to physical life eternal lies somewhere in the genome. What they really offer is a final loss of meaning because life and death are complementary and interdependent. As Joseph Chilton Pearce says, without death the meaning of life is lost. To take it further, to live in fear and ignorance of death is a perversion of life.

Ego-intellect is busy compounding the problems it made, incapable of comprehending, much less embracing, wisdom. The solution we seek for a better life in the body lies in development.

The behavioristic models of psychology and biology have led us to despair precisely because they left out everything that makes us tick, the purpose and meaning of life, and left us with mere reflexes, instinct, conditioning and selfish genes. Idiot savants and fire-walking are glaring examples of the fundamental failure of mechanistic models.

The model of ourselves must lead us to freedom, be open-ended though structured and allow room for intuitive and non-verbal awareness including, for example, the Dream Time of Australian aborigines, the ecstatic dance of the Kalahari Bushman who communicate and heal via invisible energy cords, the visions and dreams behind great scientific breakthroughs such as the benzene ring and DNA, and the communication between hunters and prey, women and children.

And now more than ever we require models that inspire us to achieve what Joe Pearce, I and many others have experienced, which he terms "unconflicted" states of complete faith and trust which allow us to accomplish the unthinkable. Unconflicted behavior is a state of fearlessness, another word for love, and is what is meant by "perfect poise" in athletics and martial arts when one moves adroitly without effort and at times with awareness outside the body which also may occur in hunting. Sex within the mantle of spiritual love also can be a gateway to transcendence.

The Developmental Blueprint

The developmental blueprint we inherit prompts us to seek in the outside world appropriate models and interact with them. For example, if an adolescent fails to find a suitable model to emulate then his blueprint may atrophy and sink into a dormant state leaving a depressed, disappointed young adult who feels and acts more like a child. Or a young man who is unaware that his anger and distrust towards older men has its origin in their failure to nurture and initiate him.

Nature's agenda is a lot like an architectural blueprint. We can't live in the lines drawn on paper, but if we follow the blueprint with the appropriate content soon we'll have a house. The quality of our intelligence, like the quality of a house, will be determined by the quality of the content with which we construct it, i.e., the quality of the models we follow and by our interaction with those models, thus the critical significance of mentoring.

Though Piaget, Pearce, Shepard and others have defined the blueprint for human development, we still send kids to school and expect them to sit in desks, and utilizing intimidation, law and fear of punishment force them to learn what they "have to know" to become worker bees. But ultimately we do them and our society great harm. Joseph Pearce summarizes the frustration that I and countless boys and girls have experienced, and why school is disastrous.

> "At age seven, for instance, my sense of betrayal on being forced to sit at a desk all year was because the blueprint within me set up a tremendous expectation for something different. Schooling could elicit no response from my blueprint because there was no match between model and agenda. A mismatch of stimulus and response brings on a sense of outrage, a violation of self, for the growth of self is thereby truncated or retarded. All that my early schooling did was to teach me to hate schooling, for we hate anything that thwarts our development, which is the basis of our survival. This learning to hate school, which is practically universal among children, is doubly tragic since we equate school with learning and the brain is constructed to do one thing – learn. So a double-bind sense of despair is the only result. If the model for learning matches the

needs of the learning period, then learning is spontaneous, natural and impeccably thorough."

About 95% of what children learn comes from observation and modeling adults, only 5% from school, but how much more of value would children learn from schools without walls in which their proclivities are playfully aligned with nature?

By the middle of adolescence, our house of intelligence should be primed for full occupancy and employment. At this point in our development we are supposed to make a radical shift in agenda to a very different form of intelligence. Just as we are born to grow, mature and become parents, maturation leads us beyond biological development to become one who accesses higher knowledge and creates. Once we have identified with creation, it is natural for us to move on to identify with nature and the Creator, ultimately accepting life and death and our own death gracefully.

But our biological development has been so seriously disrupted that we have generated dysfunction, and what is worse, we have resigned ourselves to a dysfunctional state as revealed nightly on "reality" TV. Our conceptions of self and the world have been shaped by dysfunctional models. Because we have no concepts of normality, we pass on to our children our own dysfunctional state – from every direction dysfunction is mirrored back thus reinforcing our pathology as normality.

We administer drugs to boys because they are bored or have difficulty paying attention in school. What if it is normal and natural for them to be outside playing and learning in nature? What if the sickness is not in them but in schooling? What of formula, circumcision, crib death, growing up without wild animals to name and imitate, schooling and teen pregnancy (the average age of woman at their first birth in Bushman societies is around 20)? And these are as unnatural as nuclear families living by themselves, children growing up with merely one parent in their lives, and elders being confined to "homes" where they do not interact with younger generations. A book could be written just about the adverse effects of living by the clock instead of "Mother Time."

Brain Development, Heart and Mind

We actually have five brains in one. The oldest is the reptilian brain, which was dominant for hundreds of millions of years. Superimposed on it is the old mammalian brain, which took on a giant leap of new possibilities, and finally the neo-mammalian brain or neocortex associated with dolphins, whales and humans. The old mammalian brain uses the reptilian brain, and the neocortex utilizes both older brains in yet another quantum leap of possibility.

These three brains work this way: the reptilian handles physical imagery – through it we sense and respond to the physical world, except for smell; the old mammalian brain processes internal images and emotions; and, the neocortex is the intellectual brain that handles extremely abstract images. The things we learn to do so well they are seemingly automatic, like driving a car, are handled by the reptilian brain. The old mammalian or mid-brain evaluates quality including relational character or condition between ourselves and our experience. It processes love, hate, fear, aversions, attractions, as well as all our bondings between child and parent, child and nature, male and female, person and society and so on. The mid-brain is cohesive; it ties things together. Sensory information coming through the old brain is given meaning and emotional content by the mid-brain, which also integrates the reptilian brain with the neocortex.

After centuries of bad remedies prescribed for a disease that has been wrongly diagnosed, new research gives us that opportunity to remove blocks to transcendence and allows us to develop a nature that lies beyond violence and rage. A major clue to our conflict is the discovery that we have five different brains within us. These five brains, four of which are housed in our head, represent the entire evolution of life before us: reptilian, old mammalian and human. Pearce says, "Nature never abandons a good idea but instead builds new structures upon it; apparently each new neural structure we have inherited evolved to correct shortcomings in or problems brought about by nature's former achievements," and he sees brain evolution as another example of transcendence, "rising and going beyond."

The mid-brain is the heart of this three-part brain system, and also is directly innervated with the heart itself, a vitally important connection with the function of bonding. Traditionally, emotion always has been associated with the heart, and the mid-brain actually does take directives from the heart and communicating with it in turn. Long intuited by poets and saints, the fifth brain lies not in our head but in our heart, half or more of which is composed of neurons, a hard, biological fact. We really do think with our hearts! This heart-head dynamic reflects, determines and affects the very nature of our resulting awareness even as it is, in turn, profoundly affected. Within this mutually interdependent system lies the key to transcendence and the resolution of our tendency toward violence.

If spirit is the unknown power impelling us to rise and go beyond, the intelligence of the heart brain embodies this elusive driving force, a fact we can grasp if we distinguish between intelligence and intellect as we must between spiritual and religious, heart and ego, love and fear. In an efficient biological unfolding the intelligence in our heart and the intellect in our head should function interdependently, but their reciprocal action is broken down by the cultural counterfeits of civilization, namely the predominance of ego/fear, which blocks the "unconflicted" state.

Pearce discovered that he was capable of unconflicted behavior "through a kind of willful and voluntary throwing away of self-preservation....a genuine acceptance of death...Therefore there was nothing left to lose! I found that in this state not only did fire not have to burn me, but also gravity did not have to hold me..." Twice I observed levitation by a man who was praying intensely. While giving a demonstration speech in college on how to treat a poisonous snake bite, I had intended to gesture with a razor blade where one would cut Xs across the imaginary fang punctures in my arm, but instead and much to my surprise, actually made the cuts, though I did not feel them. The class was impressed and the professor gave me a high mark.

Which seems as nothing compared to the Sufis who not only walk across 1300 degree coals, hot enough to melt aluminum, but who hang from hooks on which they swing for hours without harm; moreover, after they descend and remove the hooks the wounds quickly disappear. The Sufis playfully practice what Jesus taught: in knowing ***what*** we are, we know there is nothing to fear so we are entitled to miracles.

Joe Pearce discovered that the structure of reality is negotiable when he was free of all internal conflict which is generated by fear of harm or death. Acceptance of death carries us beyond the fear of death and opens us to another reality, one in which we are literally invulnerable – from Viking to Samurai, the ancient warrior's code. Fear of any kind throws us into an ancient survival mentality which shuts down our higher awareness and full potential. While 97% of the Sufis who annually undertake a ritual firewalk pass unscathed, 3% become frightened and perish. While it is widely believed that because its function is defensive or protective, ego is good for survival, the frightened Sufi firewalkers might disagree. Repeatedly in my life I survived or saved the lives of others when I moved beyond fear and ego to fearlessness and inner peace. Heroes typically claim the same.

Pathways to the Heart

The path to manhood with heart requires the completion of a series of bondings, first with mother. Normal bonding between mother and infant occurs in utero, and if a pregnant woman feels unsure about having a child she communicates that insecurity to a fetus which is surprisingly aware and sensitive to the mother's emotions and even to her environment.

Civilized life is so fraught with artificiality that we have lost our bearings in the world, and nowhere is this more obvious or more harmful than in birthing and neonatal care. We cannot imagine raising a baby without diapers, but women in Africa and Latin America do it. These mothers know when the babies they are carrying close to their bodies, often in slings on their backs, are about to urinate or defecate. According to anthropologist Colin Turnbull, they anticipate the infant's need prior to any detectable signs. Women in Guatemala say a woman is stupid or a poor mother when two or three days after the birth of her baby she is still being soiled by it.

These women have bonded with their babies. They were allowed to have natural childbirth, an instinctive process mediated by the mid-brain and basically identical in all cultures. Like breathing, bonding will manifest if allowed. Bonding provides an intuitive, extrasensory kind of connection between mother and child, a felt process that is inexplicable to language, thought or intellect, a communion that transcends the reasoning mind. A mother senses her baby's needs the same way she recognizes her own bodily needs, but the communion of bonding extends beyond physiological processes.

Bonding relies upon a physical link between the mid-brain and our hearts, and bonded people connect at intuitive levels that operate below ordinary awareness at the level of the beating heart, the mid-brain's center of emotion.

"Attachment behavior" is defined by Pearce as the pathological consequence of the failure of bonding at birth, though it can also occur at any time in our development when bonding is programmed to occur. Attachment is mediated by the reptilian brain and the lowest levels of the mid-brain; the attached person can relate only through overt signals or stimuli and is not able to perceive subtle or intuitive signals as precursors of physical experience. A person governed by attachment instead of bonding is locked into hindsight – and the hindbrain – which motivates him to compensate by trying to anticipate, predict and control events in the external world, which seems like an accurate description of civilized humanity. *A Course in Miracles* says it is insane to plan our life, but we live in such fear – ego-dominance – that we cannot imagine the possibility of living in the present and trusting our own intuitive guidance, as subsistence hunters do.

The attached person is unaware of the inner power of the mid-brain and its connection with the heart. Which has serious consequences, socially and environmentally. The attached person lacks trust that his needs will be satisfied, so instead acts aggressively to seize and possess. "I can't get no satisfaction," the Rolling Stones sang in the mid-60s to the baby boomers, first generation to be industrially birthed and denied bonding with their mothers, possibly the origin of the hippy generation's protest to "make love not war." In retrospect were they asking to be allowed to bond with their mothers rather than be warred against, as they were?

The attached person feels vulnerable to an unpredictable world and attempts to incorporate into his ego defense the objects, events and persons of his external world, which means he treats another person as an object to be dominated or as a means for his own protection. The attached person lives in a perpetual state of defensive alert, a precursor for stress disease, addiction, substance abuse and violence.

Learning is a process of moving from what is known to that which is unknown. Bonding gives a person a level of trust that calls forth a response rather than a reaction; it allows a person to flow with events in contrast with the attached personality who attempts to analyze the future and predict outcomes, obsessed with forcing the unknown back into the known, again an apt description of science and Western culture. A bonded person's receptivity allows him to integrate experience into ever widening circles of possibility. His deep trust in the connectedness of everything mirrors the creative principle that binds a diverse creation together, from subatomic particles to ecosystems, galaxies and minds. ***Attachment behavior is a metaphor for civilized life obsessed with control, bonding is a metaphor for foraging life and its acceptance of what is.***

Though bonding is well established in utero, after birth it must be reconfirmed, and if re-established well the child will move far afield integrating the old into the new. If not, then the attached infant's fists will remain clinched long after birth, and later it will cling to the parent fearing loss of contact, afraid to explore the world, like Harry Harlow's rhesus monkeys clinging to their artificial surrogate mothers.

If two living heart cells are separated on a slide they pulsate at different rates, but if the cells are brought closer together, at critical distance before they actually touch they will start to pulsate in synchrony and function as a miniature heart should. They have successfully communicated with one another, overcome a gap of separation. They are bonded.

Proper birthing and the brilliant start it gives to learning is a model for the movement from known to unknown that will be carried out in all the subsequent shifts that must be made with each stage of development.

Nursing continues to signal well being from mother to child. The infant's heart sends these messages on to the mid-brain which gives it a sense of emotional security in a stable world. The child that is breast-fed is more intelligent than the bottle-fed child, and the longer it is breast-fed, up to three years, the more intelligent it will be. If the child's future developmental shifts are met with successful bonding, his superior intelligence, sociability and suitability as a parent are assured.

Before we look at the ways in which bonding processes have been disrupted by industrialized birthing and caused an epidemic of attachment behavior, which may impair our ability to cope with the social-environmental crisis, we need to take a deeper look at healthy bonding between heart and mind.

The heart plays a major role in our consciousness. Feature films and books recount actual events from heart transplants in which the receiver takes on proclivities or expressions of the donor. A woman who received a man's heart awoke from the operation and requested hot dogs and beer for the first time in her life, exactly what the man had been eating when he died. In another case the recipient, a Mexican male, began speaking words he had never heard before, but when he met the donor's wife discovered that the peculiar language was often used by the donor. Heart recipients describe themselves after transplant as feeling like a new person has come inside their life. Quite possibly their body has become the home of a second spirit that never left its heart – which, after all, was kept alive as it was relocated from one body to the other.

In any case, activity in the heart controls and governs activity in the body and the brain. The heart receives reports from the brain about the environment, then the heart commands the brain to respond. A medicine man once told Carl Jung that white men, with furrowed brows and unrelenting anger, were insane and murderous because they thought in their heads. He explained that whole people think in their hearts.

Intellect is dangerous without intelligence, which is the ability to function for our well being. Intelligence is designed to incorporate intellect into its service, but to do this intellect must be developed right along with the intelligence of the heart. The problem we face today is the dynamic of the relationship between heart and brain, intelligence and intellect. Pearce says,

> "Since all intelligences are coded to unfold within nature's timetable, intellect opens on target whether an intelligence of the heart has developed or not (just as sexuality unfolds at puberty whether we are ready for it or not). And therein lies the problem. The dynamic of the heart and brain is the dynamic of intelligence and intellect, the principle dynamic on which our life is based. If we develop intellect and fail to develop intelligence we are then subject to a novelty seeking mind that operates without regard to our own or others' well-being. Anything is possible to us, but what is appropriate?"

Intelligence of the heart is the foundation of all bonding. Without it people do not nurture one another or the earth. There are at least two stages of heart development. The first starts at birth and follows the natural stages of childhood development that impart emotional security and trust. The second opens at middle adolescence with the development of the pre-frontal cortex, which may have appeared only 40,000 years ago. This fifth and final brain was described by neuroscientist Paul MacLean as the angel lobes, because they are the center for empathy, compassion, understanding and higher intellect. The prefrontals become active at around the age of 15 years, a stage that allows us to develop an awareness that incorporates animal emotions into a higher human state in which the biological links up with the spiritual, as when we fall in love with another person or through hunting with nature, when truth, metaphor and poetry acquire significance.

In each case, the new stage of development must be met with a nurturing environment. The heart-limbic system may appear primitive, but its solid connection is absolutely critical. The first teacher of the heart is the mother; the bonding between mother and child must be established at birth. The mother then awakens the undeveloped intelligence of the infant and serves as the model for ongoing development until the child's intelligence is self-actualized and is no longer in need of nurturing. The child becomes a person at home in a world of movement and change, someone who stands firm in the strength of the living earth.

The heart's intelligence is not merely a sweet sentiment but a biological necessity and the basis for all bonding. Bonding develops in clear stages: mother-infant from birth to 1.5 – 3 years; infant-father/family from 1.5 – 3 years; child to nature from 3 to 12 years; adolescent to society (and males to nature) from age 12 to 16; and, male-female mating bond, from 18 to 21.

The 20th century incurred the loss of the bonding power that holds family and society together. As a consequence of the failure of the mother-infant heart bonding, there has been a corresponding loss of intelligence, love and nurturing that has left us living in a dark, reptilian world of exaggerated ego-defensiveness. No wonder so many films feature rampaging reptiles ranging from escaped crocodiles and giant snakes to Godzilla.

Breaking the Bond

Our relationship with Mother Earth is an extension of our relationship with our own mothers. Likewise, some have argued that lack of bonding with our earthly fathers stands in the way of a relationship with the Father in Heaven. Are society and the earth dying because we have not honored our most fundamental human needs? Awareness and important insights on the behavioral and emotional needs fulfilled by human development came from classical ethology, the biological study of animal behavior, especially the work of Nobel laureates Konrad Lorenz and Niko Tinbergen, from whom I learned at Oxford. Lorenz's well known studies of imprinting in geese who were exposed to him soon after hatching and thereafter followed him as though he were their mother, pointed to critical periods for bonding in human development.

In the later 60s, my professor, a classical Lorenzian ethologist, and I spent countless hours speculating on the disaster of modern birthing practices: yanking babies out of women with stainless steel forceps, removing newborns from their mothers and placing them alone in a nursery, bottle-feeding instead of nursing and so on. Unfortunately, we were proven right.

Perhaps the greatest insult to generations born since WWII was taking babies away from their mothers and keeping them in nurseries. Finally, someone in medicine wondered why babies are so quiet there, even though they cry out at first. Perhaps the newborns are adapted to be quiet to reduce the probability of being found and killed by predators?

So a study was done on nursery babies to discover what is going on internally, and the results are most distressing: after crying for a while, which in natural circumstances would attract the mother, the babies went into shock! Why wouldn't they be severely frightened? In the same way that a baby's mouth and sucking response – finely coordinated use of more than twenty muscles - is innately adapted to the mother's nipple, the newborn's instincts program it to be held closely by its mother. To an infant abandonment signals danger; it is astonishing and incredible that it has happened to millions of babies throughout the civilized world. Though industrialized birthing has begun to recognize the needs of infants and mothers to bond, the baby boomers are now the age of elders with economic and political power, but they suffer from severe attachment. So can they serve as elders capable of mentoring youth through rites of passage, essential to self-replicating communities? Or will they simply be olders? My guess is that many older people may need to be called to service and trained as mentors. Perhaps abundant play in nature and belated rites of passage would help prepare them.

Other medical geniuses did an analysis of mother's milk and found it wanting: way too low in protein and fats, they said. So formula was invented and with it a highly profitable industry to replace breast-feeding. Why no one asked how babies managed to grow into healthy children for the past few million years is a real puzzle. But following WWII, 97% of the babies born for several decades were bottle-fed with formula. As it turns out, babies are adapted to nurse from their mothers 60 times per day, a frequency of intimate contact that assured effective bonding. With bottle-feeding babies were fed much less often and had less contact with their mothers. Equally bad, while being bottle-fed babies are held at arm's length rather than to the mother's breast close to her heart, thus depriving the child of the heart-to-heart communication it needs for bonding and proper subsequent development.

What has the high sugar content of formula done to the population and its proclivity for sugar and carbohydrates? High carbohydrate consumption has been identified as responsible for the diseases of civilization, ranging from diabetes and obesity to high cholesterol. For another thing, sugar deflates the immune system. In the 1950s when a physician in North Carolina warned the populace about a correlation he discovered between the incidence of polio and summer consumption of sugar in the form of ice cream and pop, the incidence of polio declined sharply for several years until reversed by PR men backed by the Rockefellers who had major ownership in the soft drink industry. Something you would not expect to happen in a hunting society.

And what of the insult to mothers? Is post-partum blues something natural or is it the result of industrialized birthing which also deprives the mother of bonding with her baby? The mother and the baby are a co-adapted system of heart, emotion and body interface: the mother is programmed to nurture as well as receive rewarding feedback from nursing, holding and caressing the baby that is unparalleled in adult human life. How has this deprivation influenced mothers' relationships with their children? Their sense of wholeness and cosmic connectedness? Their attitudes toward men? Their hearts? The earth?

On top of all these insults to mother and child the boy infant is hauled away by strangers and under blinding lights has his penis foreskin whacked off. Even though there is no good reason known to perform circumcision, the practice persists apparently because parents are concerned that little Johnny might grow up, see other boys' penises and think he's different. He's not different. Chances are he's just as insecure and lacking in trust as the next unbonded kid. Brain wave studies demonstrate that it more than hurts a little while before they "fall asleep". Like the infants removed to nurseries, circumcised infants go into a state of shock.

Does infant circumcision sentence a male to a lifetime of fear and defensiveness? Could the barbaric practice of infantile circumcision be a contributor to the growth of male violence and sexual dysfunction? Does it up the odds that males will be more willing soldiers?

But the real disaster is the separation of mother and infant at birth, leaving us psychologically and emotionally crippled. Pathetically, an unbonded child has no choice but to try to possess his experience so he holds tight to the blanket, his only stable source of stimuli in his world. Human awareness develops and exists solely through relationship, but when the intimate relationship is lacking, an infant's only choice is to establish whatever relations he can on the shallow sensory level provided him. Then he will perceive every encounter as an object of possession, and when he is older that possession will become domination because emotional bonding will be beyond his capacity.

The inability of people to relate on an emotional level is epidemic. Unbonded males see females as objects of gratification, physical possessions to be dominated which leads to physical abuse. Each developmental shift contains a quantum step of possibilities, but the unbonded ego cannot make the leap and be integrated into the higher level of integration. A bonded child automatically makes the shift and easily relinquishes an earlier identity.

The unbonded child becomes an obsessive-compulsive consumer who can never get enough stimulation. Thanks to industrialized birthing, generations of Americans are helplessly addicted to everything from TV and computers to food, sex and material possessions. They can't get no satisfaction. The greed that is devouring the earth comes from a lower brain identity – reptilian humans on the take.

Parenting has become a major national issue, but most remedies are intellectual in nature. There is no intellectual substitute for bonding. We need mothering far more than a bigger house, second car or the latest in entertainment centers. When people are locked into the sensory-motor system of the reptilian brain because they were never bonded in infancy, do they crave stimulation and self-protection and so choose a life defined by materialism, money and consumption? Meanwhile, the hundreds of thousands of violent attacks by students against teachers are blamed on TV violence, a symptom as much as a cause. School shootings are blamed on everything from Ridilin to bullying and firearms, but what if lack of bonding and fearful enculturation are the real influences behind high divorce rate, single-family homes and fragmentation at every level?

Facing an annual expenditure of four billion dollars for crime and violence, in 1979 the State of California conducted the first major study of the basic causes of crime and violence. At the top of the list was the violent way children come into the world.

We need a developmental plan that accomodates our evolutionary human needs.

We do not need more therapy: "a hundred years of psychotherapy and the world is getting worse," but recovery of certain irreplaceable elements of the sane lifestyle of our Pleistocene ancestors, including prolonged and intimate association between children and mothers, between children and nature and society, and effective rites of passage for adolescents, coupled with "rising above and going beyond" the negative culture of fear.

If true intelligence means thinking with the heart and that is dependent upon proper bonding and positive enculturation then it should not surprise us that things are awry on planet earth. Perhaps what we really should ask is how all this came about? It came about because of male dominance in civilization. Because we have been living in the shadow of Hercules, whose first and greatest feat, killing the Nemean lion, made herding possible, we find ourselves living in a patriarchal society that wars and worships heroism and competition. Dominating animals and nature is equivalent to domination of women and the heart. The untempered egoism of pastoral life that gave birth to intellectualism and then to science and technology reached its apex with the domination of child birthing and culture by men.

Pearce adds this discouraging reflection,

> "No good comes from discussing any of this. An enormous literature has appeared over the years to no avail. These obscene practices have become not just acceptable but the model for childbirth. Our current generations are the unbonded victims shaped by the system, terrified of the thought of birth outside the medical umbrella, willing to pay any price to avoid personal responsibility for what is considered a dreadful experience. As my New Zealand physician friend Dr. Stephen Taylor, put it, this is really a basic war of man against woman. In the male intellect's long battle with the intelligence of the heart, the real trump card was found in catching the woman when she is most vulnerable and stripping her of her power. Now, it seems we have her – and are surely had. Beneath it all grows great anger: children angry at their parents; men angry at women because they didn't get what they needed from woman at life's most critical point and still fail to get it; women angry at men for robbing them of their power and, identifying with their oppressors, rejecting motherhood and men in the process. This has caused a rising tide of incompetence and inability to nurture and care for offspring....Home birth under any circumstances is safer and more successful than hospital birth...the death rate is six times higher in hospitals than at home...Male doctors' intellect has interfered with woman's intelligence and in effect, destroyed a major segment of their lives. Medical childbirth is one of the most destructive forces to issue from the mind of man and a most destructive force on earth today....the violence done to infants and mothers at birth...is the primary cause of our explosive rise of suicide, drug abuse, family collapse, abandonment and abuse of infants and children, deterioration of schooling, and social disintegration...Only television...comes close in destructive force."

The origin of the male intellect being at war with nature's wisdom, in this case, feminine intelligence and the intelligence of the heart can be traced back to the domination and control of nature required of herding and agricultural life. Even though men were bonded with their mothers for thousands of years in civilization, increasingly they were separated from nature during childhood and barraged with the culture of fear, then put through rites of passage during adolescence that incorporated earlier development into the defensive ego-consciousness of the warrior for whom conflict, domination, subjugation and conquest are the meaning of life.

Adolescence

Part of the programming of adolescence involves a scrupulous examination of our culture, and if we find it wanting, we rebelliously reject it. On the one hand we seem driven to identify, adopt and conform to life as it has been; on the other we are reluctant to accept what is pathological. Adolescence is a stage of development during which shifts can be made in the greater social and economic fabric.

Here is what my 14-year old son, Drake, had to say in a poem he wrote for school:

> "I used to hate change/Now I am change/I used to believe in this world/Now I can only resist it/I used to be a stale pond/But now I am an ocean of raging waves!"

Popular music today features screams of agony, hate, desperation, self-pity, anarchy, loneliness and suicide. Hopeless.

Adolescence also is the sensitive period for the awakening of spiritual life and acquisition of wholeness. If we have not been bonded, then we are driven to maintain and protect our state of dysfunction. Instead of moving our physical, emotional and mental processes into an all encompassing higher structure of spirituality, we resist and rationalize our inability to integrate and devote ourselves to the maintenance of a fragmented psyche. We grow up surrounded by slogans that reinforce our counterfeit culture, "Be a man," "Stand up for yourself," "Be assertive," "Get even," "Get ahead in the world," "Be somebody," "Survival of the fittest," "It's a jungle out there," "He made a killing in the stock market," "Be a strong individual," and so on. Implementing these pseudo-virtues of the pastoral myth underlying industrial civilization is won at the cost of true society. Development of spirit is what generates community, but imagine what a 17-year old boy encounters if he walks away from football practice to undertake a vision quest or gives up partying to meditate! His pursuit would be branded as selfish, self-indulgent, anti-social, even pathological, and yet what could be more appropriate at that time in his life for his personal development and ultimately the benefit of his future family and society?

Do not mistake me, adolescence is a biological adaptation that prepares boys for adult life, and that life includes the assumption of risks as a protector as well as being a provider. It's just that all earlier developmental stages and growth are being reassembled under a spiritual umbrella that must be embraced for adult life to take on a correspondingly higher level of meaning. Just as the newborn is adapted to bond with its mother, and the child is adapted to identify and imitate animals to develop cognition and differentiate itself, the adolescent male is primed by a critical period to encounter a model that will facilitate his adult bonding to society as protector and provider. That model consists of adult males and an initiation process commonly known as rites of passage, the original form being the hunt. Boys are primed to take risks and prove themselves worthy as providers, and in the process of killing an animal to confront death and the necessity of self-control and to adopt moral reflection. They also are ready to respond to this pivotal experience by opening the heart to spiritual influence, tempering their instinctive fire, bonding with nature and acquiring humility.

Anthropologist Carleton Coon believed that unlike the children of hunters, boys and girls today have no adults to guide them through the puberty ordeals that they need in order to maintain social continuity. It is no wonder that they create age-graded micro-societies of their own, including gangs. Coon also thought that saving our planet from human destruction is only half of the problem. The other half is for us to learn how nature intended human beings to live and reestablish continuity with those who may still be living after the rest of us are dead.

Males come out of properly initiated adolescence with their intellects integrated with intelligence. Intelligence is the means by which the life process interfaces and synthesizes divergent parts into symbiotic relationship resulting in well-being, success of individuals and societies, and proper relationship to nature. Intellect, on the other hand, is a tool of intelligence, a process meant to operate in a logical, analytical and non-judgmental manner. The integration of intellect into the higher integral structure of intelligence is accomplished in spiritual development of adolescence during which we move beyond the body to identification with the divine.

The shift associated with adolescence opens us to a qualitatively different kind of awareness than we knew in the first fifteen years of life. The shift requires an authentic rebirth; we must become as little children in order to be remade. We embark on a new development that means relinquishing development up to that point.

Joseph Campbell views rites of passage as a hero's journey. Without tearing, blood and pain, there can be no growth, no new life. To discover the divine within we muster the courage to leave society and find spiritual bliss. Society is the enemy because it imposes its structures on us, but when we enter where the dragon dwells we must kill it because everyone of its scales says, "Thou shalt." It is imperative that we throw away yesterday as the snake sheds its skin. The very dark place we were afraid to enter turns out to house what we were looking for: the mysterious treasures of life. Deep within our own psyche there shimmers the eternal jewel of peace. Embracing the spiritual we cannot despise the earthly because the ultimate purpose of our journey is compassion, our goal to bring the jewel back to the world. Though separateness appears real, beyond the world of opposites is radiant unity everywhere, and our job is to recover that rapture and integrate it.

Campbell shares the advise that was given to a Native American at the time of his initiation: as you travel the path of life and come to a great chasm, jump. It's not as wide as you think. To leap across the chasm to the new life of adulthood, the hero needs the fearlessness of unconflicted mind. Like a Samurai warrior, he must go into battle ready to die so he will live.

The shift in adolescence differs from earlier transformations in so far as our own volition enters into the process. If bonding has taken place, then we are apt to choose to move ahead with initiation to adulthood. But if unbonded we may not be able to surrender to the new blueprint and move on, but instead will remain attached to the old identity, to body, childish emotions and rage, intensified by the onset of sexuality at puberty. The bonded person who rises to the occasion offered has the potential of gaining immense personal power. The unbonded adolescent may turn to technology for a weak imitation of power, including cars and video games. The dwindling recruitment of boys into hunting and the outdoors over the past few decades indicates a lack of bonding and a paucity of role models in their lives.

Because we have not provided the social context in which adolescence may flower into spiritual power, we have instead a populace of despair that endeavors to find in technology what they did not find in themselves at adolescence. On top of which is despair over our feeling of vulnerability which motivates us to invent more and better machines and gadgets to substitute for our eroding power, until we are entirely dependent on technology because we have no power to embrace life as it is. Our final retreat is to artificial existence over which we have a semblance of control, and that leads to a perpetual state of anxiety over losing the ease and comfort technology offers, until we are ready to wage war against anyone who threatens our technological lifestyle and the oil it depends upon. We have identified with the things we made and we are lost in them, unlike the hunting societies who identify with creation and find in a natural life wholeness and fulfillment. The same applies to many recreational hunters.

Technology has locked our consciousness into the lowest level of our brain system, the reptilian. On every front it pollutes and destroys, hidden by consumerism and the ceaseless demand for more technological products. There is an apocalyptic awareness around the planet that we cannot keep going in the same direction, but there also is massive denial of the simple fact that we reap what we sow. Jerry Mander is right that our faith in scientific breakthroughs that will save the day is pure illusion. Technology has always created more problems than it has solved, and the new technologies created to solve those problems generate more of the same. *A Course in Miracles* teaches that we already have everything we need, something the Pygmy fully understands but which we, being unbonded and living in the defensive ego-consciousness and madness of artificial life, cannot possibly comprehend. And yet the proof is there in the coherence, humility, peace and joy of the hunting peoples and recreational hunters for whom life is sacred. Pearce's unconflicted state of being, one without fear or doubt, is that same "everything we need".

Are we willing to make the changes necessary to avert the coming catastrophe? The mechanistic scientists and the behaviorists deny the existence of mind, spirit and soul, but then they are offended that the culture produced by this denial exhibits insanity. But we still have it in our power to recover the wisdom of nature and true intelligence in our lives and the lives of our children. The very least we can do is make every effort to see that our infants and children bond with us, that they grow up hearing stories rather than watching TV so their imagination will blossom, that we recognize they need to play much more and work less, that we maximize their exposure to nature, that we ourselves redefine the meaning of life based on heart and make lifestyle choices so as to be worthy models, and that when adolescence appears we offer them the opportunity to embrace the power within themselves adjusting our life in whatever ways will facilitate their movement toward adulthood with sacredness.

"Nature Deficit Disorder" Revisited

Those critical years of childhood from 3 to 12 during which we are meant to interact and bond with nature prepare us for the transformation to adulthood. Regarding this development period it is unfortunate that Richard Louv's important book, *The Last Child in the Woods*, overlooked the seminal insights of Joseph Chilton Pearce (*Magical Child* and *Magical Child Matures*) and human ecologist Paul Shepard (*Thinking Animals* and *Nature and Madness*). Shepard said, "His nine-year mission is to build confidently from his good-mother symbiosis a lively relationship…to slowly master new patterns of nonhuman life that will, in time, serve his identity shaping when he enters the adult social world as an adolescent….

> "And what difference can it make if those nine years are played out in a fabricated environment?….
>
> "First, life in a made world slowly builds in the child the feeling that nonlivingness is the normal state of things. Existence is shaped from the outside or put together. Eventually, he will conclude that there is no intrinsic unfolding, no unique inner life at all, only substance…
>
> "Second, when he goes back into society after adolescence, having missed the initiation into the world of final mysteries and poetry, he will believe either that (a) all life, including people, is, in fact, machines…or (b) the only truly living things are people; this opens the door for all the dichotomies that separate the human from the nonhuman on the basis of soul, spirit, mind, history, culture, speech, rights, right to existence, and so on…."

Shepard is correct that the consequences, philosophically, of an artificial perspective dominate the Western mind: God is the maker working from the outside rather than spirit that dwells within; the reductionism of Greek atomists and their scientist progeny; the paradigm of the universe as machine including the human body; and relativistic thought from the psychology of self-help to existentialism which culminates in the conclusion that reality is whatever we make it.

The task of youth is to discover structure in nature: continuity; patterns that are predictable; regular rhythms; relations that are stable, a coherent world that remains during his own changes. The child in the city is expected to move directly from bonding with his mother to mastery of social relationships, and to skip over his intimate indulgence in nature and get on with adult life. During these 8 to 10 years his inherited need will be deadened with the portrayal of nonhumans as entertainment rather than oral tradition which actually complements his hunger for otherness. Inadequate substitutions abound in the form of toys, videos, films and zoos, an arbitrary, superficial mix of nature. It should not surprise us that the boy of 13 is keenly interested in machines. The image of nature that has been given him has proved incoherent. The boy is destined to a life of alienation, fearful helplessness and a sense of himself and the cosmos as nonliving.

Shepard says,

> "The archetypal role of nature...is in the development of the individual human personality, for it embodies the poetic expression of ways of being and relating to others....Indeed, the real brittleness of modern social relationships has its roots in that vacuum where a beautiful and awesome otherness should have been encountered....The multifold, otherness-with-similarities of nonhuman nature is a training ground for that delicate equilibrium between the play of likeness and difference in all social intercourse and for affirmation instead of fear of the ambiguities and liveliness of the self."

Adolescence and Life as Sacredness

> "Tribal people everywhere greeted the onset of puberty, especially in males, with elaborate and excruciating initiations – a practice that plainly wouldn't have been necessary unless their young were as extreme as ours....The tribal adults didn't run from this moment in their children as we do; they celebrated it. They would assault their adolescents with, quite literally, holy terror; rituals that had been kept secret from the young until that moment....rituals that focused upon their young all the light and darkness of their tribe's collective psyche, all its sense of mystery, all its questions and all the stories told to both harbor and answer those questions....The adults had something to teach: stories, skills, learned well and completely, or the tribe could not survive.... Tribal cultures satisfied the craving while supplying the need, and we call that initiation. The practice was so effective that usually by the age of fifteen, a tribal youth was able to take his or her place as a fully responsible adult."
>
> ~ Michael Ventura, *The Whole Earth Review*

Among foraging cultures and in the past, children in the early teens were put through rites of passage and assumed a place among adults in their society. The modern world has no economic niche or spiritual horizon for young people, and we have forgotten the special importance of rites of passage. As Robert Bly says, confirmation, barmitzvah, a letter in football or a driver's license do not suffice.

Anthropologist Colin Turnbull cannot think of a single culture that handles the crucial stage of adolescence more abysmally than western civilization. The consequences are to be seen all around us in the neurosis, violence and loneliness of our youth, our adults, and our aged, many of whom never approach the richness and fullness of life that could have been theirs had their adolescence been handled with more wisdom, respect and understanding.

The holding pattern we have created keeps youth in limbo. Each year children enter adolescence earlier and stay in it longer. Michael Gurian (see Foreword) says it now spans from age 9 to 21. They are alienated and each generation more lost than the last, a dismal situation exacerbated by commercial exploitation of the age group's lack of models and their deep longing to belong. The young naturally want to participate in adult life as adults, and males are especially primed and eager to prove themselves worthy of following the footsteps of their elders. A disciple is one who "follows the exemplar," the exemplary model appropriate to a new, adult life. We see a lack of "discipline" in our young precisely because there is a breakdown in the biologically encoded program for following the model. The failure is ours, not theirs; it is anomalous for an adolescent to resist initiation rites and refuse to take his or her role in society.

The genetically encoded imperative is for the adolescent to follow; the model is what the adolescent seeks, and without emotionally rich rites of passage led by mentoring elders, our youth bond with media personalities, Rambos, victimized heroic figures alone in the world whose lives are committed to vengeance, or to sports heroes, many of whom are glory hounds, and to the ever present anti-heroes of popular music whose vehement social protests speak to the alienation and anger of youth waiting impatiently if unknowingly for someone to intervene and reorient their life toward meaning.

The failure of bonding at birth is the fault of the adult, not the infant's, and the failure of adolescents to follow is the failure of adult models. Our failure to meet their need to follow may redirect identification from an adult role in society to a place in the gang. The gang offers the opportunity to "be somebody," to face risks and prove self-worth, which accounts for much violence and teen death in the cities of America. **In the same way that we blame school violence on guns rather than our failure as parents to provide bonding, we pretend that gun control is the solution for gang violence which also is a consequence of our failure to provide bonding with models.**

Starting at about age 12 until the mid-teens, we develop an idealistic image of life, and around 14 to 15 a feeling arises that something great is supposed to happen. Adolescents also feel deep within themselves that there is something great that must be expressed. It is a sense of destiny, and their efforts to express this is often accompanied by pointing to the heart, a clue to a dawning love affair with life on a new plane.

How tragic it is that in our world the "something tremendous" that is supposed to happen rarely happens. That pitched feeling of expectation may be felt as an acute longing. It is not about sex because what the young person anticipates is unknown. What they anticipate but seldom find is death and rebirth of the psyche. Becoming an adult includes dying to childhood and being reborn as something new and as someone with a special mission to fulfill. Some Jungian psychologists believe that the unfulfilled need for psychic death and rebirth contributes to teen suicide, another perversion of what is natural precipitated by our failure to provide rites of passage.

Because our youth appear cynical and pursue anti-heroes, it might be difficult for us to perceive the idealism spontaneously unfolding in them. Through the framework of idealism, they scrutinize society, adults, parents, teachers, coaches, and discover our vulnerabilities and weaknesses, not out of disrespect but from the necessity to construct a new model for adult human life, to become the best they can be as an adult and to contribute to the reformation of society.

On Role Models

The hidden greatness a young person feels calls for exemplary models, the emulation of which may facilitate success. This is where myths and stories of heroes of immense stature served youth well for millennia.

In the tradition of India, the Bhagavita and Ramayana legends of superhuman feats by godlike women and men are woven into the highest spiritual teaching. Pearce says,

> "The power of these great epics lay in the paradox that the highest reaches of humanity arose from people depicting every human failing, failings so magnified as to be unmistakable, yet finally overcome. Incorporating god-like greatness, which we long to possess, and human weakness, which is already ours, these models of transcendence meet us where we are in order to show where we can go. Our evolution toward greatness begins, after all, in a most animal-like body. The bridge in childhood is between a specifically mammalian brain and a human brain, while in adolescence the bridge is between the human brain and the human spirit that can transcend it. The great and lasting cultures of history held before their young people symbolic figures who rose above their lower natures, making transcendence the highest and most noble of all quests, the ultimate achievement and model for becoming....Brought up on models of such stature, we identify with a general...notion of a 'higher aim of life'...all are lifted up just by the acknowledged presence of them. And for some, at least, such images act as their first stage in the cycle of competence: a rough model about whom we feel impelled to 'fill in the details' and to become like through practice."

Six decades of research on brain development and function led Paul MacLean to conclude that the critical human needs are audiovisual communication, nurturing and play. Pearce believes that these needs sustain us from birth and also serve as a springboard to transcendence itself. To fulfill these needs it is imperative that models are provided at each stage of development. Pearce says, "Recall that the model is the living embodiment of the child's inherited capacity or talent and that its stimulus – a possibility demonstrated by the model's presence – brings about a like response in the child, building structure of knowledge or imprint within him." He emphasizes that there are no exceptions to this necessity for modeling, and that, "The character, nature and quality of any intelligence or ability are determined... by the character, nature and quality of the model." Which is all the more reason to recover community life, meaning authentic society, so that appropriate models are present and available for young people.

At each stage of maturity the inherited program of development extracted our sense of self out of one stage and moved us into an expanded potential. By the age of 15 or 16, with sexual drive in full swing, we are "all gonads," but also engrossed in logical intellect and social involvement. We are obsessed by the heroic impulse to prove ourselves worthy as men, often taking extreme risks; until the mid-20s we are ideally suited as soldiers. (The only changes in the brain after age 15 are a growth spurt of the prefrontal lobes from age 18 to 21.) Both cerebral hemispheres are fully myelinated, and if we civilized (domesticated) people who have been deprived of bonding and suffer from "nature deficit disorder" have at that point developed no more than 5-10% of the neocortex, as has been proposed, then the adolescent feeling that something great is coming may have a neurological basis.

The secondary prefrontal development at age 15 represents the highest level of brain coordination and development. When the higher incorporates the lower into its service, it transforms the lower into the nature of the higher, the key to nature's plan for our biology.

The sexual instinct evolves in us to magnificent levels of spiritual love as immortalized in the legends of Tristan and Isolde or Romeo and Juliet. At mid-adolescence the prefrontal cortex incorporates our instincts of the lowly serpent which are subsequently transformed into transcendent power. This is Pearce's model of brain development, and it converges precisely with my own model of behavioral development: the sexual instinct links up with the heart and transforms us, just as the instinct to hunt links up with the heart and transforms males.

The idea that only a small percentage of the cortex is needed to operate and interact with the lower centers to handle the external world, while the rest of the cortex deals with a vast, open-ended, literally infinite spiritual world is supported by the fact that Abos appear to utilize much more of the cortex than we do, and the spiritual life of Kalahari Bushman is much more extensive than our own. Civilized living and its focus on ego consciousness may demand much less use of gray matter.

We have touched on some of the costs of our failure to provide young people with proper initiation to adulthood, but the toll is enormous for society and the environment. When the something tremendous that was supposed to happen didn't – rites of passage and discovery, as in vision quest, of an individual's unique mission in adult life – our youth knuckle under to the paltry models and commercial curricula provided. We measure our self-worth monetarily and are schooled accordingly. Before the age of five a kid watches 6,000+ hours of TV and the pattern continues after starting school. By the age of adolescence, a young person will watch 18,000 murders and learn that life is violent and expendable. What of noble aspirations, virtue and restraint?

Our youth are sabotaged by TV, commercialism and our compulsive buying into materialism and consumerism. Several decades ago it was estimated that every day six teenagers committed suicide and over 3,000 ran away from home, that on any given day over 1,500 children were in jail and about 2,500 babies were born out of wedlock. Each year the percent of black males who are either in prison, awaiting sentence or on parole increases. The rate of recidivism is over 95%.

Pearce wrote about a hit rap album the lyrics of which describe anal-oral sex with a 12-year old girl. Attempts to remove the record from the market brought an outcry of infringement of rights and freedom in the marketplace. Plato said he could predict the shape of a society by the music of its youth, in which case our situation is gloomy. Carol Gilligan found that girls at age 11 were confident, had clarity and purity of mind as well as strong self-image, but by age 16 were confused. Pearce adds, "Millions of dollars are made from this destruction, and the destroyed child becomes the destroying and consuming adult."

What is the cost of not belonging to the fraternity of men, the sorority of women? Without rites of passage that culminate in acceptance into and identification with adult circles and their responsibilities leaves young men few alternatives other than membership in gangs. One is joining the military and giving allegiance to a government that has eroded the Bill of Rights for the sake of imperialism, another is the empty path of egoism which makes us more vulnerable to manipulation and control by industry and government.

It is not true that history repeats itself. Since WW II a range of phenomena without historical precedence have confronted our inherited makeup so severely that we are unable to cope. We have been so altered by industrial thinking and technology that we are not even capable of grasping cause and effect. Hospital childbirth, day care, schooling, TV and the decline of child play have taken their toll, and now we face the final insult from computers on every desk and video games in every home.

There are many factors contributing to premature sexuality, and one of them is industrialized farming. "A better life through chemistry," the DuPont slogan proposed. Have hormones in our meat, eggs and milk contributed to a younger onset of puberty and an accentuated sexual drive among youth? Rape by 12-year old boys has become common. It all comes down to the strategic invention and alteration of products that will sell better and make higher profits irrespective of the costs to the quality and integrity of human life. **Unbridled intellect coupled with reptilian motives set free in a world without intelligence anchored in the heart can only go bad.**

The Cost of Stimulation

The mounting crisis for youth today includes the crisis in the family, education, structure of society, declining health and well-being and multiple forms of violence, all spilling over increasingly into adult life. A century of disruption of natural developmental processes also has taken a toll on human awareness, sensitivity and consciousness. Research indicates that the brain is not synthesizing an ever increasing disparity and intensity of information, but instead is tuning out. Enjoyment and aesthetic levels have dropped. According to Pearce, twenty years ago people could distinguish 300,000 sounds, but now many children are unable to go beyond 100,000. Twenty-five years ago subjects could distinguish 350 shades of a particular color, but today the number is 130.

Either young people have a steady input of high-level stimulation from TV, computers, video games, game boys, cell phones and Ipods, or they are sinking into sensory anxiety and isolation. Last weekend I took my 14-year old son and two of his friends camping, but whenever we weren't active one boy had his cell phone out and was texting, unresponsive to my questions. Many young people today have little interest in visiting parks or undertaking outdoor pursuits because they lack intense sensory input. German psychologists have speculated that a generation with such altered brains may create an environment of such intense stimuli that a normal brain might not survive. The total sound of a preliterate jungle society is about equal to that of a modern refrigerator!

What Unfortunate Children Have

An independent child psychologist, Mikulak, developed extensive tests of sensory awareness in children, and applied them to cultures ranging from the preliterate societies of Latin America and Africa to those of Europe and America. She found that children of primitive settings averaged levels of conscious awareness of their surroundings and sensory sensitivity 25 to 30 percent more than those of the children of industrialized nations. Preliterate children were more aware of what was happening among people around them, also what was said to them. They also were more aware of the sights, sounds, taste and touches of daily life. And they knew the names of plants and animals in their environment, which few of the children and adults of industrial culture do. Mikulak's studies have been ignored.

In his book, *Evolution's End*, Pearce described studies in the late 1980s of the learning ability of children in so-called primitive groups of the third world with severely low standards of living. When these "deprived" children were put into a learning situation equal to those provided for our fortunate children, the deprived children showed a three to four times higher learning capacity, rate of attention and comprehension and retention than the fortunate children. About this Pearce comments,

> "Deprived of advanced electronics, these primitive children were given the most necessary things – love and nurturing – and they played continually and developed to the maximum their society afforded."

Why Unschooling?

The negative enculturation that civilized peoples impose on their youth is not instinctive though it capitalizes on our survival instincts. Convinced that we must pass on survival knowledge and engender fear, distrust, competitiveness and self-centeredness, we pound it into our offspring for their own "good" just as it was pounded into us. We treat schooling in a similar way, regardless of how much pain it may have caused us, having lost the richest, most wonderful years of our life, we insist that it must have been good for us. Then we subject our children to it and they prove our point by becoming just like us, joining the ranks of mass anxiety, confirming our insane worldview. We have little choice in the matter, but hope springs eternal that this time "we will make schooling work." Pearce reminds us that, "It never has."

In a poem entitled "Space Man Society," my son Drake said,

> "The school is a prison where you go almost every day to learn yet I learn nothing/ The government is an organization meant to protect us yet all it manages to do is take away freedom and collect taxes.../I am not the cowering mind trapped by fear/I am the courage of the eagle chick at its first attempt at flight..."

Competition or Cooperation?

Turnbull believes that we must consciously aim adolescents toward transformation. Do we choose a society in which people want to cooperate rather than compete? A world in which each individual becomes fully integrated and applies his whole being to whatever he does? Adolescence is when it is possible to bring together the heart, mind, body and spirit to function simultaneously so they reinforce and vitalize one another. In so doing we inculcate the spirit of cooperation rather than competition, the spirit of incorporation and integration rather than the mechanics of isolation and fragmentation, and we promote a shared belief system in spirit as the glue of society rather than legality. Greater fulfillment, equality and security are the rewards offered by true society compared to the State. Primal societies inform us about what we have forgotten: the ecstacy of divinity. Have we lost our human potential in the bloody business of survival and the endless fear of loss?

This sorry state of disintegration can be traced back to our ancestors shift from the humble interdependence of hunting life to immodest domination of nature and the commitment to progress it entailed. When moved to a reservation and told to take up the plow one Indian complained that it was wrong to rip and tear the flesh of mother earth, that humans are meant to share her bounty. A few years later the same society removed babies from their mothers and stuck bottles in their mouths filled with cow's milk containing hormones and excessive sugar, then put a TV in every home. Up from Eden? Hardly!

"In the first place, God made idiots. That was for practice.
Then he made school boards."

~ Mark Twain

Chapter 6

The Reinvention of Nature: Woman the Hunter?

"Man and Woman each have gifts the other doesn't have...So let us treat each other with respect. Let us look upon each other in a sacred way."

~ Oren R. Lyons,
Spokesman, Traditional Circle of Elders

Taking Grandson Fishing

Yesterday I took my four year old grandson to a nearby lake in the middle of the jungle where I live in Mexico. Had the whole place to ourselves and tied up to trees and fished for large mouth bass. Caught a huge one, his first ever. Now, his Mom is a vegan and has raised him accordingly. We brought the fish back to camp and since it was strong and unhurt, I asked if we should release it. My daughter (his Mom) said yes. But my grandson said, "Well, Mom, we should ALWAYS let the baby fish go, but this one is old and lived a good life and wants us to eat him I think." I told him if we did he would have to do the thank you ceremony, kill the fish, gut it, and help me cook it. He said OK. We did the whole thing and he ate it on an open grill over the camp fire and loved every bite. He has not quite been the same since. Sort of a worldliness that is grounded in a new level of understanding.

~ Don Four Arrows Jacobs

The men's movement followed the woman's movement which came after the rebellion of youth we knew as the hippy revolution. A leader of the men's movement, Robert Bly, understands the fundamental relationship between masculine instincts and the lifestyle of men in prehistory. He said,

"Many boys become fascinated with hunting, and make small bows and arrows, form hunting bands, and shoot rabbits or birds. It doesn't always turn out well. The boy enthusiastically brings home a dead cottontail or a killed robin, but many women, and some men, feel that a boy's hunting instinct is deplorable and he should be educated out

> of it. New Age parents usually want the boy to bypass hunting and go directly to ethics. The trouble with such a bypass is that the boy is mythologically living through the past history of man, which includes century after century of joyful hunting....During the hunting era, the man's emotional and even his religious life, resonated to the empty spaces of forest and plain, and he learned about God through hunting animals....If a shaming mother or father blocks a boy from living that time through, he will never arrive at contemporary time."

On a jet flying home from a lecture in North Carolina a young woman saw that the book I was reading was about the sacred hunt. She had written a senior thesis in college on male initiation and had interviewed Robert Bly. When she heard my point of view on hunting as male initiation she politely encouraged me to read Sam Keen's book, *Fire in the Belly*.

Keen emphasizes the importance of men committing themselves to the ecological stewardship of a place. He believes that there is no dignity for men unless they assume the role as earth fathers and protectors of place. Keen knows that men need to fully embrace life as interdependence, but for him that movement is focused on other humans and on place, and it does not originate from or encompass hunting wild animals for food.

Hoping to recover fierceness and wildness, the men's movement took up drumming and dancing as well as rituals of Native Americans. I agree with Keen and Paul Shepard who saw these symbolic efforts as adequate only to the partial discovery of psychic wildness and a temporary sense of fraternity.

Keen echoes Bly when he writes about the unparalleled importance of directly encountering wild places, and he insists that wildness first comes from identification with the actual wilderness – mountains, forests, tundra, the haunts of untamed grizzlies, undomesticated wolves, fierce cougars. Wildness, he says is not a metaphor the meaning of which we may learn while comfortably housed in a city or within the boundaries of the civilized psyche. Keen feels that we need great expanses of untouched wilderness to remind ourselves of the fundamental truth of the human condition, that we are merely a single species within a community of sentient lifeforms.

Keen insists that the modern city fails to provide the type of initiatory ordeals young men need. He adds that sport, drugs, and membership in gangs does not replace the confrontation with the wilderness and its strange animals and unpredictable dangers.

Untamed grizzlies, undomesticated wolves? Strange animals? Unpredictable dangers? These usages suggest that Keen is a city boy, and judging from Keen's account of his maturation, he did not grow up hunting or fishing. Perhaps, like the apartment cat that bypasses predatory experience for several years and runs from a mouse, Keen's hunting instinct atrophied from lack of use. Wild animals figure into his mind as challenging confrontations, but apparently not from directly participating with them in the food chain.

I admire Keen for quoting Wendell Berry, who said that we may best serve civilization by being against what usually passes for it. But much of Keen's definition of manhood is founded on civilized concepts from classical Greece, such as heroism, which appear to reflect Keen's background in Western philosophy. Heroism and husbandry both smack of civilization and herding life; both are related to the domination and taming of wild nature, within and without.

Keen sees the progressive lifestyles of humans as something that is to be abandoned because they are no longer useful in time, and he sees each new age, by which he really means culture – way of making a living – as bringing forth a virtue. There are categorical errors here. For one thing, universal virtues are never counterproductive. More serious, he fails to glimpse the virtues of the hunting life. He does credit hunting as the crucible in which man identifies with the animals he hunts, and he sees that identity as mystical, which it surely is. He admits that the hunter knew and respected the animal he was to kill, but then he says that the hunter created a story in which the animal offered its life as a sacrifice to feed humans.

There was a time when, like my 15-year old son, I could not possibly imagine that any animal would offer itself to a hunter. Unknowingly, I had absorbed and adopted the civilized culture of prowess: to hunt successfully meant to master stealth and deception and the use of advanced weaponry. My conviction was shaken the moment a doe stopped underneath my tree stand and looked straight up into my eyes when my bow was drawn and I was ready to loose a lethal arrow at her chest. She not only paused as if waiting for me to release the arrow, she even blinked at me, which, years later I would learn from a Lakota holy man, is the signal given by a deer to a hunter that he may take its life. There was a moment of truth looking into the doe's eyes that would chart a new course in my life, one that would lead me to doubt the civilized culture of ego-intellect and search for a culture of the heart. In that momentary connection I knew that she was offering her life to me. In retrospect I see what the Western Shoshone elder meant when he said that if the majority of men in this country had been properly initiated to hunting, it would be a totally different world.

For a number of years I was not aware that the belief in the animal giving itself to the hunter was shared by nearly all the tribes of North America. How could it be so widespread among distinctly different cultures unless there were a genuine foundation for it? Neither did I know that the same belief existed among African and Australian Abo cultures and ancient European hunters. I had not yet discovered in world mythology the consistent story that in the very old days humans could communicate with the animals, which freely gave up their lives for people, and that weapons existed solely as a means of dispatching animals quickly and humanely. I did not comprehend the significance of Biblical references to early humans having the ability to communicate with animals.

Had Keen been a lifelong hunter or spent enough time with aboriginal hunters of North America perhaps he'd know that when the preparations are made and permission is given, the animal really may offer itself. It is not merely a story or a justification, and had I not observed it myself as a hunter and also as a student of carnivore behavior, I never would have believed it. Most veteran hunters positively testify that certain animals were meant for them, i.e., came to them deliberately. Likewise, in my youth and in the lives of many youngsters I took fishing, I have noticed an uncanny level of beginner's luck - we might well ask why the expression exists. Like Don Four Feathers Jacobs' story about his 4-year old grandson, at the front of this chapter, my 3-year old son caught the biggest trout I've ever seen, and when I was fishing in the Spoon River with my father and grandfather, both experienced fishermen, I hauled in a 10-pound fish, a family record. Another summer on the Orca Project in Puget Sound there were many sophisticated fishermen going out daily, but the only person to catch a salmon was a teenage girl who had never been fishing before. One summer in British Columbia I took two experienced adults fishing with a 13-year old boy who had never been salmon fishing. The boy's single mother told me he desperately needed a rite of passage so I prayed the night before to the Spirit of the Salmon Nation to grant him a salmon. They all used exactly the same gear from rod and reel to line and lures. There were two salmon caught that day, both by the boy.

Perhaps it is wise not to judge or assess a matter when we have no direct experience of it.

Life as Interdependence

The Russian ecologist, Kropotkin, saw life as cooperation. His view of life much influenced that of Aldo Leopold, father of the land ethic and wildlife management in the western world. For thousands of years Native Americans have viewed life overall as cooperation, despite the competition that organisms including humans exhibit.

The scientific perspective from ecology and evolution, which rests on Darwinian natural selection, is that cooperation is in reality a way of competing for reproductive success. Sociobiology interprets social behavior as a product of competition.

While all living things are in degree and much of the time selfish in their behavior, the greater reality is one of cooperation and interdependence. Ecological interdependence is, in principle, hypothetical, but life as interdependence is not. The philosophy of Ortega puts sociobiology into perspective. His philosophy of co-existence conjoins the true halves of realism and idealism, "I am me and my circumstances." For Ortega, life is the mutually transcendent, interdependent relationship between ego and world. Neither ego nor the world have the luxury of existing without the other. Ego is a necessary but insufficient condition for the co-operative whole that is a life. In this sense, sociobiology points to life as co-operation.

Predation Or Cooperation?

It is true that deer deliberately give themselves to some hunters, contrary to what anti-hunters and many wildlife biologists imagine, and it is true that wild animals sometimes give themselves to predators. So I learned one hot day in Nairobi National Park.

I had been following the mother cheetah and her half-grown young when they came upon an old male impala whose horns were blunt and worn. He was a bag of bones and had no harem of females accompanying him. He was, in biological jargon, a post-prime adult, senile from all appearances. I was relieved to see the old impala because I hoped that the cheetah family might feed on him. It had been several days since the mother had made a kill.

The cheetah stalked close and rushed at the impala who simply stood there watching her. It made no attempt to flee or defend itself in any way. The cheetah knocked the impala over and called her cubs with a bird-like whistle. The four cubs fed on the hind-quarter of the impala as the impala lay there with its head cocked up watching them tear skin and take bites from its body. The mother stood back staying alert for the approach of dangerous predators – the largest cause of death among cheetah kittens. The impala had not been strangled by the cheetah, nor in any other way impaired, and as the cheetahs ate its body it made no effort to stand or escape. It uttered no alarm calls or moans of pain. It simply watched its body move into the cheetahs' bodies until, apparently from loss of blood, its head collapsed and it died.

For years I reflected on the death of the impala, and I still am humbled by the feeling that it was an event I was meant to witness. The impala did not resist, and for all practical purposes, it cooperated with the cheetahs that ate it. I understood what had occurred that day in the African sun when, six years later, a whitetail doe offered herself to me.

Later still when I studied orca whales I came across two references in the literature to encounters between orcas and their prey which were more like cooperation than predation. One observation was from a well-known marine mammalogist, Vic Scheffer, who watched a pod of orcas following a small herd of gray whales along the northern coast. The orcas were several hundred yards behind the grays when both the grays and the orcas stopped dead in the water. After a few minutes one of the gray whales left its herd and swam directly to the orcas. It did not attack the orcas or in any way exhibit aggression to them. It simply swam to the orcas and allowed them to kill and eat it.

The other account came from the Eskimos who said that when orcas follow blue whales along the coast sometimes they both come to a stop though separated by several hundred yards. They say that the orcas are talking to the blue whales underwater, asking one of them to give itself to them because they are hungry and need to eat. They go on to say that the blue whales decide which one will feed the orcas, then that whale swims back to the orcas and gives itself to them.

I asked Rob Arnaud, a hunting guide and outfitter in southwest Montana, to read and comment on this chapter and the next which begins with a story about an elk that offered itself to me. He commented that, "After 20 years of work with elk, I really find no mysticism in them....I have a great deal of respect for them and I do believe that most of life's lessons can be learned in hunting wild elk!"

Then Rob began to wonder about animals giving themselves up, and he shared with me his observations of how Cheyenne Indians hunted buffalo and the rituals they employed. He was helping a film producer document the hunt. The goal of the Cheyenne hunters was to kill a two-year old bull. Rob parked the vehicles a half-mile away from a herd of 7-800 buffalo. It was August and the rut was on. While the cameras were rolling the Cheyenne sang and chanted in their language. Doubting that they would succeed in attracting a buffalo, Rob grabbed his binoculars and began walking toward the herd. The author of the script asked Rob how he was going to find and separate a two-year old bull from the herd. Killing one bison in a herd is very dangerous and difficult. At that point a Cheyenne man looked at Rob incredulously and said, "You don't get it! I was singing and praying for a two-year old bull to come out of the herd and sacrifice itself to me!"

Rob thought, "right," and kept on walking toward the herd. "We got within 400 yards of the herd and a two-year old bison bull left the herd behind him and walked the entire distance directly to us, then turned broadside, and the Cheyenne shot him in the heart!"

I wrote back to Rob, "You might want to try it sometime. Knowing as I do your connection with God, nature and wildlife, I encourage you to pray sincerely from your heart to be given an elk, and to promise to honor it and share it with others. It will come to you and it will not run. That is the beauty of the sacred hunt. It teaches us that when we are humble the power of the Creator far surpasses our prowess."

A German hunter whom I recently mentored in the sacred hunt reported that after thirty years of hunting by prowess, a deer finally offered itself to him. As a hunter educator he starts by teaching the principles of the sacred hunt to initiates.

The Meaning of Cave Art

Keen does not mention trophies at all in connection with male rites of passage, though he does refer to totem animals with which men identified. He describes the famous charging bison painting of Lascuax, and speculates that it all amounts to sexual symbolism and represents the philosophy of hunting, "I hunt; therefore, I am."

The etching is of a charging bison trailing its intestines. Its head is striking a stick figure of a human with a penis and bird-like head, which is falling backwards. Nearby is the etching of a bird.

The function of cave art could hold valuable insights about the life of Cro Magnon hunters, the ancestors of modern Europeans. Thirty years ago I developed a theory for the origin of art as trophyism, some of which I summarize here. The distribution of species conforms perfectly with universal trophy values, from the smallest big game, deer and chamois, at the entrance, to large big game – wild horse, bison, elk – in the main chamber, to rhinoceros and bear, dangerous animals, in the ante chamber, and, finally, the most sequestered and rarest figure being the lion, definitely the most dangerous species.

Art historians have praised European cave art, but they have been baffled by the fact that the artists rotated the horns and antlers of big game species 90 degrees to face the viewer. If trophies were measured by the size and spread of horns and antlers, as they are today, then we might expect the artists to feature them.

The theory that the art represents hunting magic makes no sense considering that some figures may have taken a full week to create. What if the wild horses or elk have moved on by the time the art was finished? When pygmy hunters practice hunting magic, they make a quick drawing on the ground of a generic antelope and then pray for success in the hunt. The figures in the cave art are not generic but highly individualistic, for example, an 8-point elk or a pregnant horse, which suggests that the animal depictions are records. Moreover, clay tablets have been discovered in the caves with sketches of the animal that is fully embellished on the cave wall, which indicates that the artist sketched the animal outside the cave before depicting it in the cave. More evidence in favor of the art as record.

Often figures of animals are superimposed on one another, though there is plenty of suitable empty wall space between clusters. If the figures represent trophies, perhaps each set represents an individual hunter's kills – his personal trophy case. Placement of a handprint on an animal figure could constitute a signature, "I killed this animal."

In one of the caves there are fossilized footprints including those of a young man whose age is estimated as 16. The footprints show that he stood with his back against the cave wall and that four adult males stood around him in a semi-circle.

Behind the young man is a deer etched on the wall, which suggests a rite of passage ceremony. Young Cro Magnon hunters were buried with the canine tooth of a deer around their neck, the very trophy worn by European hunters to this day.

According to my theory of the origin of art as trophyism, the wounded bison art communicates, "I who record this event killed this dangerous, wounded bison that killed another hunter; therefore, this bison is an exceptional trophy and I am a brave hunter." During my lecture on cave art at the University of Nevada, a Swedish anthropologist infomed me that the bird-like head and the bird are universal symbols of death, i.e., the man's soul has taken flight.

If the central function of cave art was trophyism as a form of competition for social status, then perhaps it was trophy hunting that led to human domination of large predators and ultimately to civilization and the global crisis.

Hunting, Virtues and Culture

Keen says it is impossible to know exactly what elemental virtues early hunters added to our definition of man. Then he reminds us of the opening scene of "2001" and the use of a weapon by a proto-human, but weaponry is hardly a virtue. It may be characteristic of the human species to use weapons, as it is to use language, but these are not virtues per se.

Keen asserts that because hunting cultures are nomadic, they cannot create cultural complexity, that since they have to keep moving they have to limit themselves to portable "cultural" objects. Many hunting societies are not nomadic, such as the coastal natives of the Pacific Northwest and others that occupied very productive environments, but a bigger shortcoming is Keen's equation of culture with objects. Because anthropology has relied upon investigation and examination of tools and objects to infer cultural life, we come to think of these artifacts as the equivalent of culture, when they are merely tools. The cultural life even of nomadic hunters is surprisingly complex, whether we consider construction of shelter, clothing, weaponry or ritual art, but the heart of culture exists in the stories told about creation, culture heroes, the behavior of animals often as teachers, the place in which people live and its resources, the history of the society, the cosmos. If anything, the mythopoetic life of hunting peoples is more complex than that of other peoples. I also suspect that when it comes to measures of imagination and comprehension of symbols and metaphors, the hunters come out on top.

Like so many civilized thinkers and their doctrines as seen in school textbooks, Keen thinks that civilized humans have more time and energy to devote to creation of culture, when in reality, it is the hunting peoples who have more time and energy for culture, more than farmers, more than city folk, and the richness of their story-life confirms what ethnographers have discovered.

A brief but scrupulous examination of hunting societies or of contemporary recreational hunting would reveal a number of "elemental" virtues fostered by hunting, and these include patience, courage, fortitude, generosity, humility – a reflection of spirituality, compassion, inner peace, cooperation, respect for living things, gratitude, creativity, moral reflection and more. I find it impossible to exclude any of these virtues at any stage of cultural evolution, and I am certain that hunting still can evoke the development of these virtues in males as well if not better than any other activity. Many of them are also learned by female hunters.

What About Pastoralism?

Keen moves on to discuss man as planter, skipping pastoralism altogether. Like a Neo-Marxist anthropologist, he paints a picture of women creating agriculture, which they may have done, but he imagines that it was planting that gave rise to mathematics and science. While the eco-feminists may approve of Keen's perspective, there is good reason to say he is wrong, that it was hunting that promoted science and math. It is hunting that calls upon formation of hypotheses, deduction and experimental testing, i.e., problem solving. Even Einstein recognized subsistence hunting as proto-science.

It is no mere coincidence that boys tend to score higher in mathematical aptitude than girls – and girls in language. If women did store grain, create surplus wealth and start civilization, it was men who protected the women and children and fertile fields from other farmer societies and the aggressive, dangerous pastoralists who wanted to graze their cattle there.

Keen and cultural historians may prefer to imagine that early agricultural life was a time of relative harmony, when there is much reason to think the opposite. Farmers are forever in conflict with nature; their life is not one of acceptance of nature, as it is for the hunter. For farmers are in competition with wild animals as well as the domestic animal herds of pastoralists, not to mention insects and weather. On a higher plane, the spiritual life of farmers tends to center on fear, insecurity and control, and their actual life is drudgery as Paul Shepard says. (Notable exceptions include the Hopi and Tibetans, discussed below.)

It is not farming that expanded human consciousness to the cosmos, it is hunting. Long before any fields were plowed, hunters were keeping close tabs on lunar, solar and seasonal cycles, as reflected in their calendars and in their stories.

From Farmer to Warrior?

When Keen arrives at "Man as Warrior" he states that it is not clear why man changed from farmer to warrior. It is conceivable that farming grew out of pastoralism, as in growing food for animal herds, but in any case pastoralism is opposed to farming as a lifestyle, and the conflict between herders and growers has its origin in competition between herders and big predators that wanted their "game." From there it would have been warfare between different groups of pastoralists, competing for grazing grounds or water, then with the farmers who settle in productive growing areas. The threat of attack by awesome herders would have favored formation of armies by growers, and then the armies of different cities would have come into competition for grain and ground to grow it.

Keen imagines that the farmer expressed his manhood in nature, but that simply isn't so. The farmer is not at home in nature, the hunter is. Farmers live a life of opposition to nature, in an eternal effort to control it. Surely, he is wrong when he proposes that after a few centuries without hunting or hunger, men began to get bored with farming, and that is what motivated them to violence and warfare.

Warfare and violence are incipient in the hunter from millennia of defense against predators, but it is pastoralism that favors full-scale offensive aggression against carnivores as well as other humans. The farmer became a warrior against the herders and the armies of other farmers.

To this very day, woman holds her highest status not among farmers but among hunters. Like pastoralism, the farming life exerted control over plants, animals and women as men became warriors.

Keen's focus on place is about ownership of land, typical of civilization but nonexistent among nomadic hunting societies. Like Wendell Berry, Gary Snyder and Keen, we all are locked into a civilization that pretends it owns the earth. Snyder's commitment to the resurrection of abused, marginal lands in the lower Sierra is admirable to be sure, but what concerns me is that the life of foraging cultures is not the model being followed. What we own owns us: when we enslave the land it enslaves us – hardly the "old ways." On the other hand perhaps the best any of us can do in the civilized world is to steward land and promote the diversity of natural plant and animal life.

Why the Men's Movement Denied Hunting

As I "plowed" through some of the more popular literature of the men's movement I noticed that, like Keen's book, it seemed to deny, overlook or deliberately ignore hunting as the prototypical male activity. How could this be, I wondered? After years of deliberation I have come to the conviction that the men's movement rejected hunting as masculine because men fear their own anger, especially they are afraid that their anger is innately masculine rather than cultural artifact, so they fear hunting and blame the masculine instinct for their anger. The confusion comes from categorical error: first, the rage of men is not inevitably derived from instinct, but is a deplorable result of a combination of the long-term pastoral mythology of war that permeates our culture, and incomplete bonding including industrial birthing that stuck males into the heartless state of attachment behavior – what we later came to identify as co-dependency. And I think Robert Bly is right that many men carry anger over the fact that they never underwent real rites of passage as adolescents. There are different kinds of instincts. The potential for aggression is inherited, but it is not a trophic drive like sex that builds up over time and has to be released. The rage of modern American men is not natural but pathological.

Second, hunting may be instinctive but it has nothing to do with anger, aggression or violence toward humans so fear of embracing it as fundamental to the male psyche is categorically wrong. The only similarity between hunting and non-predatory aggression is that weapons are associated with both, but beyond that superficiality, they are distinctly different. Whether subsistence or recreational hunters, men do not feel rage toward animals they hunt and kill for food. It is true that killing an animal is a violent act, by definition, but hunters do not feel anger when hunting or killing anymore than lions or wolves in contrast to their behavior when combating other groups of their own species or other predators.

"Hunting" big predators that are dangerous is normally not undertaken for food, but to protect food, kin or associates. The aggressive interaction between predators, whether lions and hyenas, wolves and bears or humans and other carnivores is not hunting, predation for food, but warfare between species, which, as I said above, primed us for warfare with other human groups once we became the dominant predator and began herding. We see enemy humans the way our ancestors saw lions and bears, as subhuman, worthy of genocide.

Men are immobilized by rage and feel guilty about it, but they also live in dire fear that their condition is something natural to men so they find themselves in a double-bind. Unaware that they were severely violated as newborns and that their culture operates on the basis of a relatively recent myth of power/war, they threw hunting out the window with their masculinity. While they received a degree of therapy from temporary bonding with other men, they never resolved the origins of their pain and anger. They didn't learn that the wild man within is at peace in wild places gratefully participating in the food chain, and that killing, as part of that process, engenders compassion. If those impotent gatherings of men had been grounded in feasting on venison or salmon caught by their own hands and blessed by a unified voice, the movement might have reoriented a sick culture. If nothing else it would have meant a recovery of hunting as a rite of passage with deeply profound consequences for the world.

From a broader perspective, while the men's movement was the end of the road for many men suffering from millennia of power mythology topped off by the insult of industrial birthing, it also was the final outcry from the wastelands: we need our mothers! It was the last in a series of warnings about the collapse of civilization itself. We need our Mother Earth.

His-*story* or Her-*story*?

Since the mid-80s there have been intellectual uprisings primarily in the ranks of academe, that question our views of ourselves, our cherished theories and myths about history and reality. Female anthropologists have questioned time honored theories about the nature of masculinity and femininity. Hunting and its role in human evolution has been challenged and revised. Some are busy reconstructing his-tory to her-story, others known as deconstructionists insist that reconstruction is a waste of time because all knowledge is merely symbolic, i.e., we can't actually know anything outside our own use of language so why bother? There's nothing better than hunting or a vision quest to discover knowledge beyond language. The eco-feminist reconstructionists blame men and myths of masculinity for the abuse of women and the environment, and there are many splinter groups with radically different points of view and agendas all taking pot shots at one another. Frankly, it's a bit overwhelming and difficult to sort out, but altogether the man-bashing women seem nearly as ego-based as the men they judge, blame and attack.

There is much room for revision of our scientific culture and its mythologies about who we are and our roots. The biggest problem with science is that it is a human enterprise, and as such is incapable of living up to its ideal form as put forth by Jacob Bronowski and others. Each science has hundreds of subcultures within it, and each of these operates more or less the way hunting societies do. They have their shared doctrines, which really amount to their religion, their culture heroes – an example would be Aldo Leopold, the father of wildlife biology - but most conspicuously they have their own language, their own specialized terminology appropriate to their field, and members of the culture as opposed to strangers may be identified accordingly. Strangers may be tolerated but are not necessarily welcome or taken seriously. Any real shift in doctrine within the subculture succeeds only after rejection and resistance. Bronowski recounts the effort of the European physicists to oust Einstein and his ideas, by convening a special meeting for that purpose. Einstein wasn't invited but went anyway; moreover, he applauded some valid criticism of his ideas, a true measure of the man.

Why do small academic groups behave in ways that ultimately are counter to their professed purpose of helping society find its way? I believe their behavior reflects millions of years of adaptation to hominid society, which until very recently was typically small and closed. Essentially, without knowing why, we naturally want to be accepted by and associate with a society, to espouse its beliefs and speak its language, and once we have been initiated as a member of a professional cult - often by procuring a doctoral degree, be it in wetlands biology, sociobiology or subparticle physics – we identify with that society and its culture, and often that leads to ritualized competition for status in the group, determined by trophy value of publications rather than size or ferocity of animals killed, though it comes to the same thing.

Largely at the unconscious level, our social instincts regulate our behavior and tend to inhibit our creativity as scientists or intellectuals, and that wouldn't matter in a world without crisis. Such a world does not exist for us. Our life, as Ortega said, consists of problems in urgent need of solution. Admittedly, our assumptions about the nature of life influence our perceptions, choices and actions. That is the point entirely: it is absolutely essential in our time that we question our assumptions about reality so that we may redefine life and set ourselves on a new course, one with promise for our future. Our commitment to survival of our species and the biotic community and energetic matrix on which it depends is a reflection of our own meta-programming as living things. Success means to follow, and in the final analysis there is no meaning to life-in-the-body that does not include successful reproduction. That is the unquestionable assumption of life itself, the ego's ultimate measure of meaning.

This book represents revision, reconstruction of modern ideas about the nature of civilization and the nature of human nature. I am not alone in calling for a recovery of Pleistocene values; perhaps I have few allies in terms of my views about the future of civilization, but irrespective of the fate of civilized life, the task at hand is to redefine and encourage the development of young men who are well suited to survive a crumbling world and make a new beginning. Part of the prescription I propose rests upon hunting as fundamental to the male psyche.

"Man the Hunter" has been under attack, viewed as a distortion by chauvanistic male scientists in anthropology and biology. The revisionists have been associated with the men's movement or the woman's movement, and often claim affiliation with the humanities – history, philosophy, literature, mythology. Some of their objections are valid, to be sure. Scientists are human and anything but objective, despite what they claim. In general most biologists are imprinted on and committed to uphold the doctrine of evolution: no matter what evidence might be presented in support of creationism, they are not apt to buy it. Physics, on the other hand, has achieved the unthinkable by moving beyond a Newtonian worldview to one that not only encompasses the contingent nature of human knowledge, but which insists that objectivity is an illusion, that the scientist necessarily influences the outcome of science. More far-reaching are indications that the universe is permeated by intelligence: the new physics has converged with spirituality, something the mechanistic biologists refuse to accept. Physicists are sitting down with and looking for answers among medicine people of native tribes about the multi-dimensional nature of reality and the human mind! Physics may have its origin in the hunting life and now is finding answers among hunting cultures. Real wisdom there and we would do well to follow suit.

But physicists stand out among thinkers in the civilized world. After studying the behavior of orca whales for 25 years I never cease to be amazed at the fact that other biologists who have studied these creatures have ignored the peoples who know them best, the native societies of the North Pacific rim from the Makaw of Puget Sound to the Ainu of northern Japan. These peoples have been living alongside orca whales day in and day out for thousands of years. They have fished, hunted and whaled in the same waters, and just like all foraging peoples around the world they have an outstanding knowledge of the fauna and flora of their environment based on accurate and attentive observation and frequent direct encounters. Why wouldn't scientists seek answers and insights from the coastal societies?

Because they belong to their own scientific societies and they imagine that only their members can possibly know something of value. It simply doesn't occur to them to consider the merit or value of information from non-scientists. Their colleagues probably wouldn't acknowledge it anyway.

I can assure you that the native people of the northern coasts do in fact know much about orcas, and that their knowledge is incredibly significant in so far as what it implies about the intelligence of orcas and their ethical nature interacting with humans. They interact with orcas in ways that we cannot even imagine possible, much less credible. But my efforts to communicate these findings to other scientists fall on deaf ears…too far outside the box of scientific culture.

As a human enterprise, science is fraught with all the difficulties of civilized human life including its vaulted pride. There have been volumes written about rock art in southern Africa, for example, and they present the usual range of explanatory ideas about the art and its original function. But then along came Adrian Boscher, a young Englishman who decided to travel to South Africa with naught but a hunting knife and bag of salt to live in the outback of a Bantu tribe. Because he was an epileptic - a word that in ancient

Greek means divine disease and which also is recognized as divine by the Bantu – he not only was accepted but was the first white person to become a full-fledged medicine man in an African society.

Archaeologists had speculated about the significance of vulvar inscriptions on the walls of caves in southern Africa, but they had never asked any Bantu what they signified. Boscher found out from the actual people who made the etchings that the caves were birthing locations and that each vulvar figure stood for the birth of a child there.

In 2007 the news media announced that scientists just discovered that the first place humans focus their vision on another person is their eyes. It has been said that science is the art of proving the obvious.

Among the academic species I most respect are cultural anthropologists because, owing to the nature of their work, they tend to be more aware of cultural differences and how their own culture has conditioned their perceptions. That tends to pull them out of their own professional subculture, though I know some who are just as stuck in scientific mythology as the man on the street. Recently after I lectured on the fundamentals of male initiation to anthropology students at a Canadian university I sat down with the professor, a cultural anthropologist, who assured me that he had been fully initiated into manhood by smoking dope, driving fast and drinking beer as a teenager!

My point is simply that there is plenty of room for criticism of science as cultural artifact. So what about "man the hunter" and "woman the gatherer"? Are these notions about masculinity and femininity genuine or merely the fantasies of male scientists in a patriarchal civilization?

Woman the Hunter

Mary Zeiss Stange wrote *Woman the Hunter*. The cover of the book is a rendition of perhaps the best known piece of rock art in southern Africa, the "White Lady of Drakensburg." The figure is that of a running person carrying a bow in one hand with arrows across its back. It would seem most appropriate as an artistic expression from prehistory of "woman the hunter." But wait! Did anyone ask the Bantu people who have lived in southern Africa for several thousand years about the meaning of this particular piece of art? Perhaps they made it. None of the archaeologists have, but the white witchdoctor, Adrian Bosher did, and here's the answer he received: it is not a woman at all but a white man with red hair, a prince who loved hunting, the son of a king who ruled much of southern Africa long ago. The Bantu people have a precise oral tradition associated with the art their people made centuries earlier.

Stange's mistaken choice of art does not in itself discredit her book, but much else does. It is an old song in a new skin. The woman's movement started off with an effort to prove that men and women are really the same, save their obvious anatomical differences, so as to justify social equality of the sexes. For years the debate and dialogue focused on the biological sameness of men and woman. In *The Human/Animal Connection* I made the following comment in 1985:

> "With the wave of critiques on civilization and humanity's need to surrender itself to Nature, it has become increasingly popular among Neo-Marxist anthropologists and feminists to discount the role of hunting in human evolution. Their arguments are unfounded, but they bear testimony to the gravity given to hunting as though it were to blame for humanity's predatory posture to itself and the planet. The anthropologists who tell us that meat makes up a portion of hunting societies' diets much smaller than the plants ought to know that nutrition is not simply a matter of quantity but quality. It's as though the predilection of the hunters themselves for meat were some universal figment of imagination foisted on the women and children by vain men, or that the highest standards of living being set by per capita consumption of beef appeared from nowhere without an historical, organic imperative.
>
> "And one may suspect the ecological knowledge of anthropologists if they suppose that humans diverged from the primate stock to gain world control by any route other than hunting and competition with predators. If gathering plant foods were enough to account for human evolution then it must be explained why other primate gatherers, such as baboons, chimpanzees and gorillas did not follow a comparable course. It is hardly the ability to gather plants that separates humans from their primate kin, but rather their formidability as predators and competitors.
>
> "When an accurate assessment of historical life may be the vitally significant key to our future, we must be extremely careful to avoid rewriting history to conform with the ebb and flow of social taste. However much we should like to hold up the relative egalitarianism of hunters as a desirable alternative for ourselves, or however much we feel the necessity of recovering the balance of male and female in a dangerously over-masculinized world, nonetheless we must grapple directly with the facts of human life as it has been lived. Great intellectual humility is required now more than ever precisely because human and world survival hang in the balance. To confuse historical reality with our emotional certainty about how the world of tomorrow ought to be different from yesterday is to invite disaster."

Stange is a hunter and she wrote a book that proposes that women have been hunters all along. I am totally in favor of hunting by women and I promote and encourage it because I think it is valuable experience for them, and, because hunters are the foremost environmental conservationists, I want there to be as many hunters as possible. Stange's case is built upon her interpretation of mythology from ancient civilization, the fact that Pygmy woman participate in group hunts, and the existence of a single hunting culture on earth in which women regularly hunt.

The "hunting" that Pygmy women undertake is not really hunting at all, but cooperation in net hunting. The women and kids help string up long nets in the bush into which small game is driven and then clubbed to death or speared. It is the responsibility of adult males to dispatch larger animals. It's difficult to see how natural selection would produce "woman the hunter" from net hunting.

It is fairly common among foraging societies for women to hunt, trap and kill small game, but only among the Aka negritoes of the Phillipines do women hunt the same relatively large species as men – deer and wild pigs. Hunting by both sexes is done with bow and arrows and women are supposedly as good or better hunters than men though they spend less time doing it, owing to childcare.

Does the occurrence of hunting by women in a small island culture support Stange's hypothesis? It does not, anymore than the extremely rare occurrence of women monopolizing men in mating prove that humans are fundamentally polyandrous. The fact remains that the woman hunters of the Phillipines do not kill animals larger than themselves, i.e., they are not big game hunters. Chimpanzees often kill baboons and vervet monkeys, but these prey are smaller than chimps. A majority of the primate species are in fact omnivores that kill small animals. Equally important, I think, is the total absence there of big predators which would be more much dangerous to women hunters than men.

Consider the difference between an adult male pygmy killing a full-grown elephant by himself and a pygmy woman clubbing a duiker – a small antelope about the size of a domestic cat - to death in a net. Consider the findings of Eibl-Eibesfeldt, a German ethologist who studied over sixty cultures globally and found that in all of them little boys between the ages of four and five years compete with each other throwing stones – and girls don't.

The feminists would like to be able to say that throwing stones is encouraged by men or imitated by boys, or that little girls are discouraged from throwing stones. The problem is that there is no evidence to support that objection. Little boys throw stones whether adult men throw them or throw nothing at all. The shaping and throwing of stones as weapons for hunting or defense may go back millions of years among our ancestors. Its appearance at a predictable age among human males indicates that it is firmly established in the developmental blueprint of "man the hunter," but not in females.

While Stange and others have uncovered biased sexism among anthropologists regarding "man the hunter" and "woman the gatherer," that does not disprove the theory that hunting and gathering have been the primary division of foraging labor between the sexes. The confusion extends beyond feminism's social agenda to fundamentals of ecology, embraced by anthropology only in the past few decades. The evolutionary path of humans began with carnivory.

Carnivory 101

In hunting societies, choice of mates by women depends upon the capability of men to provide meat for them and their children. Ethnologists agree that among foraging cultures everywhere meat is by far the preferred food. An amazing coincidence unless of course selection has favored humans who prefer meat. The amount of flesh food sets the standard of living for hunting societies just as it does for modern societies descended from hunters. It is not essential for contemporary humans to eat meat as long as they make a concerted effort to compensate for it nutritionally; however, it is doubtful that a healthy non-meat diet was possible for most foraging peoples. Moreover, those people who ate more meat more of the time would have been healthier, more robust and more likely to pass on surviving offspring, which is why hunting evolved as the most successful human lifestyle around the globe until a few thousand years ago.

Even the most nutritious and energetic plant foods – seeds and nuts – are small, seasonal and unpredictable. A nut tree that produced last year may not produce this year; when it does it may last a relatively short time. Much effort is required to collect, process and store or transport plant foods. Compare a nut-eating strategy with hunting: pound for pound, animal flesh not only surpasses plant foods nutritionally, it comes in large packages weighing up to thousands of pounds each.

Modern Europeans savor meat over all other foods despite the ecological and economic inefficiency of eating cows in contrast to soy beans and the threat of heavy meat consumption to health. Cows are bred and fed to be fatter than their wild cousins not only because weight equals money for the cowmen but also because people love fat meat. The natural affection of people for "juicy" steaks has its origin in the hunting life. Fat is high in energy and easily stored for periods of scarcity. Like big cats, hunting peoples often lead a feast or famine life which favored the evolution of fattism. The preference for juicy beef steak is a case of super-normal stimulus, the classic example from ethology being an exceptionally large artificial egg which the nesting bird attempts to incubate or enlarged breasts among women. In the hunting life people could not get enough fat so when super-fat cow meat came along it was much preferred. Cow flesh is high in saturated fat, but wild game is not only much lower overall in fat, it is higher in polyunsaturated fats, important to brain function.

The research of Loren Cordain at Colorado State University is significant because it demonstrates through controlled experiments that wild game flesh enhances athletic performance. The same can be safely assumed for hunting performance in foraging cultures.

Just because contemporary human carnivory has gone out of control – and civilized people exercise much less than foragers – does not mean that the more active hunting peoples suffered from eating lean, wild meat. Quite the opposite: consider, for instance, the immediate ancestors of European man, the Cro Magnons, who reached the zenith of big game hunting and who were significantly larger in height, stature **and** brain size than us. Consider, too, the impressive vigor, size, and beauty of the Maasai who made the ultimate carnivorous adaptation of consuming blood and milk. (The pastoral Maasai are awesome warriors who, armed only with spears and clubs, were never defeated in battle even by western armies with machine guns.)

Humans instinctively love meat for good reason. To quote the mighty hunter, Toma, of the !Kung Bushman, "From the day I was born, I was born for meat." As a rule, survival of the !Kung and other hunters' infants probably depends largely on abundance of animal flesh, especially during limiting seasons, when both plant and animal foods are scarce. This crucial point has been missed by some anthropologists who describe hunting peoples as having an abundance of plant resources and males as hunting animals merely for sport! The knowledge of the hunters themselves has not been taken seriously. For example, during seasons of food scarcity, !Kung hunters said that if they did not kill game their wives' breasts would dry up and their babies would die.

Food sharing is found among all hunting societies. No doubt it has social significance, but it's important that the food that is shared is meat. Plant foods usually are consumed by the family that gathers them.

Glynn Isaacs identifies food sharing as uniquely human (which of course it is not, for example, orca whales cooperatively killing and feeding on great whales), but what he and other anthropologists have overlooked is that while meat is shared it is not always shared equally, but instead distributed according to culturally established protocols. Often who killed the animal or delivered the first wound receives the most, then the other hunters that helped according to their respective roles in the hunt, and so on down lines of kinship. On the other extreme, it is not uncommon among indigenous North Americans for a young hunter to give up his kill to elders, but in either case, the elaborate rituals surrounding the sharing of meat point to its supreme value.

Early in his studies of the Kalahari Bushman, Richard Lee concluded that meat wasn't important because it made up only about 20% of their diet, and that since women gathered 80% of the food that plant foods were much more significant. He also was the one who proposed that, since meat is a relatively minor portion of the diet, that the men hunt for sport. The extreme importance given to meat by Bushman culture, as in elaborate distribution rituals, and the preference of all Bushman for animal foods ought to say something about the actual value of meat.

Lee did not then understand what ecologists refer to as "limiting factor." The limiting factor refers to that resource in short supply, meaning that its availability is what limits a species' population growth. For pheasants in parts of the midwest it is calcium in the soil. The distribution of pheasants and the distribution of soil containing calcium are identical.

Stange asks why men would go hunting when they didn't need to. For humans living a foraging life, plant foods do not have the same value as animal foods. Though animal flesh comprises merely 30% or so of the Bushman's diet, it is by far the most important component. Plant foods may be relatively abundant, but the critical resource for Bushman survival and reproductive success is meat. Which means hunting by men is something more than sport. Why would Bushman hunters regularly expose themselves to dangerous predators and poisonous snakes without real benefit to themselves and their kin?

If more roots would have been sufficient to assure the survival of Toma's baby, we can be confident that he would have gone looking for roots instead of the giraffe he and his hunting partners killed. The Bushman are not stupid; they know what makes a difference even if the professed scientific authorities on their life do not. The whole drama of human life is founded on who was able to procure more meat more often and more predictably. The advantages of carnivory have selected for qualities and characteristics among males that enhance their hunting success, thus, man as hunter.

We are not diminishing gathering or the contributions of women to human evolution and society. As a niche, gathering favors an entire gamut of adaptations from intelligence and learning to social and communication skills, in which, by the way, females tend to excel. Gathering requires keen alertness of food sources and dangerous creatures in the environment. Women who are gathering accurately observe and interpret tracks and other sign and report their observations to hunters. Gathering does not favor adaptations for use and construction of weapons nor the stature and physical prowess conducive to hunting nor its surges of emotion and finely coordinated behavior.

The evolution of gender differences is related to the survival and success of both sexes. It is not a matter of one being better than the other but strictly a matter of each being better adapted to perform certain functions. Men can gather and they do; women can kill smaller game and they do. Men are significantly adapted to hunt and kill big game. Women aren't. Today, women are just as capable as men of using a high-powered rifle to kill an elk or a grizzly bear…and some do.

Stange's "woman the hunter" not only overlooks the size of animals killed by men compared to women, it also overlooks gender differences in ability to compete with predators. Baboons offer a model of what early hominids may have been like, at least in niche. They are "gatherers" that collect plant foods as they move along, and they also are opportunistic predators that kill smaller animals, such as young antelope. Males are much bigger than females, in part because it helps them protect the troop from predators. Four adult baboons can actually kill a leopard.

In a now classic experiment conducted on a game ranch near Gilgil, Kenya, the large carnivores were all removed. Observations on the behavior of baboons showed that in the absence of predators such as lions and hyenas, baboons hunted more frequently, killed bigger prey and ate more meat. Predators limit the extent of carnivory among baboons.

My scientific addition to the "hunting hypothesis" is the absolute significance of competition between our hominid ancestors and larger carnivores. It doesn't do any good to succeed at big game hunting if you can't eat the meat, and you can't eat the meat if other predators steal it from you and possibly kill and eat you while they're at it. One of the chief advantages to wolves from living in groups is their ability to defend large carcasses from bears, or if need be, to employ group size to steal food from bears. The same principle applies to lions and hyenas. There are some lion prides in Tanzania's Ngorongoro Crater, for instance, that survive solely by stealing kills from hyena packs, and the reverse is often the case for hyenas that steal food from lions. If there are enough hyenas they may even kill and eat the lions, too.

Our ancestors were right in the thick of this longest war on earth for hundreds of thousands of years, and some people on the planet still have not achieved fully dominant status to the biggest predators in their range.

If you think contesting a lion for a zebra carcass 15,000 years ago was easy, think again. Your weapons would include bow and arrows and spears. Several brave and experienced men bearing spears might be able to drive off a single lion if sufficiently motivated. A female lion would be a whole lot easier than a male because males are bigger and much more powerful, according to my analysis able to successfully contest ten times as many spotted hyenas as a lioness, though only about 25% larger in body size.

Let's use the Maasai as a model. They ritually hunt lions as part of their initiation to adulthood. For pastoralists as they are, lion hunting is practical – the greatest threat to their cattle are lions. Moreover, the bravery and skills required to "hunt" lions prepared and tested them, until very recently, for warfare with other human groups.

Now the Maasai, as I said above, are among the finest warriors ever to live. They are large, robust and athletic, and the males comprised finely coordinated armies able to run double-time in formation for twenty miles in the tropical sun carrying 60+ pounds of spear, shield, sword and clubs. In the 1950s, it took twenty or more adult Maasai to successfully pursue and kill a single male lion. Even then there were risks. The first warrior to grab the wounded lion's tail – or deliver the first wound – received credit for the kill.

It has been argued that throughout most of human evolution social groups would rarely have more than six adult males. But these "postdictions" are based on the study of hunting societies that live today in marginally productive environments and so probably are low for the Cro Magnon hunters of Europe and elsewhere who occupied environments rich in big game as well as large predators. In any case, if twenty Maasai with razor sharp German steel spears face risk against a single male lion, what do you suppose it was like for our ancestors? What if they encountered a group of three or four adult male lions? An entire pride of a dozen or more males and females? The most unlikely achievement of the human race was dominance over awesome carnivores before firearms.

In the same way that a male lion is far more dangerous to hyenas than a female lion, a male human that is 25 – 35% larger than a female might be far more successful in defending or stealing food from predators. The optimal reproductive strategy for human ancestors would have been for men to hunt and protect and for women to gather and bear and nurture children. Sarah Hrdy is right to say that intelligence in general would not be sex-linked; however, analytical ability as related to weapon use and hunting strategy could be sex-linked and that is suggested by the excelling of boys in math.

Bettelheim's study of dreams in children found that at about age four boys began to dream about big predators, girls about spiders and snakes. The great threat to grown males throughout almost all of human life has been big predators; the threat to gathering/domestic women has been snakes and spiders.

Stange is right that women are capable of aggression and violence. About one-fourth of the teen homicides committed these days is by girls using knives. But that does not mean women are well adapted to make war, against other predators or humans. It was at this point in my debate with Stange that I asked her to tell me what she would do if she and her husband were stranded with their children and hungry, but only one of them could go out with a spear or bow to hunt deer or elk where brown bears abound. She did not respond.

Stange cannot explain why it is that a large percentage of boys spontaneously kill animals and girls don't. It can't be imitation since these days few boys actually witness any adult males hunting.

Stange's suggestion that gender roles are a relatively recent invention seems weak in light of extensive studies of foraging peoples whose lifeways have not radically changed for thousands of years. Of course, gender roles in civilization have been extremely influenced by pastoralism and farming life which promoted the patriarchal hierarchy and warring, but that has been only in the past few thousand years. The feminist argument is with civilization and its myths of masculine dominance, not with hunting-gathering life. Until one can think about human behavior in terms of adaptation to environments and how those adaptations influence reproductive success, all the rest of it fails to fly.

Like *Fire in the Belly, Woman the Hunter* makes a fundamental error when it equates predation and aggression. Hunting is human predation, the killing of animals for food, though also to prove oneself worthy as a provider and qualify for marriage, which is the origin of trophies (raptorial birds, some spiders and bobcats also demonstrate their worthiness as mates by trophy hunting). The emotional base is definitely not one of aggression or anger towards animals. Foragers and recreational hunters do feel fear and aggression toward dangerous predators, a relationship between possible enemies. If a confrontation turns into war the emotion behind it may become hate.

Like many writers, Stange imagines that the hunting adaptation is connected with violence towards humans and that male aggression is channeled through hunting, but they are distinctly different instinctual systems. Male cats may fight for rank in the neighborhood, but aggressive – fighting – energy is not channeled through hunting mice. For one thing, aggression is not a trophic drive like sex that builds up over time and drives the individual to search for an appropriate stimulus. Even though the emotional rewards of hunting are intrinsic, the hunting instinct in humans does not accumulate. We have here confusion about the nature of aggression and hunting in men, and much of it is a result of projecting the pathological behavior of civilized men backward in time or onto the foraging lifestyle. Men in civilization have been subjected to negative enculturation including the mythology of warring and recently to deprivation of bonding with their mothers and absence of initiation to manhood, the combined effects of which include rage.

It is an insult to me and other hunters for Stange to suggest that we feel aggressive or angry toward animals we hunt for food. Nothing could be further from the truth. According to questionnaire surveys I conducted no hunters indicated that they feel anger or violence toward the animals they hunt, but nearly all chose "respect," "admiration." or "reverence." Stange also quotes Washburn and Lancaster's comment about the "pleasure" of killing, but there is no evidence among aboriginal or recreational hunters that the actual act of killing is pleasurable. As an instinctive system hunting has its own intrinsic rewards. In this sense civilized humans are basically no different than civilized cats. Both are well fed and neither need to hunt for food in the strict sense, but both derive satisfaction or pleasure from hunting nonetheless. Nearly all hunters I surveyed said they feel sad about the death of the animal, corroborating Ortega's comment that hunters do not revel in the death of the animal.

How do you think Stange and other feminists would feel if I wrote at length about emotions associated with child birth? But Stange seems to be an expert on everything male. She thinks that hunting estranges men from animals and nature when if anything it does the opposite, and that is exactly what men reported in my survey. There are eco-feminists who see men as rapists of the earth and of women, and to them hunting is a form of rape of nature. Rape is a violent act of domination, but it has no connection with subsistence or recreational hunting, both of which represent ritual communion with animals and nature.

The eminant psychiatrist, Erich Fromm, wrote *The Anatomy of Human Destructiveness*, and in it wrote about men who hunt for subsistence or recreation. He believed that in the act of hunting, a man becomes part of nature again, and based on a considerable body of knowledge about existing primitive hunters concluded that hunting is not conducive to cruelty and destructiveness.

Hunters have been accused of being sadistic, but Fromm disagrees, saying that sadism is far more frequently found among frustrated people and social classes who have little pleasure in life and who feel powerless.

Stange adds injury to insult when she proposes that men feel no remorse when they kill animals. That is not what subsistence and recreational hunters report. Then she suggests that perhaps women have deeper feelings for animals they hunt and kill. It has been my experience that women find it easier emotionally to kill an animal than men, and perhaps that should not surprise us. In the same way that women are adapted to be highly sensitive and intuitive in their relationship with babies, men are adapted to assess the emotional state and predict the behavior of wild animals. Just as mothers identify with their babies, which helps them attend to their needs, men identify with and accurately imitate animals, which enhances their hunting success, but which also makes them keenly sensitive and responsive to the animal's suffering and death. Around the world, hunting societies strictly forbid causing unnecessary harm or suffering to wild animals.

As for Stange's observation that men need to prove themselves worthy, we have already said that young men around the world for millennia have had to demonstrate their prowess in hunting to qualify for marriage and manhood. That urge is still alive in each generation and we would do well to direct it in a positive manner rather than ignore it as an aspect of initiation that may become redirected and perverted. The fact that women are less interested in trophies indicates that they do not have the same genetic makeup as men, i.e., they are not adapted to prove themselves worthy as mates on the hunting field.

We have witnessed an incredible growth of women's sports in the past fifty years. That growth did not require a revision of "women in sports" in history or prehistory. Traditionally women have not competed in sports either in civilization or among foragers, but they do now and no justification is required. Fortunately women are free to hunt and compete in the Olympics.

The Hunter's Pledge to Contemporary Woman

We are sorry if you are angry at his-story, the pastoral story of domination, subjugation, patriarchy, hierarchy and war against nature, women and children. It is not the hunter's war and we are angry about it, too. Our fathers and their fathers' fathers also suffered much. Please do not debase the heritage of men as hunters whose love affair with nature is founded on providing life-giving food for women and children and the practice of which is a ritual with authentic religious meaning and the source of our spiritual food. It is our heart's desire to recover the ways before time, including the valuable, honorable and admirable role of women in our life and world. We hunters are providers for and protectors of women and children, and these purposes necessarily involve the taking of life, for which we apologize. The wild animals are our brothers to whom we are grateful and pay respect. They give meaning to our life as servants, and it is our obligation to maintain proper relations with the creatures and the earth so we all may sit together in the sacred circle of life.

"Nature is the storehouse of potential life of future generations and is sacred."

~ Audrey Shenandoah, Onondaga

We need to honor and respect our Mother Earth. She is the source of all life. The sun shines life to the earth, then the earth produces life in all forms and in a balanced way. Everything is here to serve everything else. If we interrupt the flow in any way, we leave nothing for the future generations. Before every decision is made, we should ask, and answer, a final question; "If we do this, what will be the effects on the seventh generation? What will we cause our children to live with?" We need to have respect and love for all things and for all people. We need to do this for ourselves and for all the children still unborn.

Chapter 7

Orion's Legacy: Men, Myths and Hunting

"Oh I've got something inside me to drive a princess blind.
There's a Wildman Wizard, he's hiding in me, illuminating my mind.
Oh, I've got something inside me, not what my life's about."

~ Harry Chapin, "Taxi"

Apologizing to an Elk I Did Not Kill

Three earlier seasons I had hunted elk in the Eagle Cap Wilderness of northeast Oregon where we lived. The boundary of the wilderness area of nearly 400,000 acres set a mile behind our house. A herd of about thirty elk often passed closeby and on a few occasions actually spent the night in our backyard. It was not unusual to see a few grazing in the meadow a few hundred yards away. But make no mistake about it. When the hunting season came around the elk didn't, at least not by day.

The very first time elk meat touched my mouth it was more than delicious. I had a total body sensation, and said to Barry Cox, my friend who had killed the elk, "Wow! This is power food." Living as we were in the heart of some of the best elk country, and knowing what high quality food it is, I had made up my mind to hunt elk.

The first year I went up into the high Wallowas with Lynn Burton, a U.S. Forest Service wildlife biologist who had been successfully hunting elk most of his life. We packed in on horses and set up camp and hunted with bows for several days but never got close enough for a shot. Tracking elk up and down mountain sides I developed great admiration and respect for them. It seemed that they let us tediously poke our way closer and closer then they would bound away easily and wait for us to catch up. If a creature ever were at home in that rugged environment it is the elk.

There was a grand old, trophy bull with a harem who answered our bugle calls. His response not only was thrilling it gave us a fix on the old boy's location. So we would do our best to move as fast as we could in his direction before bugling again, hoping he would think another bull wanted to challenge him to a duel for cows. In which case the bull would come toward us looking for the challenger, and we might get close enough for a shot. That is a typical hunting strategy during the rut or fall mating season.

After covering 600 yards or so, we'd stop and bugle again, and again, the monarch would reply only farther away. We spent the entire day chasing the bull and wearing ourselves out.

An expert who had called in many bull elk, Lynn was stumped and finally concluded that the bull was bugling deliberately to evoke our call so he could get a fix on our location and evade us!

The next year Lynn and I packed into the high country to hunt elk in October with rifles. There was snow at the higher elevations where we camped. It was conducive for spotting elk and tracking them, and the second day out Lynn shot a young bull which we packed out that evening and then skinned and butchered at his house.

Lynn relocated to Bozeman so I bow hunted by myself the following fall above our home in the wilderness area. I never saw an elk, but someone shot a large bull in the abandoned apple orchard right behind our house!

My fourth season I decided to hunt in the traditional way I had learned from a Lakota medicine man.

I had befriended a Choctaw/Cherokee Indian, who had heard me on a national radio show talking about why hunting is good for youth. Dave lived near John Day, Oregon, about three hours away by car, on a 4,000 acre ranch which he was allowing to recover from overgrazing by cattle. A clinical psychologist by profession, in Viet Nam Dave had been in Black Ops, meaning highest security clearance and secrecy, an experience which led him to distrust the federal government. He was an avid hunter who believed in living off the land.

For a week before elk season opened I arose early and went outside to pray to the Creator for permission to take an elk. At night when the first star appeared in the sky I did the same. When I felt that permission had been given, I then began to pray to the Spirit of the Elk Nation, what in the West we refer to as an oversoul. I asked it to please bless me and my family with an elk for food. I promised that we would honor, bless and thank the elk. I did my level best that week to clear my mind of all resentment and resistance, and I systematically practiced forgiveness so I could be a clear vessel and hunt with a pure heart. As I went to sleep at night I prayed for Guidance.

The night before the season opened I went to Dave's and slept, then got up before light to drink coffee and headed out riding behind Dave on his 4-wheeler as the sun came up. Less than a mile out we saw a herd of elk trotting over the ridge we were on so we got off and walked to where we had seen them and started tracking them slowly west down into the canyon. We were a little more than half-way down the side of the canyon when Dave whispered, "There they are."

A herd of twenty-five elk led by a big bull was walking slowly up the other side. There were cows and calves following the lead bull, but the last elk was a 4-point bull, full-grown and probably two and a half years old. What a sight! The elk were grazing a little then walking a little, and several of them occasionally looked across the canyon at us 200 yards away.

Then Dave, who was squatting, said quietly, "There. There's your elk. Take him, he's yours."

Dave meant what he said, meaning that the young adult bull at the rear of the herd belonged to me.

The elk was standing perfectly still, broadside to me, the ideal shot. I watched him through my rifle scope and saw that he was looking straight at me.

Again Dave said,"Take him, he's yours. You've got a perfect shot. Aim about a foot over his back."

I just kept watching the elk watching me, and I was beaming with joy and gratitude that all the prayers really had worked. There was an elk frozen in place waiting for me to pull the trigger as the rest of his herd moved over the next ridge out of sight.

Finally, I put the rifle down and told Dave I couldn't do it. The elk turned to walk up the hill after the herd.

Neither of us spoke on the walk back to the 4-wheeler. We hunted the rest of the day without seeing anymore elk. That night back at camp while we cooked dinner, Dave said, "In the morning, we'll have to do a ceremony for that elk."

I laughed and said, "Why? I let him go!"

Very seriously he said, "That elk offered himself to you and you didn't take him. Now you have to apologize." That's what I call respect.

Over corn mean the next morning at sunrise I apologized to the elk, to the Spirit of the Elk Nation and to Creator, and thanked them for the blessing they had offered me.

I got what I had come for, though I knew that had we actually needed the meat I would have pulled the trigger.

~ RANDALL L. EATON

Charles Bergman is a humanities professor who is erudite and intellectually sophisticated. His book, *Orion's Legacy*, is a cultural history of man as hunter. Like Stange, he thinks that the scientific basis for believing men were shaped by hunting has been thoroughly discredited. Though the feminists have uncovered chauvinism in science, certainly the vast majority of biologists, anthropologists and psychiatrists remain convinced that it was the hunting-gathering life that shaped humanity, men and women both.

Anthropologist Cartmill wrote a serious book about hunting throughout human history, concluding that there is no reason to believe that hunting is natural or instinctive in human beings. He believes that hunting is not "natural" to humanity in any meaningful sense, and goes so far as to say that the majority of humans who ever lived have never hunted, but that is unfair considering that the majority of humans born have been in civilization. One might as well insist that since the majority of Manhattan's pet cats have never hunted mice that it is not natural for them to do so. Cartmill might be surprised about the proportion of boys born in civilization who found themselves carried away by the untrained and unlearned impulse to use weapons to kill animals. Like Bergman, Cartmill ignores evidence and sound deductive argument from evolution, ethnography, mythology and human development in favor of hunting as natural and instinctive.

Bergman's interest is not the debate about prehistoric man as hunter and his influence on contemporary masculinity, but in the prehistoric hunter who has taken up residence in the mythical landscape. Bergman says that if you're a modern man, you've probably imagined yourself as a sort of primal hunter, a prehistoric hero battling with saber-toothed tigers and mammoths. This myth of the prehistoric man has lodged the hunter in our psyches as the primal patriarch. It is the standard stereotype against which every man secretly measures himself. The prehistoric hunter is the true source of our masculinity, and contemporary men are taught to trace their ancestors back to the campfires of a weapon-bearing, big-browed predator.

From Bergman's point of view, hunting is part and parcel of modern masculine identity, whether there is a biological foundation for it or not. He's right to say that men long for a return to primitivism. He is hunting for the meaning in the fact that our persistent notion of the real man – a cave man, a jungle man, a man on the savannas, the original man – is that of a hunter

Bergman wants to see what the hunter in our heads has to say for himself. As the most emotional figure for men, Bergman seeks the hunter, not as an archetype, fact of nature or ecological niche, but as a cultural phenomenon. He treats the hunter as metaphor that men have created, not as what created men, but as a mythical theme that shapes our fantasies. Following words like tracks we can see how pervasive the hunter myth is in our consciousness:

A buck: is a dollar, from buckskin, frontier unit of trade with Native Americans;
A young buck is a young man;
Job hunt, witch hunt, fortune hunt, bounty hunt, bargain hunter, headhunter, manhunt;
Open season;
Closed season;
Fair game;
Straight shooter, long shot, cheap shot;
Cut to the chase, thrill of the chase;
Take a stand;
Make a killing, kill or be killed, dead meat;
Hot on the trail;
Pick up the scent;
Killer instinct.

Regarding the sexual hunt there is the prowl, poaching, stag party, love trap and so on, and the way men refer to women as prey is a bestiary of terms: bunnies; chicks; beaver; foxes; pussy. Which is to say that of all the things a man might call himself – lover, criminal, lawyer, doctor, fool – he is more or less a hunter in the way he thinks and imagines himself, whether or not he has a gun rack in his pickup. From Elvis's hound dog to *Leatherstocking Tales*, from Daniel Boone to Hemingway and Melville to Teddy Roosevelt, the hunt is our historical identity.

In his search for the origin of our identity with the hunt, Bergman concludes that, unlike the Inuit whom he observed hunting in the far north, for civilized humans the hunt is a statement of power. He is right about the ***image*** of the hunt in our civilization being a statement of power, but for most recreational hunters, men and women alike, hunting is anything but a power statement. It may be for a very small elite group of men and women, wealthy business tycoons, military leaders and power-hungry politicians, the new royalty, but it is not for the rank and file hunter.

Bergman is right about the ancient and modern myth of hunting, that the hunt's primary emphasis and justification have little to do with sensitivity, but are grounded instead in anxieties about power. As much as Ortega has been praised for his understanding of the inner side of hunting as religious, his view of hunting does suffer from the typical distortions of Western civilization and its prevailing myth of power over nature, domination and war. Ortega says, for example, that to hunt is to take possession of some other being of a species basically inferior to the human. Aboriginal hunters do not view wild animals as inferior to humans, and for them hunting is not taking possession or an "act of acquisition," as Aristotle said, but reception of a gift earned by "proper relationship," a term frequently used by some Native American tribes.

From the beginning, civilized men have deliberately employed hunting as preparation for war, and that is what has produced a distortion of hunting as a mythology of power. When Plato talks about the hunting of animals and the hunting of men, he reflects the way in which hunting and war became linked in culture. As I have said repeatedly, hunting in its pure form pertains to the pursuit and killing of animals for food and other products, but war is between humans (and their hominid ancestors) and big predators or other human groups.

With civilization and the overwhelming importance of war, hunting of typical food species continued by farmers and warriors to train themselves in warring skills including weapon use, patience, tracking, physical stamina and so on. For the same reason that Maasai ritually "hunt" lions, the men of early civilizations "hunted" dangerous animals to prove themselves worthy and gain status as warriors. The taking of a lion, for example, required great courage and skill, and was far more esteemed than killing a boar, deer or hare. These were warring societies and men were ranked according to their deeds in war or against wild animals, which were measured as trophies.

Though aboriginal hunters collect trophies, first when they prove themselves worthy for manhood and marriage and then as they continue to hunt, their success on the hunting field is not aimed at power over the animal or human. The power they gain in killing an animal is spiritual, a gift from the animal to the man.

When warring with humans becomes significant, as it was for the plains Indians after the horse, which made mobile herds of bison defensible, then the "hunting" of dangerous predators becomes a pursuit of power transferable to warfare. A warrior who had killed grizzly bears not only held high esteem among men and women in his society, but he wore the claws of the bears around his neck as a trophy signifying his power to enemies - those who are inferior, "them," "animals," those we destroy. Genocide appears when humans of competing groups replace big predators as enemies.

While it was the hunt that brought us into competition with big predators – the original war on earth – it was possession of resources, wealth, whether in the form of bison herds that could be defended with horses, or livestock or grains, that shifted human life to a systematic pursuit of masculine power. That shift colored our stories accordingly and gave rise to the myth of Orion, who, though widely claimed to be a hunter, may actually be a symbol of the warrior, the archetypal male of civilization.

Bergman sizes up the myth of Orion as the emblematic heroic hunter whose prowess is celebrated in the constellation that bears his name: no image defines more accurately how the hunter "planted" notions of violence and rape deep into the male psyche.

But Xenophon and others say again and again that hunting among the warrior elite of Greece was undertaken to enhance warrior skills. The adolescent impulse of heroism becomes a component of the pastoral myth of domination. According to the myth of Orion he was anything but humble about his hunting exploits and frequently bragged about them. Perhaps it was his unbridled pride that got him killed and banned to heaven. Perhaps, like the myth of Narcissus, Orion's story is actually a warning to civilized men about the danger of hubris.

The many stories of Orion emphasize destructiveness, the dark side of the masculine. He even rapes the King's daughter whom he had intended to wed. Bergman says that,

> "This intersection of the hunter and the rapist, of hunting heroics and sexual appetite, is disturbing. The killing of animals, the seizing of women…the two slide into each other in the story…The elision can take place in the psyche of the great hunter because identity means all others must be reduced to serving his appetite – both hunting and sexuality coincide in narratives of erotic domination….Many men, I suspect, if they were honest, might admit that they fear a figure like Orion lurking in the nether regions of the soul – unbridled, drunken, violent. The stories of William Golding suggest that this night-marsh descent into primitive violence is a modern obsession as well, that under the thin veneer of civilization is a violence and rapacity embodied in this primitive hunter."

There are many clues to the true identity of Orion and the meaning of the myth, not the least of which is, according to one version, that he was killed by Artemis, his hunting companion whom he hoped to wed but tried to rape. In another version in which he threatens to kill all the animals on earth, the earth goddess Gaea is offended and sends the scorpion to kill him.

Orion does not represent the hunter in the male psyche as Bergman keeps insisting, but he does represent the archetypal dark side of the masculine, which is greedy and barbaric. Orion's male instincts have gone awry because, like Hercules, he was not initiated properly into manhood.

Bly says that one of the three components of male initiation is discovering our dark side. Rites of passage found among hunting societies are deliberately designed to temper the fire of masculine instincts with the cooling waters of feminine compassion. Among Australian aborigines the rituals extend as far as sub-incising the penis full-length so that young males bleed profusely, mimic menses and identify with the feminine within their own psyches.

With pastoralism and the importance of warring, the initiation of boys to manhood shifts from successfully killing a typical big game animal to demonstrate one's hunting prowess and suitability as a mate and parent, to the ritual slaying of very dangerous predators. The emotional pitch of violent aggression among young Maasai warriors confronting a lion reaches an extreme – they literally go berserk, a term from Scandinavia that refers to the same intensity of fighting emotion associated with killing bears and combat with enemy humans. Nowhere on earth at any time have males of hunting societies exhibited warring instincts toward animals hunted for food, and that behavioral pattern also typifies recreational hunting among civilized males.

Orion is the untempered male whose instincts are beyond his own control, a product of warring culture. That he rapes the very women he wants to marry tells us that he is incapable of embracing the feminine, and that because his masculine passions never linked up with feminine compassion, the goal of male initiation. Though Artemis hopes to wed Orion, she slays him. Orion is a man without soul. So dangerous is the untempered male to women, creatures and the earth that he must be killed, the very situation we confront today.

Male initiation among hunting peoples may be relatively simple and last up to a year or two, but among pastoralists it is more extensive and may take as long as ten years. Initiating young men to enhance their warring prowess but also temper them sufficiently to control aggression and violence within society is a demanding process. However well different cultures have man-aged, their men may still end up psychically unbalanced. The story of Orion may reflect the period of early Greek pastoralism, which is indicated by the fact that Orion wiped an entire island clean of all wild animals in order to marry the King's daughter. The skin that Orion in the sky carries in one hand may be that of a lion. Both these components of the myth indicate that in Orion's time the people were competing with wild animals. Again, this suggests that Orion's great feats had nothing to do with hunting for food, provisioning, but with warfare against predators or wild species that competed with livestock.

Bergman wonders why these ancient images of men as hunter-warriors are so persistent. He sounds a lot like the eco-feminists when he proposes that the hunter planted notions of violence and rapacity deep in the male psyche. Orion is but one of many myths that portray and reveal the meta-myth of civilized life as domination and subjugation. A few thousand years of continual warring among civilized nations has equated masculinity with warring and the role that hunting has had in preparing men for war. But it is not the hunter in prehistory or in our psyche that "plants" notions of violence and rapacity in the male psyche, but the farmer and pastoralist, the warrior. Orion is a warrior, not a hunter.

It is a common theme among civilized humans to project their own violence and rapacity upon primitive cultures, as we have seen in Bergman's interpretation of Orion and in Golding's *Lord of the Flies*. It is not only unfounded but harmful to our efforts to discern what is natural and healthy for us compared to what is artificial and pathological.

Behind the myths of Orion and Artemis is another myth, the myth of agriculture and its perversion of the hunting life. In his lustful pursuit of power, Orion, a civilized man, abused and corrupted hunting, the original lifestyle of goodness. Despite 5,000 wars in as many years, there dwells in the deep structure of the male psyche a longing to abandon the life of power and recover the good life of hunting. Like many men of our time, Bergman has his wires crossed. His attempt to understand the hunt leads him to read books and observe the Inuit hunting, but that would be rather like reading sexual physiology texts and watching pornography to understand what it means to fall in love. One could know everything in the world about sexual physiology but know nothing about what it means to make love. There simply is no relationship between intellectual knowledge and observation of hunting and the personal experience of hunting itself. Which is to say that Bergman's faith, like that of Western civilization, is in reason, the intellect, ego, not the intelligence of the heart. The answer Bergman is looking for lies in direct experience of the hunt. We can – and I think we must – go back to first things. Van der Post understood the Bushman and what civilization is missing because he, too, was a hunter. The hunt invites a man to surrender the hopeless futility of a life of power to the earth and receive its blessings with an open heart. Tears may fall.

Narcissus, the Wild Man and Hercules

In his poem, "Chicago," Carl Sandburg says he has seen the painted women under the gas lamps luring the farm boys. Gilgamesh employed a harlot to seduce the wild man, Enkidu, whose desire weakened his connection with the wild animals and led him to the city, then to his moral corruption and finally his death.

The Greek myth of Narcissus makes the point well. As the story opens Narcissus is out hunting with his companions when he leaves them to drink at a pond. When Narcissus looks down into the water and sees his own reflection, he falls in love with himself, but when he later realizes that his own desire leads back only to an empty reflection of himself, he commits suicide by drowning.

Bergman interprets the Narcissus story as a relationship between desire and quest for power within the context of hunting. I see it as a warning and a lament about the risks of leaving the cooperative life of the hunter to pursue the self-glorification and vanity of power-hungry, civilized men who are, as Bly suggested of Narcissus, stuck in their own circuits. Narcissus turned his back on the ways of the wild man and his love of things wild, and chose instead self-infatuation only to come up empty. The path of Narcissus ends in self-destruction precisely because it glorifies the superficial, material level of reality. For the hunting life that he spurned in favor of the desirable possessions of civilization, Narcissus lost his very soul.

In the story of Iron John, the boy ends up by a magical pond and looks in it to see his reflection. Unlike Narcissus, he does not fall in love with himself, but rather with nature. He breaks free from himself and becomes deeply connected to the power, beauty and intelligence of nature as well as his inseparable relationship to it. The outcome for the boy in the Iron John myth is radically different because behind him stands the wild man, a mentor who serves as a model for the boy's initiation to manhood. The tragedy of Narcissus is the tragedy of the modern era in which young men have been encouraged to turn their backs on "first things" and pursue egoism instead. Most have no mentors, no rites of passage, only a meaningless life devoted to chasing what is superficial and unenduring.

Without the help of the wild man, we end up like Narcissus, infatuated with ourselves, the glamour of cities and the illusory power of technology. When we let the wild man out of the cage and go with him to the wilderness he will reward us with great fortune and gifts: manhood founded on nature.

The Initiation of Hercules

Still the greatest heroic figure of Western civilization, Hercules was so strong as an infant that he killed two snakes in his crib, and as a boy taking music lessons he struck his teacher over the head with a lyre and killed him. With too much power for the world, Hercules was sent into the highland pastures to shepherd flocks. There he killed all the wolves and lions surrounding Thebes, and for his unparalleled achievement in killing big predators became a great hero.

In time Hercules married and became a father, but in a rage of insanity killed his own children. To appease his crimes he was given twelve tasks, the first of which included killing the dreaded lion of Nemea, which he did by squeezing it to death. After accomplishing all the feats Hercules became an even greater hero by virtue of his deeds. Again he was overtaken by rage and killed many of his fellows. He sought repentance, and Zeus sentenced him to three years of feminine duty during which he had to wear woman's clothes and daily endure women's work.

Then Hercules reentered society again, and, as before, assumed the life of a heroic warrior. The woman he was to marry was kidnapped by a Centaur, but Hercules shot the Centaur with one of his poison arrows. As the Centaur died he gave Hercules' fiancé drops of a potion that supposedly would redirect Hercules' attention to her if he should ever wander. That day came and Hercules' wife gave him the drops of love potion, which actually were the centaur's blood mixed with the poison from Hercules' arrow.

Hercules was so strong that the poison could not kill him, but the pain was so enormous that he had a funeral pyre prepared and the trophy skin from the Nemean lion put over it. The gods of Olympus came to admire Hercules' strength and bravery so much that they drew him up to heaven and welcomed him. The goddess who had plotted for so long against him and stricken him with fits of murderous rage, gave her own daughter – the goddess of everlasting youth – to Hercules in marriage.

Unlike the savage Orion and the unmentored Narcissus, Hercules' father, Zeus, stood over his son the way the Wild Man, Iron John, mentored the boy. With genuine wisdom, Zeus placed Hercules into feminine life so his ego would be tempered and he could acquire humility. The killing of predators that made him a hero as a young man in a pastoral culture reinforced his egoism and eventually drove him to kill his own children. The atonement by heroic feats only had the same result: more uncontrollable rage.

The story of Hercules is the story of pastoral man and the terrible cost of a lack of rites of passage that temper the male ego. Preferring to wrestle and fight the young Hercules even killed his music teacher who might have had a softening influence. It was Hercules' initiation to the feminine that put an end to his insanity and rage, and which ultimately won him divinity and marriage to the everlasting feminine, a symbol of his eternal soul. **The message for civilized, warring humanity is clear: initiation to manhood must encompass compassion - the route to divinity is through the heart.** And that is precisely what hunting offers our young men today. The instinctive fire that drives the boy to pursue the animal is tempered by compassion when he actually kills one, and the entire process transforms the boy to a man of heart.

In Jungian terms, the heroic flights of Hercules were destructive and the only way he could recover was through a more comprehensive identification with his whole psyche. Henderson explains that the essential function of the heroic myth is the development of the individual's awareness of his own strengths and weaknesses so that he will be equipped for the arduous tasks with which adult life confronts him. Once the male has passed his initial test and is allowed to enter adulthood, the hero myth loses its relevance. The hero's symbolic death becomes the achievement of maturity.

The symbolic death of the hero occurs when the young man kills the animal. Socially, his feat earns him manhood, but at a deeper level, killing the animal also kills himself so that he may be reborn. Taking the life of the animal is the death of the child and the birth of the man. When the boy dies his childhood wounds die with him, but when he kills to become a man he also wounds himself in the heart. Just as the animal sacrifices itself so the boy may become a man, the man wounds his own heart to honor the sacred animal that died for him, the meaning of reciprocity: one sacrifice for another. The word "sacrifice" means "to make sacred," the meaning of hunting as a rite of passage to maturity, not unlike the woman who sacrifices her body and heart for the sacred child.

Hunting and the Archetypes of the Mature Man

Carl Jung charted fertile ground with his psychology of the unconscious mind. He and his disciples demonstrated that there is a vast realm that reveals itself to the conscious mind through dream, myth and art. Jung understood that much of the unconscious was the consequence of repression resulting from civilized humanity's separation from nature. He saw the failure to integrate the unconscious into the conscious as unhealthy and dangerous.

The Jungian psychologists have identified archetypes in the unconscious. The archetypes are like blueprints or models of behavioral conduct. The hero archetype expresses itself in males during late adolescence as a powerful drive to strike out on one's own and prove oneself worthy as a man. For example, the Hollywood movie, "The Right Stuff," is about the hero archetype including its negative aspects.

The Hero was born in the hunting life when the young man went out to kill a large animal and demonstrate his worthiness as a provider-mate. Once he did that his society went to great lengths to regulate his egoism and promote maturity. With the arrival of civilization and the emphasis on ownership, wealth and war the Hero was unleashed. The old European myths, for example, tell of the young man going out to "make his fortune," which meant to conquer, vanquish, kill and steal. The heroic hunt as a practical demonstration of masculinity turned to lust. Civilization still is governed by the immature Hero archetype, a threat to life on earth.

David Moore and Douglas Gillette wrote *King, Warrior, Magician, Lover*, about archetypes of mature masculinity. Feminists have severely attacked male dominance and the patriarchy as oppressive and abusive, and they have argued that connection with love and gentleness comes only from the feminine side of the human equation. Moore and Gillette disagree, saying that the patriarchy is not an expression of deeply rooted masculinity, but of the immature, shadow, "crazy" or stunted side of masculinity. They go on to say that the patriarchy is based on fear, of women and men. As I discussed under the myth of power, I believe that the patriarchy arose with domestication of animals as an adaptive response to protect and defend herds of animals against predators and other men, that it is not founded on fear of women. I view it simply as an embellishment of the dark side of the masculine ego.

In any case, are men missing development of the inner feminine or are they missing connection with the mature male archetypes, described by Moore and Gillette as the "deep and instinctual masculine energies," which they identify as King, Warrior, Magician and Lover? They believe that mature masculinity has been blocked by the patriarchy itself, even by the feminist critique, and I agree wholeheartedly with them that men were being blocked by the lack of meaningful and transformative initiatory process by which they could have achieved a sense of manhood. For them, the crisis of masculinity does not call for less masculine power but more of the mature masculine. For example, the archetype of the Lover is one of relating through feeling, commonly associated with the feminine.

Whether we define it as masculine or feminine, there should be general agreement that men do need to develop their feeling nature. Where Moore and Gillette fall short is their emphasis on civilized men. They define mature "individuated" men by their patients who fall short of maturity. It is true that you can learn much about lions by studying them in captivity, but you could never imagine the ferocity of their hunting or warring instincts by observing them in zoos. Likewise, to know what mature men are really like it helps to spend time with some in primal societies. The mature men of hunting societies do exhibit the calm strength and compassion that is uncommon among pastoralists, farmers and city men. In fact, I am convinced that masculine maturity reached its zenith in the hunting life and has been eroding ever since, though it still resides in many older hunters, warriors, athletes and artists whose life experience has been conducive to awakening the archetypes and integrating them into consciousness.

As psychoanalysts, Moore and Gillette have seen men acquire genuine inner strength and centeredness by getting in touch with male archetypes via meditation, prayer and "active imagination." These processes are effective precisely because they permit ego transcendence and identification with the unconscious, what I refer to as Spirit or the inner Voice of God and Tolle means by Being. And each of them is derived from hunting as alert presence and as prayer. Properly initiated males whose rites of passage include hunting, vision quest and art may access the archetypes of mature masculinity at a relatively young age.

Some Jungian psychologists perceive the King as the central male archetype around which the rest of the psyche revolves. In human life, the king as leader-chief is a relatively recent innovation. Most hunting societies, for example, do not have a chief, counterpart to the king. As a group elders may serve the purpose of leadership and resolving tribal conflicts. If the King is central to the mature male then it must be primeval, but kingship is an outgrowth of the shift from hunting and a horizontal circle of power to agriculture and warring with its vertical hierarchy of masculine power.

If the Jungians are right the King is the spiritual essence of a mature man: ordering, wise, calm. The King is the source of concepts and ideas in the sense that Plato described the shadows on the cave wall as reflections of a realm of perfect forms. The King appears to be the intermediary between the unmanifest and creation, and it is true that young men need the blessing of the King from older men whose lives embraced Him. When accepted and acknowledged by a mature man who is spiritually developed, a young man undergoes inner transformation. Essentially, recognition from the King in a mentor awakens the King within the young man so one day he similarly may bless and heal young men.

I do agree with Moore and Gillette that when we access the King energy correctly we will have a sense of being a participant in creating a more peaceful, fair and creative world. We will have a transpersonal devotion to our families and friends and also to the world. We will have some form of spirituality, and we will know the truth of the commandment around which human life seems to be based, "Thou shalt love the Lord thy God with all thy Heart, with all thy soul, and with all thy might. And thy neighbor as thyself."

Since the King emerged only recently with civilization, perhaps it is an aspect of a more primordial archetype, namely the Hunter. Tom Dolph is a member of the Orden der Valknut, until recently a secret male society which has its origins in Pagan times in northern Europe. In hopes of attracting more young men to the Order, Dolph wrote *Book of the Hunt: Initiations into the Life of Honor* which describes their initiation rituals, and claims that in ancient times the huntsman ranked above the king. I asked Dolph to explain,

> "...the entire concept of Chivalry grew out of the Hunting traditions. The Huntsman was actually considered THE authority (even above the King) in matters of Chivalry. In the long version of Tristan and Isolde, Tristan's noble character is recognized NOT by his good manners and social discretion, but by his expertise in the 'un-making' of game. NOTHING teaches common sense, self-control, generosity, patience, acceptance of the inevitable and accurate insight into the true nature of things like the life of a Hunter. It is an exercise in ABSOLUTES. It is survival at the most basic level, and it's not just me against the wild, it is the entire village depending on ME to do exactly the right thing in exactly the right way with exactly the right attitude in every situation. A long and dangerous hunt brings out the true character of everyone in the party. Those who are not or cannot be self-correcting will be corrected by his companions. Those who will not or cannot accept this refining process simply will not survive. Those who rise to the level of Huntsman are clearly men of Honor and discretion."

So what of the other archetypes: Warrior, Magician and Lover? I believe that they stem from the original mature male archetype of the Hunter, which somehow the Jungians missed. The Hunter is so present in us that it is largely transparent. In a sense the Hunter is the male prototype, as Ortega said, "the original man," without historical precedent. Wolfgang Giegerich, a Jungian psychologist, even proposes that the human soul was given birth through the act of killing. The genuine archetypes, Hunter, Warrior, Magician and Lover, are not exactly instincts, though they may have physiological correlates that are actual instincts, for example, the Lover archetype and the sex drive. The mind is to the brain as the archetype is to biological instinct. They are "spiritual instincts," in the sense that they are innate and have a spiritual origin.

The Warrior does not appear first in civilization, but as I have said repeatedly, he appears first as an aspect of the Hunter. Competing for animal carcasses, hunters have made war against dangerous predators for hundreds of thousands of years. The Jungians describe the Warrior as the source of aggressiveness. By this term they do not necessarily mean combative behavior towards other humans or animals, but rather the determination to get up and go and keep going. The Warrior energy arouses, motivates and energizes, exactly what the Hunter energy does. When Moore and Gillette say the Warrior embodies a "positive mental attitude," that he has an unconquerable spirit, great courage and self-discipline, they describe the Hunter. If a few Jungians had been hunters, they would know that it is the Hunter within that stirs a man's blood and rouses him hours before daylight and pushes him to go out into subfreezing weather and sit quietly but alert for hours on a tree limb or in a marsh. It is the Hunter inside that drives a Bushman out into the veld to pursue meat amidst lions and cobras for three days, and it is the same Hunter that holds an Eskimo's spear steady at an ice hole waiting 24 hours for a seal to emerge. Successful hunting requires years of self-discipline and training. Before the Warrior was the Hunter is.

Before the Magician is the Hunter. The Magician is considered to be the energy behind the shaman and the scientist, he who discovers how the world works and applies that knowledge. He is the knower and master of technology. It is the Hunter who arouses a man's curiosity about the nature of things, that leads him to carefully observe ants, eagles and deer and discover the medicine in their food. The Hunter's keen alertness teaches him to read nature like a book. His life is one of relentless proto-science, formulating and testing hypotheses empirically. And he is the original technologist. Like the shaman who emerged from the hunter, the Magician understands the links between the unseen world of spirits and the world of nature. It was the hunter who first communicated with the spirit world and who honored it in his life. It is the Hunter inside who lies behind the recovery of magic and mystery in subatomic physics and depth psychology. He is the quiet observer, the detached witness, the eyes and ears of God/Spirit/Being, and therein lies his power as healer of the psyche.

The shadow or perverted form of the Magician appears in modern science and technology which strive to master nature and control it. The original Magician, the Hunter, seeks and honors harmony, cooperation and reciprocity with nature.

The Lover is also an aspect of the Hunter. It is libido in the sense of vital energy, vividness, passion and creative energy. The Lover is deeply sensual and feels connected to all things, just as hunters primitive and contemporary see their prey as their kin. Moore and Gillette say this about the Kalahari Bushman whom they view as lovers who are aesthetically attuned to everything in the environment. They are like hunters everywhere whose dance, music, song, speech and art either derive from the hunt or imitate and honor the wild animals they hunt.

The Bushman accurately can imitate the sounds of over 300 species of their world. Their expertise at imitating animals reveals their unparalleled affection for them and their sense of oneness with them. The foundation of mysticism is the Lover archetype of the Jungians, though it, too, is an aspect of the Hunter: the hunter's mystique.

The intuitive sensitivity of the Lover gives a man the capacity to feel at one with other beings and the world, even to feel their pain, again, a primary dimension of the

Hunter who identifies with his prey. So it is with the Hunter that we are deeply and profoundly connected to the suffering of the world.

Moore and Gillette share a common misconception about civilized life compared with the hunting life, and being biased by their experience healing civilized men, they imagine that there never has been a time when the archetypes of the mature masculine have been dominant in human life. But they are wrong. They are dominant among the Tibetans and Hopis and many hunting societies. Like other writers, Moore and Gillette point to Golding's *Lord of the Flies* as an illustration of the savagery of primitive society, but what it actually depicts is the brutality of civilization. Civilization favors infantilism, not maturity.

It seems to me that the re-creational hunt awakens both the Warrior and Magician, and that the kill awakens the Lover. The demands of subsistence hunting are so extreme that they awaken the King. Vision quest also activates the King, and the Lover stirs us to create art.

The answer for the long haul is not psychotherapy employing masculine archetypes, but it is proper initiation of boys to manhood utilizing critical experiences that are transformative and maturing. The Hunter connects the human male with the Creator, just as birthing awakens a woman to the Great Mother. When Bly said that the hunt taught men about God, he was absolutely right.

"A good heart and a good mind - those are what you need to be a chief."

~ LOUIS FARMER, Onondaga

The combination of heart and mind is very powerful. The Medicine Wheel teaches that two worlds exist - the seen and the unseen. The seen world is the physical and the unseen is the spiritual world. Both of the worlds are necessary to discover true reality. The seen world is easiest seen by the male side. The unseen is easiest seen by the female side. The heart is the unseen and the mind is the seen. Blessed is the leader or person who has developed the heart and the mind. Truly, the person is of tremendous value to the Creator and the people.

Chapter 8

From Boys to Men of Heart

"When I was a boy of 14, my father was so ignorant I could hardly stand to have the old man around. But when I got to be 21, I was astonished at how much he had learned in seven years."

~ MARK TWAIN

Among the Greatest Things I Never Did

A few weeks after being face to face with the lion, I was driving far north of Nairobi on a straight highway. Cathy and I were en route to an outdoor African market in the tiny Morris truck I had just bought. As we came over the crest of a hill I saw something in the road four or five miles ahead. Though my first thought was that it was a body, I said nothing to Cathy. Then I noticed that cars driving by the thing in the right lane of the road slowed down or even came to a stop before driving on. I told myself that if it were a person the cars would stop.

"Do you see that thing in the road?" I asked Cathy.

"Yes. I wonder what it is?"

"You don't suppose it's a person's body, do you?"

"No, it couldn't be that."

A little farther down the road we both said, "Oh my God."

It was an old Kikiyu man with extended ear lobes, wearing a First World War surplus wool coat, as I had often seen there in the equatorial highlands. Next to him was a crumpled bicycle. As I got close in the car I saw two African men standing by their truck at the roadside staring at the old man. I parked, and as I ran to his side in one stride I leaped onto the bed of the truck, grabbed two burlap bags and leaped off, something I normally could not have done. As I ran past, the African men standing there yelled at me, "No, Bwana, don't touch, Bwana! Bad juju, Bwana! Him dead!"

They were warning me that spirits hovering near the old man might invade my body, and apparently that's why no one would offer him assistance.

As I reached the old man and leaned over to put the bags on him, I was sure he was dead. One leg was snapped, broken. Blood coagulated in a large pool beneath his fractured skull, and his eyes were open, the whites pointing up at the intense mid-day sun. He was not breathing.

What happened next was astonishing. As I knelt down closer to him it was as though some other power placed my hand on his shoulder and held it there firmly. Within twenty seconds the limp body miraculously recovered life. His deflated chest expanded slowly upwards drawing in air.

Like the experience with the lion, that moment is one of several that are imprinted indelibly in my mind for I was merely a witness, not the director of my body or will. It was not my conscious mind that took command and touched the old man.

By then several cars had stopped and I was surrounded by Africans. Judging from his car and clothes, one man was a bureaucrat whom I begged to direct traffic while I went to find help. Reluctantly he agreed. I asked the crowd to step back and give the old man some space then jumped in my little truck and flew down the highway 15 miles to the first village where I asked about the location of the District Commissioner, the local mayor. I found him drunk in a bar, unable to help. Next I tried using the pay phone but was not proficient enough in Swahili to get the operator's help.

I kept driving another ten miles and came upon a police station. The two officers on duty were tall, robust Africans whom I would bet had served in the Queen's Rifles in WW II. I stood at the counter and burst out,

"There's an old man on the highway down there whose been run over. He needs help. Can you help him?"

With a bored look of disgust one of them slowly pulled out a form and set it on the counter, then asked,

"You hit him, didn't you?"

I was shocked at the man's disinterest.

"Hit him? No, I didn't hit him. I'm here to tell you that he needs help."

"If you did not hit him then why are you reporting the accident?"

"Cathy, do you have a pen and piece of paper?"

She handed me both from her purse. I put down the piece of paper on the counter, looked at the man's badge and wrote down the number on it.

"Now, if you don't get down there as fast as you can I swear I will do everything in my power to see you lose your job."

The men hopped to it and were heading down the highway before I could get in my car to follow. As we arrived at the scene, I saw one of them throw the bicycle on top of the old man in the back of the Land Rover pickup. As they drove away, I shook my head and let out a big sigh as tears streamed down my face. We drove back to Kiambu, outside Nairobi, both in a state of grief.

The next morning at the university I shared with my colleagues what had happened the day before. They were shocked that I had stopped to help the old man because, they explained, when other white men had done that Africans assumed that the white man had run over the African and they killed him. They begged me never again to stop and help an African on the road.

Was I protected from harm that day by the same power that guided me to touch and revive the old man?

Years later I learned from Polynesian Kahunas what may have happened there on the tarmack. The laying on of hands is the oldest form of healing we are aware of. It is used effectively by the Kalahari Bushman to this day, as it is among certain churches. The Kahunas say that we can transmit mana or life force directly by touch. According to them, when I held the old man's shoulder, he was given a dose of my vital energy which brought him back to life.

The old man was released on crutches from the hospital one week later.

Whenever I did truly wonderful things I was not directed or guided by my conscious mind. I simply knew what to do, without thought or reflection having any part in the matter. When we dare to surrender to the heart do we act flawlessly and receive perfect guidance? Does heart-intelligence equip us for life better than formal education, "training," and technology?

Of one thing I am certain: The greatest things I ever did, I never did.

~ RANDALL L. EATON,
The Greatest Things I Never Did (in progress)

Nobel laureate, Albert Camus believed that a man's work is to rediscover through the detours of art, those one or two images in the presence of which his heart first opened. Michael Meade, author of the wonderful book, *Men and the Water of Life: Initiation and the Tempering of Men*, sees art as including myth, emotion and ritual, and men's work as rediscovery of "the doorways to their hearts and the territories of the soul." The proper initiation of young men to adulthood aims at many targets, but its success is measured by opening the heart.

Wherever men are they hold within themselves the potential to protect and provide, which throughout almost all of human life has carried the awesome and terrible prospect of killing whether to procure food or fight with enemies, animal or human. Male initiation rituals intend to balance the destructive potential of masculinity with the compassion and caring of the heart. The essential process of rite of passage was defined by Van Gennep: There is a departure from daily life, a suffering of ordeals and dramatic episodes, and a return as a marked and different person. Turnbull characterizes rite of passage as separation, indoctrination or preparation, and re-incorporation.

There is within each of us a program and desire for shifts of identity as we pass through the primary stages of the human life cycle. Eliade says each initiation is a creative death, meaning that as we move from one stage to the next we need to look death in the face, as Ian Fleming said. The brush with death may come from risking survival in the external world or it may be psychic death, but in either case the previous stage dies and out of it we are reborn into a fuller life. The classic stages are birth, childhood, maturity, elderhood and death, with initiations between successive stages.

I would emphasize that ordeal is central to male initiation precisely because it promotes ego transcendence. Left alone to survive in the wilderness without previous training leaves the boy at a loss. When he realizes that his ego is not capable of guiding him through, he discovers another guide he can trust. Spirit is not analytical, nor does it call on memory files, intellectual training or preparation, and in my personal experience of ordeals it has been perfect, infallible, examples of what Joseph Chilton Pearce terms "unconflicted" state of being.

Without ordeal, without facing real danger, challenge or hardship beyond the capacity of the conscious mind, the young man never discovers that a greater power is available to him, and that he accesses it through his heart.

Without culturally established rites of passage centered around the primary developmental phases of the human cycle, life presents us with initiations like mine in Africa confronting a lion and rescuing an old man against all odds. As Meade says,

> "They can be provoked by any unexpected, dramatic event: accident, divorce, abortion, the death of a loved one, the loss of a career, an eruption from nature that destroys the shape of a life. All severe separations in life evoke the sense of initiation in the psyche and open a person to psychological and mythical territories of unusual depth. Initiation is the psyche's response to mystery, great difficulties, and opportunities to change. The ground of the psyche shifts and breaks and opens. Past and future frame this opening – the past can be re-viewed and the future can be glimpsed and felt. Once the opening has occurred, the psyche is animated with the expectation that the beginning will be carried through to a new organization of inner and outer life.... Traumas, shocks, mistakes, and losses that we are encouraged to 'put behind us' and 'get over' often contain detours that did, and often can again, open our hearts and our inner resources for change....
>
> "Initiatory experiences carry a person away from what they know and outside the normal rules, beliefs, and boundaries. While in that separated state outside of normalcy, radical change can occur and radical healing is possible. Initiation involves both suffering and healing, makes the 'self' a territory of great learning, and connects a person to the essential mysteries of life..."

Tribal initiations often include deliberate woundings, such as scarification, which permanently mark the initiate. Usually the scars are visible and inform everyone that the marked individual has passed into a new stage of life. A person's relationship with everyone in his society is changed by initiation.

Modern life lacks rites of passage, but initiatory experiences may leave physical marks though more often they leave psychological and emotional scars. The wounds may serve as doorways between inner and outer realities.

One of the fundamental dimensions of male initiation to adulthood is descending into our wounds. Mentoring in which older men present stories about their and the ancestors' wounds, reveals that everyone is wounded, that wounding is a part of life and that grieving our wounds is what transmutes them into gifts for the community, as Robert Bly says. Grieving is a core routine for a man of heart.

In the absence of traditional rites of passage, there is no clear demarcation between death of the old and birth of the new, and that results in much confusion. According to Meade,

> "Initiatory experiences inhabit the same deep psychic ground as birth and death... Seen through the eye of initiation, death is not the opposite of life, death is the opposite of birth. Both are aspects of life....Seen through the eye of initiation the scars of initial woundedness and of life-changing events turn out to be the openings to imagination and the heartfelt experiences of life. When these experiences are contained in art, in

poetry, story, song, and dance, the limits of the individual and of time are shed, and the timeless territory of the heart and the imagination opens."

Turnbull's assessment of rites of passage for adolescents is that we are like empty, organic receptacles, fully formed but still growing and waiting to be filled. Like receptacles we are capable during adolescence of embracing our total being. Sexual and spiritual awareness are modes of experience just as valid as physical and intellectual awareness, and like those other modes of apprehension they may be pointed in any direction, outward or inward, restricted to the individual or encouraged to encompass the infinitely greater social self. They can be poured into our empty receptacle to perform the wonder of transformation, or spilled upon the ground, leaving us unfulfilled and empty. Socialization and education may be accomplished in the solitude of the rational domain, but it is the intensity that these other modes of perception bring to every experience that gives such education an inner significance, endowing it with vital force. It is intensity of perception combined with integrity of being that makes a human society a truly thriving, loving, joyous and exuberant organism, rather than a cold, hard and empty theoretical concept. That is the magic of transformation, and the potential of adolescence.

Meade is a master story-teller who has employed ancient stories to heal grown men who were not initiated to adulthood via rites of passage. In tribal societies, stories, legends and myths that teach a culture's principle morals and values and what it expects of adult males are part of the initiation of boys to manhood. There are stories about initiation itself that symbolically reveal its process of transition. One such story comes from Africa and is entitled, "The Hunter and His Son."

Heed this tale of father and son!

A hunter and his son went to the bush one day to pursue their prey. They hunted all morning but all they found to sustain them was a small rat. The father handed the rat to the son to carry. It seemed unimportant so the son threw the rat away. They saw no other game that day so at dusk the father made a fire and asked the son for the rat so they could roast it and have something to eat. When he heard that the son had thrown the rat away, he became angry and struck the son with his axe and returned home, leaving his son lying there on the ground.

Later that night, the son arose and returned to his father's village. He waited at the edge of the village until every one was asleep, then went into his parents' hut, gathered up his things and left. He walked late into the night following a path that eventually led to a large village where everyone was asleep. At the center he came upon the chief's hut. The chief was awake. The son of the hunter entered the hut, naked.

The chief asked the boy where he came from.

From another village, the son told him.

The chief asked how the boy was.

The son explained what had happened when he and his father had gone hunting, why his father had struck him and how he had come to this place.

The chief asked the boy if he could keep a secret.

The son asked what is the secret.

The chief said there had been a war and his only son had been taken captive and killed. "Now I have no son," he said. "I want to tell the people that you are my son who was captured, and that you escaped and have found your way home. Would you keep that secret?"

The son said, "It will not be difficult."

The chief started to play his drum – boom, boom, boom, in the middle of the night which awakened the mother of the house who came out and said, "O Mighty King, he who causes all to fear, why are you playing your drum in the middle of the night?"

The King said, " I am celebrating the return of my son."

Then the mother shouted out in joy and awakened the whole village. Everyone was asking, "What has happened in the king's hut that they are playing drums and singing so late in the night?" A messenger went around to tell everyone that the king's son had come home. Some of the people were joyful, others were doubtful saying, "Indeed."

At dawn, the son was bathed and anointed, dressed in fine clothes. The chief gave him gifts and presented him to the entire village to be welcomed. Some of the chief's counselors doubted it was his son, but others said that it was.

The counselors called together the sons of the village, dressed them in fine garments, and called for their best horses. The counselors told the sons to go to the house of the chief and call out the chief's son. Tell him to bring a horse and his sword. Say you are taking the horses for exercise, then ride out to the clearing and dismount. Take your swords and slay your horses. Observe what the chief's son does, then report back to us here. The counselors gave swords to their sons, and the young men headed for the chief's hut.

There was an informant present who heard the counselor's plan and quickly revealed it to the king. The king made preparations and called the son to him and said, "Take this sword and horse, and when the sons of the village call for you, accompany them. Whatever they do, you do it, too." When the sons of the counselors came and called for the king's son, they all set out together and rode to the clearing. When the son of the king saw the others slay their horses he did it, too.

The sons of the counselors returned and reported to their fathers that the king's son had slain his valuable mount. They exclaimed, "Only the son of a king ever would display such complete disregard for valuable property!" The counselors still had doubts and said, "Indeed." They decided to make further tests. The next day they gave a slave girl to each of their sons. They told them to invite the son of the chief to bring his slave girl and accompany them to the clearing. Then they should slay the slave girls and observe what the son of the chief did. Once again the informant was present and informed the king, who told the son to take his slave girl when they came for him, and to do whatever he sees the sons do. At the clearing, the sons of the counselors took their swords and each slew a slave girl. The son of the king did it, too. The sons returned to the counselors saying, "Only the son of a king would act as he has done." This satisfied the counselors who offered no more tests.

Time passed and the son lived with the king. Then one day the hunter appeared, looking for his son and questioned the people, asking, "Have you seen one who looks this way, who acts like this and that?" The people responded saying, "No, we don't know him, we haven't seen your son, but the son in the king's hut looks like that." The hunter went to the hut of the king, entered and greeted the king, who was seated with the son. The hunter spoke to his son, "Will you get up and return home with me and live as before?" The son was silent, but the king said, "Hunter, if you would keep the secret with me, I will give you however much gold you wish." The hunter said no. The king then offered one hundred times whatever gold the hunter would request. The hunter refused despite all the offers and begging of the king. The son remained silent.

The king asked for three horses to be saddled and one sword to be delivered. The three of them, the hunter, the king and the son, rode off to the clearing. When they reached it, the king handed the sword to the son and said, "We are unarmed, though you hold a sword. There is nothing left to do. Either you must kill me and take my goods and return with your father to his village or you must kill your father and return with me and live as we have been living in my village."

The son didn't know what to do.
If it were you, what would you do?
Kill the father or the king?
What would you do?

The father and the son are both joined and separated by the wound the son receives early in the story. The son is not simply hurt by the wound, he awakens to his own life through the wound. The emotions surrounding the wound generate the rest of the story and propel the boy into manhood. Meade says, "A genuine community of men forms around shared wounds." In a sense it is the woundedness of the boy that wins him admission to the fraternity of men. It is the glue that binds them together.

Robert Bly makes much of the inevitable shaming of boys that leaves them with the wounds into which they must move to transfer the dark side of the personal to the light side of the collective.

The father's gifts to the son are the rat and the fire: food and warmth. But they cannot satisfy the son's passion for life. Full of great expectations for the success of their hunt and his future life, the son easily discards the rat. In a sense it indicates the faith the son has in his father and his father's world. But the expectations of the father and the son are not the same. The father is hoping that the son will learn something about the uncertainty of life and the value of embracing gratefully whatever life provides.

Following the father's footsteps presents the son with what may be the most primal and yet significant lessons of initiation: the fact that something will die to sustain their lives. The father's footsteps lead to the issue of life and death. The son knows deep inside that one day he too will kill to provide as his father has provided for him.

The wounding of the son is what separates him from his father and leaves him alone outside his parent's village looking for a second father, a new king. Though Michael Gurian proposes that fathers accompany their sons on rites of passage, fathers cannot initiate their own sons. In order for a boy to give up his previous life as a child he must separate himself from his parents and their home then prove himself worthy in the eyes of other men. Without the shaming the father gives to the son, he would never be compelled to separate from his childhood and family and seek outside approval for his new life as an adult in a community of adults.

In leaving the father and entering the king's hut, the son has awakened a king in his psychic village. The parents no longer rule the son's psyche. Meade says,

> "The dynamics of this story reflect the instincts in the depths of the human psyche, for somewhere we know that if we accept loss fully [as we must accept death to be unconflicted and capable of transcendence] we open up to unknown possibilities both within and without...The son is looking for something that will father what is royal in him....The king becomes the second father by accepting the grand imagination that seized the son and caused him to toss away the rat. The sense of self-importance that flooded the son with spirit and feeling is the secret that is shared by the king and the son. And this sense of grandness allows the son to step into a symbolic world where he has another father."

Meade suggests that below the family guilt and shame, the negative enculturation that generates fear and doubt, there is a carefully guarded belief that in the core of the soul there is a seed of royalty, and around that core the soul grows. Each of us has a royal heritage, an inherent claim to mythic life, but those who are destined to become royal are at first abandoned, the function of "separation" in rites of passage. It is that feeling of abandonment that forces a person to be close to the part that is hidden – one's true self. Proper initiation finds boys alone, abandoned and naked – the "ordeal" in rites of passage – with naught but the true self and its heroic destiny, the true self being divine spirit, transcendence its heroic destiny.

The slayings of the horses and slave girls are not about hurting women and animals, as some women fear are the eventual consequences of hunting by boys. Stories are full of swords and heads rolling; Meade tells us, "for this is how the psyche changes – by being cut off and then growing again." The horse is a metaphor of the instinctive power of masculine force. To become the son of a king – a king within himself – the boy must slay his drive to power, his tendencies to charge about and get on his high horse. In another word he must transcend his ego to become the son of a king which is God.

The slave represents an habitual way of seeing and doing. To become the son of the king, the boy needs to slay his habitual self, not only his egoism but the negative conditioning and programming of his culture. The clue to where this slavishness exists lies in his attitude toward "girl" and his own immature, feminine self, Meade says. So the son must cut through two areas of his psyche that he takes for granted: the dimension of masculine instinct, power and force; and, his inner feminine. The son kills the horse before he slays the slave girl because the war-horses in a man's psyche must be cut down before he's able to cut through his habitual view of the feminine. Which is to say that only by overcoming the power of masculine instincts can a man set free the feminine within – his own heart. The slayings of the literal layer of the masculine and feminine is what opens "the full emotional and imaginal life of the man."

Deer symbolize gentleness, and in slaying a deer many young men have slain the habitual image they carry of girls and thereby discovered and opened their hearts.

At the story's end the son receives a sword, a symbol of what the son has become.

The sword represents the temperament he has received from the father's wound and the king's blessing. The pain and anger carried in the wounds of the son may turn inward and destroy him or break out and become a threat to others.

> "If the fathers and elders of a culture don't meet the sons on the grounds of their wounds and tempers, everyone is in danger of feeling the sword. The core of grandness in the sons, the spark of royalty, won't be released without drawing out the fire that surrounds it....The sword metaphor combines the capacity to judge with the ability to feel. In the sword, thinking and feeling come together and the capacity to slay is tempered with the feeling to protect."

The sword is a symbol of the son himself. Just as the sword is made by tempering the blade from fire to water, hot to cool, the son moves back and forth between father and king until he learns to separate them. The story is part of an old idea that a man is not born but made, "forged from the blows of his family and the hammerings of the kings that temper him."

Though ancient, the story of the hunter and his son comes from an era after domestication of animals, as seen by the existence of horses, village life and its social hierarchy. Yet the father was a full-time hunter, indicating that the culture was still a mixture of foraging and subsistence agriculture. The initiation of boy to man among some hunting societies consists simply of demonstrating hunting ability by killing an animal of sufficient size to establish worthiness as a provider. Among the Kalahari Bushman, for example, the killing of an antelope qualifies a young male as an adult.

As the original rite of passage, the hunt includes separation from family and dependence on it, ordeal in terms of facing wilderness and risks alone for the first time, taking an animal's life which is a symbolic death of the young hunter's childhood, and reincorporation or rebirth as an adult provider.

"...the greatest strength is in gentleness."

~ LEON SHENANDOAH, Onondaga

Chapter 9

Male Initiation Rituals

"I believed then and still strongly believe that all truth and knowledge is to be found in the wilderness."

~ *Ingwe*

The Green Fire Die

"In those days we had never heard of passing up a chance to kill a wolf. In a second, we were pumping lead into the pack, but with more excitement than accuracy: how to aim accurately downhill is always confusing. When our rifles were empty, the old wolf was down, and a pup was dragging a leg into impassable sliderocks. We reached the old wolf in time to watch a green fire dying in her eyes. I realized then, and have known ever since, that there was something new to me in those eyes – a thing known only to her and the mountain. I was young then and full of trigger itch. I thought that because fewer wolves meant more deer, that no wolves would mean hunter's paradise. But after seeing the green fire die, I sense that neither the wolf nor the mountain agreed with such a view."

-Aldo Leopold, *A Sand County Almanac*

Ingwe's Initiation

The story of Ingwe's initiation gives us an insider's view of male rites of passage in a contemporary Kenyan forager-farmer culture in which masculinity is defined by hunting and warring.

Norman Powell was born in South Africa in 1914. He was given the name of "Ingwe," which means leopard, by the Zulu. He spent most of his youth in Kenya where he grew up with the Akamba tribe, and after WWII was initiated as a warrior into that tribe, which, before the coming of white man, had preyed upon elephants with bow and arrow. Ingwe had grown up hunting and trapping wild animals with his Akamba friends.

The place of initiation was occupied by forty young men and a group of elders gathered in a small clearing. The ceremony is secret and limited to males. The initiates are told that if they ever divulge certain parts of the ceremony they will die. Though white, Ingwe had been invited because of his life-long intimate relationship with members of the Mbua clan to which he was being admitted.

The first afternoon the initiates were instructed in matters concerning the ceremony while some elders scouted the surrounding bush to assure that no one else was in the vicinity. The codes and beliefs Ingwe heard helped him better understand the Akamba's harmony with the earth. When evening came they were marched in pairs to certain places where they were told to sleep. No one had been allowed to bring anything except the clothes on their backs, nor were they permitted to build shelters. Ingwe and his friend, Kiloo, dug into a hollow they filled with grass and leaves to stay warm. Just as they were falling asleep they heard a loud wailing noise, but could not decipher its source.

Kiloo and Ingwe slept for a while then heard a great roar accompanied by voices shouting, "Don't kill our sons, don't kill our sons!" Then they heard sounds of fierce fighting followed by cries, "Oh our sons, cover your eyes, for you must not look upon the Mbabani who has come to steal your soul. We your elders will drive him from this place." For three nights they listened to the elders drive away the evil monster.

The morning after the third night the initiates were gathered into a clearing deep in the bush and were ordered to sit. The evil monster they had heard for three nights rushed in at them covered in animal skins. It mocked and spat upon them while doing a demented dance. The elders came rushing back and used sticks to drive it away.

Four goats were sacrificed. After they were skinned and their entrails buried ceremoniously, each initiate was given a piece of meat and told to go to a quiet place to cook it and pray to the spirits for guidance. Kiloo and Ingwe built an altar of sticks at the base of the sacred mumbo tree where the good spirits come when they visit earth. They put bits of their meat on the altar as an offering in their quest to become true warriors of the tribe.

Each morning they were divided into four groups to receive instruction in the traditions and mores of the tribe and manhood. They were taught of Engai, the creator of all, of the coming of man, and of the good and bad spirits. They also learned of legends, folklore and the prophecies of such great medicine men as Munei, who had prophesied the coming of the white man. Interspersed with the teachings were bouts of competition in wrestling, running and archery.

On the evening of the seventh day they were told to strip and form a single line facing a double line of elders holding thin branches about four feet long. The initiates were told to run through the double line, and as they did so they were struck across their backs by the elders. Every warrior had to endure the ordeal of pain several times. Though the pain was intense, no one cried out as this would have disgraced themselves and their fellows.

When they had finished running the gauntlet, the initiates were told to go down to the river and bathe for they would then be reborn into warriorhood. The cold water burned their lashed backs as they stayed alert for crocodiles.

Next they were led to a clearing where a fire burned and they were ordered to be seated. The medicine man called upon each in turn and handed them the *kithito*, a horn filled with medicinal herbs and sacred objects, to be used in the same way as Christians use the Bible. The medicine man had each one repeat the warrior's oath as he held the *kithito* above his head. When the ceremony was complete the warriors were allowed to sleep.

The next morning they went three miles to a clearing in the bush where an ox and several goats were roasting over coals. A group of women and young girls entered the clearing with gourds of beer and milk, bowls of honeycombs, sugar cane and other delicacies. There was much laughing, congratulating and praising as the feast continued until mid-afternoon.

Ingwe Seeks a Vision

Having been reborn as an adopted warrior of the tribe, Ingwe felt that he must seek a vision about the direction and meaning of his new life. He went to seek council from Musomba, the father of his blood bother Kiloo and medicine man of great wisdom. Musomba advised Ingwe to go to where the Athi and Tsavo rivers meet to form the Sabaki, a location both Ingwe and Kiloo had dreamed about the night after initiation to warriorhood and their bonding as brothers of blood. He was told to fast for two days asking his ancestral spirits to help in his quest. Kiloo was told to accompany Ingwe and pray with him for the first two days, then on the morning of the third to travel down river and leave Ingwe alone until Kiloo received a sign indicating that he should rejoin Ingwe.

Kiloo and Ingwe went to where the rivers meet and recognized the very place Ingwe had seen in his dream. There they camped, fasted and meditated, and when Kiloo left Ingwe he "felt so alone in this seemingly endless wilderness that stretched away on all sides, yet I was filled with the urge to enter the unknown, for there I felt I would find the answer for life. I believed and still believe strongly that all truth and knowledge is to be found in the wilderness."

Ingwe climbed to the top of a rock outcropping, prayed to the spirits for guidance then began to walk into unknown country. Soon he came onto an oryx in a clearing. The bull lowered its rapier horns, capable of fending off a leopard, then raised his head to look at Ingwe. Ingwe followed the oryx to a hillock, which turned to look at him again, then ran off. Ingwe sat under a thorn tree on the hillock and felt a sense of well-being come over him. The medicine man had told Ingwe that he would know the appropriate place to seek his vision, that an animal track, a feather or some other sign, such as an animal would inform him.

Ingwe relaxed and became one with the place, and toward mid-afternoon, he looked off to see a small group of people trotting toward him. They were twelve young warriors who raised their bows above their heads as they passed, a sign of peace. As they passed they looked straight ahead except the last one, who turned to look at Ingwe and pointed his bow at him. Then they suddenly disappeared. He examined the ground carefully and found no tracks; Ingwe had had a vision, but did not know its meaning.

As he headed back to the camp by the rivers, Ingwe came across the bull oryx, and when he arrived at the camp Kiloo was already there cooking stew. Kiloo said that a leopard had appeared momentarily before him and he took that as a sign that Ingwe had received a vision so he returned to camp. After a dinner of guinea fowl and coffee, they talked about the theory of animals serving as guides to visions, but they would seek Musomba's interpretation of the vision.

The next morning Kiloo and Ingwe departed the river camp and started the trek back to the Land Rover, but they came upon the tracks of someone wearing sandals and limping, leaning on a bow, and then found the young man along the trail groaning in pain from an injured hip. Ingwe went to fetch the car and when they got the young man inside and Ingwe looked at his face he recognized him as nonc other than the last one in his vision who had turned to look at Ingwe. Ingwe was shocked: how could this be, he wondered. The lad had been hunting with his companions when he was injured and had come out to the road hoping for a lift. Ingwe asked him how many were in his hunting party and he answered that there were twelve. Ingwe asked no more questions for he understood that there are things beyond the minds of men that belong to the realm of vision and dream. They took the young man to his home village.

Musomba interpreted Ingwe's vision quest as follows, "Ngo (Akamba for leopard), you once told me of a dream you had, the dream in which the medicine man said that you would receive the spirit of the leopard and that one day you would be a teacher among the people. That day has now come.

> "When you were a boy you listened to the words of the grandfathers and grandmothers, learning the ways of the tribe, but today our young people no longer listen to the words of their elders, so they know not of Engai, the great spirit; they know not of the ways of the tribe, and their ears are deaf to the voices of the wilderness. Now the time has come, my son, for you to awaken them and all young people to the truth and wisdom that the wilderness holds. Those twelve young warriors you saw in your vision represented youth calling you to fulfill your mission. Go Ngo, go my son, go bring the truth to the youth of Ukambani and to all who have lost the way."

Ingwe used Scouting to bring back the ways of the tribe to the young people. He started a troop on the farm he grew up on, and also ran training courses for Scout leaders. He taught not only the wilderness skills of Scouting but also brought back the elders to teach the ways of the tribe, its history and traditions. Later he returned to South Africa where he was a leader in Scouting, and then did the same in America, where he mentored Jon Young and became the elder of Jon's Wilderness Awareness School.

Rites of Passage Among the Ojibway

Kohl's classic book, *Kitchi-Gami*, about his time with the Lake Superior Ojibway in the mid-19th century, gives us first-hand information about the way in which boys were initiated to manhood. The Ojibway of the time were hunter-gatherers who did have enemies among the Sioux, though warring generally was not as important to manhood as hunting.

Unlike the Lakota, for whom rites of passage centered on the hunt, the Ojibway recognized a boy's hunting successes over a number of years. Among the Nez Perce, Horace Axtell writes, a boy's first kill, which was often a bird, was honored with a feast normally given by his grandparents.

A boy's first kill of a big game animal, such as deer, elk or bear, was a major event in his initiation process, and was accompanied by religious rites as well as a feast.

Every adolescent Ojibway also sought a vision of his life's mission through fasting and dreaming, and successful completion of the dream vision completed his initiation to manhood. Kohl was fascinated by the courage of the young Ojibways,

> "When was it ever known, among us Europeans, that boys or girls were able, at the tenderest age, to fast for days on behalf of a higher motive, return to the most remote forests, defy all the claims of nature, and fix their minds so exclusively on celestial matters, that they fell into convulsions, and attained an increased power of perception, which they did not possess in ordinary life? What courage! What self-control! What power of enduring privations does this presuppose!...every Indian without exception, displays such heroism."

Kohl sought detailed information from an elder named Cloud who explained that Kithci-Manitou, the Ojibway's name for God, sent prophets who laid it down as a law,

> "that we should lead our children into the forest so soon as they approach man's estate (puberty), and show them how they must fast, and direct their thoughts to higher things; and in return it is promised us that a dream shall be then sent them as a revelation of their fate – a confirmation of their vocation – a consecration and devotion to Deity, and an eternal remembrance and good omen for their path of life."

Cloud told Kohl that his grandfather had taken him in the spring into the forest and prepared for him a bed in the branches of a red pine. He was told to remain on the bed and to take no food or water, but on the fourth day he got up and ate a number of plants. He went home and confessed to his grandfather. Cloud was not punished but he was told that he had done wrong and felt ashamed. He was reminded that had he persevered he would now be a man, i.e., the vision-dream quest was the Ojibway's final rite of passage to manhood.

The next spring Cloud ventured to an island in the lake and prepared a bed as before. The first three or four nights he could not sleep for hunger and thirst but on the fifth day he felt no more annoyance and fell into a "dreamy and half paralyzed state, and went to sleep, but only my body slept; my soul was free and awake." On the eighth night, a man appeared on the branches of the tree and spoke to Cloud asking him why he was in the tree. Cloud told him to fast and gain strength and know his life. The man told him that is, "good for it agrees excellently with what is now being done for thee elsewhere... This very night a consultation has been held about thee and thy welfare... the decision was most favorable. I am ordered to invite thee to see and hear this for yourself. Follow me."

Cloud explained to Kohl that the communication with the spirit was heart to heart, not spoken aloud. Cloud rose from his body and followed the spirit until they arrived at what seemed like a summit where there was a wigwam with four men sitting around a white stone. Cloud sat on the rock, but then a deer skin was put on it and he resumed sitting. The lodge was full of people. He saw the earth below and a glorious sky above and was asked if he wished to return to earth or travel higher still, and he chose to go up for that was the purpose of his fasting. One of the four men gave the command to ascend and Cloud climbed a ladder higher and higher until he came to four white-haired elders. Cloud wanted to keep ascending but was ordered to stop. He was told that he had no permission to pass higher, but that enough that is good and great is already decreed for him. He was told to look around,

> "Thou seest here around all the good gifts of God – health, and strength, and long life, and all the creatures of nature. Look on our white hair: thine shall become the same. And that thou mayest avoid illness, receive this box with medicine. Use it in case of need; and whenever though art in difficulty, think of us, and all thou seest with us. When thou prayest to us, we will help thee, and intercede with thee with the Master of Life. Look around thee once more! Look, and forget it not! We give thee all the birds, and eagles, and wild beasts, and all the other animals thou seest fluttering and running in our wigwam. Thou shall become a famous hunter and shoot them all!'"

Cloud gazed in amazement at abundance of game and birds and then was told by the four elders that his time had expired, that he could not go any higher and to return. Cloud descended back to the four men and the stone where he was welcomed and told that he had done a brave deed and had gazed on what is beautiful and great. They said that they would testify that he had performed the deed, and that he should forget any of what had been said to him, that all who sat there would remember him and serve as his guardian spirits.

Cloud awoke after three more days during which time his body had lain motionless as a corpse. He was so weak he could not stir. He heard his grandfather who had come on the tenth day. The ice on the lake had melted so the grandfather went to fetch Cloud's uncle and together they got him down from the tree and across the water in a canoe. As they helped him walk to camp, they saw a bear and his uncle wanted to shoot it but Cloud and his grandfather said no, that on return from his fasting dream a man must not shed the blood of any creature for three days. Cloud walked to the bear and spoke to it telling it to run away and it did.

A day later Cloud finally took food and in three more days was fully recovered and strong, "'And from that time I was, and remained, a perfect man!'"

Some Ojibway preserved their dream of life in art, using pictographs etched or painted onto tools or weapons.

The Sacred Hunt as Rite of Passage

Raised primarily in the modern world, Barry Moses is a Native American who was reluctant to hunt. He describes his rite of passage via a sacred hunt in which he discovered the powerful connection between his people and the deer.

Hunting: A Spiritual Tradition

by BARRY G. MOSES, Sulustu

Edward Moses was my father. He was a member of the Spokane Tribe and lived at a time when our traditional ways began to fade beneath the pressures of a modern world. His elders had always lived amid the ponderosa pine and basalt-covered hills of northeastern Washington State and survived from whatever foods they found on the land: roots, berries, salmon, and venison. But years of forced assimilation, cultural displacement, and especially the destruction of the salmon fisheries, drove the people into poverty. As a result, they learned to hunt from both tradition and necessity. My father passed this tradition to me, though sometimes I refused to learn.

From the earliest days of my childhood, my father *made* me hunt, even if I only sat in the car while he and his brothers disappeared into the woods. They never went far before the sound of rifle-shots cracked the air someplace beyond the trees. I always turned my face toward the sound and waited, quiet and breathless. The forest assumed a lonesome and deafening silence, until the men finally re-emerged and offered some sign of the outcome. Words were never necessary. If they returned to the car all at once, I knew the hunt had failed, but if they succeeded, my father would stand at a distance and wave. That was my sign to follow him and help in any way possible.

On the reservation, hunting is a normal way of life, but as I grew older, a different worldview pressed upon me. My parents separated when I was six years old and so I spent nine months of the year in a city far removed from my father's world. My new friends and classmates had no need for hunting and many of them responded with disgust to my stories.

The cultural differences drove a wedge between my father and me. Every summer I returned to the reservation, and by then I had learned to hate hunting. As we drove to the woods, I tried to discourage my father by repeating the arguments I heard from my friends. "We don't need to kill animals," I pleaded, "We can go to the store."

It was a weak attempt, which he dismissed with barely a sideways glance. "Where do you think the store gets meat?" he said as he looked away.

"But don't you feel sorry for the deer?" I continued, "It makes me sad to see them suffer."

My appeal to pity provoked an unexpected reaction. His eyes narrowed like knife blades and his words fell heavy on my chest. "Quit now!" he scolded. "The deer will hear you and be offended. If you feel sorry for them, they'll think we don't want them anymore. You'll make it hard for us to get meat." The blunt force of his words startled me, and then I just felt anger. I crossed my arms and glared at the back of his head.

Despite his quick reaction, he never spent much energy on arguments. He made his point and moved forward with silent persistence.

When I realized I could not change my father, I attempted to excuse myself from any further hunting trips, but the old man would not budge. "You do not have to kill the deer," he said, "But you *will* help me feed the people. This is how we take care of each other." He required me to help with every stage of the process from gutting and butchering, to smoking and distribution. This was perhaps my earliest cultural education, though I did not realize the importance of his teachings when I first received them.

My heart began to change when we delivered venison to family members and tribal elders. Many of our relatives were too old to hunt, and many lived in poverty, loneliness, and isolation. Sometimes my father made me present the meat as an offering, and without fail, the elders responded with emotion and gratitude. More than once, the old women wept and thanked me.

When I reached my sixteenth year, I finally agreed to hunt. My father sat me on a hill overlooking a small meadow. "This will be an easy place to start," he said. "Just before nightfall, the deer will pass through this field as they look for water." Just as he predicted, the deer arrived, dozens of them in fact, but my hands shook so much that I never got a single shot. When my father returned he asked, "Did you see anything?"

"No," I lied.

Sometime later, I asked my father, "How will I know it's my time to get a deer?"

"You'll know," he said, "Because the deer will stop and look at you. Deer are like people. Some of them run from their purpose, but others know when it's time to help the people. When they give their permission, you'll know because they'll stop and offer themselves to you."

During our next hunting trip, his words proved true.

On a remote mountain road, a young deer stood motionless in the tall undergrowth. Startled by the unexpected appearance, I struggled with my gun. The lever jammed and rattled as I fumbled to take aim. I felt certain the noise would frighten the deer, but to my surprise, the animal waited. Finally, I took one precise shot and the deer crumpled to the ground.

I ran into the field and found the deer lying with its head curled back. For one brief moment, the eyes still glimmered with life and connected with mine. The mouth opened and closed several times, and then breathed a final sigh. There was no pity, no victory; but rather an upwelling of humility and *love*. Tears fell down my cheeks, and I felt like those old women weeping for gratitude. "Thank you," I whispered over and over again. "Thank you."

I never became a great hunter, but I finally began to appreciate the spiritual teachings of our people. My understanding deepened after my father died. I was 23 years old, and I inherited many spiritual responsibilities, including the commitment to obtain food for ceremonial dinners. As always, the deer holds an essential place among the sacred foods.

Now I am the hunter, though I never wanted this role.

Not long after my father's death, I wrestled with feelings of grief and inadequacy. All the old doubts returned and made me question my skill and purpose as a hunter. During this time of struggle, I had a dream. A man stood at the edge of the forest and offered me a rifle. He said, "Take this gun and kill me. I give my life to the people." With trembling hands, I accepted the weapon, and in that moment, the man changed into a deer. Our eyes connected and I finally understood the deep relationship between our people and the deer spirit.

Our ancestors once depended on the deer for their survival. Now we depend on the deer to connect us to the ancestors. Our tradition creates a sacred circle where the land, the animals, and the people share one heart forever.

Initiation Among the Bassa of Cameroons

Nauk Bassom wrote "Baskets at the Crossroads" as an account of his initiation to manhood among the Bassa tribe of Cameroons, Central Africa.

Shortly after a young man was admitted into adult society he is given a test by seven to nine elders who come one morning early outside his father's compound. They ask him to step outside, and when he does the elders stand between him and the door. They tell him it's time for him to depart. Nauk's mother ran after him but the elders prevented her from hugging him. Nauk heard one elder tell his mother to go away, and he explained to her that for the next 18 moons her son will have nothing to do with the people of the village. The elder declared that this is the law and to let her son go. Nauk was not entitled even to look back as he was escorted out of the village. He was thirteen.

Nauk's mother yelled after him to be humble and compassionate and to give praise to the Father daily. She also said that he should not forget to put his baskets at the crossroads.

Three months prior to his departure with the elders, Nauk had to spend three months deep in the forest where he and 27 other boys had to survive in a hostile and dangerous environment. They had to subsist off what they could gather, trap or hunt, cook it and share it with one another. They had a mentor who was their instructor during this period. Before his father handed Nauk over to the mentor, he hugged his son, held his head against his chest and told him to listen. He asked Nauk if he hears something, and Nauk said yes, his heartbeat. The father nodded and whispered for Nauk to go.

Nauk went his way and crossed the river to where the mentor was waiting and greeted him with the same hug and questions as his father had asked. Nauk heard the mentor's heartbeat. The mentor sighed and said simply that they should go. That same morning the mentor explained the meaning of crossroads to Nauk. He told him that when he walks on a path heading north, he will meet people coming only from the north, but at the crossroads, he'd meet people coming from the east and from the west. Nauk said he understood this first lesson but he paid it little attention.

On another day, the mentor came and said that he and Nauk were from different age groups, but that their coming together creates crossroads between generations. Nauk was asked if he understood. That same day and following night, Nauk learned that the crossroads are not only where people from the four directions come together but also the intersection of the old and the new, the traditional and the modern, youth and aged, visible and invisible, the world of the living and the world of the dead.

Three months later the time to depart came and the mentor hugged and asked Nauk to put his head to his chest and listen. He asked if Nauk could hear anything. Nauk said yes. The mentor asked him what he hears, and Nauk replied that he could hear his father's voice. The mentor asked what the father says. Nauk responded that he hears a long song, a very long song. The mentor asked to hear the first words. Nauk said that the song says to keep the flame burning in the father's house and there will always be someone to feel the warmth of the legacy, to keep the flame alive. The mentor shouted with pleasure and told the boy to go.

Nauk crossed the river where he was greeted by his father who hugged him and put his ear against his chest and asked him what he heard. Nauk said that he heard the father's voice saying to keep the legacy, to increase the vital force, keep the fire burning even if there is no one to feel the warmth of Father's house.

Nauk's father was pleased and proud because it was important for his son to know the myth of his people's origins. Nauk went home with his father and was admitted into the adult society. Nine days later he was admitted into the "High Order of the Hunters." During the rites of passage, an elder said to him that he must learn to keep the fires burning in Father's house and he must experience the crossroads. In one voice the audience replied affirmatively. They meant that the neophytes had to become wanderers, to learn how to sustain their traditions and culture and learn to open the third eye – the eye of spirit – so they could see clearly.

At one point in the ceremony a patriarch told the boys that if they come back to their native land their return will be celebrated, but if not that they were not meant to be part of Bassa society.

Initiation of Bassa boys is designed to open their hearts and teach them compassion. Bassomb explains that it is at the crossroads that we learn kindness, love, respect for the elders, protection of children, compassion for the weak and the meek. Being generous, compassionate, humble, hospitable, all help to fill our baskets. His mother had asked him to check his baskets often. She had taught him to pray, to put his empty basket at the crossroads. Nauk says that he checks the baskets often and understands them as source of all personal growth and wealth. His baskets now are full of stories, teachings, experience and wisdom.

Nauk explains that he has made bold choices in his life, to go east or west or south. The best way to keep the flame in the Father's house alive is to consider the children – and their children. So he keeps filling his baskets, not with silver and gold, but with experiences and stories, which one day as a grandfather he'll spark the imagination of children.

He believes that children need to be put in a position to wander freely when their time comes. Each story, each exotic landscape, magnifies their idea of the world and their vision of themselves-in-the-world. It's in everyone's reach to tell stories, to describe places and share experiences. Everyone can go out and meet the likes of the African wanderer. He encourages everyone to place their baskets at the crossroads.

Athabascan Peter John's Initiation to Hunting

In my TV production, The Sacred Hunt, Peter John at age 95 described his initiation to hunting as a small Athabascan boy. When he shot his first moose, he was five years old, and there was a lot of traditional ritual that followed. Peter John had to give his first moose to the old people. It was customary for a boy's first kill to be given to the old people, and that generosity is also what earned social recognition for him.

He said,

> "When they go out to catch a moose they look for the best one to make a potlatch for 7, 8 or 9 families together. Moose meat is special, how they take care of it, how they smoke it, everything's connected with that. The early part of the Athabascan culture stands for a lot of things that we don't have right now. We've lost nearly all of it. A long time before our time, people used to know what to take and what not to take. The animals you take is very important to your grandchildren. The Athabascan way is not like the white man's way."

Peter John means that it was traditional among his people to treat the flesh in a way that honors the moose, and to rely upon spiritual guidance regarding what animals to kill and what animals to leave alone…hunting from the heart. The respect shown to the animals has consequences for our descendents in terms of their cooperation in the future; this native form of wildlife management amounts to reciprocity on the spiritual plane.

> "The first moose you catch, the first moose I want him (a young man) to take is good moose. One shot, that's all it's going to take to catch that moose. If he takes two or three shots that's the way the bullets going to travel all his life."

The preparation given a boy prior to his first hunt will have life-long consequences.

> "I'm an Indian. That's the kind of life I choose – I don't know the kind of life you choose. You're white and you got way farther education than I've got, but the education I got you'll never get it because I'm the last one that knows about it."

Peter John offers the wisdom of his spiritual ecology derived from a long life as a hunter,

> "By looking across the country here, I think about my great, great grandfather. He didn't have no tea, no sugar, no flour, no vegetables yet he made it. God made this world and everything that's in it. And when he done that he put the animals in it – in this world. And these animals have to eat the leaves, the willow, and whatever there is. That's what the animals live on: the medicine, God put medicine in there so when we eat that (animal) it helps our body to be strong and healthy.
>
> "This world is not the way God made it, it's altogether different, so, therefore, we are giving the animals the hard time which they didn't earn, but us, we contaminate

the water, the air, even the grass, the leaves. Everything what animals live on is contaminated. The white people, well, I don't blame them; it's okay. I am not against them, but we should understand that God made this world and everything that's in it so you and I can live, but then we destroy ourselves by destroying what God made."

Initiation Among the Ainu

The Ainu of the Northwest Coast of Southern Sakhalin are hunter-gatherers. A boy is recognized as entering puberty when the pubic area darkens with hair, at which time he receives a covering for his genitalia. What marks his transition to manhood is his participation in male roles, especially hunting. Traditionally, when a boy successfully shoots down his first bird with an arrow, his hair style is changed to that of a man so that the small portion of hair in front with beads attached is shaved off.

Anthropologist Emiko Ohnuki-Tierney explains that during the period of gradual transition to manhood, a boy undergoes the exciting experiences of his first hunting and fishing and participates in adult male activities progressivley more as he becomes older. The most significant rite of passage is when he receives two sets of knives, one exclusively for ritual purposes.

Jim Swan's Rite of Passage

Jim Swan is an environmental psychologist and author of several books including, *Sacred Places, Nature as Teacher and Healer, In Defense of Hunting,* and *The Sacred Art of Hunting*. He describes his rite of passage to manhood as follows,

> "My father gradually and progressively introduced me to hunting, but...the initiation experience took place when I was about 14 or 15. We were bow and arrow deer hunting in northern Michigan on Drummond Island...We shot a deer and I was the person who actually followed the blood trail of the deer through the woods and found the deer. That evening we brought the deer back to this hunting lodge. Well, they took that deer and painted blood on my face. The other boy who was about my age also had the same painting, and we stood there, and everyone congratulated us. Then we had a special pie that's made out of the heart, the lungs and kidney of that deer – a special ceremonial feast you could say.
>
> "The other custom, too, that I recall is actually an old German one that was part of that process I learned. When you killed the deer you put a small piece of green vegetation like it would eat and put it in its mouth, then you say, 'Thank you.' It's last meal. That's one way of showing respect to an animal that you've killed.
>
> "There's a sense of sadness that you feel for the animal, and out of that there's a sense every time that you shoot at an animal you say under your breath or in your mind, 'I hope I either miss this cleanly or I kill it cleanly.'
>
> "Beyond that there is an enormous sense of upwelling of reverence that comes as you realize you're part of the food chain and so is this animal, and in taking this life you're reenacting an event that is as old as mankind itself. It's a very religious experience, you might say, especially the first time."

Dave Watson's Initiation to Hunting

Dave Watson sang for years with the Oak Ridge Boys, and he produced the much acclaimed video, "A Year in the Life of a Bow Hunter." The following excerpts are from an interview he did for "The Sacred Hunt II: Rite of Passage," he describes how simply a mentor may communicate effectively a sense of respect and reverence for animals taken.

> "My uncle had a farm in Ohio of about 600 acres. He raised corn and soybeans, and there was an abundance of wildlife. We'd go out in the morning and shoot quail for breakfast, and it was just the neatest thing because it was the ritual of the preparation of the hunt and then preparing the meal, all in one short time period…from shotgun blast to start of digestion was probably one hour, and it was just a neat way to go out and then get food from the land, cook it, eat it and say, 'Hey, this is something that I did,' and I was probably ten years old. That was my first experience with hunting.
>
> "Hunters have this tremendous power and this tremendous ability to influence young people, whether they realize it or not. They have the ability to change a young person's life forever in a positive way or in a negative way, just depending on their initial experience. And with me it was a very, very positive way because my uncle would go out there, and yes, we would shoot these quail, but he'd pick up each one we'd shot and neatly straighten out all the feathers and gently put it in his vest. And he truly respected the animals that we were taking, and yes, it was an incredible moment for me, and yes, I would call it a rite of passage."

Hunting as Initiation: The Ordeal of Gray Elk

Though we are concentrating on the role hunting plays in initiation to adulthood, it also can be a form of initiation of adult men to a new life. A poignant example is that of Tom Rael whose native tribe was dispersed far and wide by the government when he was a boy. His parents resettled in Denver and raised him without contact with his people or other natives. He grew up with whites, blacks and Latinos, ignorant of his own racial and cultural heritage.

Tom was an ambitious young man who, while still in high school, had his own construction company which made him financially successful at an early age. He loved animals and kept a menagerie at home. He was a passionate hunter.

In the Rockies Tom shot a monarch elk one afternoon. It had the largest harem of cows Rael had ever seen, over 100. He had placed his shot carefully, sure it was lethal. He watched and waited for the bull to go down, but dusk came and then darkness as the bull remained standing. The cows came to the bull one at a time and sniffed his body as though to say goodbye.

After midnight as the bull was still standing among his harem, Tom wept to think he had killed such a beautiful and magnificent creature. He went back to his cabin and slept, sure the bull would be dead by dawn. When Tom arrived back at the meadow he found the bull still standing, leaning against an aspen for support. He shot the bull six times, point blank in the head with a .38 revolver to kill it. Then as he reached over to slit its throat and bleed it, the bull revived and charged him, carrying him forty yards before finally it died.

Two of Tom's vertebra were dislocated and both his hamstrings severed. Three days later he was admitted in a wheelchair to a hospital where he was told he would not walk again. After he came home, bound to a wheelchair, he received an unexpected visit from an Oglala Sioux medicine man who told Tom he was on a mission to heal him of his injuries if he would agree to teach the ways of his people.

The holy man healed Tom's injuries and he began to walk again. He learned about his people and his cultural background. His life changed a lot. He gave up the construction business and now makes native art instead. He spends a lot of time teaching young people and is a master storyteller.

When Tom and I met he told me he was only nine years old. That's how long it had been since the day the bull elk nearly killed him. That elk gave up its life for Tom and transformed his life. A magnificent elk died that Tom could be reborn.

The Initiation of a Maasai, Warrior Extreme

The Maasai herding culture of East Africa is at least 4,000 years old, and for most of that time they have been at war with other pastoralists, farmers or lions. Raids against other herders to steal cattle were common until fifty years ago. The nature of male initiation among the Maasai reflects their lifestyle and indicates how rites of passage adapt them to it. It helps to view different cultures as we would different species because most cultures are comparable to ecological niches (ways of making a living).

With the exception of overgrazing and the devastation of drought on their herds, the Maasai are very well adapted to their environment. Egoism and competitiveness are promoted in male rites of passage because they are appropriate to a pastoral life. On the other hand, hunting peoples actively discourage male egoism as a threat to social solidarity. Western industrial culture has lead the world to the brink of disaster because it has clung tenaciously to the "myth of power" associated with ancestral pastoralism. Maasai life and rites of passage are especially instructive regarding the global crisis the West has created.

Tepilit Ole Saitoti's autobiography, *The Worlds of a Maasai Warrior*, will be our primary guide. Saitoti describes his life in Maasailand, where men dominate women and accumulate status and power according to their wealth as determined by the size of their herds of cattle. Men of wealth take several wives, and the wives are ranked in a hierarchy according to longevity of marriage. The Maasai are semi-nomadic, moving from one *manyatta* to the next to graze herds on fresh range.

Pre-puberty boys are sent out to herd goats. Tepilit's goat herd was attacked by a leopard that killed eight goats and took only one. He was unable to kill the leopard and was ashamed of himself for letting the incident happen. When he was 17 he worked up the courage to speak to his father about becoming a man, meaning he wanted to be circumcised. Not long thereafter he was herding calves as his warrior brothers herded cattle, and a lioness killed a three-year old calf.

Saitoti was alone. He wanted to spear the lioness but she held the calf so close to her body as she suffocated it that he could not spear her in the heart so he decided to aim for her kidney, a wound that would kill her slowly. He threw his spear and it struck the lioness who leaped into the air. Saitoti drew his sword and turned and ran as fast as he could to a tree and climbed it, thinking the lioness was on his heels. He dropped his sword and climbed as high as he could into the tree. The lioness was struggling to extricate the spear when Saitoto heard a second calf bellow and more growling. But he had no spear and no sword so he could do nothing to protect it. A pride of lions had attacked another calf.

He saw one of his older brothers running toward him and then saw an old man walking by. He was frightened that his brother would think he had not done his herding duties well so he went to the old man and begged him to intercede and tell his brother that he had killed a lioness. The old man told the brother to leave Saitoti alone, and as the brother began to strike Saitoti with his herding stick, he hesitated when Saitoti told him he had speared a lioness.

They found the dying calf but the brother still doubted that Saitoti had speared the lion. The brother saw spoor and followed a blood trail. Soon he saw his brother come running with the bent spear in his hand, uttering praise that such is the Maasai man, such is the Maasai warrior. Sambeke handed Saitoti his spear with the exclamation that he was a great Maasai warrior. Saitoti was overcome by pride and ecstacy, as well as immeasurable confidence which he felt may be known perhaps only by decorated Maasai men.

The next day Saitoti found the carcass of the lioness and cut off the tails and claws, but being still a youth he was not allowed to celebrate his achievement.

Two months later, Saitoti's father called all his children together and announced that Tepilit was going to be initiated into manhood because he had proven before all that he can now save children and cattle. His killing of the lioness was not conducted in a ritual manner with other Morani, young male warriors, and to qualify him properly it would have had to be a male which is far more dangerous.

The circumcision ritual is a test of courage. The initiate must not budge, move a muscle or even blink despite overwhelming pain. To do so would mean that one is a coward, incompetent and unworthy to be a Maasai man. Saitoti's father sums up the meaning of the ritual, explaining that the pain is symbolic of a deeper meaning. Circumcision represents a break between childhood and adulthood. For the first time in Saitoti's life, he will be regarded as a grown up, a complete man, who will be expected to give and not just to receive, and to protect the family always. Saitoti is told that his wise judgement will for the first time be taken into consideration, that coming into manhood is not simply a matter of growth and maturity, that it is a heavy load, and especially a burden on the mind.

Three days before the ceremony, Saitoti was required to give away all his belongings – necklaces, garments, spear and sword. His head was shaved, even his pubic hair. All that he had done in childhood and everything associated with it had to be left behind as he moved into a new life as a new person. As the day approached great tension mounted as members of the family feared that Saitoti might fail the test and they would be shamed, spat upon even beaten if he did. As the final hour neared his closest family members acted like they hated him and recently circumcised warriors taunted and teased him.The warriors sang songs praising warriorhood and encouraged him to achieve it at all costs.

The ceremony was attended by males only. The circumciser splashed a white liquid across Saitoti's face then cut him. The operation lasted fifteen minutes. When it ended he was given words of praise and was awarded cattle for his bravery, eight in all.

Saitoti nearly bled to death from the circumcision conducted by a man who was losing his eyesight.

Two weeks later Saitoti was taken far away to join with other newly circumcised boys. During the healing period, the young warriors wore headdresses composed of feathers from colorful birds they had killed along with black cloaks. They were pampered wherever they went. Then their headdresses and cloaks were removed and their heads shaved. Saitoti describes the feeling he had as an emerging warrior, saying that as long as he lives he will never forget the day his head was shaved and he emerged as a man, a Maasai warrior. He felt a sense of control over his destiny so great that no words can accurately describe it. He said that he now stood with confidence, pride and happiness for all around him he was desired and loved by beautiful, sensuous Maasai maidens. He could now interact with women and even have sex with them, which had not been allowed before. He was now regarded as a responsible person.

Saitoti writes about the old days when warriors were like gods, and women and men wanted only to be the parent of a warrior. Everything else would be taken care of as a result, because when a poor family had a warrior, they ceased to be poor. The warrior would go on raids, steal cattle and bring them back. A warrior would defend the family against all odds.

The Maasai have a saying, "You are never a free man until your father dies." While a man's father lives he remains paramount and a man is obliged to respect him. Saitoto's father strictly controlled all his sons and their deviations from his expectations resulted in severe punishment.

Saitoti and other young warriors wandered for months from one settlement to another singing, wrestling, hunting, playing and pursuing sexual encounters. Maasai rarely "hunt" wild animals except those that attack people such as lions and rhinos.

The ritual "hunt" of the lion is surely the most extreme undertaking of a Maasai warrior. I had lived in Maasailand before I was struck by a lion in the Lafayette, Indiana zoo, where my professor and I were volunteering to expand the cage space and I served as a keeper feeding the animals daily. As I was walking hurriedly along cages carrying 40 pounds of meat, the old, flabby lioness who had occupied a 12' by 12' concrete pad for years, seized the opportunity for entertainment in her miserably boring life. At precisely the right moment she lunged forward, extended her foreleg out as far as possible between bars, and with a flick of her paw, the way a housecat bats a ball across the floor, set me backwards on my rump. I was shocked and angered by the event, but the more I thought about it, the more I began to wonder how humans became dominant over lions before firearms.

If an underweight, out of shape lioness could reverse the direction of a 200 pound man (who at that time was captain of Purdue's powerlifting team) carrying 40 pounds and moving approximately four miles per hour with no more than the flick of her paw, what must it be like to be attacked by a full grown male lion in prime condition? That unexpected event altered the course of my life; it was an initiation of sorts that invited me to rethink human origins in light of besting big predators.

Saitoti's adopted brother killed two lions, one of which had attacked him. He bore scars visible below his sword belt, a sort of permanent badge of courage. The lion had bitten him repeatedly and torn a sizable chunk of flesh from his groin, nearly castrating him. These achievements gave him exceptional status as a Maasai warrior. Before he had been initiated he had killed rhinocerus and elephant, other high-ranking trophies that gave him additional status and esteem among Maasai.

When I arrived in Kenya I already was prejudice against the Maasai whose cattle competed with wild animals for graze and water, but when I encountered the Maasai personally their grace, charm and humor seduced me. They are a proud, powerful people, to say the least; their masculine instincts are fueled and fired, forced into control by fear of a harsh patriarchy. Though the Maasai initiation process may take years, there is no place in it for the vision-dream quest of the Ojibway or Lakota, nor do the Maasai seek a vision for guidance about the mission of their life, as do the Akamba. The Maasai men know the purpose and function of their lives: to accumulate status, wealth, power, wives and children, and they do it one way, by being aggressive towards dangerous animals and humans.

We men of Western civilization tend to identify with the Maasai men because our cultural values are much alike. We, too, endeavor to excel and by excelling prove ourselves worthy to receive social status, power, women and wealth. Our fundamental assumption is that there is no gain without pain. Like the Maasai boys we grow up worshipping heroic warriors or sports figures, and soon we are stuck in a commitment to accumulate more of everything as a measure of the progress of our lives. Like Saitoti, we dream of the day when we will feel as he did when his head was shaved and he became a warrior, desired and loved by beautiful, sensuous maidens.

Saitoti's pride reminds me of the ecstacy I felt when elected unanimously as captain of my high school football team or the comparable sense of self-infatuation I experienced playing my initial college basketball game when I scored the first twelve points. That kind of pride and ecstacy that Saitoti felt when his older brother congratulated him for killing the lioness is actively discouraged by hunting societies everywhere. The Bushman explained why to Richard Lee: if they do not discourage a hunter's pride he will eventually kill someone. The danger of male pride is homicide, social fragmentation, which, to a small hunter band could be disastrous in terms of hunting success and defense against predators. But for the Maasai, accomplishment of males in stealing cattle and killing enemies and predators is praised and rewarded. In the simple contrast of the way Bushman discourage egoism and the Maasai encourage it lies the difference between the relative peace of the hunting life and the conflict of pastoral life.

Perhaps it should not surprise us that Saitoti says that a Maasai warrior is not supposed to cry. The most extensive and elaborate male initiations occur among the warring pastoralists. While the outcome is meant to emphasize masculine fire and minimize the opening of the heart, nonetheless, Maasai men must be able to control their violence. The controlling influence seems to be their fear of father and the patriarchy, which their initiation affirms they will uphold and defend. They cannot win at the adult male game if they do not follow the rules: violent rage is directed away from society at the enemy lion and human.

The life of a Maasai man is unceasing control over cattle, wives and children, predators and enemies, which Saitoti's father described as an awesome mental burden. No room here for surrendering to a higher power the destiny of one's life. The god of the Maasai dwells in a powerful volcano, much like Yaweh, the vengeful god of the Hebrew warrior-herders. Like Maasai fathers, the gods of the Maasai and Hebrews are harsh, strict and quick to punish.

The "Sky God" of the great pastoral traditions represents a polarization of divinity: He is absolute; only He is divine, though by conforming conduct with His ordained hierarchy of power on earth, the patriarchy or the church, humans (and only humans) who subscribe may ascend to divinity. Surely, the reservation of divinity found among the monotheistic religions is a cultural adaptation – with biological consequences – to the pastoral myth of power. The Ten Commandments, for example, were recorded intact among the Sumerian tablets centuries before Moses, apparently as a code of social conduct meant to control behavior of the original civilized people. The diffuse religions of the foraging cultures sees divinity in all creation, as an extension of the Creator, and so they contain respect for everything, not simply power.

Though Jews and Christians may attend church and pay their dues, are they like the Maasai in the sense that few invest in a prolonged period of deprivation and surrender intended to make them receptive to higher guidance? What of Jesus' forty days and forty nights? The law has been laid down and it is upheld by the male hierarchy of power. Here is an authentic measure of the egoism of a culture relative to its spirituality. The lack of vision quest or its equivalent in pastoral cultures indicates the relative importance of ego-intellect in their lifestyle of control. The same pattern is reflected in the initiation of males to adulthood: in pastoral, farming and industrial cultures, masculine instincts and pursuit of status, wealth and power prevail. Vision could threaten the control of the patriarchy and its vengeful deity. The same applies to the State.

A certain amount of deprivation and pain may be expected in the rites of passage of males. Meade says that, "One of the purposes of the pain of initiation is to allow the initiate to know pain himself so he won't need to put others in pain in order to learn about it." But the circumcision of the young adult Maasai is really a test of bravery, an opportunity for a male to prove himself worthy as a warrior, one who will endure at all costs the hardships and dangers of the warring life. Meade's explanation does not seem to apply to Maasai; if anything, they are expected to inflict pain and suffering.

The Maasai girls' rite of passage includes clitorectomy, surely a very painful procedure though not a demonstration of bravery. It is the way in which the patriarchy exerts control over the sexual life of women, meaning that if they are robbed of the pleasure of orgasm then perhaps they will be less likely to commit adultery. It is an act of disrespect towards women that informs them as they enter womanhood and marriage, often to a man twice their age, that they are subject to the control of their husbands and the patriarchy. While Maasai warriors glow with the pride and confidence of heroes, the initiated women are violated, debased and forced into lifelong submission, not unlike the traditional treatment of women among Muslims and Jews.

The deprivation of food and water associated with the Ojibway's vision quest is not merely a test of bravery or courage but physiologically and emotionally necessary to evoke communication with the spiritual realm (the activation of the pineal gland). Sleeping in the cold and running the gauntlet among the Akamba, serve two, inter-related purposes: demonstration of a young male's intention to submit his will to the greater good of his society; and, to demonstrate his willingness to endure the pain and suffering of the adult responsibilities to provide and protect.

Initiation Among the Gisu: Tempering Masculine with Feminine

There are cultures that take careful steps during initiation to bring males into a respectful relationship with females, and on the psychic level that means tempering masculine heat with feminine water. The Gisu people in Uganda refer to Litima as the violent emotion peculiar to the masculine gender; it underlies quarrels, ruthless competitions, power-lust, brutality and possessiveness, but also is the source of courage, independence and ideals with meaning. Litima fuels the process of individuation, including initiation and drive necessary to make change. It is ambiguous: the source of independence and meaningful ideals can also be the source of brutality.

Meade says that,

> "Societies that attend to initiation of youth provide rituals that require that everything else come to a halt. Questions hang in the air: Will this generation of youth find a connection to spiritual meaning and beauty that can lift the flames of Litima to the high emotions and ideals that keep the light at the center of the tribe burning? Or, will they be a generation of possessive, power-driven people? When the questions are not seriously entered, the eruptive forces move toward physical violence, possessiveness, and brutality."

Young men need help to open themselves up to adulthood. The raw passions and ideals need attention and expression if they are to mature toward the wisdom and skills of elders. Litima needs to channel through rituals that awaken each initiate spiritually. The fire in each youth needs to be tested, seen and educated – the word means to lead out or elicit. Litima is that which needs to be drawn out, both the capacity for violent eruption and the capacity to defend and protect others courageously. Litima is volatile, disruptive, asocial; it intensifies everything and lights up the shadow areas of society, family and the individual. The red and black colors often connected with initiation rituals symbolize the fire and ash of Litima.

Next to Litima, the Gisu culture places the value of awakening feminine awareness in men. They know that opening the channel of Litima in men presents danger to women, so the initiation of men encompasses an initiation to the power and mystery of the feminine and non-sexual bonding with women. There is a certain point in the process, which culminates in circumcision, in which the male initiate wears the adornments of women. They are given strings of beads that are worn like girdles diagonally across the male's chest and heart. The same girdles are worn by Gisu women over their wombs. The number of strings of beads a male wears indicates the number of female kin who have affection for him, and he is told that the beads will give him strength to endure his ordeals.

The strings of beads symbolize the creative power and sacredness of women. Worn by the women, the beads focus attention on the womb of the tribe, the source of all its members. The initiate's heart is shown to be like a womb for conception and giving birth. **A man's womb is in his heart.** A young man's passage to adulthood is conducted while wearing the beads which connect him with women and feminine power. Meade says,

> "The beads remind the men that a boy whose heart has been opened through the eruptions of his spirit and the affections of (ritual 'mothers' and 'sisters')....This process makes clear that more than 'male strength' is necessary to complete the initiation into manhood, but he must have feminine strength and endurance as well. While the initiate loses some male skin in the circumcision, he gains the feminine strength in his heart.... The ritual makes clear that he is made of the elements of male and female and must embody both to be in the community of man....Without rituals that bind men and women in a deep respect of the other, women are denied the capacity to know and the power to control their wombs and therefore their bodies, and men are denied the knowledge of their own hearts."

The Gisu young men face the same painful circumcision ritual as the Maasai, but the Maasai have no feminine symbols covering their hearts, no ritual sisters or mothers to remind them of the feminine strength of endurance. The psyche of the adult male Maasai is unbalanced by heavy emphasis on the masculine. The central focus of his life is power and control, domination and subjugation, the life of the mighty warrior pastoralist, ruler of his world.

In a dream-vision I was invited to a naming ceremony by a native medicine man accompanied by many of his white followers. Several of my college teachers were in attendance. In the ceremony I was encouraged to become a prayer leader and given a new spirit name, "Makes Beads for Peace." A few weeks later a Lakota medicine man who visited me at my cabin on Lake Tahoe set on the table a book with a photo of the medicine man in the dream. It was Sun Bear, whom I had never met or seen a photo of until that day. He had died before I had the dream. A decade later when I read about the role of the beads in the initiation of Gisu males, the meaning of my spirit name suddenly made sense: the beads are a symbol of feminine energy, and I was to balance the masculine with the feminine. Making beads for peace meant to conceive from my heart this book to help recover the initiation of boys to men of heart.

Way of the Grandmothers: Initiation of Rising Sun

In a lecture in the early 1990s given by Rising Sun, a Lakota, I learned about his initiation from boyhood to manhood, by a very different route than I had heard before from my Lakota teachers. Rising Sun said that the path of his initiation was the "way of the grandmothers," and that unlike the initiatory path given by the grandfathers and medicine men, he and other boys of the age of 14 to 15 went through the same rituals as girls their age.

The grandmothers took the boys and girls across the border into Canada for a summer during which the boys wore the clothes of girls and even sat in the "moon time lodges," with the women and girls who were menstruating. He explained that the path he took was much older than the way of the grandfathers, and that the latter had arisen only in the past few hundred years after the coming of the horse and the onset of frequent warring among his people as they pursued the bison herds. Interestingly, many of the Lakota holy men are quick to say that their culture already was in a state of spiritual and moral decline when Europeans arrived in their region. The Sioux had acquired horses indirectly from their introduction by the Spanish so Sioux warring life had begun before Europeans colonized their lands. Perhaps it was the shift from foraging to horse culture as a form of pastoralism that caused a degradation of the spiritual life of the Lakota. (The Hindu scholars have a different explanation for a global age of egoism based upon the Yuga, the several hundred thousand-year orbit of the solar system around a central galactic sun. According to some, the Kali Yuga or age of ego/iron, also known as the dark night of the soul, came to a close only recently in the latter 19th century).

Pre-Colonial Lakota Initiation by Sacred Hunt

From my point of view, two cultures stand out as highly exceptional because they are civilized but have not succumbed to the myth of power and domination. They are the Tibetans and the Hopis, and there is reason to believe that they are closely related. I remember well the first time I walked into Bodena, the original Buddhist temple, in Kathmandu, and was struck instantly with the similarity in appearance and countenance of the Tibetans and North American Indians. According to some sources, the red men were driven from Asia by the yellow men, save for the Tibetans who found refuge in the Himalayas. In any case, the red men of North America and Tibet have one thing in common: a profound spiritual proclivity. The Tibetans may meditate and chant and the Hopis may seek visions, but for both the meaning of life is anchored in their spiritual traditions.

John La Fountaine was a spiritual advisor among the Lakota whom I interviewed for a TV/video production, "The Sacred Hunt II: Rite of Passage." Here's what he said about the path a boy took to manhood before colonization.

> "The vision and the spiritual part was the very foundation that was laid for a child when it was quite young, and as that foundation was laid, they built upon it. In Lakota there is a word that is said, 'Wolakota.' It is but one word but it covers a huge message, a message of respect, honor, responsibility, not only to the animal but to yourself, and to the tribe and to the earth, and all these things created a vital part of the transformation of a young boy to a man.
>
> "In the transformation of a young boy to a man, prior to non-Indian involvement, it was vital to the greater makeup of the tribe that the young boy went to the shaman, medicine person or holy man to go through a ceremony. After the

ceremony he said, 'This (a sacred hunt) is the path I will be taking. Now I need assistance from the other (spiritual) side.'

"So a ceremony would be held and the individual would make an offering and go into the forest. The skills known as tracking and stalking an animal started becoming more prevalent after the influence of the non-Indian. There was a spiritual power on this island (North America) that was tremendous and it manifested in the initiatory hunt. When the young man made his offering and walked into the forest and sat at a designated spot as instructed by the holy man, and as he sat there the animal that was meant to be taken would walk to him. This warrior, this young man, would not immediately take the animal's life. He would sit and watch and look into the animal's eye.

"If you're a stalker of deer you'll know that the deer very rarely winks or blinks. For you to have the eyesight to see one blink is quite phenomenal with the naked eye. He would sit there and look at the animal that walked up to him. The deer would eat, then raise his head and look at this young warrior, and as he looked at this young warrior he would blink as that was the sign for the young warrior that the deer had made peace with the earth and with Takashila (Creator), and once it had made its sign, the young warrior would stand up. The deer would wait for him and give him one shot and one shot only, and he never missed because the spiritual arrow that he shot was charged from here (the heart). It wasn't because of prowess.

"As the experience extended into modern hunting, it became based on prowess, so a lot of these old spiritual keys and knowledge were lost, and now the hunters have become survivalists, stalkers, trackers. It's almost as if the animal isn't respected. But in that initiatory experience, all was respected, all was respected.

"There was a time when you went to the holy man for instruction, whether it was fasting to receive a vision or for (spiritual) permission to hunt. How many people sit down and say, 'Creator, bless me, give me permission to take this sacred animal's life.' How many people actually do that in their heart? And how many people once they've asked hear spirit say, 'Yes, you are worthy of it because of the path you walk.' So few, so few.

"Another part of the initiatory process is making relations with the particular animal. Often a young man was given a medicine bundle that contained a variety of sacred things. If the animal is taken in a sacred manner the spirit of the animal can be taken and used to empower the individual and the tribe as a whole.

"Deer, for example, have the spiritual power to help. The spiritual power of the deer family is such that, in most the situations you're found in, it will help you out of it, provided the proper prayers and songs are made. That deer can move you through the hardest of hardships. Each one of the animals has a certain power that was aligned with it, and you were taught all that as you grew older and as you actually entered into the field to take an animal's life, then it was more empowering for you. There were parts of the animal that were taken, prayers for the spirit of the animal, parts of the animal that were returned to the earth so that the earth would be fed as well as the spirit of the animal and yourself and the tribe.

"A microcosm in a greater macrocosm. Quite beautiful, and it flows in a circle,

> and if we stay in the flow of that circle, the animals will respect us as we respect them, and they will never run from you. They will come to you. 'So you may live I give you my life.'
>
> "We are indeed all related, and if we can come from a place of knowing we are all related, you can speak to that animal as well as it can speak to you. In looking at the initiation process, can you see how a young man has, through the very experience of moving through it, become empowered? Can you see how he has come to a place of knowing? Come to a place of making relationship? Once you have the smallest tid-bit of making relationship with an ant, you move it into a higher realm, with a bird, with a deer, with an elk, and all of that added to the very spirit of the individual. That spirit as it built became a great initiation because you walked with wisdom.
>
> "You wouldn't even have to say anything. People would look in your eyes. People would stand next to you and they would say, 'Indeed, indeed.' And the initiation is complete: Manhood, with power (spiritual), with respect (for all life) and responsibility (to society and nature)."

I am not the only recreational hunter who has followed the same basic prescription that La Fountaine describes for the Lakota during pre-colonial times. It is the path followed still by some native hunters. The key ingredients are humility and respect – enough humility to seek permission to take an animal's life, and if permission is granted, enough respect for the animal to allow it to come to you. Seeking permission can be as simple as sincerely asking if it is appropriate; the reply may be as subtle as your own deepest feelings. If it feels right to hunt, then a sense of gratitude and total faith in the outcome is likely to be met with the appropriate response from the animal. Higher guidance may encompass dreams, visions or other signs, and you still have to get yourself out there where the animal lives and maintain an open heart while there.

The Valley Bisa of Zambia are subsistence hunters, and while they do not hunt in the traditional way of the Lakota or Navajo, they do recognize spirit animals, those individual animals that do not run away and which actually come to the hunter. They feel that their ancestors play a role. A remarkably high percentage of recreational hunters have said that a certain deer or elk was meant for them, meaning that it and only it was supposed to be taken by them that season.

Imagine If You Can

Imagine how very different our world today would be if we embraced the principles of hunting from the heart in every dimension of our life. We follow our hearts in matters of love and marriage, and no one, not even the most left-brained intellectual doubts that we should. Falling in love is totally irrational, let's face it. My college existentialism professor said, "I did not marry my wife because she is a good cook, a good mother, a good driver or housekeeper. I married her because I love her!" How does he know he loves her? Because he trusts his feelings, and yet when we come to so much of our life we are afraid to trust our feelings. We suffer from "conflicted" behavior. Many students have come to me over the years and said, "I'd love to do such and such, but I can't." I'd ask them why not and they'd tell me they never could make a living at it, to which I'd respond, "You're right, you never could precisely because you don't believe you could."

It starts early. Our children observe our anxiety and stress and also feel it as we rush madly through life going to jobs we don't like, living in places we don't want to be. Even if we say to them that they can grow up and do whatever they like, they already doubt the possibility. We force them to attend school when they don't want to because they know from their own feelings that it is counter to their best interests and needs. And they are right. It goes on from there to a hardening of the heart, a distrust in the authenticity of true intelligence. Instead they cling to ego-intellect, governed by fear, and settle for the lowest common denominator rather than their great human potential.

For a couple of years I studied martial arts and discovered Chi Gung, the oldest form of energy work in civilization. It's not very dramatic, but nothing is as effective. Bill Moyers' three-part PBS TV series about health and the mind filmed a little Chinese man over 80 years old in Peking Square who stood perfectly still and at ease as five men attempted to push him over. They not only could not push him over, they were unable to move him to any extent. But all at once the five struggling men suddenly fell over backwards as though pushed by an invisible force. The old man had not moved. Exactly the same thing happened to an American martial artist who tried unsuccessfully to move the old man's arm. He was able to redirect their energy back upon them without contracting a single muscle.

Moyers was awe-struck by what he observed, and most people in the West refuse to believe such a thing is possible. There are Chi Gung masters who can send energy through a wall and knock someone down on the other side. There are others who can point their fist at a clump of paper and start it burning. After WWII, the US Army filmed an old Chi Gung master deflecting machine gun bullets at close range; his robe was shredded and he had welts from head to toe but no visible wounds.

The American Medical Association recommends acupuncture even though they do not know how or why it works. My guess is that it was a flareup in China of Nixon's flobitus, successfully relieved by acupuncture, that prompted the AMA to eventually endorse acupuncture as a bona fide healing modality. Chi Gung and acupuncture rely on a paradigm that considers energy (Chi) to be the universal force; it is not raw energy but energy intelligized, in another word, spirit. There is order in a universe of energy made possible by an all pervasive organizing principle and intelligence, known in China as the Tao.

It puzzles me that many martial artists would rather kick and punch than learn to master energy. The dynamic art has far more sex appeal. But then Bruce Lee's famous one-inch punch, capable of moving a 200-pound man fifteen feet backwards, took more than physical prowess. It took mastery of Chi. It puzzles me that NFL players spend so much time lifting weights (and shooting up steroids) when five years of standing still thirty minutes per day learning to move energy in their own bodies would enable them to knock someone over without touching them. It puzzles me that the strongest men in the world – having been a competitive powerlifter, I know some of them - who hold the records in the squat, bench press and deadlift are weak next to Sri Chin Moy, a yogi who was guided to take up weightlifting late in life as a demonstration of his faith in God.

At 69 years of age and weighing 160 pounds he was a whimp by anyone's standards, but he did the pec-deck exercise with 650 pounds, a calf raise with over 8,000 pounds – raising an elephant with Carl Lewis, the Olympian, sitting on its back - and with one arm supported 7,900 pounds!

Sri Chin Moy is famous among American orthopedic physicians who invited him to their annual conference, sure they would prove him a fake. They weighed the plates he lifted and carefully scrutinized everything. Larry Pedagana, the surgeon who operated on my knee, was there, and he said, "All I can tell you is that we don't know how he is still walking around," meaning that the feats he performed should have killed him.

In line with Joe Pearce's "unconflicted" behavior, Sri Chin Moy says that he doesn't move the weight with his mind, by which he means his ego, but with his heart. He prayed that his incredible demonstrations would inspire people to lighten the mental burden of their lives and turn to a different path, the path of the heart, the path of transcendence.

Jack Schwartz, the famous healer, was studied by physicians at the University of Toronto Medical School, where a 20-gauge knitting needle was passed completely through his bicep. The electroencephalograph monitoring his brain wave patterns and the EKG reading of his heart activity showed no changes during the procedure. After the researchers pulled the needle out of his arm one said, "Stop the bleeding, Jack." The bleeding stopped; more remarkable, the man then said, "Start the bleeding; Jack," and the wound began to bleed again.

Jack was famous for the demonstrations he gave before lecturing to medical and nursing students. He layed down on a bed of nails with his shirt off and then had everyone in the audience walk by to inspect the puncture wounds in his back. At the end of the lecture the audience again walked by to look at Jack's bare back but found no punctures there, only dried blood. All the punctures had healed.

Jack wrote a book entitled, *I Know in My Heart*, he also wrote one entitled, *It's Not What You Eat, It's What's Eating You.* Using his mind and heart to master his own vital energy, Jack accomplished the unthinkable. The last few years of his life he slept an hour daily and ate the equivalent of one small meal each week while maintaining a fierce schedule of teaching, healing and writing.

Why isn't Jack Schwartz a household name? I discovered him first on a nationally broadcast PBS TV program. Why wasn't every professional athlete talking about Sri Chin Moy's path of the heart? His feats have been performed on every major TV network in North America, and why aren't most martial artists flocking to Chi Gung? Because, as Deepak Chopra reminds us, seeing is not believing, believing is seeing. It is our assumptions about the nature of reality that preprogram and limit our perceptions and thus our capability.

Western civilization is spiritually bankrupt. It trusts the body, the ego and the machine. It trusts pills and scalpels and medicine men who see nuts and bolts where energy meridians and charkas ought to be. It trusts intellect, not intelligence. That is why many recreational hunters wear camos, use high-powered scopes and bullets that kill at 400 yards. They believe they must employ prowess to deceive and overcome a deer or elk. Perhaps we would rather play the ego game than hunt from the heart, because that is the model we've encountered from infancy. It reminds me of the incredible extent to which so many of us go to make ourselves attractive to the opposite sex: from bulging biceps to fat bank accounts and super-normal breasts because we lack faith in life as a spiritual matrix that transcends our everyday awareness. So few ask the Creator for permission to hunt a deer for the same reason that so few ask for their soul mate to come into their life: we are thoroughly conditioned to believe in prowess, the path of ego.

Despite the negative infuences of enculturation, fortunately the hunt is such a powerful experience that it opens the hearts of many hunters. If it can do that for contemporary males who have been spiritually disempowered by the myth of domination-control-ego-intellect-science all their lives, then it is powerful medicine indeed. Likewise, many are the young men who set sail with the ego at the rudder in quest of "scoring" sexual gratification only to fall in love, find their heart and discover divinity.

How Killing a Wolf Opened Leopold's Heart

Leopold stands out among intellectual prophets of modern America because he advocated a land ethic. Yet it is obvious that what he proposed was well established among Native Americans and other primal societies around the world. His plea to recover tribal values in a civilized world was expressed best when he wrote about the wolf, his greatest teacher.

Over a gun barrel and his victim, Leopold discovered humility. In the best of his musings, he shares the milestone in his momentous journey,

> "A deep chesty bawl echoes from rimrock to rimrock, rolls down the mountain and fades into the far blackness of the night. It is an outburst of wild defiant sorrow, and of contempt for all the adversities of the world. Every living thing (and perhaps many a dead one as well) pays heed to that call. To the deer it is a reminder of the way of flesh, to the pine a forecast of midnight scuffles and blood upon the snow, to the coyote a promise of gleanings to come, to the cowman a threat of red ink at the bank, to the hunter a challenge of fang against bullet. Yet behind these obvious and immediate hopes and fears, there lies a deeper meaning, known only to the mountain itself. Only the mountain has lived long enough to listen objectively to the howl of a wolf. Those unable to decipher the hidden meaning know nevertheless that it is there, for it is felt in all wolf country, and distinguishes that country from all other land. It tingles in the spine of all who hear wolves by night, or who scan their tracks by day. Even without sight or sound of wolf, it is implicit in a hundred small events: the midnight whinny of a pack-horse, the rattling of rolling rocks, the bound of a fleeing deer, the way shadows lie under the spruces. Only the ineducable tyro can fail to sense the presence or absence of wolves, or the fact that mountains have a secret opinion about them.
>
> "My own conviction of this score dates from the day I saw a wolf die. We were eating lunch on a high rimrock at the foot of which a turbulent river elbowed its way. We saw what we thought was a doe fording the torrent, her breast awash in white water. When she climbed the bank toward us and shook out her tail, we realized our error: it was a wolf. A half-dozen others, evidently grown pups, sprang from the willows and all

joined in a welcoming melee of wagging tails and playful mauling. What was literally a pile of wolves writhed and tumbled in the center of an open flat at the foot of our rimrock.

"In those days we had never heard of passing up a chance to kill a wolf. In a second, we were pumping lead into the pack, but with more excitement than accuracy: how to aim accurately downhill is always confusing. When our rifles were empty, the old wolf was down, and a pup was dragging a leg into impassable sliderocks. We reached the old wolf in time to watch a green fire dying in her eyes. I realized then, and have known ever since, that there was something new to me in those eyes – a thing known only to her and the mountain. I was young then and full of trigger itch. I thought that because fewer wolves meant more deer, that no wolves would mean hunter's paradise. But after seeing the green fire die, I sense that neither the wolf nor the mountain agreed with such a view."

Not every budding naturalist will have to stand in Leopold's shoes to see the green fire die, but owing to the impact of civilization on the landscape, few will discover the howl of the wolf and what it means to think like a mountain. The killing of a wolf transformed Leopold's life and thought from a civilized man-against-nature to a nature prophet, one who thought like a mountain and saw with the fierce eye of the wolf.

Some readers may take Leopold's highly sensitive rendition of killing a wolf to indicate that recreational hunting is wrong, but that is not his point at all since he was an avid hunter throughout his life, and it was his passion for hunting that led him to develop the field of wildlife management. Neither is he saying that he was wrong to kill that wolf: after all she gave up her life that he might champion her kind. Her death led directly to the recovery of wolves throughout much of this country as well as to the creation of extensive wilderness areas.

Leopold is saying that the prevalent attitude of his time that wolves and other predators ought to be exterminated for the sake of having more deer to hunt is wrong. Elsewhere he tells us that humility is required in the preservation of predators precisely because our egotistical impulse is to destroy those beings that compete with us for food, homes or anything. Not only was Leopold a hunter, it was being a hunter that taught him that wolves have a right to kill deer, too, what the Indian hunters took for granted all along. The notion of eradicating predators did not originate with hunters anywhere but with civilized humans who own livestock. Here is the cardinal sin of civilization against nature and the human soul, and what one wolf's sacrifice meant in the transformation of a young trophy hunter to a truly alert man who discarded the myth of power for a life of the heart, a holy man in the halls of science.

"Speak to the Earth and It Shall Teach Thee," Job

The radical problem is not whether it is right to kill animals; it is our perception of nature, and that is a measure of how we live. The wolf symbolizes wilderness not because wolves and humans are incompatible, but because the materialism of civilized humans opposes them to nature. Materialism is a philosophical term for the egoism found only among agricultural, pastoral and civilized peoples, those who own. For

Leopold the howl of the wolf symbolized the anti-thesis of this basic disease,

> "We all strive for safety, prosperity, comfort, long life, and dullness. The deer strives with his supple legs, the cowman with trap and poison, the statesman with pen, the most of us with machines, votes and dollars, but it all comes to the same thing: peace in our time. A measure of success in this is all well enough, and perhaps is a requisite to objective thinking, but too much safety seems to yield only danger in the long run. Perhaps this is behind Thoreau's dictum: In wilderness is the salvation of the world. Perhaps this is the hidden meaning in the howl of the wolf, long known among mountains, but seldom perceived among men."

Living by the heart extends beyond connecting with animals in the hunting field. Does it mean that it is possible for us to know where to go, when to go there and what to say to whom? Incredible? Didn't Jesus say the Kingdom of Heaven is within us? Doesn't that mean that the Holy Spirit is there to guide us perfectly when we listen? The Kalahari Bushman regularly receive and send "wires" from heart to heart. Like many indigenous peoples, they have a deep, abiding faith in the whole of life and accomplish more with their innate faculties and inner guidance than we do with hypertrophied intellect and highly technical inventions. The day of the moon landing, Wallace Black Elk was at the United Nations where a reporter walked up and asked him what he thought about it. He said, "Seems to me we was always flying in space and we didn't have no suits like them astronauts."

The good news is that we do still have it in us to live life at a higher level than the machine. The hunt offers a crucible for a boy to become a man whose life is anchored in nature and the heart. Such a man, according to John La Fountaine, would embody spiritual power, respect and responsibility. If we are to present adolescent boys with rites of passage, we will need to give new meaning to ritual as the foundation of our life.

The Old Ways from Europe

Hollywood has cashed in on our fascination with the romantic illusion of medieval Europe where the route to status and fortune was defined by victory in battle. Even men born outside nobility might become knighted if extremely successful in combat. Not unlike the long path taken by a Maasai warrior, a boy's training for knighthood usually began at the age of eight, and at about 14 he would become a squire in service to a knight and continue his preparation. After a few years the squire would be elevated to knighthood via a ceremonial rite of passage, and his life of conquest began in earnest.

Europeans have been busy killing one another and others in the name of God and King since the llth Century, but what about the older ways? What did it truly mean in ancient Europe to be wild at heart?

Months after completing this book, I was contacted by Tom Dolph who wrote, *Book of the Hunt: Initiation into the Life of Honor*, which is about the "Order der Valknut," a branch of the Teutonic Knights started in Germany nearly a thousand yearss ago and largely a secret order until the appearance of Dolph's book in 2002. There are numerous chapters to this day in Europe, but apparently very few in North America. Dolph had watched "The Sacred Hunt II: Rite of Passage" and read my anthology, *The Sacred Hunt*. He sought my advise on how his chapter of the Order might recruit more young men. Like me, Dolph and his Brothers are concerned about the declining enrollment of young men in hunting and that is why Dolph's book was published.

Of special interest during this era when civilization is unraveling is a tradition of male initiation with roots that are European and ancient, ultimately pre-Christian and pagan in origin. It is, after all, Western civilization that threatens human survival and life on earth, so the Order may offer a model for recovery of proper initiation of boys. Members of the Order have included luminaries such as Robert Louis Stevenson, George Eastman and John Steinbeck, among others.

Though the Order became a Christian group for men, much of its fundamental doctrine is pagan to this day, including its view of civilization, with which I heartily agree,

> "Man is part of Nature. He was neither created nor fitted to flourish in cities. Cities are the invention of those in rebellion against God and Nature, an attempt to close ourselves away from God and the natural order of the Universe. We have rediscovered the Primordial Sanctity of Wilderness. Wilderness is conducive to the spiritual life. Cities corrupt our relationship with God, nature, each other and our own inner selves."

Having just spent two months in total wilderness in British Columbia with groups of people composed of both sexes and all ages from children to elders, I emphatically agree with Dolph. Quite unconsciously, simply being there means an expansion of awareness and self until one no longer feels separate from others, be they human or nonhuman. The ego shrinks as spirit soars; cooperation among people flows as easily as ritual, a deep sense of gratitude and laughter abound. We discover in the wilderness immeasurable peace and joy, our true nature, along with our dependence on nature.

The formula for emergence of the sane human is simple: wilderness subsistence; small social group with all ages present; and, animals as teachers.

Dolph continues, "Domesticated man is subject to constant and needless discontent in life, what Thoreau so aptly called, 'lives of quiet desperation'. Domesticated man is utterly blind to the advantages, the serenity, the strength, wisdom, contentment, beauty, truth and majesty of nature." He comments that a visit to a national park may arouse awe in us, but it does not deeply connect us. The hunt is, "a way of experiencing life as a part of life," and initiation to the hunt is a catalyst to change. "These changes make you what you ought to be, and that turns out to be what and who you really always wanted to be, but didn't know it," Dolph adds.

So how does the Order define a good man? He is self-reliant, trained, tested and initiated into a social context of Honor, regardless of what he does for a living. The True Man is committed to principles by which he lives, and these help him survive with honor. Dolph says, "These are qualities that allow him to provide for himself and others without appropriating or endangering the means of survival of those around him. A True man can and will go so far as to relinquish his own life and property in order to protect and assure the survival of others…the initiation process is an almost mystical, magical experience."

Certainly, initiation into the Order is archetypal in general and in many of its details, and there is no doubt in my mind that for the most part these rituals and ceremonies effectively integrate the conscious with the unconscious as well as they connect a man with nature and society. At first glance, the Christian overlays may seem out of place in an initiation process that otherwise much resembles those of hunting peoples, who decidedly do not take animals and nature for granted. For example, like the Bible, Dolph states that man was given dominion over the animals, but unlike many Christian sects who abhore nature, the animal, the body and the unconscious, Dolph considers man's God-given dominion over the beasts as both a gift and a responsibility which has been abused and dishonored. In any case, we may have in the Order's rites of passage some of the oldest surviving remnants of European initiation. With minor deletions, their extremely archetypal nature makes them appropriate for men everywhere, and ideal as they are for Christian men.

A Life of Honor: How a Huntsman is Made

In the ancient times, the first initiation took place when a boy was seven years old. Today, most men who enter the Order do so as adolescents or adults, but they still undertake the first initiation, which is aimed at severing the ties with childhood. After the apprentice has spent some time with his "Anwalt," his mentor, he is instructed to gather a bundle of dry sticks and tinder, flint and steel. In ancient times he also was told to steal his mother's wooden spoon with which he was fed as a child. Nowadays, the apprentice is asked instead for a photo of his mother as well as a childhood toy.

Sometime after the fall equinox and first frost the initiate receives word that, "The Sackman is coming for you." The mentor arrives carrying a sack and escorts the boy to remote wooded area with no sight or sound of civilization. At a convenient place the mentor stops and tells the boy to dig a hole in the trail. Sitting crouched across from the initiate, the mentor asks what the boy has that belongs to his mother. The boy answers and then the mentor says, "Bury it!" The photo is placed face down in the hole so as to avoid throwing dirt in her face. The mother is being buried, not insulted.

The procedure is repeated with the toy, and after a handful of dirt is scattered over it the mentor asks, "Do you do this willingly?" The initiate answers, "With all my heart and no regrets." The mentor then grabs the boy by the upper arm firmly and grufly says, "Be thou henceforth a man forever!" The Sackman then tells the boy to finish it, and the hole is filled and tamped. The mentor then arises and blindfolds the boy, leads him down the trail out of sight of the place where the past was buried, and then leads him home.

The second initiation is undertaken when the boy is 14, also after the equinox and first frost. The initiate is led blindfolded further down the trail to a clearing on the edge of the woods where the ground is clear and flat. The blindfold is removed and the initiate is given a peg of antler, bone or wood with a length of cord about the height of a man. The other end of the cord is attached to the end of the mentor's staff. The initiate is instructed to drive the peg into the ground and describe a circle with the staff. He stays inside the circle as he marks it out on the ground, and then is told to sit in the center of the circle. The mentor walks around the outer perimeter of the circle in a clockwise fashion while saying to the initiate,

> "This is you. This is your world. This is your little self. It is nothing but a circle in the dirt. It is cold, damp, dirty and useless. And there you sit in the middle, the king of dirt, the king of nothing! Get up and build a fire."

The initiate builds a fire in the center of the circle, and the mentor sits on the north side watching. Normally, the ritual is done at sundown. The mentor asks the initiate to sit down with his back to the fire facing him. The fire may cast a shadow, and if so the mentor draws the attention of the initiate to his shadow.

The mentor says, "Now your world's a bit warmer, but you can no longer be the center of your little kingdom, you would be consumed by the fire. You must ever move around the center. You must tend the fire to maintain the light and warmth. You must ever tend the flame in order to reap the benefits of light, warmth and protection from the demons of night. And yet, wherever you sit, a shadow remains in the circle with you. The flame doesn't create the shadow, you do. Only if you stood in the midst of the fire would the shadow vanish, but you would be consumed by the fire. You have the power of the fire, but you are not the fire."

These instructions are symbolic, loaded with initiatory meaning: to become an adult is to give up being the center of one's world (ego) and to serve others instead; to be a man is to keep the masculine fires burning, i.e., ever committed to providing and protecting; accepting the shadow, the dark side, of one's self; and, knowing that the ultimate source of fire/power is not the ego, but the unconscious. The circle created around the initiate is a symbol of his total self or psyche, including instincts and archetypes. The fire that he must ever tend brings light or awareness into his unconscious with which he is being connected.

The mentor now tells the initiate that he wants to enter the circle and share more words with him, and the initiate invites the mentor in to sit. The mentor rises and is given the peg and cord. "He then drives the peg into the ground some distance to the north of the initiate's circle and with his staff describes an arc which cuts across the initiate's circle and creates a space known as mandorla." The mentor does not draw a complete circle, but leaves the arc open to the whole of creation. The mandorla is large enough for both the mentor and initiate to sit. The mentor asks the initiate to sit on the west side as the mentor sits cross legged in the east facing him.

The mentor asks the initiate if he wants to live or die. The initiate answers that he wants to live. Then the mentor asks, "As a man of honor?" The initiate replies, "As a man of honor. I would be your Brother." The mentor says, "Then I must first be to you an uncle." Here the mentor takes a small bag of dust and with it draws a small cross on the ground between them, and says, "The decision is made, a new course is set. For a thing to live, something must die. It is the Law."

The mentor takes out a dagger from the sack and lifts it to catch the light of the fire and while slowly turning the blade recites, "Behold the dagger and the runes (ancient Celtic symbols) I make. Behold the blade honed for my blood's sake." He opens his shirt and pierces his own left chest over the heart, and with the blade scoops up the blood and instructs the initiate to open his own shirt. With the bloodied blade he draws the odal rune upon the initiate's left chest and recites this verse, "My blood will die and yet it lives, in ages to come for the life it gives."

The mentor then presses a clean white folded cloth against the initiate's chest to soak up the blood rune as a lasting reminder. The mentor binds his own wound and says yet another verse as he wipes clean the dagger while turning it in the firelight, "Watch and see the sheen and shade as the Raven perches and turns on the dagger's blade. Never can I turn the edge to thee that its edge is not turned as well toward me. I send you turning like an oak leaf in the winter wind, return with honor that my wound may mend."

The mentor gathers some cedar chips and spreads them on the flame. Next he takes a burning stick from the fire and puts it out and lays it on the ground to cool. He presents a drinking gourd and places it on the earth between the initiate and himself. Into the gourd he drops a small stone engraved with an odal rune and fills the gourd with water from a jar, and says, "The fire you tend reveals your griefs." He takes the charred stick and smears its ashes on the initiate's right palm, saying, "This is your guilt." He smears ashes on the initiate's right cheek saying, "This is your shame." Smearing ash on the left cheek of the initiate he says, "This is injustice in the world." He smears the initiate's left palm and says, "This is the straw death." Finally he asks the initiate to stick out his tongue on which he smears ash saying, "This is the desire of your heart."

Again the mentor smears ash on the initiate's right palm , forming a cross as he says, "The guilt is what you have done. For this you deserve to die." Completing the cross on the initiate's right cheek he says, "The shame is what you are. For this you deserve pity." Smearing his left cheek again, he says, "Injustice is the way of the world." Smearing the left palm again he says, "The straw death is the death without purpose." Again smearing the initiate's tongue he says, "The desire of your heart is withheld from you."

The mentor takes the gourd and pours some clean water on a clean white cloth and wipes the right hand twice, saying, "We share your guilt, but God forgives guilt."

Wiping the right cheek twice he says, "We too feel shame, but God takes away shame." Wiping the left cheek twice he says, "We stand with you against injustice. God will punish the unjust." Wiping the left hand twice, he says, "May God bless your endeavor as we honor your martyrdom."

Then the mentor hands the gourd to the initiate and asks him to rinse his mouth with the water and spit it outside the circle. The mentor pours a small amount of mead in the gourd and gives it to the initiate asking him to take a drink. The mentor takes the gourd and says, "May God grant you the desire of your heart as surely as we are your companions on the quest." The mentor then drinks the last of the mead and water.

Next the mentor gives the initiate a smooth stone saying, "We honor your quest and extend to you the favor and protection of the Brotherhood of the Sircarii, Order of the Valknut; to you and your house." (The favor and protection are extended upon the initiate, all female relatives, male relatives under the age of 14 or over 50, and to all his property.)

As the ceremony comes to an end, the mentor gathers his instruments and walks down the trail to wait for the initiate who is saying his prayers and contemplating the events of the day. He puts out the fire and scatters the circle and picks up the stone and the cloth with the mentor's blood and then joins his mentor, as they head off to share a meal.

Tending the fire is the next step of the process; it occurs sometime between the second and third initiations, usually at age 18. It is remarkably similar in form and purpose to the vision quest of several native tribes of North America. It lasts three days during which the initiate, now considered a hunter, fasts in the wilderness. He is given instruction, but undertakes the quest on his own. He selects a secluded spot where he will not be disturbed for three full days. Ideally, the place is located at the edge of a clearing in the woods, and the questor must supply himself with ample drinking water and firewood as he must not leave the fire. His vigil should start shortly after sunset. He inscribes a circle with the additional arc thus creating a mandorla (also known as a penumbra), but once he has built the fire he must stay inside the circle until dusk three days later. He may bring a sleeping bag, additional clothes, toilet paper, a shovel to build his latrine in the circle, a journal and pen and any weapons of choice. He will have brought the stone given him by the mentor. It is called a kinstone (or kenstone or soul stone).

During his fast the young hunter is expected to tend the fire, pray, contemplate his life and his eventual death, his purpose in this life, and to record any insights or thoughts he may wish to enter in his journal. Otherwise, the only ritual he pursues daily is "shadow casting" when the sun is at its zenith. He places the kenstone in the center of the mandorla, steps back and raises his hands in the sign of the Raven, symbol of the Order, so it falls on the stone, and then repeats a prayer, the first aspect of the initiation process that reflects the infusion of Christianity:

> "Oh Lord God, Creator of the universe and all that dwells therein, I beseech Your pity for my life of sin, as the Raven overshadows and darkens the stone my soul is burdened as I watch here alone, release from my hearts the elements of old, fill them with light and turn them to gold, warm this stone of my soul, give it wisdom and grace, that I may serve Thee with honor til we meet face to face, in the name of your Son and the Holy Spirit I pray, till the Morning Star rises and brings the New Day. Amen."

The Third Initiation at age 21 brings the questor to full manhood, and it focuses on the death bond, which links the initiate and Brothers directly with their ancestors and the traditions of the Old Brothers. It is the magical connection between those who died with honor and those who live with honor. It is a complex undertaking that embraces archaic blood-letting and symbols along with Christian vows, more suggestive of Christian warriorhood than the hunt. The Fourth Initiation is for men of 50, who at that age are considered elders deserving special honor and respect.

Following the third initiation ceremony, the New Brothers are taught the Four Truths and the Fifth Truth, a delightful mix of hunter wisdom, pagan humor and Christian ideals: You may serve the king, but you must never be the king's man; You are the dagger, the dagger is the hunt, the hunt is honor, honor is mercy; The hunter and the Raven will fight against the antichrist; we are the bands of Orion; God gives us the power of laughter, the Raven gives us cause to laugh; and, Every time you fart, say, "Life is good!"

Perhaps if the Brothers were aware of Orion's true nature, that of a domineering, egotistical warrior who never found humility, they would delete their truths accordingly. Anyone who has spent much time with ravens can appreciate their comic, trickster nature, their uncanny intelligence, astonishing repertoire of sound and the gifts they bestow on hunters whom they lead to prey and from whom they in turn benefit as scavengers when a kill is made.

Two weeks before I first heard of the Order, I was contacted by Duba Leibell, an award-winning script writer and film producer who six years earlier had purchased my video, "The Sacred Hunt," as a present for her husband and when she watched it was converted from anti-hunting and anti-gun to pro-hunting and pro-gun, and not only did she take up hunting, she committed herself to raising her two children to shoot and hunt. I already had written an extensive scene for one of Duba's productions about the initiation of a young man via a vision quest. Duba asked if I had any suggestions on rituals they could perform for her son's 13th birthday, to be celebrated by going on his first hunt with his father.

My recommendations included a family gathering led by a mentor, an adult male such as an uncle or hunting companion of the boy's father, designed to recapitulate the boy's childhood as a way of putting it to rest. I suggested that the boy present a childhood toy to be burned in the fire that had been built by his mother. A line was to be drawn in the earth and when the boy's childhood was duly honored and given up, he was to be pulled loose from his mother's tearful embrace by the mentor and taken across the line where, as his family left, he would light his own fire, receive instruction from the mentor and be left alone for a vision quest in which he would pray for a vision about the purpose of his life and seek permission to take the blessed animal on his initiatory hunt.

Paganism is on the rise in Europe and North America because people feel spiritually impoverished and disconnected from life and nature. The way of the hunter was well known in Celtic society because hunting was important to life. The animal was seen as more than a resource for food and garment, but also as a guide in the "Otherworld," or world of the spirit, much like totem animals are guides for shamans. The hunter is hunted because when he consumes the animal's flesh the animal's spirit lives again in him, which is why so many cultures ingest the blood of their prey. The animal's wisdom is given to the hunter. It was believed that the animal allowed a hunter to take its life if the hunter was worthy. Their relationship was not competitive but one of kinship. Reciprocity was as fundamental to Celtic life as it has been to Native Americans.

I find it fascinating that years before I learned about Druidic traditions I wrote these words in an essay about an ancient European shaman,

> "In truth a man is what he eats. The right hunter's right mind connects with the right animal's right thought, and they join from that day onward. **The wisdom in a certain animal is meant for the man who receives it**. It is truly a marriage and it continues throughout the man's life and after. That is the secret of hunting."

The Order warns against enrollment in any non-Christian hunting tradition; however, for young non-Christian hunters, male and female alike, amalgamation of the first two initiations followed by the vision quest – without the noontime prayer - would amount to an adequate initiation process. Vows are important and these could be non-denominational, e.g., to respect, honor and protect the earth and creatures, be thankful for wildlife and wild places, take only what is needed and use what is taken, preserve wilderness and the hunting tradition, serve as an ethical model and suitable mentor, cause no unnecessary harm to wildlife and environments, respect the rights of others, practice safety at all times, and conduct one's self honorably in the field. Personally, I also would recommend these vows, "Life is sacred. Honor it," and "Follow your heart in all things." I also would encourage daily thanksgiving, regular practice of forgiveness and daily prayer for Guidance

Males are adapted to submit themselves and suffer ordeals to earn admission into a group of adult males whose values and virtues they uphold. Like so many institutions, formal hunter education falls woefully short not only in terms of sacred rites of passage but also socially. The Order exemplifies what may be achieved by a private hunting group in meeting the social and emotional needs of males who choose service to nature, God and humanity over individualism, materialism and self-glorification. Men, nature and society would prosper much from the prevalence of sacred hunting groups. It would be "a totally different world" if a majority of men in this country had been properly initiated to hunting and were firmly established in hunting groups with the spiritual strength and emotional solidarity of the Order – whether pagan or Christian.

It is worth noting that, according to Joe Pearce, the pivotal ages in brain-mind development are 7, 15, 18 and 21, nearly identical to the initiatory ages of 7, 14, 18 and 21 recognized by the Orden der Valknut centuries before scientific study of the brain.

City Shaman

You were meant to live in cities
And point to the hills
To make dreams for the steel-grey heart

Resonating the sound of geese never heard
You chant to saints and whores
The song of another Kingdom

~ RANDALL L. EATON

Chapter 10

Buddhism, Hunting and Ethics

> *"One should not talk to a skilled hunter about what is forbidden by the Buddha."*
>
> ~HSIANG-YEN

Zen and the Art of Killing Raccoons

Now I happen to be a person who loves raccoons. I've had many pet raccoons and raised some from infancy. At one time I had eleven. My college thesis was about how to keep raccoons out of wood duck houses, no easy task. When I left high school for college, I succeeded in reintroducing three of my raccoons back into nature, though one of them, Suzy, would still scramble down a giant maple tree, climb up my body and sit on top of my head and lick my face when I called her with the trill-whistle. There are few people with more affection and admiration for raccoons.

Still I am on the verge of killing one. It has been raiding the cat food supply in the barn for almost a year. And in true raccoon fashion, it has managed to undo all my efforts to keep it out of the feed can. For a while, the bungee cords over the top of the can worked, but then the raccoon chewed through the plastic lid. Next I moved the garbage can into the tack room, but the raccoon crawled through a crevice between the rafters along the ceiling and got into the food.

Live trapping the raccoon and releasing it could be just a pretension to kindness since the raccoon is likely to encounter severe competition from existing raccoon residents, not to mention the difficulty of adapting to a new location.

If I do kill a raccoon, it will take a few months before one of the youngsters raised here on our cat food will move back into the vacated territory and go looking for Purina. But if I see one on the road, I just might kill it.

We moved instead.

To define the way in which hunting develops a young man's ethical nature, I present a dialogue with Gary Snyder's essays on Buddhism, ethics and the environment. Gary is a practicing Zen Buddhist, a Pulitzer-prize-winning poet and environmental philosopher whom I have known for twenty-eight years.

Snyder and the "beat" generation, including Kerouac and Ginsberg, were poets and intellectuals different than their predecessors because they detached themselves from professional academic life and sought instead to be fiercely independent. Modern Taoists, they forecast and helped to shape the hippy movement of the next generation.

Gary is right at home with Mother Earth and he knows that our relationship with her is exceedingly more important than abstract knowledge. Considering how the hippy generation entered this world, yanked and poked and cut and isolated, deprived of the beauty, bliss, comfort and love of their first rite of passage, is it any wonder that they protested vehemently against their parents? Demanding an end to the war, not only in Viet Nam, but also the war of ego against heart, of men against women and babies and the earth?

Those of us who grew up outside the big cities bonded with and trusted nature and animals, and many of us found a kind of nurturing from the earth we had not known originally with our mothers. But with so much wounding at those critical stages in the life cycle, birth and puberty, and even before birth, we were first in line behind the beat generation to raise the flags of protest. The year I graduated from college, the hippy revolution just had begun when my closest friend went off to fight and be wounded in the Viet Nam War while I was wandering the university district in Seattle signing anti-war petitions with a copy of the *New Republic* under one arm.

Michael Meade says that the hippy revolution still has to be resolved, that no generation since has successfully closed the door that our generation rammed wide open. Is that because the arrogance that victimized us, our mothers and the Earth is still on the loose? How many of us have healed our wounds? We approach or have passed the age of 60, when the Greeks said a man was ready to be a philosopher, but many of us who have managed to survive the insane onslaught are emotionally barely more than adolescents wondering if in our lifetime genuine maturity is possible. We envy the beat generation because they played the game with more or less of a full deck: if not properly initiated into adulthood at least they had been well mothered and nurtured.

What concerns me most, however, is whether we'll be able to heal our wounds and transmute them into gifts for the community. For us, life has not been an experimental party of creative exploration, but one of enormous disconnection, fragmentation and alienation, first from our mothers then from our fathers and therefore from ourselves. Even if individually and collectively we do come out of it all with gifts capable of healing the gap between mothers and infants, which will bring us back together with the earth, and the gap between boys and men, which will bring us back to responsible stewardship of society and nature, will it be enough?

Like Snyder, I happen to believe that protecting the viability of the earth and preserving her many lifeforms is of the utmost importance, but in asking why we follow the inane policy of expanding economy or keep filling our rivers with mercury that poisons tuna that we eat, I came around first to the lack of initiation of boys to adulthood. And within that context I especially looked at the role hunting has played in producing men who are avid stewards of the earth. The facts are exceedingly significant. There simply has never been a group of men (and women) who have given so much of their time, energy and money to the recovery, maintenance and improvement of the environment.

Few people today know that the National Wildlife Federation, largest conservation organization ever, was founded by hunters. The Nature Conservancy has conserved over 100 million acres, more than any other organization, and hunters are behind it, too.

Snyder points to the conservation revolution of the early 20th Century as the dawning of the environmental movement, when people in this country began to demand the setting aside of public lands to be held or managed wisely in perpetuity. But the real conservation movement was born, of all times, during the depression when hunters and fisherman stepped up to the plate and took charge. That was when Ducks Unlimited was born, and to this day they have set the pace for environmental conservation. (Anyone who wants to enjoy masculine energy at its very best should attend a DU fund-raising banquet.)

Gary Snyder and I have the same goals: to protect, honor and cherish the earth and all its things wild...including imagination! We've stood on the same stage, we've written in the same publications, he's taught my students and admired my women – and I his, and I even wrote a poem about him that he liked.

I met Gary first in Wyoming where I was a visiting professor. When the college brought him in I went to an open discussion he held at the student union. He read a poem entitled, "One should not talk to a skilled a hunter about what is forbidden by the Buddha," a quote from Hsiang yen, a Chinese philosopher.

"One Should Not Talk to a Skilled Hunter About What is Forbidden by the Buddha"

HSIANG-YEN

A gray fox, female, nine pound three ounces 39 5/8" long with tail
Peeling skin back (Kai Reminded me to chant the Shingyo first)
Cold pelt. Crinkle; and musky smell
Mixed with dead-body odor starting.

Stomach content: a whole ground squirrel well chewed
Plus one lizard foot. And somewhere from inside the ground squirrel
A bit of aluminum foil

The secret

And the secret hidden deep in that

Snyder asked the audience what they thought it meant. I piped up and said something about the spiritual side of hunting, which appealed to Gary, and soon we were friends. The year was 1981.

The next year I was teaching at a humanities school in Reno, and the year after brought Gary and a number of other speakers in for a series of lectures on "The Human/ Animal Connection." When I picked up Gary at the motel next to the college to go to the site of his poetry reading, he opened the door wearing black, lace underpants, and offered me a shot of tequila, saying he drank one before every reading.

During the program he told a story about the raccoons that invaded his outdoor summer kitchen; it finally got so bad that he killed one and the others stayed away for a few years. The audience seemed caught offguard by that account since they perceived Gary to be a Buddhist, non-violent and incapable of killing sentient life.

The next morning I picked Gary and his friend up for breakfast before they drove over the Sierras to Nevada City, his home. I told him my theory on the evolution of homosexuality, that selection had favored the evolution of a male type that could be left behind with the women, when the heterosexual males went off to hunt or make war, without having to worry about the wives they left behind being unfaithful. We were eating bacon for breakfast, and I was a little surprised that, being a Buddhist, Snyder ordered it for himself. When I finished, he giggled and said, "Why I don't know if I'd trust any man whose not interested in my wife."

Snyder

Old lady coyote face
Sexy underpants
Shot of hard stuff before every show
(shouldn't tell them about killing raccoon)

Eating bacon for breakfast
With scorned intellectuals he giggles and says,
"Why I don't know if I'd trust any man
whose not interested in my wife."

Nothing hidden deep in that

No secrets.

A few years later when I organized a program of lectures, seminars and a symposium on "Animals as Teachers," Gary was one of the participants. At the fancy house by Lake Tahoe where I was staying, we held a cocktail hour for the speakers, faculty and some guests. In a discussion, I told Gary that my favorite poem of his was "One should not talk to a skilled hunter about what is forbidden by the Buddha." He asked me what I thought it meant, and I said, "It means that we're all hunters, that hunters know something the Buddha does not know." He nodded approvingly.

But during the symposium when I promoted the virtues of hunting, neither Snyder nor anthropologist Richard Nelson spoke up in my defense when the young women from Berkeley attacked hunting as a vice. That evening at my girlfriend's mansion known as "Rocky Roost," built among huge granite boulders along the north side of the Lake, I served dinner to about forty people from the symposium. When they were about halfway through with dinner, I made an announcement that they should be careful eating the pheasants, all of which I had killed, because they might contain lead shot which could break their teeth. There was a period of silence, but the anti-hunters chewed on, delighting in what they had been sure was chicken.

Just before dinner I went to the table occupied by the anti-hunting, "environmentalist" college girls from Berkeley, and asked them who was the first person to write about women's rights. They sat there shaking their heads and said they didn't know. I proudly told them it was Theodore Roosevelt, this nation's greatest conservationist and most famous hunter.

I remained perplexed why Snyder had said nothing in defense of hunting; after all, along with his poem, "One should not talk to a skilled hunter about what is forbidden by the Buddha," I had read at least two poems of his about hunting and shooting deer, so naturally I assumed that he was pro-hunting.

In 1985, I published a booklet on *Zen and the Art of Hunting: A Personal Search for Environmental Values*, which ended with a question from a reviewer about what the book had to do with Zen followed by my response:

> "Zen teaches that life is paradoxical. Zen is the way of no way, a path without a path. It is a way of fearlessness, which is the way of love. A classic teaching of Zen: 'If you see the Buddha on the road kill him.' The Zen masters know that worship of the Buddha and his teachings stands in the way of Buddhahood. To kill the Buddha is to kill dogma, belief, thought, and set the mind free to experience what is. Another way of saying that a man thinks with his heart, not his head. Such a man is alert, like the hunter, and such a man lives with compassion for al1 life, including what he kills and eats.
>
> "Gary Snyder considers himself to be a Zen Buddhist. He receives a lot of heat from the Japanese Buddhists because he writes about hunting, and I can speak from direct experience that many people who revere Gary Snyder's writing are shocked upon hearing that he hunted (turns out I was mistaken about this, having assumed that his poems about shooting deer were animals he hunted, not deer wounded by other hunters – its always a good idea to get your facts straight!). In their minds, a good Zen Buddhist or environmentalist shouldn't kill deer – the Buddha forbade the killing of sentient life. But Snyder is closer to the heart of Zen than his Buddhist critics precisely because in killing deer, he killed the Buddha.
>
> "Some Buddhists, including priests I've known, blindly adhere to the teachings of the Buddha, and in so doing miss Buddhahood altogether. By being his hunter-self, Snyder properly practiced Buddhism. He was alert enough to know what was right for him. He lived up to himself rather than deny his Buddha nature and succumb to idealistic piety
>
> "Hunting taught me the meaning of Zen: living by the heart. It taught me to

stop hunting except for food I really need. I have learned since that I need to hunt and eat wild animals, which is why I have resumed hunting. Still, I may never kill another animal because I hunt with my heart. Thanks to hunting I know that living is paradoxical, and that is how I hunt. Though I don't practice zazen, sitting, I do practice Zen in hunting.

"The paradoxical nature of my hunting points to similar paradoxes: the people who most love roses, who spend hours pruning them, kill them; the people who most love vegetables are those who grow, kill and eat them; the men who most love waterfowl, who adorn their den walls with paintings of ducks and geese, who study and observe them for decades, who invest in their habitat and protection, also kill and eat them. Not much different than the hunting peoples whose myths, songs, art, adornments, dance and language imitate and celebrate the sacred animals they kill. This is paradoxical only to the men and women who live from the head, suffering from centuries of separation from Nature and thus their true nature."

Except for a visit to Gary's home in the Sierra foothills and his involvement as an advisor to the Asian Elephant Survival Foundation, which I had helped start, we didn't have much interaction over the next few years. Then Gary sent me something he had written with a note that "This is what I think about hunting," apparently as a correction to what I had said in *Zen and the Art of Hunting*. I wrote him back and said, "You said it all with the title of your poem, 'One should not talk to a skilled hunter about what is forbidden by the Buddha'." Meaning that the skilled hunter knows something the Buddha does not know, that like it or not, we are all hunters. If the new physics is right about everything in the universe being conscious in some degree then we all take sentient life.

So, what, exactly does Gary think about hunting? It all comes down to his interpretation of Buddhism and its First Precept, which he explores in an essay entitled "Nets of Beads, Webs of Cells." As it turns out, the First Precept, *Ahisma* in Sanskrit, actually means to "cause no unnecessary harm." Snyder continues:

"Not eating flesh is a common consequence of this precept in the Buddhist world, which has largely consisted of agrarian peoples. This has posed a thorny question for normally tolerant Buddhists in the matter of how to regard the spiritual life of people in those societies for whom eating fish or animals may well be a matter of economic necessity. My own home place is beyond the zone of adequate water and good gardening soil, so my family and I have grappled with this question, even as we kept up our lay Buddhist life.

"I have plenty of neighbors for whom Buddhism is not even on the map. I know hunters and antihunters, usually decent people on both sides, and have tried to keep my mind open to both. As a student of hunting and gathering cultures, I've tried to get some insight into fundamental human psychology by looking at the millennia of human hunting and gathering experience. I have also killed a few animals, to be sure. On two occasions I put down deer that had been wounded by sport hunters and had wandered in that condition into our part of the forest. When I kept chickens, we maintained the flock, the ecology, and the economy by eating excess young roosters

> and, at the other end of the life cycle, by stewing an occasional elderly hen. In doing this I have experienced one of the necessities of peasant life worldwide. They (and I) could not run their flock this way, for anything else would be a luxury – that is to say, uneconomic.
>
> "Also my hens (unlike commercial hens who are tightly caged) got to run wild and scratch all day, had a big rooster boyfriend, and lived the vivid and sociable life of jungle fowl. They were occasionally taken away by bobcats, raccoons, wild dogs, and coyote. Did I hate the bobcats and coyotes for this? Sometimes, taking sides with the chickens, I almost did. I even shot a bobcat that had been killing chickens once, a fact of which I am not proud. I probably could have come up with a different solution, and I now think that one must stand humbly aside and let the Great System go through its moves. I did quit keeping chickens, but that was because it was not practical. Happy loose flocks cannot compete with factory egg production, which reduces hens to machines (but protects them from bobcats)...."

Let me pause here to say that Snyder is hardly a peasant, and having been to his place, his lifestyle is not flamboyant but economic. We also raise chickens where we live in the foothills of the Wallowa Mountains of northeast Oregon. The flock started with 24 poults who arrived in a priority mail box plus a rooster from a friend. We let them run free by day, and predators – skunks, coyotes, great horned owls and dogs – took their toll, as did drowning in the horse trough when a neighbor failed to keep the water level up while we were out of town. Now there are but seven of the original hens left, though the total flock size is about twenty excluding three batches of small chicks hatched this summer.

Last year I decided to kill six of the young roosters when we were unable to place them with flocks. Free ads on the local radio station resulted in no calls. It bothered my son, Drake, a lot. They were all offspring of the hen, Patty, a wild-spirited arcana that he caught in a chicken scramble at the county fair. I let them live for a year so they would experience their chickenness (an ethical criterion I adopted from Mike Fox – before his humaniac period – for the treatment of domestic animals). Most of them even managed to sneak in a few copulations when their father and chief rooster, Rocky, didn't notice. Since I discovered that "veal" is a euphimism for calf meat I haven't eaten it, and for the same reason I won't eat lamb. If we are going to eat an animal the very least we can do is allow it to live to an adult age and experience its own "Buddha nature." Forcing a calf to live in a small stall so its flesh will be tender or confining a chicken to a tiny cage so it will put on weight faster is a violation of respect. It causes unnecessary harm.

I let one rooster from Patty's first clutch live for another year, but I killed him yesterday. Drake had begged me to let his favorite young rooster live so I did. As Max matured, he began to fight fiercely against Rocky for domination of the flock, and both of them were being harmed. Many times I broke them up or one of them would have died. Max took to roosting outside the coop in the juniper tree by the shop, with younger hens and roosters. But after three years of sweeping and hosing chicken poop off the deck around the house, my wife, Cathy, began to plead with me, "Isn't there something you can do?" I kept saying that it was no use having chickens if they couldn't run free.

My resolve broke when Max kept crowing under my wife's bedroom window and waking her up at four in the morning. When a chicken's freedom begins to conflict with your wife's rest, possibly her health, its time to act in favor of your wife. Drake and I doubled the size of the outdoor chicken yard to about 450 square feet, nothing in comparison to the several acres the chickens covered on a typical day, but a whole lot better than living in an industrial chicken factory. At least here they could scratch, a chicken's God-given right, defend their rank in the pecking order, copulate at will and be safe from predators.

I told Cathy and Drake that keeping Max safe in the yard with Rocky was unlikely, but we'd give it a try. For several days it worked, but when the serious combats started Max flew over the seven feet high fence and started roosting again in the juniper. He also resumed wakeup calls before dawn.

I had done my best for Max, but his time was up. After blessing and thanking Max, I asked the "Spirit of the Chicken Nation" for its forgiveness, and killed him. More beautiful than his father, Max will not be forgotten. He was ambitious enough to leave 16 surviving offspring. (We resumed letting the chickens out of the coop by day.)

There's another generation of yearling roosters about ready to crow and take on Rocky, and the day will come when I kill them (or let one of them replace their grandfather). We'll eat them. We like eating chicken, and we'd much rather eat our chickens than those from the store that were factory-raised with hormones and antibiotics in their feed.

That's the whole point about raising chickens for eggs and meat. It is not simply a matter of economic practicality, about this I disagree with Gary who on this point resembles an ag major more than a nature poet. It is a matter of *ahisma.* If its wrong for chickens to be raised as they are for the market then its wrong to eat them, and while we do occasionally buy eggs at the market when our hens aren't laying, I would rather not. They are organic eggs, which means the food the chickens eat is organic so the eggs are safer and healthier for us, but the hens are nonetheless violated. They deserve better. So do we. Meaning that to buy factory eggs is to encourage unnecessary harm.

While we're on the subject, nutrition counts. The agrarian peasants Gary refers to do not eat fish or animals always out of necessity, as he says, but because these foods are desirable, and they are desirable precisely because they are more nutritious, despite the persistent claims of vegetarians. Not only was human psychology formed within the crucible of carnivory, which is why Snyder has studied closely hunting societies, so were our bodies. The surprising drama of human evolution had nothing to do with the necessity of eating meat, since in primitive situations it was far more difficult and dangerous than eating plants, but with the advantages and benefits of meat – including fatty acids associated with meat that are critical to brain function – in terms of survival, health and reproductive success.

Recently I saw a bumper sticker that said, "I didn't fight to the top of the food chain to become a vegetarian." Joseph Campbell said that vegetarianism is the first step away from life, that vegetarians are just eating something that can't run away. It is alright for humans to eat meat because it is better for them. Where do we end up if we cause unnecessary harm to our bodies out of fear of causing unnecessary harm to other bodies?

I do sympathize with Gary's regrets over having killed a bobcat. Both he and I are great fans of the predators. When I met Gary in Wyoming I was quick to load him down with copies of the journal I published and edited: *Carnivore: Carnivorous Mammals Including Man*. I could tell he was pleased. Ten years of my life had been given over to the study of the behavior, ecology and conservation of carnivores, especially big cats, and from there I went on to develop grandiose theories about how competition with carnivores had shaped human life and culture, another intersection of our interests.

I had raised a margay, a bobcat, a black bear, red and grey foxes, raccoons, a cougar, two great horned owls. Though I've been a hunter since the age of 13, I have never had a desire to kill a predator. From my point of view we are kin under the skin.

Vegetarian or not, the fact is that we all are killers; we all take life, even if we would rather not. One cannot build a home, hoe a garden, drive a car, walk or breathe air without taking life. From all accounts including the seemingly miraculous implications of Bell's Theorem, even electrons are sentient. And if so then the Buddhist distinction between sentient and non-sentient life is artificial. In which case it seems to me the principle of *ahisma* is still intact: avoid causing unnecessary harm not only to most types of animals but also to plants, perhaps rocks, everything.

Which brings us back to the nearly universal ethic of hunters, subsistence and recreational both, to eat what we take and take only what we need. If there is a difference between people it is their attitude towards consumption, not only of food. I am convinced that greed comes from materialism and that materialism comes from identity with the body, which is egoism, meaning we identify with the ego whose function it is to protect and defend the body (and its offspring).

Ahisma or living by the hunter's code, "take what you need and use what you take" is a natural outgrowth of proper human development. If we are to promote *ahisma* then there must be a recovery of healthy birthing and child-rearing practices which result in deep emotional bonding at each stage. That in turn will mean that adult humans are living under the aegis of heart-intelligence, instead of ego-intellect and its disasters.

If the truth be known those who are most aligned with the First Precept of Buddhism are hunters precisely because they have participated directly in the food chain, and in doing so, in actually taking life, they have been initiated into the life of the heart. The passionate instinctive fire of the masculine has been tempered by the cooling waters of feminine compassion. In another word, the ego-intellect, which is masculine or yang, has been softened by intelligence, which is feminine or yin.

Those of us who participate in the food chain come to feel about it as a love chain. We know that animals suffer and die that we may live, and as hunters who identify with wild animals, the taking of a life is a matter of pain and suffering. As Ortega y Gasset said, no hunter revels in the death of his prey. In recent years it has become an ethical axiom of hunting that if you do not feel some sadness over killing an animal then there is something wrong with you.

It is true that hunting is transcendent, that the supreme alertness that is hunting connects us not only with the animals we hunt and imitate to the point of identity, but with their habitats. The land ethic was proposed by Aldo Leopold, whose life work and vision were founded on hunting. Real ecology comes down to respect for the living earth. Roosevelt was more than a staunch egoist bent on collecting trophies. He also was a true ecologist whose actions reflected his commitment to protect the earth. Now you know why I pointed out to the young eco-feminists that the forerunner in women's rights was also a hunter and the greatest conservationist the world has known. **Hunting not only leads to *ahisma*, avoiding unnecessary harm, it also promotes stewardship of the living earth.** No wild places, no wild things, it's as simple as that! The hunter has been and still is the foremost champion of the wild.

The second ethic among contemporary hunters is to put back more than they take. There are more deer in America now than at any time in its history, more wild turkeys, more Canada geese. It was the hunters' dollars that paid for the research and nesting and wintering habitat that recovered the bald eagle. The list of merit from the hunter's fire exceeds all other groups combined.

After studying orca whales for twenty years I sought guidance on how I could best serve life. The answer I got was to make a film that would help hunters and non-hunters alike better understand how hunters really feel about hunting, wildlife and nature. Anyone with a background in wildlife biology knows quite well that hunters are by far the most powerful force for environmental conservation, so it is not surprising that I set out to make "The Sacred Hunt" as a creative communication that might promote hunting and reveal its true nature.

Michael Meade and I agree that birthing by women and hunting by men represent the fundamental polarities of human life. As woman expresses one pole of life in giving birth, man represents the other by taking life – for the nurturing of it. That is the evolutionary matrix in which we were formed, and it is the psychic matrix in which we still live. There are fundamental experiences in life that transform us; we call them initiations. A woman's peak initiation into the fullness of life, the one that profoundly connects her with the earth, the creatures, other humans and the divine, is birthing a child. For a male, hunting and killing an animal launches him into responsible adulthood and opens his heart.

Men must resolve a paradox unknown to women, and they do it by flexing biceps and bowing heads. Together, birthing and hunting constitute the field of human life from which all true religious inspiration flows. Within hunting is the prototype and most powerful of all koans – "and the secret hidden deep in that."

Birthing for women and hunting for men initiate them into the sacred dimensions of life. When life – all life – is sacred we walk a sacred path. We avoid causing unnecessary harm, and if we men have been fully initiated in the sacred hunt we put back more than we take. Hunters epitomize the Buddhist principle of compassion, and if Snyder wants to save the quality of the Sierra Nevada mountains of northern California, it might help to enlist his strongest allies: the men and women who hunt deer there! Even under the harshest population control, on ethical grounds none of us would deny a woman's right to birth a baby. If we want to promote the ultimate ethical significance of *ahisma* – stewardship of the biotic community – then we would do well to offer the sacred hunt in a young man's rite of passage.

Dead On the Road Deer

Collecting road killed deer for food, as Snyder and his family have done, will not engender the fierce protection of nature exemplified by hunters. Gary says, "And by keeping a sharp eye on the roadside I have saved myself the quandry of whether to hunt or not to hunt deer." "The practice of the wild" is anything but pious, and surely does not insulate itself from quandry. Elsewhere Gary points out that Zen meditation sets sail for the unknown, that it takes on equally all dimensions of consciousness. He reminds us that no one ever said it is comfortable or easy. Neither is life, of course; the Buddha said, "Life is pain and suffering." Gary is right to say that the nature of life as suffering is no justification for ignoring it, but if the First Precept does mean to avoid causing unnecessary harm, it does not mean to avoid unnecessary suffering. I suffer when I kill our roosters as when I shoot a pheasant or goose. If Gary is going to eat dead-on-the-road deer to relieve his suffering, then can he also accept the nature of life as suffering and kill a deer for food? Nobody ever said it was easy.

Good Hunting to All that Keep the Jungle Law

Norbert Weiner, progenitor of cybernetics, wrote a book entitled *The Human Use of Human Beings*, and in it said that in spite of all the machines we must function on our own level – the human level. C.A. Meier, the disciple of Carl Jung, asks,

> "And what of the self-regulation of nature, when she is no longer left to herself, when she is excessively interfered with, and too badly wounded to be able to recover?... One thing is certain: we are in great danger of losing our humanity as a result of this unrelenting process of destruction. If therefore you equally relentlessly make attempts at preserving the wilderness, you are not only doing something idealistic or idealogical, but rather something substantial for the health of men globally."

Meier asks how we can maintain sanity in the face of the destruction of the wilderness without, which is at the same time a direct attack on the wilderness within. He answers, "First of all, we must frankly admit that, in spite of our culture, we are still mammals, natural beings. This aspect of our being, last but not least, is forgotten by that selfsame culture; we are, as we say, unconscious of its archeological, prehistoric existence and reality in the unconscious part of our psyche." He ends his provocative essay with the quote from Rudyard Kipling's Jungle book, "Good hunting to all that keep the Jungle Law!"

Like Zen, Jungle Law is paradoxical: life lives on death. Coyote is sheer paradox, the divine devil. It is Coyote who reveals our nature to us. Coyote is creator and destroyer, a trickster-genius and a moron, fire and water, ego and soul. He is a walking contradiction whose message is simple: life *is* paradox, get used to it.

Until quantum physics, western science viewed all paradox as yet unsolved mystery which will be resolved by reason. And if we can't find the moral of the story then we see it as having no real usefulness, to which Coyote says, "Lighten up!" Science conducts controlled experiments to isolate variables and their causal influence, all to give us more control over nature, our bodies, our enemies. Once I wrote in a whimsical poem that being in control means knowing what is out of control. It is our fear that motivates us to control others and our world; those who are fearless, who live with faith and trust are not concerned about exerting control to protect themselves from the unknown. Coyote teaches us to accept the things we may never understand.

Coyote is the sportiveness of life, "random, bawdy, irreverent, foolish, inconsistent and destructive, a frightening package...these qualities imply anarchy and chaos....he is also the creative force to Native Americans in the universe."

Coyote's wild adventures often land him in big trouble, and he often gets himself and others killed in the process, but life goes on as coyote remakes himself from some remnant of his former self. Coyote embodies things we can't change or understand, and he must be accepted for who he is. For all his infantile behavior, coyote is actually about maturity and accepting our limitations. But he is not without power because he also has the power to change the things he can. He is a risk-taker secure in the knowledge that no matter what happens tomorrow is another story and he'll be there to live it.

If we were more like coyote we would enjoy life more, much more, precisely because we would not live in fear nor the anxiety of uncertainty. Coyote knows there is no end to the story, there are only more episodes – reminiscent of Buddhism's doctrine of reincarnation. We profess to believe but we really do not. We have lost the spirit of coyote and for us time is running out every second of every day. As Chopra says, those who have all the time in the world live longer than those who are always running out of time. Coyote will never die.

According to the Caddo people, in the very old times there was no death and soon the world became crowded. The chiefs of the different animals assembled and agreed that everyone should die for a while then return to life, but coyote disagreed saying that it would become just as crowded even though it might take longer. Coyote was outvoted. The chiefs built a special lodge facing east, and when the first animal, a human, died, its body was put in the lodge and the medicine people sang a renewal song. As a whirlwind blew in from the west, coyote rushed into the lodge and shut the door. The whirlwind blew away and ever since that time death has lasted forever.

Because coyote sabotaged the will of the other chiefs, he was afraid, which is why, to this very day, he slinks across the prairie often looking back over his shoulder for whirlwinds and angry animals.

Coyote was the wise one in this story since he knew that life and death feed each other, something the animal rightists really don't fathom. They would prevent us from participating in the food chain, if they could, and for many of them, all living creatures should live forever in their present bodies until there would be no space left for anyone. They think it is immoral for a man to kill and eat a deer just as it is morally wrong for a lion to kill a wildebeest. But they are not aligned with coyote, nor even the deer, which, though a teacher of gentleness, nonetheless gives of its body and spirit willingly for the benefit of its animal and human kin. As my friend, a lama, said, "They don't get it, everything has consciousness." Well, perhaps everything except humans separated from nature.

So to those who claim to be fighting for the rights of animals, ask them to listen to brother coyote: life and death both are necessary whether we like it or not. Bodies die, spirits don't. "Accept the things you cannot change or control." The path to happiness is not resistance of what is inevitable. The path to happiness is simple: it means to choose happiness. Coyote knows we have free will, but the masses of humanity who suffer from victim programming as a result of buying into Newtonian thinking, believe that they are subject to the whims of so many universal laws, so many causes. They feel powerless. Feeling powerless they identify with the animals which they see as being helpless against the hand of humanity, so they strike out in anger without seeing that their fundamental beliefs about themselves and reality lock them into a prison they built.

Prayer to Deer

I HAD NEED.
I HAVE DISPOSSESSED YOU OF YOUR BEAUTY, GRACE AND LIFE.
I HAVE TAKEN YOUR SPIRIT FROM ITS WORDLY FRAME.
NO MORE WILL YOU RUN IN FREEDOM
BECAUSE OF MY NEED.

I HAD NEED.
YOU HAVE IN LIFE SERVED YOUR KIND IN GOODNESS.
BY YOUR LIFE, I WILL SERVE MY BROTHERS AND SISTERS.
WITHOUT YOU I HUNGER AND GROW WEAK.
WITHOUT YOU I AM HELPLESS, NOTHING.

I HAD NEED.
GIVE ME YOUR FLESH FOR STRENGTH.
GIVE ME YOUR COVERING FOR PROTECTION.
GIVE ME YOUR BONES FOR MY LABORS,
AND I SHALL NOT WANT.

If Buddhism is interpreted to mean that killing sentient creatures is wrong, then it is a denial of the fundamental nature of the human as hunter. As such it denies our inner wilderness, our Buddha nature. If, on the other hand, one interprets Buddhism as Snyder has, to avoid causing unnecessary harm, it is an affirmation of human nature or hunting as the original lifestyle that still is the foundation of human psychology, spiritual life and ethics.

Taoism always has appealed to me as it often does to European people who undertake a brief but scrupulous examination of eastern religions. If ever there were a religion that speaks to the heart of civilized humanity it is Taoism; after all, it points to the vaulted pride and folly of civilization and calls us back to nature and the fundamental forces of life. When in doubt, one should go fishing! Joseph Campbell was an avid fisherman, and his understanding of the innocence of hunting and fishing represented by Taoism was reflected in his work. The first precept of Taoism appears to be harmony, living in balance, in the wilderness of the psyche and outwardly in nature. From harmonious living, the First Precept of Buddhism flows naturally.

Machine Worries, Machine Hearts

There is a famous story from Chuang Tzu, a Fourth Century B.C. Taoist, about "The Arts of Mr. Hun Tun," also known as "The Chaos." It is a timeless message for civilization, which invariably devotes itself to "expanding economy," at the expense of nature and therefore the soul of natural man.

Tzu-kung traveled south to Ch'u, and on his way back through Chin, as he passed along the south bank of the Han, he saw an old man preparing his fields for planting. He had hollowed out with an opening by which he entered the well and from which he emerged, lugging a pitcher, which he carried out to water the fields. Grunting and puffing, he used up a great deal of energy and produced very little result.

> "There is a machine for this sort of thing," said Tzu-kung. "In one day it can water a hundred fields, demanding very little effort and producing excellent results. Wouldn't you like one?"
>
> The gardener raised his head and looked at Tzu-kung, "How does it work?"
>
> Tzu-kung explained how a well sweep works "so fast that it seems to boil right over!"
>
> The gardener flushed with anger then said with a laugh, "I've heard my teacher say, where there are machines, there are bound to be machine worries; where there are machine worries, there are bound to be machine hearts. With a machine heart in your breast, you've spoiled what was pure and simple; and without the pure and simple, the life of the spirit knows no rest. Where the life of the spirit knows no rest, the Way (Tao) will cease to buoy you up. It's not that I don't know about your machine; I would be ashamed to use it!"

Essentially, as Miyuki says about the story, it attempts to articulate the "feminine functioning of the ego," in contrast to the ego's masculine functioning, as seen in Sam Keen's "homo faber," the controller, manipulator and dominator of nature. The ego's feminine functioning is, as Confucius reminds us, an art and it is closely related to the healing process of nature within and without. The boy's instinct thrusts him into nature to pursue and overtake the wild animal. But in the process he is seduced by his own keen alertness with which he transcends himself and becomes one with the animal and the environment. Then, when he kills the beautiful animal, with which he has identified and which in life gave him meaning, he feels at one level as though he has killed himself. And indeed he has. No wonder he adopts "ahisma," the ethic of avoiding unnecessary harm. No wonder he champions nature. It has become his true home and it lives now within.

The old gardener is ashamed to use a well sweep because it represents "excessive interference with nature," neglecting the purity and simplicity of the heart. Excessive interference with nature is the same as "unnecessary harm."

When Pearce refers to "ego-intellect" he means what Miyuki does by "masculine functioning of the ego," and by "intelligence," Pearce means what Miyuki does by "feminine functioning of the ego." Just as Michael Meade sees the hunt as the fundamental experience by which instinctive passion is tempered by feminine compassion, in the initiation of a boy to manhood, Miyuki says, "It is, then, of primary importance...

to cultivate the feminine way of ego functioning, although it may appear somewhat nonsensical for the masculine ego and will certainly require painstaking work." In primal cultures, that work is known as initiation. It produces men who are able protectors and providers but who also are men of heart, men who will not interfere too much with nature, take more than they need or cause unnecessary harm.

Not Who You Eat But Who Eats You

Up north in British Columbia where we were befriending wild orcas in the wilderness, I took Jim Nollman fishing for salmon. Jim had his own crew at Boat Bay where they focused on musical communication with orcas. One of his guests was a Tibetan Buddhist lama from Vancouver who heartily ate the salmon Jim and I caught that day. Soon the lama and I were launched into a far-ranging discussion about carnivory. He said to me, "Why it's a wonder you people don't moo!" Meaning moo like a cow because we eat so much beef, but it was not the quantity of beef to which he referred, but the fact that we don't consciously interact with the spirits of the cows we eat to help them on their journey. Instead, he said, we take that cow energy into our bodies, and, I suppose, become more cow-like, like Ted Nugent's sheeple.

So I said to him, "But you people (meaning Tibetans) eat cow meat!" "Yes," he replied, "but we do something with it." Months later I shared the lama's comments with my poet friend, Charles Cameron, who laughed and said, "So what's important is not who you eat but who eats you."

As he sat there devouring salmon, I asked him if he were accumulating karma by eating the salmon, and he said no, that the person who killed it received the karma. I became a bit infuriated at that point and said, "You mean to tell me that Jim and I have the karma from killing these salmon, but those of you who eat it get none?" He nodded his head yes. "But what if you ask me to go out and catch a salmon for you to eat, doesn't that count for something? If the original intention is yours and I simply carry out the plan, don't you deserve some of the karma?" He shook his head no and ate more salmon.

Is karma merely a doctrine, a belief? Perhaps if you adhere to the Buddhist doctrine of karma and you interpret *ahisma* to mean it is wrong to kill sentient animals then it might be wrong for you to kill animals for food. The critical question is whether karma arises solely from our beliefs, meaning we create it, or is it an absolute system of right and wrong action. Could the lama be both right and wrong? Right that it would be wrong for him to kill a salmon, but wrong that I collected some karma because I did. If I had felt wrong about killing the salmon then I would have acquired karma. I felt sad about killing them, not wrong, and felt good eating them. Based on the universal perception of hunting peoples regarding exactment of dues for offending animals, e.g., by "causing unnecessary harm" or failure to pay proper respect, I am inclined to believe that their belief in karma is based on millennia of experience in which they have learned that the consequences of wrong action are real and based on more than human belief. Certainly the Salmon Nation has continued to be generous with me and the people I have won over to their camp. It is also true that I always have given abundant blessing and thanks for its gifts.

I don't eat road kills because I feel that they are contaminated energetically, that they did not die in a sacred way, and that the meat may be full of "fear," the hormones from a stressful death. Beyond that I believe that if a person is going to eat meat, wear shoes or do anything that contributes to the death of an animal he/she could profit from killing an animal for food or clothing. Then that person may actually make a decision based on direct experience about their actions as a consumer of other living things.

Checking Deer at a Slaughterhouse

Because I had checked deer two seasons in Illinois, the Missouri Game Department was eager to employ me over the holidays. A starving graduate student, I needed the money, and among the graduate students in zoology who aimed to become wildlife biologists, there was a certain degree of honor bestowed on those who checked deer.

They assigned me to a small town in the hills of central Missouri, a farming community where people spoke German as well as English and each year tourists came from all over the state to celebrate Oktoberfest. My station was the local slaughterhouse, selected by the department because most hunters brought their deer there to be processed, packaged and stored in lockers.

Though I had been around livestock all my life, and while my duties as a deer checker included handling carcasses, removing jaws so that future checkers could learn to age deer by examining tooth wear, and cutting eyes out so biologists could weigh lenses to improve aging technique, I had never actually slaughtered a cow or hog or seen it done. In fact, I had never killed an animal larger than a goose, and despite hunting deer with a bow and letting probable victims escape, I had sworn off hunting mammals altogether.

Actually, the check station consisted of a weight scale beneath a cardboard sign alerting hunters to report here with their tags and deer. But after hours of standing in the cold, I sought comfort inside the one-room slaughterhouse. I had caught glimpses of bodies being cut, and heard the firing of a .22 pistol which I assumed was used to kill the animals, but I was reluctant to watch.

The butcher reminded me of a character in a vampire movie, the moron who was devoted to Count Dracula, the man held in an insane asylum where he stood on his head in the corner of the cell and ate spiders. He seemed quite unemotional, somewhat bored and yet precisely professional about his trade. His two sons were preschool age. They looked like little elves scampering bare foot around steaming piles of guts and pools of coagulated blood. Like their father, the sight, smell and sound of death were old hat to them.

A large Hampshire hog was next in line from the chute leading up to the slaughter-room door. The boys kept asking their father if it was time yet, and when he said okay, the boys slapped sticks across the hog's rump until it moved forward into the squeeze-cage just inside the doorway. With lightning speed the butcher clamped the hog tight inside the steel bars, put his pistol to the hog's head and fired a shot. The hog fell to its side, screamed loudly over and over as blood spurted from its skull. It lay there struggling to right itself and flailing the air with its legs, as the butcher leaned over and cut its throat to let it bleed to death. The hog was butchered alive. I forced myself to watch and tried to hide my pain from the butcher, who never once looked my way. Within two minutes he had cut the body in half, gutted it and hanged it on a motorized pulley. His handiness with knives was awesome.

Next in line was a Holstein heifer. She reminded me of the dairy cows on my grandfather's farm, and having convinced myself that cows are mere robots, reduced by breeding to bodies without souls, I was troubled by the countenance of terror in her eyes. No doubt, she was very frightened and had to be beaten before she entered the room. Perhaps it was the hideous cries of the dying hog that alerted her to the danger lurking within. With bulging eyes and bellowing, she collapsed on the concrete from a single bullet. In seconds her intestines and stomach lay severed from her body, peristalsis moving partially digested hay further down the alimentary tract, and within a few more seconds the two halves of her body were hanging from hooks. Both halves of her bloodless heart beat rhythmically as so much meat disappeared into the cold room.

Each time I teach wildlife biology or environmental ethics, I swear that I'll take the students on a field trip to a slaughterhouse, but when the time approaches, they and I find some good excuses not to go. None of us want to witness the horror of it all. And it is not merely the killing of animals that keeps us away, but the manner in which it's done: industrialized killing, no caring, no feeling, no heart, no love or thanks for the animal, nothing sacred, which is why some meat-eating humans slaughter their own animals. A visit to a slaughterhouse leads one either to give up eating meat or humanely killing animals for oneself.

I don't believe we take on karma when we kill an animal or plant for food, if we do so from a point of innocence. When we knowingly cause unnecessary harm we feel guilty, but in either case the least we can do is sincerely thank and bless the animal or plant we kill. That's what the Lakota people call "making sacred." If it is our intention to cause unnecessary harm that brings us karma, it is also our intention that makes repentence possible. Again, we all kill, we all do harm, what we all do not do is make sacred. For me there are two fundamental ways of living: with or without sacredness. A sense of the sacred comes from feeling that we are part of something greater than ourselves. That deep felt sense of interdependence is what fosters *ahisma* and stewardship, and for many men it is the hunt that transforms life from the separation of egoism to the transcendence of interdependence.

We Are All Hunters

The hunter is the original ecologist and the original Buddhist! If you want to know something the Buddha doesn't know speak to a skilled hunter for whom *ahisma* is the First Precept. We are all hunters. We all take sentient life. Perhaps my response to Gary twenty years ago was warranted, though the anger wasn't, for which I since apologized.

In struggling with the First Precept during his training in Zen, Snyder noticed that some of the masters ate fish when they were away from the monastery.

"One time I was visiting at the temple of a roshi near Mount Fuji and asked him why it is that some priests and monks eat meat or fish. He responded heartily, 'A Zen man should be able to eat dog shit and drink kerosene.' My own teacher was a strict vegetarian. Once he said to me, 'Just because I eat pure food, and some of the other priests do not does not mean that I am superior to them. It is my own way of practice. Others have their ways. Each person must take the First Precept as a deep challenge, and find his way through life with it.'"

In response to a letter from a vegetarian to the editor of *Carnivore* journal about the many sins of carnivorosity, I said something along the same lines.

To A Vegetarian

"Thank you for your 19 points about the dangers of carnivorosity, sent to *Carnivore*.

Carnivore does not promote carnivory; it explores among other things, the role that carnivory has played in human evolution and behavior, humanity's rise to dominance over other lifeforms and the origin of the contemporary crisis (social and environmental) in these terms. However, my personal reflections on the matter of diet are as follow.

There is a Hindu yogi in Washington State who heals people, and he eats junk food from the local hamburger spot, burgers and animal-fat fried potatoes, everything. There are some highly evolved, I guess, Tibetan Buddhists who say that if we westerners knew what we were doing to ourselves when we eat meat we'd be astonished. But they eat meat! They seem to be saying what a western mystic healer, Jack Schwartz, says about smoking: it's not what we eat or inhale but what we do with it that counts. Perhaps they hold a secret about transmutation of animal flesh, some psycho-spiritual process?

Perhaps if one strongly believes that meat – or anything – is unhealthy then it will be. If Alice Bailey is right perhaps negative thoughts about eating meat actually make meat harmful for people who eat it. Supposedly speaking for an ascended master known as The Tibetan, she also says that different people need different diets.

There's also Gary Snyder, the Zen Buddhist and environmentalist, who told me once that he eats dead-on-the-road deer – I call them dords for short. He wrote about the risks of piety and self-righteousness. The vegetarian Krishnamurti says over and over that the man who says he knows does not know, and that what is is sacred. Carnivores, too.

Being careful about one's diet is fine, but being care-ful means to be full of care: for your enemies, carnivores, killers of innocent rice and beans. Forgive me, but I wonder if maybe one could eat shit and thrive if one thought well enough of it?

As the editor of *Carnivore* many people ask me if I eat meat. Only my dog knows for sure, and like all dogs, she's a shit-eater – but I don't kick her."

When Snyder's teacher said, "Each person must take the First Precept as a deep challenge, and find his way through life with it," he was saying what it means to think with the heart, what a man may learn from hunting.

Outside of hunting, efforts to maintain environmental quality largely amount to rearguard actions. So called environmentalists may win some battles but overall they are losing the war against unsustainable economic growth. **If there is a difference between**

hunters and non-hunting environmentalists, it is the depth of connection that hunters have with the earth. Hunters depend on wild animals and places at every level of their being. For them, hunting is the highest meaning of life itself. I once defined hunting this way:

> "Re-creational hunting is a ritual that establishes a relationship of mutual interdependence with animals and Nature. Hunting is a ritual that honors the animals and the earth on which the hunter depends spiritually and physically."

Snyder says that,

> "So far it has been the earlier subsistence cultures of the world, especially the hunters and gatherers, who have – paradoxically – most beautifully expressed their gratitude to the earth and its creatures. As Buddhists we have something yet to learn on that score. Animals and plants live mutually on each other, and throughout nature there is a constant exchange of energy – a cycle of life and death affairs. Our type of universe is described in sutras as a realm of *kama*, of biological desire and need, which drives everything."

Unless a person has hunted he may not fathom the truth in Ortega's description of the Paleolithic man who dwells in each of us. He says, "It has always been at man's disposal to escape from the present to that pristine form of being a man, which, because it is the first form, has no historical suppositions. 'Natural' man is first 'prehistoric' man – the hunter. But by hunting, man succeeds, in effect, in annihilating all historical evolution, in separating himself from the present, and in renewing the primitive situation."

Hunting is a unified field of human experience, our most fundamental nature, ever ready to leap into the present. The religious posture towards the animal is no different for a contemporary civilized hunter than it is for a pygmy or Bushman. Though most hunters today have not been raised in a culture of "making sacred," nonetheless many conduct their own personal ceremony for the animals they kill. This was brought home to me in my own life since I started blessing and thanking rabbits and pheasants at an early age, without any exposure to such practices. For years I thought I was exceptional until I made "The Sacred Hunt" film and interviewed scores of hunters who spontaneously had done the same.

The Heart of Compassion

In another essay, "A Village Council of All Beings," Snyder reflects on experience that awakens the heart of compassion as "The intimate perception of interconnection, frailty, inevitable impermanence, and pain..." I know of no experience more effective in awakening the heart of compassion than hunting. The burning desire of the instinct to hunt that propels us to pursue the animal, paradoxically places us into that intimate experience of the animal's suffering and death and shocks us into instant awareness of our own mortality as well as the necessity of balancing our passion with compassion.

Describing the well intentioned but misplaced compassion of early Buddhists in China, Snyder mentions monks who purchased and ceremonially released caged pigeons and fish, the focus being on individual lives, rather than populations and the habitats on which they depend. He says,

> "Even as the Buddhists were practicing vegetarianism and kindness to creatures, wild nature in China suffered significant species extinction and whole-sale deforestation between the fifth and fifteenth centuries A.D. India too was vastly deforested well before modern times....To save the life of a single parrot or monkey is truly admirable. But unless the forest is saved, they will all die."

The First Principle of wildlife management, the application of ecological principles to the conservation of wildlife, is to sustain populations of wildlife by maintaining suitable habitat. However lofty their goals, animal welfarists are like those Chinese Buddhists who saved some individual organisms but lost the species. They can not see the forest for the trees. They would put an end to hunting on the grounds of cruelty, but their efforts would not promote environmental conservation, what all wildlife needs.

Members of Ducks Unlimited kill individual ducks and geese but they also conserve vast tracts of wetlands that produce populations of millions of waterfowl, far more than they kill. Those wetlands are homes to hundreds of specics of birds and mammals, thousands of species of invertebrates and plants, the number of individual organisms being astronomical. After merely 20 years the members of the Rocky Mountain Elk Foundation have conserved four million acres while successfully reintroducing elk throughout the midwest and east where elk were exterminated 150 years ago. Once again the hunters present a model for what it means to "put back." The National Wild Turkey Federation has done the same for wild turkeys. The members of Pheasants Forever do likewise, and here in my county they plant species that provide critical winter cover not only for pheasants but countless other species.

At the end of "A Village Council of All Beings," Snyder discusses education of young people, "We must further a spiritual education that helps children appreciate the full interconnectedness of life and encourage a biologically informed ethic of nonharming." In this instance, as we've already seen, by "nonharming" Gary really means avoiding unnecessary harm.

For each member of Ducks Unlimited there have been nearly 12 acres of productive wildlife habitat conserved to the benefit of the entire community of living things. If these men and women can translate their love of nature which was fostered in a duck blind when they were young, into hundreds of millions of dollars to protect the living earth in a time when the sheer insanity of expanding economy threatens the survival of the biosphere, what do you think five million of them might do, or fifty million? Tragically, at the very time when the earth needs them most the ranks of hunters are dwindling, in part because parents and educators do not understand the immense value of hunting to development of character and virtues.

The First Precept always has been at work in my life: we live-trap mice from the house and barn and release them in the shed where we throw a week's rations on the floor to help them make a new start, but in the fall when so many mice invade the house that we cannot live-trap them fast enough, out come the snap traps. We release insects from spiders to flies and moths. But it was hunting that made me acutely aware of its meaning, and I have adhered to it ever since. The problem with doctrines is that they begin to live us, however lofty the principles, but no set of doctrines can encompass the breadth and depth of our life, which is why the Buddhists say, "If you see the Buddha on the road kill him."

A Treaty with the Deer

The Ojibwe tell a story about a time when all the deer had vanished from the land. The humans roamed everywhere looking for them. Owl, who sees the future, found them all in a large corral in the far north. The deer fed and carried on as though they were fine. The owl was curious so he flew to the corral to question the deer. A flock of crows attacked the owl and drove it away. Because it was night, owl escaped harm.

Owl reported the location of the deer to the humans who formed a war party to rescue the deer. Owl led them back to the corral, but when they arrived the crows attacked fiercely, and the battle went on for days. The deer simply watched the battle and made no effort to escape.

Finally the chief of the humans sought a truce. He asked the deer why they seemed unconcerned about the attempt to rescue them, especially since the war party had suffered so many losses. The chief of the deer explained that they were in this place by choice as the crows had treated them far better than the humans ever had. He went on to say that the humans had wasted their flesh, desecrated their bones and spoiled their land. The two-leggeds had dishonored the deer and therefore themselves. After all, the deer chief added, "Without you we can live very well, but without us you die."

The humans agreed to stop offending the lives, death and spirits of the deer, so the deer followed them back to their homes. Today the oldest and most sacred treaty of the Ojibwe is with the deer.

I pray for the cow nation because so many humans kill and consume and wear their bodies without honoring them. As Jim Eaglesmith said to me, the cow is the most abused animal on earth. Genesis may say that into our hands are they delivered, but it does not say that we need not honor and be grateful for them.

If Christians would adhere to the doctrine that "The Kingdom of Heaven is within ye," would they look inward and know better than to take for granted the life of the many organisms that feed, clothe and house us? Learning to think with the heart comes through proper initiation, and traditionally that process included the taking of a life. It still is the most powerful path a young man may walk.

It may be a great paradox, but many a young man would do well to take up hunting to find his heart and become a true hunter, one who takes only what he needs, puts back more than he takes and protects nature. Such a man would be a perfect Buddhist. If the truth be known, hunting is a model for ethical living in the world today.

Perhaps it is clear that after all these years of apparent confusion and conflict surrounding hunting, Snyder and I are still on the same page.

In Part III of *A Place in Space*, Snyder writes an essay about Reinhabitation, and ultimately urges us to follow his lead and colonize marginal lands and steward them with the 7th generation in mind. He's certainly having a good time doing it in the Sierra foothills, but then he comes out periodically, as he says, to rob the treasuries of college campuses where he speaks or teaches. Most of us would find it more difficult to live as well as he does on marginal lands. But at the rate of exploitation of the planet that's where we'll end up, if we're lucky! The wise ones will find their way clear to make the move sooner rather than later. I did it first in 1980, and then again in 1997.

He is absolutely right that the ethics or morality of interdependence is "far more subtle than merely being nice to squirrels." The science of ecology has been laying out a spiritual dimension for some time, and not merely implicitly as Gary says, but explicitly.

Aldo Leopold insisted that we need to extend the social ethic, which, after Kroptotkin, he perceived to be the universal ethic, to the land, thus the "land ethic." Snyder thinks we should integrate the knowledge of the nutrient and energy cycles into our own personal spiritual quest and these with the wisdom of the recent past. The expression of it, he says, is simple: "feeling gratitude to it all; taking responsibility for your own acts; keeping contact with the sources of the energy that flow into your own life (namely, dirt, water, flesh)."

Clearly, Aldo Leopold did agree. *A Sand County Almanac* still stands above all other nature writing of the 20th Century.

In "The Rediscovery of Turtle Island," Snyder calls for the end to human uniqueness; I have said as much elsewhere, though with the proviso that what is unique about the human race is its position as the behavioral and ecological dominant of the planet. Not the best creature under the sun, but the one whom all others fear and for good reason. The quest for dominant status among awesome predators, accomplished prior to firearms, surely is the most surprising achievement of the human race. Winning the lion's share represents a turning point in our relationship to the planet and to one another since, once we achieved top rank, other humans became our primary competitors, the fate of lions and wolves before us. The dangerous shift came with the success of achieving dominance because that transferred to an egotistical stance of domination and control over nature. It has been downhill ever since; our global environmental crisis was inevitable the day that Hercules slayed the Nemean lion.

Humanity has been living in the "shadow" of Hercules ever since. The "Users" as Snyder terms them are the exploiters of the multiple- or wise-use movement, in contrast with the savers who want to hold some parts of nature in its pristine state. Generally the users are aligned with development, the savers are against development (once they have their own wilderness cabin). Savers can be radically anti-human, ousting Bushman from the Kalahari Gemsbok Preserve where they have coexisted for hundreds of years. They can be insensitive to local ranchers, farmers or loggers whose livelihood and lifestyle stand in the way of wilderness preservation.

In developing a culture of nature, a key consideration is our ethical obligation to the nonhuman world. The central threads of animism and paganism celebrate, "the actual with its inevitable pain and death, and affirms the beauty of the process. Add contemporary ecosystem theory and environmental history to this, and you get a sense of what's at work."

The very act of hunting gives life and meaning to the nonhuman world. And if anyone celebrates the inevitable pain and death, and affirms the beauty of the process, it is the hunter.

There can be no moral philosophy that does not presuppose a radical philosophy. In our search for nature-culture, we would do well to embrace interdependence as philosophy. Ortega also said that the true psychology would be the authentic philosophy, and in keeping with Jungianism, we can say that our life is interdependent not only between ego and world but also between ego and the unconscious. It is our responsibility then to steward the wilderness without as well as the wilderness within; they, too, are interdependent.

The hunter embodies Ortega's philosophy: his life transcends his ego and encompasses his circumstances – the animal and the environment. The hunter knows full well that his life is interdependent with the animal and the environment.

It seems to me that we have in the hunt the pre-existing foundation for a "culture of nature," which represents interdependence and which is transcendent, ethical and religious.

What About Ego?

The essay on "The Etiquette of Freedom" is quite remarkable. Snyder presents a meaningful overview of the last 500 years in the Occident and its loss of contact with nature. During this period Europeans also made contact with numerous primal societies, which became a source of doubt about civilization.

All well and good until we arrive at Snyder's description of consciousness and ego. He says, as Krishnamurti often did, that consciousness is the world, "You are the world," meaning that consciousness is the content of consciousness. Ortega y Gasset came to the same point in his development of the philosophy of co-existence: if we examine consciousness we discover that the "radical fact of living" is that living is problematical at the core. The nature of problem is our interaction with and relationship to the world, another convergence with Krishnamurti who said that life consists of relationship with "other beings, ideas and the world."

Many people equate consciousness with ego, and the Buddha is credited with using the term "defensive ego-consciousness." If we define ego as consciousness and consider its primary function to be survival, protection and defense of the body – and by extension, offspring and those on whom our and their survival may depend – then consciousness is the origin of the illusory belief in separation and the enormous suffering that it causes.

While it is widely held that ego has a legitimate function – without it the human race might not have survived – the real question is how much influence does it exert in our lives? Is it true, as Krishnamurti and others have insisted, that we have come to equate the ego with the whole mind? That our identity with the body, with material reality, has given the ego control over our lives so that we live in a perpetual state of defensiveness and fear? If that is so then it is "defensive ego-consciousness" that is at the root of our conflict with one another and the world. As Jampolsky put it, love is what remains after all the fear is gone. It follows that if we were unafraid our relationship to one another and the world would be quite different, i.e., we would not be waging war or facing an environmental crisis.

Snyder takes a different point of view. He says, "The conscious agenda-planning ego occupies a very tiny territory, a little cubicle somewhere near the gate, keeping track of some of what goes on in and out (and sometimes making expansionistic plots), and the rest takes care of itself." I only wish Snyder were right; unfortunately, I side here with those who see the contemporary ego of Western man as occupying nearly the whole territory of consciousness. It is not that consciousness and ego are actually identical, one and the same, in all societies or in every individual. Snyder's ego just might be tiny compared to my own, and in primal societies ego tends to stay more or less in the corner it belongs. The global crisis generated by Western civilization cannot be understood in any meaningful way without identification of ego (fear, insecurity, materialism) as the ultimate culprit, thus the absolute importance of discovering what sorts of developmental processes, experiences and education tend to promote egoism and what tends to minimize it.

We are born with the potential of expressing a broad range of ego, of becoming extremely egotistical or nearly egoless. **Does the solution to the environmental crisis on earth eventually comes down to how we raise our children**? On the one hand that may be hopeful; on the other, it takes true human societies with wise elders and intimacy with nature to raise "nearly egoless" human beings. (See Chapter 5) It takes full bonding at each developmental stage coupled with demanding rites of passage to produce men of heart who serve and "fiercely protect" society as well as nature. Our work is cut out for us!

If we are in the period of "precollapse" of civilization, a term Snyder uses, then along with trying to save what we can of the lifeforms and ecosystems that remain, it is imperative that we begin to plan for the recovery of healthy development of our young. For many of us that will mean learning from primal peoples what they do to make young men and women functioning members of society. Since it is quite possible that we will not be able to stop or significantly retard the rollercoaster of unsustainable economy, then the least we can do is rediscover, invent and adopt the kinds of ethics and lifestyles that are conducive to sustainable living and stewardship, not only of the environment but of future generations. All of which makes Gary Snyder's writing about "the practice of the wild" extremely significant in this time.

For those of us who are elders or soon to be, it comes down to choosing what we really want for our descendents. Is it shopping malls and grand estates or the prospect of living simply in cooperation with one another and the land in ways that permit perpetuation of meaningful living? If we are at the edge of collapse perhaps it is something to welcome.

It is true that the fork in the trail we call Cartesianism is responsible in the West for what I have termed "the great corruption." Which happened in China and in every civilization in the history of the world. I once described civilization as dehumanization because that is exactly what it is: a deterioration of active, aware interdependence, socially and environmentally, coupled with rising egoism.

Snyder is right to point out that the country folk have always known the facts of life and death, just as the primal societies do:

> "...they have understood the play of the real world, with all its suffering, not in simple terms of 'nature red in tooth and claw' but through the celebration of the gift-exchange quality of our give-and-take. 'What a big potlatch we are all members of!' To acknowledge that each of us at the table will eventually be a part of the meal is not just being 'realistic.' It is allowing the sacred to enter and accepting the sacramental aspect of our shaky temporal being."

City people tend to forget that there is more to mind than human consciousness, and most seem blind to the wisdom of their wild ancestors who saw each creature as a spirit with intelligence. They also saw other creatures as their kin, and for all these reasons asked permission to take their lives and gave them thanks. Snyder says, "The precept against needlessly taking life is inevitably the first and most difficult of commandments. In their practice of killing and eating with gentleness and thanks, the primary peoples are our teachers: the attitude toward animals, and their treatment, in twentieth-century American industrial meat production is literally sickening, unethical, and a source of boundless bad luck for this society."

The First Precept of Buddhism is adopted directly from universal hunting life and is carried on today by recreational hunters who choose to participate in the practice of the wild to glean those very lessons Snyder would have us learn from the primary peoples.

I once asked Cliff Young, an elderly man who sat on the Nevada state supreme court and who, as president of the National Wildlife Federation was responsible for the ouster of James Watt as Secretary of the Interior, how he would characterize in one word the hunter's relationship to his prey, and his answer was, "kinship."

Hunters **know** animals are intelligent. Hunters **know** that they sit at the same table as mice, groundhogs, bobcats, crows, deer and elk. Unfortunately, many farmers do not know what hunters know today; their relationship to nature is modifying it in ways that turn a piece of ground into a suitable substrate for production of domesticated crops that translate into money in the bank.

The hunter deliberately submerges himself in nature, at foolish expense, precisely because he wants to "practice the wild," and to find himself connected with the actual. He does not aim to dominate nature, as does the farmer, but to enjoy the feeling of being a part of it, subject to its discomforts, whims and excesses. The entire experience is humbling; moreover, it is consciously sought for that very reason. Who else gets up at 4 AM to sit on a tree limb when its ten degrees or stand all day long in a driving blizzard at twenty below zero? For a few pounds of deer meat or a duck one doesn't really need? It gets him outdoors but also out of himself. If the hunt is anything today it is ritual homage to nature. Every true hunter is a Taoist at heart, negating the civilized to honor the wild and the wild in himself.

The entire issue of the commons and the confusion surrounding its shared use historically is expertly addressed by Snyder in his essay, "The Place, the Region and the Commons." When common property was held and managed locally it worked well for everyone and abuses were rare or corrected. The commons are not to be confused with public lands managed by a central government, which have been abused. Snyder says,

> "The commons is a level of organization of human society that includes the nonhuman. The level above the local commons is the bioregion. Understanding the commons and its role within the larger regional culture is one more step toward integrating ecology with economy."

Snyder is adamant that there is no "tragedy of the commons," greater than this, "if we do not recover the commons – regain personal, local, community, and peoples' direct involvement in sharing (in being) the web of the wild world – that world will keep slipping away. Eventually our complicated industrial capitalist/socialist mixes will bring down much of the living system that supports us. And, it is clear, the loss of a local commons heralds the end of self-sufficiency and signals the doom of the vernacular culture of the region."

I am sympathetic to the urgency to govern bioregionally; I also suspect that the recovery of the commons is more likely if the hunters are engaged. Time and again since the Great Depression, they have proved themselves as the most able group at conserving wildlife and wild places. Traditionally, the commons use to provide fish and game to supplement the agrarian diet. License fees and taxes on firearms and ammunition have resulted in billions of dollars for wildlife and millions of acres of wildlife habitat (National Wildlife Refuge system and state lands) which are used by many segments of society for recreation and education. In the State of Washington, license fees have purchased well over one million acres of wild lands that are used for hunting and fishing as well as other recreational and educational purposes. Granted, these are public lands, but their existence speaks to the power hunters possess. Increasingly, recreational hunters in Canada and the US are finding less private land available; even the public lands such as those under the U.S. Forest Service are essentially being made unavailable to them.

Most states now have hunter federations who work to maintain hunter rights but also conserve wildlife and wild lands. Why not enlist hunters into the campaign to recover the commons? Why not unleash their great enthusiasm to establish local commons anew? Who else has been as successful at working together to make things happen for shared wild places? The wild men and women are the first line of defense for things wild. The new environmentalists have something to learn from them.

The Central Issue

In his essay on "Good, Wild, Sacred," Snyder comes back to the central issue facing humanity and the environment. It is one and the same issue that Aldo Leopold confronted in his plea for a land ethic that demands an extension of the "social" ethic of cooperation to the nonhuman community. In short, what motivates people to care as much for nature as they do one another?

The ancient Taoists felt that all social values are false and cater to self-serving values, not much different really than sociobiology which identifies altruism as self-serving, i.e., cooperation can evolve if it serves the reproductive interests of individuals.

Buddhism, says Snyder, takes the middle road by allowing that greed, hatred, and ignorance are intrinsic to ego, but that ego itself is a reflection of ignorance of not seeing who we truly are. Organized society can influence or exploit these weaknesses or it may encourage generosity, kindness and trust, and the outcomes are very significant for us and our world. It boils down to bonding and whether enculturation is positive or negative.

It is true that in hunting cultures stinginess is the worst vice. Snyder says, "We can all agree: there is a problem with the self-seeking human ego. Is it a matter of the wild and of nature? I think not: for civilization itself is ego gone to seed and institutionalized in the form of the State, both Eastern and Western. It is not nature-as-choas which threatens us, but the State's presumption that it has created order." Joe Pearce says that order has been achieved through law, justice, judgment, fear, shame, guilt and punishment, which have generated massive conflict at every level while robbing us of our human potential.

A foremost biologist recently was featured on the cover of a major newsweekly, and in the article he reduced virtually all of human behavior down to selfish genes. It is true that a mallard hen does not nurture all ducklings equally; she nurtures her own ducklings and ignores, even drives away others. According to actuarial data, maternal grandparents are more likely to adopt orphaned grandchildren than paternal grandparents. Because, sociobiology argues, the maternal grandparents know absolutely that the grandchildren are their genetic descendents but the paternal grandparents can not be sure.

We say we love all children, but do most of us give a stepchild the same amount of attention as our own? Even in small hunting/warring societies, such as the pre-colonial Lakota, in which many adults may be identified as father, mother or grandparents, every child still knows its biological parents, and in a crisis will parents come to the aid of their own children first?

Is selfishness our biological nature? Or, is our selfishness an artifact of civilized living which promotes egoism? Do we enter into cooperative relationships solely because they may benefit us – meaning our reproductive fitness? It makes sense that wolves hunt together because they kill bigger animals and eat more meat than they can by hunting alone. Baboons in troops have a higher probability of survival against predators than baboons that forage or sleep alone, and so on.

The fact is that there are genuinely altruistic acts in which individuals sacrifice themselves for the benefit of others without any hope of reproductive benefit to themselves or their kin. Regardless of the influence of reproductive selfishness in human evolution, each one of us is free to be as truly altruistic as we choose even to the point of denying food and dying from starvation.

Snyder is right that civilization encourages egoism, and it also is true that authentic societies are extremely rare in the civilized world. No longer are the survival and reproductive success of individuals directly dependent upon one another, and in a relative sense the value of each individual is diminished as societies dissolve into hierarchies of power filled by anonymous herds. As war machine, civilization places value on acts of heroism against the enemy and rewards its heroes for their individual achievements with status and wealth, both of which feed the ego and may translate into reproductive fitness. It also encourages non-violent competition that results in the accumulation of wealth and power.

So what has all this to do with the practice of the wild, with saving the earth? Snyder claims that more than self-interest inspires his neighbors' undaunted love of the land. I wonder if there is a difference between what Snyder terms self-interest and others call enlightened self-interest? With a world at stake perhaps it is no time to quibble; however, clearly this question of self-interest is a stumbling block about which something needs to be said.

Towards a General Science of Love

"Don't you know what it means to be related to the world?...to feel you are the world and the world is you. Unless you change completely, radically, and bring about a total mutation in yourself, there will be no peace for man."

~ KRISHNAMURTI,
The Awakening of Intelligence

Co-existence means assuming responsibility for the world, "I am me **and** my circumstance, and if I do not save it, I do not save myself." It connects humans to one another, to non-humans and to their world. Only awareness of ego can lead us to the greater reality of life as co-operation; this practical necessity for human survival makes sociobiology acutely appropriate for its time. But, let there be no mistake: it is an old song in a new skin. The separativeness of idealism, what the Hindus ascribe to the illusion of *maya* is the same as Robert Trivers' self-deception: if we deceive ourselves into believing we are unselfish when we are not, then we prevent self-knowledge and ultimately the enlightened self-interest that promotes co-operation.

All this amounts to "profound emotional education" for individuals whose development did not consist of proper bonding coupled with the cultural conditions that discourage egoism and promote cooperation. To transcend ego, what Maslow said is the pinnacle of self-actualization, means to start with recognizing it, accepting it, from moment to moment, non-judgementally. I say non-judgementally because judgement is the work of ego: to condemn ego is simply egoism. Ego cannot be exorcised, extirpated, suppressed or repressed, but awareness of ego through acceptance of it, is a long-established path to psychological freedom, which means peace of mind. The real question then is love. *A Course in Miracles* defines love as wanting good things for others. How do we move from inner conflict, which surely is the origin of conflict between humans, to inner peace and peace among ourselves and with our environment?

The great teachers started at the same point as sociobiology. The Christ and the Buddha saw that human suffering stems from the ego, and that full acceptance and awareness of the process of ego could lead to transcendence – at-one-ment. As Krishnamurti has argued, full acceptance and awareness is love. In other words, it's entirely a matter of how well we live with ego...how well we love ourselves.

The Buddha's essential message is that while personal development must entail self-definition and a livelihood, too great an emphasis on individuation produces a defensive ego-consciousness that becomes closed to change through fear concerning its own maintenance. This closure is a sign of ignorance which only a profound emotional education can dispel.

From the self-love that involves attentive self-awareness, the fear-based process of ego may be transcended. As the Buddha said, "Self is the Lord of self. Where else could the Lord dwell?"

In another word, as we discover that self is the problem we begin to reorder perception in light of self-awareness. Which is to say that awareness of self in the world expands self-interest in that world. If we are to survive, adapt to ourselves and cooperate to make a better life, our philosophy must become, in Ortega's words, "the general science of love." Ortega's philosophy of co-existence, Leopold's ecological ethic, Krishnamurti's radical truth – "you are, there is" – all comply interdependence. When we fully embrace the adaptive truth of interdependence the evolution of self and greater cooperation are possible

Now that we have pushed our environment to its carrying capacity by exploiting the forests, the seas and the earth, by leaving our tracks and smell in every niche and nook, the success of our competitive selfishness may be at an end. We will have to adapt to a world where resources are scarce, where there is overpopulation.

Our new adaptation must involve a major change of viewpoint, so that we can see that competition severely threatens our self-interest, while cooperation between individuals and societies and between them and the environment represents the new adaptive strategy which recovers the Old Ways and Pleistocene values. Today, to have reproductive success, individuals will have to expand their self-interests to encompass more people and more of nature.

To be effective, environmentalism must of necessity incorporate vital human interests and instincts. In recognizing our selfish reasons for doing so we are changing behavior which ultimately will save ourselves. As living beings we cannot escape self-interest. As living beings whose self-interests depend upon the health, viability and diversity of the biosphere, we must take a genuine interest in protecting it.

But all this is intellectual philosophizing. The crucial question remains: why is one person more or less egotistical than another? If all living things have self-interest, what varies is the extent of that self-interest. One person's may extend as far as his body (body, too, is circumstance) or his children, another's may encompass his whole society and the place in which he lives. Or more. The horse rider's interest extends to horses; he/she may protect and nurture them as well as what they depend upon – good pasture, quality range, pure drinking water, etc. A deer hunter's interest extends not only to deer meat, but to all deer, in and out of season, their behavior, their foods and haunts, cover and escape requirements, how they communicate, and the entire living community on which they depend – the key to understanding the extreme extent of hunters' interests.

The Buddha hit on something indispensable when he said defensive ego-consciousness in the extreme requires profound emotional education to dispel. Our (self) interest extends to those beings/things to which we **feel** connected. Which is why it is so important to comprehend bonding processes: they are what influence the extent and strength of our emotional connections to the other. If we are not truly bonded to our mother at birth and infancy, we may never be able to bond with Mother Earth or anything else.

So the question of environmental protection comes down to properly nurturing a young person's spontaneous urge to bond with nature. For boys in adolescence hunting is the archetypal rite of passage that bonds them to nature.

The bonding that occurs at each stage of development is primarily emotional in nature, even though along with secure bonding there may be an intellectual dimension of myth, story and abstract knowledge that reinforces bonding and adds a layer of aesthetic beauty. In young hunters, for example, this intellectual overlay may include the fine intricacies and interdependence of nature – natural history. The imprinting-like state of adolescent males during rites of passage also makes them keenly receptive to the teaching of mentors about adult responsibilities to society, nature and the divine.

By itself, intellectual knowledge of our interdependence with nature will ***not*** bond us to it anymore than a thorough knowledge of economics bonds us emotionally to the baker or electrician or assembly line worker we'll never meet. Professors, teachers, parents and scientists who think abstract concepts, textbooks or TV nature documentaries will bond our youth to nature are wrong. Extensive and intensive interaction with nature is what bonds us to nature.

To grow up and protect nature means identifying with it at each stage of our development. Mother is nature first. We need to be held by her and suck at her breast, and we need dynamic interaction and rough-house play with father, and we need to attend the real school of nature for years before we enter into the rite of passage that will grant us the great responsibility of parenting. Boys become capable providers and men of compassion when they feel inexorably connected to nature and the animals that feed, teach and entertain us.

As an infant sucks at his mother's breast, so the deer sucks at the breast of Mother Earth and when we nurse from the deer we take care of Mother Earth and sing her songs and offer prayers of thanks and put our own bodies back into the earth to feed her deer who one day will feed our children. That feeling of sorrow and deep well of tears that rise up when we kill the deer is a sacrament, a holy communion with all our relations of every tribe, human and nonhuman. A profound emotional education, indeed.

Deep Ecology

The final essay on "Survival and Sacrament" brings into focus the meaning of "Deep Ecology," a field in which Snyder has been a leader. In recognizing the importance of biodiversity and the necessity of preserving species, he tells us that we are in danger of losing our souls, that we are ignorant of what it means to be a human being, and that the meaning of his book is a meditation on what it means to be human. That is not the same justification we discover in books by biologists who plea for biodiversity on practical and aesthetic grounds. Kellert, Wilson and others have made a case for "biophilia," as an evolved trait, as though somehow that would justify it. It seems certain that curiosity is innate, and it leads us to nature, but I suspect biophilia is a potential outcome of bonding processes, and when they are fully realized we do come to feel that the environment has just as much right to existence as ourselves.

Snyder defines Deep Ecology as a belief that "...the natural world has value in its own right, that the health of natural systems should be our first concern, and that this best serves the interests of humans as well." Deep Ecology thinkers, Snyder adds, "... are well aware that primary people everywhere are our teachers in these values..." He acknowledges the conservation thrust of the 1930s, primarily by hunters and fishers, who brought about public land reform and private acquisition of wildlife habitat. In the 1970s, the wildlife conservation movement graduated to environmentalism as concerns evolved beyond the wilderness areas to forest management, agriculture, pollution, nuclear power and so on.

In major sectors of the world, such as the Orient, environmentalism has grown out of concerns for human health, though one could argue that it was the reproductive failures of eagles and other raptorial birds in North America caused by agricultural pesticides in the 60s that gave birth to the "age of ecology." In which case, health concerns were responsible for the rise of environmentalism also in the West. Interestingly, it was wildlife research funded by hunting that provided the strongest shot in the arm for the environmental movement. It also was hunters' dollars for research and wintering and breeding habitat that primarily paid for the recovery of the bald eagle and peregrine falcon.

Snyder says that it is proper that the range of the movement should run from wildlife to urban health, and that "A properly radical environmental position is in no way anti-human." The critical argument now within environmental circles, Snyder says, is

> "...between those who operate from a human-centered resource management mentality and those whose values reflect an awareness of the integrity of the whole of nature... The latter position, that of Deep Ecology, is politically livelier, more courageous, more convivial, riskier and more scientific."

Deep Ecology interfaces Zen at the "Four Great Vows," the first of which is "Sentient beings are numberless, I vow to save them." It is an urging to give life, to undo harm, what the hunters mean by giving back and what they still do better than anyone else.

It all comes back to our attitude about taking life.

> "Primary people have had their own ways of trying to understand the precept of nonharming. They knew that taking life required gratitude and care. There is no death that is not somebody's food, no life that is not somebody's death....The shimmering food-chain, the food-web, is the scary, beautiful condition of the biosphere....A subsistence economy is a sacramental economy because it has faced up to one of the critical problems of life and death: the taking of life for food....Our distance from the source of our food enables us to be superficially more comfortable, and distinctly more ignorant. Eating is a sacrament....We too will be offerings – we are all edible...."

Resolution: "All My Relations" or "All Is One"?

It has become clear to me that the ego-intellect's highest level of comprehension is interdependence, what science calls ecology and what is meant by "all my relations," widespread as a holy phrase among Native American tribes. All living things are related either by sharing DNA or by having a common Creator. When we take responsibility for the world because our survival or success depends on it, our motive may be enlightened but no less in our self-interest.

There is a higher level of awareness and it is unity, as expressed in "though art that," and in Christianity's New Commandment, "Love thy neighbor as thyself," not merely as thy brother. Perhaps we should love our enemy because he is more than friend. Perhaps he is us. Eastern Wisdom asserts that "all is one," and when the Mayans part company they say, "I am another you." The sacred phrase of the Puebla tribe is "Sey Hano!" Which means, "all is one." *A Course in Miracles* claims that while body is legion, mind is one.

Nature is a doorway to Spirit because when we leave the human world behind ego shrinks and spirit expands outward and unites us. In another word, we move from self to Self. Nature is a doorway to spiritual truth.

When Gary Snyder was a logger he killed and "ate" a lot of trees. Now he is busy saving the forests. Members of Ducks Unlimited kill ducks and geese and eat them, and they are busy saving wetlands. Is it impossible to negate self-interest? It is possible to expand it, which means to embrace otherness as much as self, precisely because they are more than interdependent, they are ultimately one and the same life. Every path of transformation teaches us the unity of life.

If I am not mistaken, Gary Snyder is a Buddhist who thinks like a hunter, and I am correct in saying that hunters think like Buddhists. By direct participation in the food chain and bonding with nature we enter the sacred dimensions of life. Then compassion awakens and we vow to avoid causing unnecessary harm and also to give life – to put back – the foundation of conservation.

"I believe much trouble and blood would be saved if we opened our hearts more."

~ Chief Joseph, Nez Perce

Chapter 11

The Healing Power of Ritual

"When a community does something together, that community is very happy, jovial, connected and unified."

~ Larry P. Aitken, Chippewa

Malidoma Some' was born to the Dagara tribe of West Africa, but he was taken at the age of four to be indoctrinated by French Catholics to become one of a generation of black priests. For fifteen years he was isolated from his family, abused and intimidated in an attempt to make him forget everything about his tribal background so he would see the world through the eyes of French culture and the Church.

Remarkably, Malidoma was given continual guidance by the spirit of his grandfather who helped him to resist brainwashing and hold onto his tribal heritage. Finally, after fifteen years of captivity, he escaped and walked 125 miles back to his home village; however, he was unable to use his native language to speak to his mother and father, and the people looked upon him with suspicion because he had been contaminated by the sickness of the colonial world. He had become an outsider in his own world. He decided that the only way to reconnect with his people was to undergo the traditional initiation rites of the Dagara, a month-long ritual that nearly killed him. Eventually, he became a tribal medicine man who also earned advanced academic degrees. He lectures and writes about the important role of ritual in healing the individual and society. He says,

> "The inability of material accumulation to replace the craving for spirit, the loss of viable forms of community, and the all-out epidemics of isolation and individualism, are symptomatic of the crushing effects of the abandonment of rituals....Social decay creeps in when everyday living displaces ritual as the focus. The fading and disappearance of ritual in modern culture is, from the viewpoint of Dagara people, expressed in several ways: the dangerous weakening of links with the spirit world, the general alienation of people from themselves and each other, the frightening violence spreading like a gangrene from the middle of cities, and the militaristic approach to its resolution...there are no elders to help anyone remember, through rites of passage, his or her important role in community and in life...To be able to face our fears, we

must remember how to perform rituals. To remember how to perform rituals, we must slow down… The indigenous world, in trying to emulate Nature, espouses a walk in life which is slow and quiet. The modern world, on the other hand, steams through life like a locomotive, controlled by an intimidating sense of power, carelessness, waste and destruction. Such life eats at the psyche, as it moves its victims faster and faster along, they are progressively emptied of their spiritual and psychic fuel. It is here, consequently, where one's Spirit is in crisis, and speed is the yardstick by which the crisis itself is expressed."

Ortega once said that the only person who hurries through life is sick or insane. Ishi, the last surviving member of a northern California hunting tribe, "considered the white man to be fortunate, inventive, and very, very clever; but childlike and lacking in a desirable reserve, and in a true understanding of Nature – her mystic face; her terrible and her benign power." Anthropologist Kroeber, who befriended Ishi, characterized him as "…the most patient man I ever knew. I mean he had mastered the philosophy of patience, without trace either of self-pity, or of bitterness to dull the purity of his cheerful enduringness…His way was the way of contentment…to be pursued quietly, working a little, playing a little, and surrounded by friends."

Not only do we move too fast, making a ritual life impossible, we also perceive pain as undesirable. Women are given drugs to relieve the pain of birthing, which also drugs their baby at its first and most important rite of passage – bonding with its mother. Michael Meade told me that now people are being given pain killers before they die! What if death is as a passage to a new life, deserving of a ritual at which we are present? We are so insulated from life and death that we live in dire fear of both. In writing about the tendency of parents to sneak a child's sick or aged pet off to be "put to sleep" at the veterinary office, I also addressed the fact that our society considers it "humane" to sweep the streets and alleys of our cities clean of cats and dogs without a proper meal ticket and kills millions upon millions of them each year. Here, too, is a condemnation of the most fundamental assumptions of the animal rights/anti-hunting movement:

"…we project onto animals our own fear of pain and suffering, then kill them to put an end to our pain, not theirs…I suspect that it is our fear of death that prompts us to kill millions of animals in the name of humane treatment.

"Those fortunate enough to have experienced death or at least looked death in the face, no longer fear it. Facing death leaves one in fear only of not having lived well. In other words, our fear of death may account for our failure to live well and to die well. Ignorant of the fact that Life contains death, it isn't really death we fear but the loss of life. Our fear of losing life is so strong as to be a source of much anguish, pain and suffering. Which is why we think that a suffering animal would be better off dead.

"Let me put it this way: if we weren't afraid of dying (loss), we wouldn't be afraid of living, and if weren't afraid of living we wouldn't suffer so much, and if we didn't suffer so much we wouldn't project our fear of it onto animals and kill them.

"Because we don't accept that death is not a loss, and because we don't accept that life contains pain and suffering, our ethics are as perverted as our lives. The problem is that we resist pain and suffering as the radical fact of life, only to create further pain and suffering in futile efforts to escape it. The Buddha said, 'Life is pain and suffering,' and the basic Christian doctrine is that life is a vale of tears. The Spanish philosopher, Ortega y Gasset, defined living as problematical at the core. These doctrines agree and they are right. What isn't right is resisting what is undeniably true.

"The ultimate tragedy is that our ignorance of the fact of living is used to justify killing animals. If the prolongation of suffering were legitimately unethical then we would set about killing ourselves after we'd killed everything else.

"Echoing the ageless wisdom, Jidu Krishnamurti says that what is is sacred. What is includes pain, suffering, misery and death. It seldom occurs to us humans that we could love our misery as much as our joy. That is because we are afraid of life, and in our insecurity forever trying to change an unchangeable reality. There is only one true freedom and that is fearlessness, the state of loving. If Life were sacred to us, if we considered all there is to be sacred, then many problems would suddenly disappear. Here is the only genuine ethic regarding all our relationships, with humans, nonhumans, mountains, oceans and God. What is is sacred."

A ritual life is impossible without the acceptance of pain as a vitally significant communication. Some' agrees,

"More often than not, the fast pace of life, made worse by so many drug substitutes, does not allow us to work through our pain. ..a body in pain is a soul in longing. To shut down the pain is to override the call of the soul to change....Is it possible then to say that pain is good, primarily because it is a call to growth? The Dagara elders would say yes.... The person hears pain as a creative action, and this connects that person with his or her highest self. This connection is in itself a ritual experience awaiting acknowledgement. It pulls the person into the neighborhood of mystery and spirituality. So pain at least teaches us something. It is commotion, emotion, and a call for rebirth. It teaches us that one must return to a code of living that begins with life itself. It draws from nature and seeks to align with what ancient tribal communities have valued for thousands of years: a code of living that allows room for the entire person to exist...ritual means a return to the ancients with a plea for help directed to the world of the spirit...in order for the modern world to heal, it must return to the past, to exactly the point where it began to forget ritual."

Indigenous village life revolves around hunting and/or farming and the practice of ritual. Subsistence interconnects humans and ritual links them to the divine. A life in which everything undertaken is first given ritual treatment generates a sense of belonging and wholeness. The ancestors are there and each day thanks are given to nature. Human output incorporates spirit, and without the inclusion of spirit human achievement becomes dangerous to everything that lives.

It is in this greater context of human life as it has been lived and to which it must return that rites of passage must be based. Entering into ritual is a response to the call of the soul. There can be no sacred life without community. The loss of real community in our life has meant spiritual erosion; we no longer can discriminate between sacred space and profane space. We want everything to "be barren, clear in a predefined way, and ultimately controllable." With the loss of community that comes with a loss of shared subsistence that connects us with the earth and the divine, we have pushed the sacred off into buildings.

Genuine society is founded on interdependence, as we have said, and that interdependence refers to accomplishing with others what cannot be done alone. There can be no ritual life without community. Individual problems and needs become community problems; solving those problems and meeting those needs is founded on mutual trust. Community is necessary to meet the intrinsic needs of every individual, and one of those needs is a deep craving to be seen and honored for who we are. No elder can be an elder without a community in which to be an elder, and no boy can become a young man with a hopeful heart if there is no elder present in his life when his soul calls him to be reborn.

In initiation, Eliade says, death has a positive value. It becomes a womb of transformation to a new identity. Meade adds,

> "Loss of identity and even feeling betrayal of one's self are essential to rites of passage. In that sense, every initiation causes a funeral and a birth; a mourning appropriate to death and a joyous celebration for the restoration of full life. Without conscious rituals of loss and renewal, individuals and societies lose the capacity to experience the sorrows and joys that are essential for feeling fully human."

In this sense, the delightful feature film, "Harold and Maude" was all about rites of passage: Harold and Maude met at funerals – of strangers – they frequented. Maude initiated Harold into manhood and he oversaw her final passage from life to death. The film "Fight Club" likewise expresses the longing of young men to endure pain and suffering to prove themselves worthy and transcend ego. The hero of the story passes through a death and rebirth as psychic reintegration. "Dances with Wolves" is a rite of passage for the hero who leaves behind the sick world of civilization to find in his isolated vision quest a better life, a ritual life founded on nature-culture, and in the end he returns, transformed, to share that vision with his people.

We need to be fully conscious of community and ritual life, but we also need to be fully conscious of the need for rites of passage. The evidence surrounds us that they emerge as misinformed and misguided efforts to transform our lives. Underneath the surface of schools, fraternities, military organizations, fraternal groups, gangs, rap bands and prisons lie the flesh and bones of initiatory rites and symbols. It is time for us to elevate rites of passage from miscarriages and ghosts to purposive soul work.

Not until I participated in my first sweat lodge ceremony did I grasp the deep significance of ritual. In the same way that two heart cells start beating in synchrony when they are a certain distance apart, though not directly touching, the hearts of people standing together in a circle holding hands soon begin to beat as one. Which is why that book title, *All I Ever Needed to Know I Learned in Kindergarten*, rings true.

For over 20 years I took people into the wilderness to discover the majesty, power, grace and mind of the orca whale, a giant dolphin with a brain larger than ours that rules the seas of the world but for some unknown reason does not make war, the only large predator that doesn't. Though it started as a scientific study, within a few years it was clear to me that the volunteers were undergoing radical transformation, and that I was delivering the finest education possible not by pontificating but merely by setting the stage for people to connect at a deep, relaxed level with one another, the earth and the creatures. Dozens of unified communities were formed just by dividing into subteams and sharing the responsibilities of preparing food and observing orcas. Yes, I was a mentor who carried profound admiration and respect for the orcas, who were the real teachers, and I also gave the experience a ritual foundation by leading people in prayer and giving thanks: thousands of people were waiting for someone to give them permission to "make sacred." Telling stories, recounting the day's experiences, joking, singing, making music and dancing around the fire at night proved far more rewarding than TV or live concerts.

I took many people fishing for the first time in their lives and when they caught salmon we blessed and thanked them and paid our respects again as we prepared the food and when we ate it. I learned again and again the hunger people have for working and living together close to the earth: Pleistocene bands eager to form. Members delight in "intimate environmental experiences," ranging from hardship and foraging to cooking and story-telling. They proved time and again the power of prayer when hearts are joined.

Most important in my own education was awareness that life is a ritual waiting to happen.

"If I destroy you, I destroy myself. If I honor you, I honor myself."

~ Hunbatz Men, Mayan

Chapter 12

The Meaning of Trophy in Male Initiation

"From the day I was born I was born for meat."

~ Toma of the ! Kung Bushman

Your Good Heart

Levi Carson is Nez Perce, a robust man who used to ride bulls in the rodeo. He described to me his first deer hunt, mentored by his grandfather. When they came upon a buck, Levi's grandfather gestured to the deer and whispered in Nez Perce, "There. Your good heart." His grandfather was saying to Levi that in taking the deer, his intentions must be pure. With tears in his eyes, Levi said that those very words gave deep meaning to his rite of passage, and that without them being passed on there will be no reverence for the animals. Perhaps there will be no good-hearted men.

"I'm not a trophy hunter," my hunting partner declares. So I ask him, "If there are two identical bucks, same size, weight and condition, standing side by side facing you, but one is a four-point and the other is a six, which one would you shoot?" His answer is the same as every "meat hunter" I've asked, "I'd shoot the six-point buck." I ask him, "Doesn't that make you a trophy hunter?"

My friend can't stand to think of himself as a trophy hunter, but in the shed behind his house are the racks of a dozen deer and elk he's saved for years. The head of the big bull his son shot at age 15 is mounted and hanging on the wall. No one is in the house for long before learning that the trophy bull scored 360 points.

So is he a trophy hunter or isn't he? And why are so many hunters ashamed of the term? According to a survey conducted several years ago, the vast majority of non-hunters disapproved of trophy hunting, but so did 85% of the hunters surveyed. Yet I am convinced that nearly every one of those hunters collects trophies of one kind or another.

When a hunter saves an exceptionally long tail feather from a cock pheasant, he is collecting a trophy. He might wear it in his hunting cap or put it on the dash of his pickup or in a vase on the mantle at home, but it's nonetheless a trophy.

The problem is semantical. To most non-hunters and hunters alike, trophy hunting means to hunt and kill animals strictly for the trophy, not for food. A colleague of mine at the University of Georgia annually gave a lecture to the new wildlife students. "Shoot 'em and Leave 'em Lay" was the title of his talk. He argued that killing animals for trophies made a whole lot more ecological sense than meat hunting. When a hunter kills a deer and takes only its antlers, the rest of its body decays and returns to the ecosystem, supporting all sorts of living things, including future trophy deer.

My buddy is not what Professor Gene Decker of Colorado State University calls a "competitive shooter," meaning that his motivation in shooting animals is to compete for records in the Boone and Crockett Club book. His goal in life is not to shoot the elk with the biggest rack or have more record big game species to his name than anyone else. But he's still a trophy hunter and so are most hunters. If he can challenge himself by investing the extra time and energy required to take a better specimen, then he will, even if that means coming home empty-handed and often it does.

I live in western ranch country where elk hunting is the ultimate challenge in every sense, and though most of the men and women who hunt elk here are not competitive shooters, strictly speaking, they are likely to hunt for extra miles or days to take a trophy animal. One rancher told me that as a young man he despised hunting for meat until he discovered the challenge and rewards of selectively hunting bigger or better bucks and bulls. He took me to the barn and showed me their racks, recounting each hunt in detail.

In those days at the University of Georgia most wildlife students were hunters, and being hunters they were distressed by the professor's message. It was logical, but it bothered them at a deeper level. They didn't feel it was morally right to kill an animal and waste the food. National surveys indicate that non-hunters feel the same: most agree with hunting as long as it's done for food. The fact is that given a choice most hunters take a better trophy animal, even though they eat it.

Where does trophy hunting originate? Why do we do it? Those are the questions I began asking in 1975 when I was hunting ducks with Sievert Rohwer, my colleague in zoology at the University of Washington, the only other hunter in a faculty of sixty. While we were eating breakfast before sunrise at a restaurant in eastern Washinton's pot hole country, a guy walked by with a curly tail feather of a mallard drake stuck in the front of his cap. "Why do hunters put feathers in their caps?" I asked Sievert who replied, "It's a trophy I guess."

Today we are most familiar with the awarding of trophy cups, which originates from the late stone age hunters of Europe who used the trophy skulls of enemies as drinking cups, a practise continued by civilized European warriors until a few hundred years ago. The discovery of human skull caps in Late Stone Age caves of Europe suggests the tradition may be thousands of years old. But trophies of all kinds originate from hunting.

A trophy is any part of an animal that communicates a hunter's achievement. A tail feather advertises to others that a hunter killed a mallard drake or a cock pheasant. Antlers on the wall tell us that a hunter has killed a deer. Typical trophy values include size, rarity or elusiveness and ferocity. Species that are difficult to kill symbolize power precisely because power is required to kill them. Usually larger antlers or horns correlate with larger size of the animal, and the larger the animal the better the hunter which is why a six-point rack carries more status than a four-point. An albino deer may carry more trophy value than a normal deer of the same size because they are less common and harder to find, thus greater hunting skill is required to take them.

An animal that is extremely difficult to hunt, such as mountain sheep or goats, may not be very large or rare, but still they demonstrate a hunter's prowess, fitness, determination and perseverance. The highest ranking trophies typically are from animals that are dangerous, such as Cape buffalo, grizzly bear, rhinos or big cats.

Evidence from European caves indicates that the Neanderthal hunters collected the skulls and leg bones of bears as trophies which they stored in the oldest known stone chests. In Chapter 6, I mentioned that the fossilized footprints of a 16-year old Cro Magnon boy in one cave suggest that he was ritually initiated into manhood after killing his first deer.

Teenage Cro Magnon males were buried with the single canine tooth of a deer around their necks. To this day in Germany and Switzerland, young hunters collect and wear the same tooth from their first deer, often throughout their lives. When I lectured in Slovenia to an international conservation group, I explained my theory to a Swiss hunter in his mid-50s, and the man unbuttoned his shirt and presented to me the trophy tooth of his first deer taken forty years earlier. It appears that some hunting traditions haven't changed much in 30,000 years!

In fact, our lives are measured by trophies of all sorts, from the hides and heads of game animals to diplomas, graduation rings and expensive cars, all of which symbolize and advertise an achievement worthy of a certain degree of social esteem. Trophyism – the love of trophies – is fundamental to understanding human nature, and how, indeed, we gained dominion of the planet.

Contrary to the assertions of anti-hunters lobbying for the cessation of using dogs to hunt black bears and cougars, trophy hunting is hardly a recent invention of the Euro-American male ego! In contemporary hunting societies and during humanity's vast hunting existence, the hunting success of males has been crucial to survival. Because the ability of males to kill large animals directly influences the survival of themselves, their mates and children, it is not surprising that among hunting societies women evaluate the suitability of males according to their trophies. Any male who has killed a trophy animal stands to gain in competition for mates if his hunting prowess relative to other males is verifiable. Now you know why males take possession of part of the prey to advertise its kind or communicate its size. Manhood and candidacy for marriage are earned by demonstration of minimal hunting ability. The groom usually gives his prospective in-laws a present in the form of meat he has obtained by his own hunting; the only way a young man could marry was by proving himself as an able provider.

A male !Kung Bushman cannot marry until he has killed a "buck," some type of antelope. Those men who never prove themselves worthy by killing an antelope never marry and never father children.

Nomadic hunters can't afford to transport large animal parts, but any portable item constitutes a trophy if it clearly identifies the prey or its esteemed size or sex. The semi-nomadic Akoa pygmies wear elephant hair bracelets as trophies. An Akoa legend links hunting ability to such trophies and reproductive success of males: according to the story, the hunter's arrows felled all game, and he had already killed two elephants and wore a necklace of hairs from their tails. It is said that all the women ran after him.

Greatly admired for having killed four wildebeests in one hunt, a !Kung hunter displayed this feat with their tails. Bushman customarily cut strips of skin from the foreheads of the antelope they kill and make them into bracelets worn on their wives' arms. The forehead skin communicates the particular species killed, a measure of hunting prowess. Bushman also fashion their hunting bags from the identifiable skins of trophy species. The abundance and kind of these trophies correlate with the success of the hunter and his social esteem.

Among Alaskan Eskimos the completion of full eligibility for marriage came after a male had killed a succession of animals of increasing size and difficulty, ending with a bearded seal or polar bear, the former being especially difficult, the latter very dangerous.

We are saying that for hundreds of thousands of years boys became men, husbands and fathers, according to their hunting success, which they demonstrated by presenting a trophy animal as proof of their hunting prowess and suitability as a mate and provider.

Collecting that first trophy is a turning point in a young man's life, from boyhood to manhood. For males, the trophy has been an essential component of their rite of passage. That is why many hunters still value their first trophy above all others, even if it is rather paltry. My friend Russell Grieve is a perfect example. He has a wall full of fine deer head mounts, but the one that sets right above his desk and about which he speaks most fondly, telling visitors that he kissed the deer as soon as he shot it, is a little forked horn buck.

Jim Posewitz wrote a fine little book entitled *Beyond Fair Chase*, widely used in hunter education; unfortunately, it does not acknowledge that to a young hunter especially the trophy is symbolic of his passage into adulthood and the self-esteem and social respect that deserves. Which is why Aldo Leopold said, "Trophy hunting is the perogative of youth."

The advantages of trophy hunting extend beyond qualifying for marriage to status in male groups. Status among men influences a male's mating success, for instance, number of wives, as well as wealth, influence and power. Display of hunting prowess to other males affects the probability of a male being accepted as a hunting partner. Contrasted with solitary hunting, cooperative hunting can be far more lucrative in terms of food and much safer in terms of risks from dangerous carnivores. By proving hunting ability to other males a man is accepted or sought for group hunts and thereby increases the amount of food available to himself and his kin. The same principle applies today.

Marksmanship can be a trophy value. If two bow hunters both shoot a 100-pound doe, but the one hunter fired one arrow and the other fired two, then the first hunter's achievement ranks higher. Rock guitarist Ted Nugent was quick to tell me, "I'm no trophy hunter." But he also went on to tell me exactly how many deer he'd taken that year and how many arrows he loosed to get them. To the "Nuge" number of deer taken and shots fired accurately are trophies.

The ability to kill a large animal such as an antelope or a deer is normally sufficient to earn marriage status and minimal rank in male groups. Those men who obtain more meat more often earn higher status among males and gain more wives or more surviving children. Competition among men of groups favors those who kill the largest, most elusive or most dangerous animals irrespective of their food value or even the need for food. The overall reproductive advantages of high status among men can be so great that males risk their lives against terribly awesome beasts. As competition for status, trophy hunting is a conspicuous expression of male egoism, and it explains why men, primitive and modern, kill animals for reasons other than food.

Among Zambia's Valley Bisa people, the social ranking of hunters is determined by the kinds of prestigious mammals slain, these being largest or most dangerous – eland, lion or elephant. In bear hunting by Eskimos, a hunter's prestige is measured by the risk of injury presented by the animal. As anthropologist Elliot Spiess said, sometimes prestige is the motivation behind a hunt, as in winter hunting of denned black bears, or when an Eskimo who has plenty of food and skins sets loose his dog team on a polar bear.

Many of the native cultures of North America were hunting bear and cougar trophies using dogs when Europeans arrived. Which means that for millennia, trophy hunting has kept these species avoiding and evading humans. Scientific work I conducted on the development of predatory behavior in big cats further supports the conclusion of every rancher in the west, "If we stop hunting them they'll soon be hunting us."

Killing of predators is not only beneficial in reducing predation on humans and competition for big game, it is also very difficult. For all these reasons predator trophies carry especially high status. The advance of human societies from hunters to effective competitors against large carnivores, and, finally, to warriors against other humans, has been recorded in their trophies. At any point in time the trophy values of a people reflect their rank among larger predators and the importance of competition with them versus other humans.

When humans are subordinate to predators, warfare against humans is relatively rare or insignificant and the highest trophy values are for large game species. The !Kung Bushman are a good example. Until recent intervention by Europeans with firearms, they were at best co-dominant with the lion which they still fear and normally avoid. The outcome of a confrontation between Bushman and lions depends on a range of factors including motivation from hunger, how many of each are present and so on. When Bushman occasionally kill leopards they do so in groups and with the aid of dogs. Leopards are not killed for food but because they pose a threat or have stolen prey wounded by the hunters. Their elimination can have a long-term benefit. Among !Kung trophies there are no risky carnivores or humans; their trophies are large herbivores.

The Tapirare Indians of Brazil are comparable to the !Kung in that their highest ranking trophies are herbivores. Like the !Kung, they do not make war. Rarely, they kill jaguars close to camp with the aid of dogs, but never hunt them for trophies. Their and many low-ranking peoples' tabus against killing the largest game animals appear to be a cultural adaptation to avoid direct competition with big predators.

Among those societies that are equal or higher in rank to the largest predators, the most esteemed trophies may be dangerous carnivores or enemy warriors. Among several warring societies of South America, only the jaguar rates as high in trophy value as an enemy human. After the introduction of the horse, the Plains Indians' primary resource, the bison, was mobile but also clumped in herds and relatively defendable. Such semi-nomadic societies warred among themselves and hunted large carnivores as trophies, among which the grizzly bear symbolized power. In numerous hunting societies of the north, brown bears have ranked as high or higher than a human trophy, such as a scalp taken in war, as evidence of warring ability.

The Eskimos' major competitor for seals, their most important food resource, is the polar bear. Prior to the advent of firearms, Eskimos were at best equal in rank with the awesome white bear. If a man killed one he was held in high esteem. According to Richard Nelson, one Eskimo had killed a polar bear with his knife, a feat which ranked him among the best of the old-time hunters.

Among pastoral societies, hunting ability is not directly important to the reproductive success of males; nonetheless, the advantages of predator control are obvious since the major food resource, livestock, is vulnerable to predation. As a way of life pastoralism would be impossible unless males were able to defend livestock against predators. For semi-nomadic pastoralists such as the Maasai, who typically warred with agrarian societies for grazing lands, the hunting of large carnivores can be ritualistic, done in such a way as to give individuals the opportunity to demonstrate warrior skills. Other examples include the Zulu, Suk and Turkana males who adorn themselves with the skins of trophy leopards.

High-ranking, dangerous and difficult-to-kill predators such as the lion, bear and eagle symbolize might and aggression in warring peoples. Warriors not only don the skins and weapons of predators, they also label their groups with these animals' names, for example, the Leopard Group of the Turkana and the Lion Hunters of Niger. We all are familiar with fraternal societies with the names of Eagles and Lions. Similarly, on a raid, Hidatsa Indians likened themselves to wolves and wore wolf skins.

Pseudo-trophies are found among some Indian societies of the Amazon Basin, the men of which trade with other tribes for jaguar claws and teeth that they wear around their necks, giving the impression to enemy warriors that they must be powerful adversaries. The illegal market in grizzly claws comes from a demand for pseudo-trophies that suggest a man's prowess as a hunter.

Men who are able to demonstrate their warring skills by taking dangerous or difficult game benefit from perfection of skills transferable to warfare, as well as from gaining status in groups. Warrior skills are highly valued by agrarian societies, wherein trophyism prevails. With civilization the opportunity arose for display of otherwise burdensome parts of large animals, such as tusks, heads and whole specimens. The cultural extensions of trophyism as the pronouncement of power include sculpted concrete lions and eagles adorning buildings of state.

As weapon technology accelerated to the level of sophisticated firearms, the risks of hunting dangerous animals was lowered, shifting trophy values from what previously had been dangerous animals, indicative of the hunter's bravery and suitability as a warrior, to extremely rare or difficult species, indicative of leadership qualities. Among males of agricultural-industrial societies, a trophy of an extremely rare species has become as significant as one of a dangerous species, so that, today, the most esteemed trophies are the rarest on den walls.

The previously esteemed "Big Five" of Africa – elephant, rhino, Cape buffalo, lion and leopard – include exceptionally large or potentially dangerous species which are not especially rare. The "Grand Slam" includes trophies of North America's rugged mountain game, valued not for rarity, size or danger, but because the successful hunter has to possess qualities desirable in a warring society. These are self-control, physical conditioning and stamina, patience, tenacity and wealth. It is no mere coincidence that disproportionate numbers of men with high status or great wealth in modern American society, business tycoons, military leaders and holders of high state office, are trophy hunters.

Because trophies carry so much importance, confirmation of the kill is often required in hunting societies. Today, organizations such as Boone and Crockett Club are detectors, demanding clear proof of the kill. Some recent oil millionaires have purchased trophies and hung them on their walls, but nothing is more contemptible among trophy hunters.

For thousands of years trophies have signified manhood and virility. A man is described as "randy" if he is especially virile or has a high libido. The term "randy" actually originates from an old Latin word, "randall," which means "wolf shield." In the pre-Roman era, men qualified for marriage by killing a wolf, the threat to herds of sheep and goats, the important food supply. By killing a wolf, a man demonstrated that he could protect herds and therefore be a worthy provider, and he signified his achievement by carrying a wolf-skin, trophy shield. To this day in northern Italy when a man asks a woman to marry and he offers her a single hair from a wolf the people of the village say they will have many children!

Lycanthropy or werewolfery also has its origin in pre-Roman trophy hunting. A Greek historian who witnessed the annual carnival during the winter solstice wrote about the men of the wolf cult – those men who had killed wolves – donning wolf skins. His description later was mistranslated to say that they "took on the appearance of wolves," thus giving rise to the myth of men transforming into wolves.

Because trophies are associated with virility, rhinos are killed for their horns and tigers for their organs. The belief in the Orient that consuming rhino horn will revitalize a man and elevate his sex drive can be traced back thousands of years to when robust men killed rhinos to demonstrate their prowess.

During most of human history, god was a tiger, lion, jaguar or bear. Man's original gods were ruthless, they ruled his life, stole his food, ate him and his kin and terrified him by day and night. As man progressed as a hunter, winning a place among carnivores by common defense and weaponry, a few brave men acquired the power of carnivore gods by killing them. The original good was a predator trophy because it pointed human destiny towards greater freedom, security and material wealth.

Every culture known in the history of the world has a hero who killed an awesome beast. The last immense stride made by humanity was pastoralism and full domination of large predators, made possible by trophy hunting. However, while domination of predators meant lower risks and less competition it also promoted the growth of human societies, possibly the overkill of game, and, eventually, extreme competition and warfare among human societies.

As mentioned in Chapter 7, the hero archetype is a spontaneous expression of male adolescence, essentially an instinctive call to rites of passage to achieve acceptance as an adult which surely began as trophy hunting. With civilization and accentuated resource competition among societies came increasing competition among males within societies and extension of the hero archetype into adulthood and its dominance over archetypes of the mature male. In my opinion the Hero has come to rule the world because young men do not undergo rites of passage that temper masculine fire. They need cultural mentoring by elders.

Contemporary life resounds of trophyism and the social esteem associated with the domination of predators. A cover of *Newsweek* depicted Jimmy Carter and his cohorts lionlike "in the lion's den," a common phrase. Dozens of beers, some for over 600 years, are symbolized by the lion. Lowenbrau means "lion beer." According to the Oxford English Dictionary, the most common name given to taverns for hundreds of years has been "Red Lion." A red lion is a dead lion, and the fraternity of the red lion are those men who killed lions. Automobiles named Jaguar, Cougar and Panthera are powered by putting a "tiger in your tank."

As an anthropologist said about these ideas, "Perhaps this is enough to explain the failure of the Edsel. Driving a car with a name like that is not going to affect the reproductive success of an American male." Regarding mate selection, the most esteemed fur coats, have been those of big cats, and imitation fur coats have the same appearance.

The Sacred Trophy

There is more to trophyism than male egoism. There is a positive, spiritual side to the trophy, too. At the age of 13, I collected my first trophy, a mallard hen, which I very carefully skinned and preserved. That skin was sacred to me and it stayed there in the basement of my parents' house in "my" old hunting room for decades, just as it survives even now in the "basement" of my mind. Every hunter remembers his first kill vividly and can accurately recount it, not unlike the first time he made love. (That does not mean that killing an animal is erotic for men, as many ecofeminists have asserted. It means that both sex and hunting may activate spiritual instincts.)

For me that mallard hen was not merely a symbol of my first big step to manhood. By preserving her skin I also honored her life as well as the spirit of her nation, and above all else it is a public statement of gratitude for the gift of her life that I might become a man worthy of her sacrifice. So it is that at the deepest level the trophy is a personal statement about connection with life and a commitment to serve life with respect, the unspoken, common commandment of all true hunters.

In Chapter 6, I mentioned a famous taxidermist, Mike Boyce, also an artist and an articulate spokesman for hunting, who told me he keeps a bear mount in his den so that he can be in communication with the essence of the bear, which means to him the spirit of the bear. I've learned from native people why an eagle feather is a prized trophy. It might require climbing a very tall tree and risking your life to get one as nesting eagles dive at and strike you, but on the other hand that Indian will tell you that his trophy connects him with the Spirit of the Eagle Nation. The Kahunas of Hawaii and the Kalahari Bushman would say that the trophy connects us via an "aka chord" of etheric energy with the spirit of the animal.

So in an egoic sense, trophies rank a man socially, but they also are a record of that man's deep connections with the creatures he killed. A trophy is an egoic statement and a spiritual symbol, but also may be a conduit to the spirit of the animal.

On one hand, trophies may explain how humans came to rule their world. On the other, the overwhelming success of trophy hunting may have precipitated the modern crisis of declining resources and threat of global war. Now that "the lion's share" is ours, only the regulation of ourselves and our relationship to the environment can save us and our precious natural heritage. It is no surprise that World Conservation Force and its affiliated high-ranking trophy hunters are at work to conserve the remaining lion population in Africa. Outside of national parks, the lion's only real ally is the trophy hunter.

From a conservation perspective in a severely beleaugered world, the popular moral judgment against trophy hunting isn't valid. Throughout the history of civilization, powerful men have established preserves for the purpose of perpetuating trophy game. Otherwise, many species would have been eradicated owing to their competition with humans, livestock and farmlands. The Asiatic or Biblical lion, for example, survived into the modern era solely because it was protected by Indian royalty as a valuable trophy species. Its value as a trophy animal is what brought the white rhino back from near extinction to a secure population level. Similar programs may help recover the elephant in Africa, and could do wonders for the grizzly bear and tiger.

In recent history, the greatest conservationist of wildlife and wilderness was this nation's best known trophy hunter – Theodore Roosevelt. Even if we do not agree with their motives, we owe a vote of gratitude to Roosevelt and the men and women like him whose love of trophies is a powerful conservation force.

What cannot be denied is that a young man's trophy signifies his passage from childhood to manhood, and if we intend to initiate young men properly then it is essential that we encourage them to collect a trophy from the animals that make their passage possible. The trophy symbolizes an achievement worthy of manhood, and it plants a sense of self-worth and confidence at a subconscious level, but it also represents a spiritual connection with the animal from which comes a sense of the unity of life.

A young man's trophy holds his heart.

Trophy Animals

The animals I never killed
Lie in gutters and hang on walls watching me
Stand up from their graves and follow me down the road

The deer I never killed wonder why I refused them
They blink and ask, "What kind of hunter are you?"

In dreams I caress their hides
And feel their empty hearts beating
In coffee houses and truck stops
I touch the painted black noses
Of trophy elk and bears and say a silent prayer:

"Next fall I'll pull the trigger.
Next season I'll bring you home."

~ RANDALL L. EATON

Chapter 13

Awakening Instincts

"If peace and love can prevail on earth, and if we can teach our children to honor nature's gifts the joys and beauties of the outdoor world will be here forever."

~ JIMMY CARTER, *Outdoor Journal*

Cleveland Amory Killed A Sparrow

On the truck's radio tonight, I heard Paul Harvey tell the story about Cliff, who like millions of boys, was not satisfied shooting his new BB gun at tin cans. He shot a sparrow and wounded it, and when his father saw what he had done he told him he had to kill it so he tearfully stomped it to death. That was young Cleveland Amory who as an adult became a champion for animal rights and staunch anti-hunter.

The most horrifying experience in my life was similar. At the age of six, I awoke before sunrise on an August morning and crept downstairs to sneak my brother's BB gun out of the pantry and through the back door. I walked down to the end of the block by Fred's Market, where sparrows were hopping out from the curb into the open street, pecking at wheat that was spilling out of grain trucks en route to the elevator by the river.

I lay down on the ground, aimed at a sparrow across the street, and pulled the trigger. The sparrow began flopping from side to side as blood spurt from its breast. Stunned that the BB actually had struck the sparrow, I cried out, "Oh, no. Oh, no." I ran to the sparrow to help it, but as it saw me approaching, it tried to escape and fell through the grate of a sewer drain and disappeared.

My first impulse was to somehow retrieve it from the sewer, but I couldn't see it in the drain. I was crying as I touched my finger to the bright red blood on the bricks. I ran home, put my brother's BB gun back in the pantry, and went upstairs to my room. I was deeply disturbed by what I had done, and over and over wondered why I had done it. I begged the sparrow to forgive me, and I prayed to God for forgiveness.

Still, the vision of that wounded sparrow is vivid, and I have contemplated the event over and over for decades. While I can understand how an experience such as I had could lead a person down the road taken by Cleveland Amory, my own feeling is that the real issue is not BB guns or killing sparrows, neither is it animal rights or hunting. The horrendous shock and confusion that I experienced was over the discovery that I am a predator instinctively prepared to inflict death. It's all the more surprising, in retrospect, that I had never seen anyone kill anything, and yet there I was doing it correctly the first time.

President Jimmy Carter had a similar experience as a boy when he used a slingshot to caste a rock at a robin, and much to his surprise, he killed it. With tears running down his cheeks, he carried the robin to his parents. His father said to him, "We shouldn't ever kill anything that we don't need for food." His mother wisely piped in, "Let's cook it up for dinner." Jimmy Carter grew up to be an avid outdoorsman and conservationist. You didn't have to agree with his policies to know he was a good man of sincere conviction, and from where I sit the last U.S. president to care more about listening to his heart than his ego.

No matter what we may be programmed to do, a person may turn his back on that program, deny his predatory nature, even make war with it, which is what Amory had done. But I believe that the greatest conflict in myself was deeper than waking up as a predator that Sunday morning. I came to believe that we are spiritual beings having a human experience, and the horror I felt was a measure of the disagreement between my spirit and my animal mind. Inflicting death on another creature is the ultimate insult to spirit precisely because on the spiritual level all is one and there is no death. That day, when I killed a sparrow, was my first conscious initiation into the nature of life in a body. I wanted to deny my animal nature and the nature of creature existence, and I suspect that is what many anti-hunters and vegetarians do.

Questionnaire surveys I conducted indicate that most men had comparable experiences, and I know many leading figures in widlife conservation who told me that as boys they killed a bird and cried about it, then the next day killed another bird and cried again and so on. As we digressively remove our children from experiences of death, fewer people confront or embrace the ambiguous reality of life in the body. From all appearances, increasing numbers deal with the terror of physical life by denial of it. While Cleveland Amory might have wanted to ban BB guns to protect sparrows from little boys, doing so would prevent individuals from having truly profound experiences. My experience led me on a very different journey towards the resolution of the enormous paradox of being a spirit with a body.

As for Amory's "animal rights," better that he might have first tackled the problem of human rights. Because he was given the freedom to own a BB gun and kill a sparrow, he came upon what were, for him, very crucial experiences in his life. The same for me. But does his experience justify his attempt to deny the rights of others? Or does it speak to the necessity of allowing others to have experiences such as his and learning whatever they need in the process?

The fact is that some of us need to kill an animal never. Others need to do so once, and still others need to kill many. Living by the heart means that we allow others to pursue the avenues of experience which call to them, and we have the humility to trust in the outcome. That's what it means to have free will. That, too, is the meaning of our constitutional republic.

I suspect that many are the sparrows, robins and blue jays who would offer their lives so small boys might one day join their camp and embrace rather than deny life. From all appearances, sparrows are overly abundant and faring well, and surely there are all sorts of logical arguments why other birds need our help. I confess that for many winters now I have fed sparrows bird seed wherever I find them, from freeway rest stops to coffee houses in the city and of course my own backyard. It is my way of giving back to the Sparrow Nation for its gift to me as a boy when one of their kin died that I might live more fully. Now we are family.

I cannot pretend to know what Cleveland Amory needed to learn in his life, but I hope it was perfectly on course. If, on the other hand, his anti-hunting obsession was a projection of his own unresolved guilt over shooting a sparrow, heaven help him.

I have made peace with my sparrow.

Amory's denial reminds me of Narcissus who failed to embrace his pain and transmute it into something positive. Perhaps the direction he took was influenced by his father's inadequate understanding and handling of Amory's awakening instinct. Jimmy Carter's parents brilliantly helped him resolve his pain by connecting his budding instinct to hunt with meaning: food to support life and a moral foundation. These are common, spontaneous experiences for boys, and they don't qualify as rites of passage; however, it is nonetheless important for parents to infuse meaning and understanding to such events, as the Carters did for young Jimmy.

The initial awakening of the hunting instinct in boys typically comes about from the impulse to employ a weapon. Kalahari Bushman boys use miniature bows and arrows to shoot beetles and set snares to catch small mammals. Those parents who fear a boy's hunting instinct do him harm by condemning him for it, as Bly said. They usually will discourage a son's use of weapons, as though he might also bypass that aspect of his instinctive nature. What they do not understand is that, like hunting, the urge to use and perfect weaponry is part of the child's phylogenetically acquired blueprint for development, and if they manage to keep air rifles or bow and arrows out of his hands, he'll use rocks or make a slingshot.

To those parents who believe that a boy's use of weapons is likely to lead him on a path that culminates in ownership of firearms and killing people, the adage that "guns don't kill people, people do," is germane. They should keep in mind the FBI and BATF studies that indicate that kids with legally owned firearms commit few if any crimes compared to kids with illegally owned firearms, and that is because they have been taught to handle them responsibly. Consider the words of Helen Smith, author of *Scarred Hearts* and a leading expert on youth violence, when I interviewed her and asked if gun control is a viable approach to youth violence,

> "...many of the troubled kids that I see say that they will commit their crimes no matter what, even if they have to switch from guns to bombs to do it. Based on my experience I think they would. So things like trigger locks or limits on gun shows belong in the same file with 'zero tolerance' and other feel-good solutions; they're more about making politicians look busy than about solving the problem..."

If anything, taking an animal's life teaches a boy the dangerous consequences of using weapons and the necessity of handling them carefully. What we ought to be asking is why aren't **all** kids taught gun safety? All the evidence indicates that it would lower accidental deaths and violent crime, at least with guns.

What We Give Children

"A generation goes and a generation comes,
But the earth remains forever."
~ *ECCLESIASTES*

Joe Pearce says we cannot give our children something we don't have. Good news and bad. Good because if we have a sense of the sacred, no matter what we do our children are likely to grow up with it, bad because if we don't have it they won't either. Unless of course we allow them to be influenced by others who do have something we'd like them to have.

Growing up as I did in a small community with frequent interaction with all my relatives from great grandparents on down, I was able to compare the attributes and qualities of my uncles, grandfathers and friends' fathers with my own father and pick and choose for myself what I wanted to emulate as an adult male. My father was not an avid outdoorsman, but my maternal grandfather was and he mentored me well. The tragic situation that most boys experience limits their exposure to one or two parents as models.

Most men who hunt were introduced to hunting as a family tradition; if their fathers did not take them hunting and fishing then their grandfathers, uncles or older brothers did. Some boys are initiated to hunting by other boys who come from hunting families, and there are a surprising number who take up hunting as adults without the influence of family.

The early dawning of the hunting instinct in boys is no guarantee that a boy will grow up to be a hunter and glean from hunting valuable lessons in life. For most boys, the instinct needs mentoring. Usually, the process is gradual and progressive. A boy only three or four years old might catch his first fish on a family outing. He might be taken along on a deer or duck hunt when he is four or five. Some men let a boy take an unloaded BB gun with them just to learn how to carry a firearm safely. My son has been going waterfowl hunting with me since he was three. He delighted in placing decoys and blowing a call, albeit poorly. He began shooting an air rifle safely when he was three, and I gave him a .22 rifle and a .410 shotgun and a compound bow at the age of six, though he shot them only under my direct supervision or that of qualified adults, as in Cub Scouts. All the shooting a boy does until he's ready to hunt should be directed at targets; these may be in the likeness of animals, but in teaching a boy shooting skills he should be taught to avoid shooting at animals - except for food.

Evolution "assumed" for a few million years that every human and its hominid ancestor would grow up with several lessons in comparative anatomy from hunters. Even very young people, in my son's case the age of three, seem naturally curious about the inner landscape of animals whether they are birds or larger mammals. In several books, Shepard emphasizes that the butchering process with the identification and naming of organs is an indispensible lesson that teaches us the sameness of interior structure across extremely diverse species with different external forms. The naming of organs, like the naming of species, contributes to categorical thinking, but it has special instruction as well, that what appears different on the outside may be the same on the inside. If our organs are fundamentally alike, perhaps we are alike in other ways as well. In the development of identification with a world of living species, and the compassion that grows out of that process, butchering animals is a necessary chapter.

Not so long ago, subsistence farming assured that young people would be exposed to killing and butchering at an early age, and that later they would participate in both, but now with industrial farming, either there is no livestock or the butchering of livestock frequently is given over to specialists who arrive in a truck with a portable slaughter facility on a trailer, and kids growing up even on ranches are deprived of the experience. There are road-killed animals in abundance for the non-hunting family to explore and investigate as Gary Snyder did with the grey fox and his boys.

In most states and provinces a boy cannot legally hunt until he is twelve and usually is required to enroll in a hunter education course before he can buy a hunting license. I know some men who shot their first deer at the age of five, and they became adults with great respect for wildlife and nature. Generally, I don't think it is realistic to set an age limit. Many boys and girls are capable of supervised hunting at the age of nine or ten.

Before and after a boy takes up hunting he learns much from elders that will influence his values and perceptions as an adult. A neighbor who farms for a living is an avid hunter who plants a small field of sunflowers each spring to attract and feed mourning doves which he and his son hunt in the fall. The seeds also feed many other species. When his son started hunting doves, he told him to go off by himself and sit quietly and contemplate the beauty of nature. But a young man will accurately access a father or uncle's values irrespective of what he says or the instructions he's given. When it comes to mentoring values there is communication between older and younger males best described as osmosis

Dave Watson, the musician and bow hunter, described above his initiation to hunting on his uncle's Ohio farm where they went out early in the morning to shoot quail for breakfast. What Watson recalls most vividly about those initiatory hunts is the way in which his uncle picked up and held the dead quail and gently petted their ruffled feathers into place before putting them in his game vest. Those non-verbal gestures communicated to Watson the respect his uncle held for the birds.

My grandfather taught me how to shoot for years before I went on my first hunt at the age of 13. He never said one word to me about respecting wild animals or nature, but his profound love for them was ever present in his enthusiasm expressed in a hundred ways from sitting and watching cat birds feed their young to calling mallard ducks into a late winter corn field after shooting time just for the thrill of watching them land and feed all around us.

Gomp grew up on a farm in southern Indiana when deer were at their all time low. The hardwood-prairie grassland savannas had been converted to croplands, and deer became rare throughout most of the midwest. Reforestation programs during the 1930s planted pine stands throughout much of central Illinois. From the shrunken but never fully conquered river bottoms, deer reestablished themselves in Mason County, including Gomp's sand farm seven miles east of town. In the corner of his back eighty acres, he had let feather-leafed locusts invade the field from the intersecting rows of osage orange, planted as wind-breaks. Within four years there were ten acres of immature forest cover just waiting for deer to take up residence.

Weekly around the year, Gomp looked for tracks, and when he found some he followed them to see whether the deer were passing through or settling down on the farm. Eventually, he told me with great pride a doe inhabited the locusts, and since I was starting to hunt then, he made it absolutely clear to me that I was not to shoot any deer on the farm and neither were my friends. In time, he said, if the herd grows, then we may hunt them, but not until then.

On hundreds of pheasant and quail hunts I walked through the locusts and paused to study deer sign, including tracks of fawns with adults, but every time I reported my observations to Gomp he already knew what I was going to say. He'd been there more often and for longer periods than I had, and he didn't simply read sign he hid, stalked and watched the deer.

Then Gomp decided it was time to get a tag and hunt deer for the first time in his life. The Illinois deer season was but a few years old, permitted only in some counties, and it lasted three days. Gomp knew the daily movements and activities of the deer on his farm, and I was certain that he'd bag one the first day out. He didn't. Why he didn't was something we never discussed. I listened to his stories about the deer and how he got close enough to shoot a buck, not only that first season but every season after it for five years. I knew that he relished hunting the deer, which brought him into their normally secret lives. That he didn't want to kill one was a secret he and I shared with the deer.

Like many farmers who uphold the hunting tradition, Gomp left extensive fence rows and wind-breaks in place long after any livestock were raised on his farm so that wild animals from cardinals and bullsnakes to rabbits, quail, pheasants and deer would have much needed habitat. The stand of locusts where deer colonized his farm still exists, years after he died and his farm was sold. The last time I went there to pay my respects to the land, the new owner's friend had a bow-hunting stand placed in a tree. Just leaving those locusts alone rather than cutting them down to add a bit of acreage and annual crop production is a deliberate act of stewardship, a choice from the heart.

A Forest for Life: A Lesson in Stewardship

My father's enthusiasm for hunting extended only as far as the opening day of pheasant season when he led me and the tenant and his male kin on an annual ritual. But his enthusiasm for stewardship far exceeded that for the hunt, though he always delighted in eating game birds. If his eyesight had been better I suspect he would have hunted more. He planted multi-flora rose bushes along the state road to provide winter cover and feed for songbirds and pheasants which gathered there in huge flocks. It was clear to me even as a small boy that he found deep satisfaction from watching the birds feed on the bushes he had planted.

When I was ten, our family began a project on the 40-acre sand farm two miles from town. We planted thousands of Christmas trees, one at a time by hand, usually in the high humidity of hot summer days. It was for me at that age a demanding, back-breaking chore. But many years later when someone asked me to list in a resume the ten greatest accomplishments of my life, I put at the top of the list, "Planted a pine forest in central Illinois," and later still wrote the following essay about the meaning of stewardship and its relationship to hunting.

"Even before we left, everyone promised over the phone that no Christmas tree would be cut until all of us had reunited. Then we would go out together with our children to the farm and cut a tree. For the first time in their lives, my son, my brother's sons and my sister's daughters and sons would get to experience an old fashioned Christmas with the whole clan, carols and finding our own tree.

"For years now I have purchased no cut trees at Christmas, only living trees. They're more expensive, but it seems better to buy a living tree that may be planted rather than one already dead. Perhaps the trend is growing because ancestral memories are waking up. Like the Druids, who saw in the oak tree the insatiable impulse for life, we are resuming a mid-winter ritual to celebrate the first dawning of a new year. Our ancestors did not sacrifice the tree's life, but rather cut its branches as life-symbols. Whatever the explanation, the taking indoors of a green living thing reenacts the primordial meaning of Christmas long before there were Christians. So pervasive and established among northern peoples as the celebration of the first longer day following the winter solstice, it is no wonder that the Christ's birthday was placed then when historical evidence indicates otherwise. Christmas today is many things to different people, but underneath all appearances it is a celebration of the organic impulse for rebirth in spite of the inevitable toll of harsh winter.

"Why, then, one may ask, would I be so enthused to cut a tree? If live trees for Christmas represent an ethical refinement more in keeping with cosmic principles would killing a tree simply be a sentimental retreat into facile, even perverted traditions of modern somnambulism? So it would seem. But the fundamental problem of moral philosophy is that it takes at its starting point intellectual abstraction, oblivious to the circumstances of living, from which all genuine ethics derive.

"It would be, for me, unethical to cut a tree unless I grew it. Such was the profound lesson of my fortieth Christmas. Turning 40 is no doubt a time when one's assessment of life involves the peeling off of decades of artificial trappings. For me, the shift in basic perspective or philosophy was away from the egotistical measures of professionalism and a return to the transcendent yardstick of stewardship– careful husbandry of the land and its resources.

"Until I went back to the Illinois farm and the forest I helped put into the ground more than twenty-five years before, I did not think that my greatest accomplishment in life would amount to planting a forest. But standing there among mature white pines with long, delicate needles that whisper wind-songs, and scaley-barked red pines with decades of dove-bearing nests tucked well against their strong trunks, and crooked jack pines still racing by tree standards for the sun and dropping their undergrowth to make refuge for deer troubled by dogs, I found a kind of ultra-deep satisfaction which thrives on silence.

"This forest is not mine. It never was, and it belongs to no man. The pride I feel, a pride that demands no voice, is for having participated in the life of a forest. Those tiny saplings that passed through my fingers into the nearly barren ground, thousands of them, one at a time are a living memorial to husbandry, that highest form of enthusiastic humility.

"At ten I wasn't capable of appreciating homespun forestry. The spade gave me blisters, the prickly pear cactus put fine, brown needles into my knuckles and the hot, humid climate sunburned and exhausted me. By sixteen I was a hunter of rabbits and quail which thrived in the young forest on land that had not seen animals larger than lizards and Carolina box turtles before the trees arrived. The small trees provided nesting cover, protection from aerial predators and shade, which, with the existing wild grasses, encouraged small game, hunting for town boys and the first inkling for me of husbandry.

"At Christmas of my sixteenth year I was elected to spend the holidays on the farm selling trees. The family figured that since I had planted many of them it was only fair that I should be the one to sell them and keep the money. Though we had purchased an old boat, retired from research by the state, and placed it on top of the highest hill in the county to be a summer cabin, "Eaton's Ark" had no heat. That left me out in the cold all day for two weeks with temperatures falling below zero and hard winds. When people weren't there looking for a tree, I hunted small game in the young forest, and in the process learned how vitally important the trees were to protecting birds and mammals from snow and wind. And as people came and went I discovered another satisfaction from harvesting trees. I knew the trees, not simply the forest, and was able to help families find the particular species of pine in the shape and size they preferred. There was a joyous communion shared between hundreds of families and myself made possible by the forest. That Christmas built relationships in my mind between the land, the trees, wild animals, people and livelihood. The toil of a few years ago had given me an introduction to husbandry and stewardship on the one hand and many meals of wild game and pocket money on the other.

"Within another four years the trees had grown a lot. Many of them were ten feet tall, and because we had planted them close together with the intention of selling them small as Christmas trees, many of the trees were overcrowded. In these patches, the environment was changing from interspersion of trees and annuals, which had been prime habitat for rabbits and quail, to a forested habitat with new species colonizing it. The mourning doves were nesting in large numbers in the stands of red and jack pine, and the dainty saw-whet owl took residence in the forest's edge, its pellets strewn beneath its roosts. The deer arrived, immigrants from who knows where. First was a young doe who occupied the end of the jack pines next to the railroad right-of-way, and every year thereafter we saw or found tracks of deer including fawns.

"Yet there remained large sections of forest with open patches created by cutting trees for the market, and these continued to support the small game with the addition of pheasants though I doubt that the forest itself may account for their invasion.

"Over the years the forest continued to mature. A local farmer stocked it with honeybees because of the shade offered by the trees, and as the pines began to produce seed, a rare bird arrived to eat them: the cross-bill is so named for its bill, specialized to remove seeds from pine cones.

"When the time came to fetch a tree, severe weather had kept my brother and sister and their families from arriving as planned so I, my son and my wife went ahead without them. The temperature was twenty below zero, and counting the wind-chill factor, it was close to eighty below. The snow was deep, and in the farm road it had drifted up to three feet. We parked along the state highway and walked into the trees. I don't remember being so cold that I felt I could perish in a few minutes, but I could not imagine getting a tree in any other way or anywhere else.

"The trees were huge, some were perhaps forty feet high. I thought that the very best we could do was to climb a smaller tree and top it. But when trees reach that size even the tops have sparse branches, and there was nothing suitable to be found. Finally we came across a cedar growing at the edge of the pines. About fifteen feet high, it had the characteristic fullness and tapered shape of its kind, and though no sophisticated tree man would normally consider the cedar as a bona fide Christmas tree, it suited us fine.

"As my son and I cut the top seven feet off and dragged it through the snow to the car, I explained to him that this cedar and others like it surrounding the pines had not been planted by me. Their berries had been eaten by birds which, roosting in the pines, had defecated the seeds onto the ground thus planting cedars.

"Having husbanded the pine trees which gave shelter to the birds which had eaten cedar berries which had given rise to our Christmas tree, I felt quite fine about cutting it. And I believe that if all of us practiced husbandry on a scale that meant we helped bring more life into the world than we consumed, then we would not be haunted by the ghosts of animals eaten and trees killed. Rather, we would feel content as part of the cycle of life and death. To tell you a secret, I did not kill that cedar tree after all. I merely topped it, and within a few years it will be as robust as it was. Not that I am apologizing, since I would have killed the tree had it been smaller. One who stewards the land with care has the right to recycle its life through himself both physically and spiritually.

"It was agreed by everyone in the family that we shared the very best Christmas of our lives. For my son there was a reunion with his kin from his great-grandmother to his infant cousin; for my wife, who grew up without extended family or siblings, it was the grand experience of ceremonious kinship; for me, it was my son walking with me through the forest I planted as a boy, and yet more. It was the knowledge that the forest who had taught me so many valuable lessons would outlive us all. And though one may not aptly express it, somehow that green-black forest rising so unexpectedly against a horizon of sandy flatland is our gift to the place that gave us life.

"Twenty-three years later I visited the sand farm again, this time with my 13-year old son and my brother who told me that a few years earlier a pair of badgers had been discovered living in a den at the end of the pine grove along the railroad right-of-way, the first badgers observed in central Illinois in a hundred years. Wherever had they come from and how did they arrive? From northern Illinois via the abandoned railroad right of way? We'll never know, but for me the mystery came as another blessing from the forest.

"With my young son I have gone back to topping rather than killing a tree at

Christmas. He and I search the forest for one then stand there holding hands and boughs as we thank and bless the tree."

For boys in the civilized world, husbandry of the land is as irreplaceable as the hunt in their development of character and ethics. In rural environments it is relatively easy to plant trees and shrubs as well as annuals to promote wildlife, game and nongame alike. Membership in groups such as Pheasants Forever, Ducks Unlimited or National Wild Turkey Federation may be one way to participate in planting food and cover species for wildlife. Pruning abandoned orchards is an easy way to promote fruit production that will attract and feed numerous birds and mammals in the fall. In the area where we live, big game foods are depleted of some minerals so we buy cheap "salt" blocks and place them in the forest.

In town, even the suburbs of large cities, a family can have a wonderful time turning their backyard into a small wildlife haven. The National Wildlife Federation provides guidelines for promoting backyard wildlife. I finally convinced the director of the Seattle zoo to develop a backyard wildlife exhibit as a model of what people there could do on their own. Every zoo should do the same.

Respect for life and the land can come from gardening: many kids are growing up without ever planting, nurturing and harvesting food, which can be done with remarkable success even in big city apartment windows. Some city schools have given up playground areas so each child can plant vegetables that they take home to share with their families. No one should grow up without hunting, fishing, gathering or growing.

I believe that our food is sacred, that the land, rain and sunshine that produce it also are sacred. I believe that the turkey served at Thanksgiving deserves our thanks. Joseph Campbell once distinguished aboriginal from civilized people according to whom they give thanks for their food. The latter thank God, the former thank the animal and the Creator. We give thanks at every meal for all our blessings, and when we do we thank the turkey, cow, pheasant, chicken or goose that gave up its life that we might live. We also thank the veges. It is an unwritten law among the Lakota that the more we are grateful for the more we shall receive for which to be grateful.

If we live from our hearts, so will our children. If we take time to admire the beauty of creation, so will our children. If we dare to be present in the moment, so will our children. If we care for our bodies and the body earth, so will our children – if this body is a temple then so is the earth that made it. If we love our children they will love their children. If we make sacred, so will they. What we honor they will honor.

Education and Enthusiasm

Like my grandfather, a mentor teaches a boy discrete outdoor skills as well as ethics, but more important than these is the sense of respect and enthusiasm for wild things. An older hunter understands a boy's passion for the hunt, and while the urge to prove himself in the field has passed, he nonetheless is thrilled by the hunt and the beauty of nature. He also finds a deep satisfaction in pointing the way for a youngster.

Life has given me a series of initiations that have redefined my understanding of education. I mentioned taking people into the wilderness and the positive influence that cooperation, foraging and ritual had on their lives. Eventually I stood before college audiences proclaiming that a few days in the wilderness was worth more than a four-year college education in terms of teaching virtues and values. Already I had come to the conclusion that public education is not only a failure but downright harmful because it "degeniuses" children, as Buckminster Fuller said. Public education amounts to day care and training for life on a treadmill of labor, stimulation and buying...by the clock.

As a visiting professor in Wyoming I was coerced into teaching a course in education, a field I had scoffed at for years. The thirty students were women, most of them in their late 20s and early 30s, married with children, in their final term before student teaching. (Strangely enough one of them came from my small home town in Illinois where she had lived a half-block away and graduated from high school with my brother.) I asked them to write an essay on their favorite teacher and to identify why that teacher was their favorite. Each student had (only) one favorite teacher in their life, and in every case the quality identified in that teacher was ***enthusiasm***. In short, every one of these women had chosen teaching as a profession because a teacher had inspired them.

Perhaps that is not too surprising. **What did surprise me was that not one of the students could recall a single bit of information they received from their favorite teacher!** I ask you then how important is content? It would appear that outstanding teachers motivate us to learn and inspire us to share the same gift with others.

That gift is enthusiasm. The word enthusiasm means "the God within." The word "inspire" means "to set on fire." Among the greatest gifts any of us may give to another is to "set on fire the God within" them.

The teachers who have inspired us were exemplary models who, at least some of the time they were in the classroom, were able to communicate with us spiritually. The content they delivered was the stuff of culture, long forgotten, but their heart-to-heart connection with us was transformative.

Jimmy Carter said, "I have never been happier, more exhilarated, at peace, rested, inspired, and aware of the grandeur of the universe and the greatness of God than when I find myself in a natural setting not much changed from the way He made it." Boys carry an instinct to hunt, and if that instinct is guided by an appropriate model, then it will link up with the heart and be transformed from excitement to enthusiasm. That young man will in turn mature and share his enthusiasm with boys.

What Hunting Teaches Youth: A Review

Hunting is a primary instinct in males, which means it operates on its own energies, and the rewards and satisfactions of hunting are intrinsic. As a "spiritual instinct," with the capacity to link up the lower with the higher and the inner with the outer, hunting expands us and makes us more whole. More than any activity, at least for males, it connects us deeply with nature and animals to which we become irreversibly bonded. The supreme alertness associated with the hunt and our spontaneous identification with the animals we hunt are transcendent, they get us out of ourselves, beyond our ego, and as a consequence the hunt is fundamentally a religious experience, one that reconnects us to the source. The transcendent nature of the hunt teaches a young man that he is part of something much greater than himself.

Hunting teaches the interconnection and interdependence of all life. Like the men of hunting-gathering societies, recreational hunters know from direct experience that interdependence is a fact of life, an ecological and spiritual principle. From awareness of interdependence humility is born.

Hunting reveals the impermanence of life and our own mortality. The taking of an animal's life evokes compassion for human and non-human life. The killing of an animal also teaches us the terrible extent of our power, and it evokes responsibility.

Because hunting teaches us that we are, like all lifeforms, dependent upon the integrity, viability and wholeness of natural systems, it inspires us to "fiercely protect nature," and to be active in environmental conservation. Though the hunt is goal-oriented, it teaches us that all of creation functions by processes and that we are part of the process. It engenders a "7th generation perspective," making decisions today with future generations in mind. As Athabascan elder, Peter John said in "The Sacred Hunt," "The animals you take are important to your grandchildren."

The hunt teaches cooperation at a social level, as in the hunt itself, and with land owners, residents and occupants, but also with the animals.

Hunting teaches us to be observant and patient. It teaches us to emulate nature and slow down, to "be here now" in the present moment.

The hunt teaches a spirit of gratitude to the animals and for the gifts of nature as well as to life itself and the divine.

The hunt promotes authentic self-confidence (tempered by humility and gratitude) and self-sufficiency (tempered by interdependence).

It teaches us responsibility in the safe and careful use of lethal weapons. Likewise, the taking of an animal's life teaches us that there are serious consequences to our choices and actions.

The hunt naturally promotes ethics universally associated with hunting. These include "ahisma," avoiding unnecessary harm, which means taking only what we need and using what we take as well as minimizing suffering of animals. "Putting back" encompasses everything from ritually placing a part of the animal into the earth to maintaining, improving and increasing habitat for wildlife. As such, hunting is the model for environmental conservation. "Thinking with the heart" means that in the hunt we learn to listen to our deepest feelings and abide by them; we also attend to our intuitions and learn to honor them.

In the realm of spiritual development, the hunt submerges us in processes that teach us the subtle realities of life. These include the power of prayer – of envisioning what we want tempered by spiritual dimension of ethical choice: the importance of asking for and receiving permission; the ability to receive guidance in the form of dream and vision; the consequences of attitude, intention and right-mindedness. It teaches us that inner peace and sanity are accessible in an insane world.

The hunt is an active form of prayer that integrates the three selves or minds: conscious, subconscious and higher. It is not merely the cerebral gyrations of rational thought, but the integration of the conscious with the emotional realm of the subconscious. Psychologist John Bradshaw agrees with the Kahunas of Polynesia, whose psycho-spiritual system predates principles advanced by Freud and Jung by millennia, that it is the linkage of conscious with subconscious mind that opens the door to higher mind. The hunt unites thought with the feeling of the desired outcome which empowers the prayer. Thought by itself carries no energy, but when we hold the feeling of the outcome, then our prayer has power. Hunting teaches us how to pray.

There are three discoveries made in hunting that are rarely articulated: that the animal has a spirit – it leaves the body at death; that we transcend the body, i.e., we also are spiritual; and, that we have the power to take life (and the act of killing itself is no fun).

The hunt engages us in skills and activities that are transferable and beneficial to our development, perception and understanding. These include awareness of our environment and self-awareness, natural history, survival skills, and especially reciprocity and stewardship.

"Look behind you. See your sons and your daughters. They are your future. Look farther and see your sons' and your daughters' children and their children's children even unto the Seventh Generation. That's the way we were taught. Think about it: you yourself are a Seventh Generation."

~ LEON SHENANDOAH, Onondaga

Chapter 14

Forging a North American Hunting Culture

"The great mystery into which every true hunter enters teaches him that a man thinks with his heart, not his head. That is the secret of hunting."

- Randall L. Eaton, *The Sacred Hunt*

It is clear by now that my own life has been carved primarily out of two traditions, the European and the Native American. I believe that if North America still has a destiny it is to forge a new culture based largely on these traditions. The European colonists made a right step by modeling government after the Iroquois Confederation, and while historians and lawyers know that the US Constitution reflects the principles of the Confederation, it falls terribly short in terms of what we did ***not*** adopt. The Confederation had the equivalent of a judiciary and congressional representation, but the power of the executive branch was diffuse. There were many chiefs with different functions but no single office like a presidency; moreover, the women were authorized to issue warnings to chiefs who abused the power of their office and even remove them. Second, decisions were made by concensus, not by majority rule. Every man and woman in five nations of the Confederacy had to agree with a proposed decision or policy change.

A thousand years ago the Peacemaker, as he became known, created the Iroquois Confederation model, and with it came peace among the member tribes which before had warred among themselves. They lived in permanent settlements as forager-farmers – they were civilized. Other foundations for peace were quite brilliant: only women could own property; and, nature reserves were established so young men could be mentored by elders in hunting as a rite of passage. The Peacemaker understood the tempering influence of the hunt. He also advocated sport for boys and men.

Imagine how different this nation and the world would be now if we had more closely imitated the Confederation. Would our life be more humane and compassionate, our environment healthier? Would it be a "totally different world?" The European patriarchal tradition was too strong for our colonist-ancestors and they were unable or unwilling to imagine political governance without a powerful executive. The combination of frenzied industrial life and the ease of manipulating public opinion has opened the door for widescale deception and abuse by the executive branch.

The North American Model

I believe that hunting in North America also has fallen short of its destiny. Though the "North American Model" of wildlife management has much to its credit, not the least of which is the recovery and reintroduction of game species, it has failed to creatively integrate with Native American hunting culture, and as a result, I fear, the future of hunting and the promise it holds for the development of young people and the salvation of the environment is in jeopardy. Effectively, we abandoned the sacred hunting traditions of Europe, but did not embrace the deep spirituality of hunting that existed among the indigenous peoples all across this continent. The cost and suffering of that failure is to be measured not only in terms of hunting as a rite of passage, but in terms of hunting as a tradition that engenders spiritual values, profound connection with animals and nature, and universal virtues generally. These in turn would have had immeasurable influence on social stability, sustainable economy and environmental quality. Perhaps it is not too late. Many are the native people who have adopted Christianity but preserved their connection to the creatures and the earth via traditional hunting practices and rites, including the vision quest. Many are the contemporary Christian hunters who speak from their hearts with respect for wild things – white men, red hearts.

Our boys are hungry to become men and they thirst for spiritual water. Might we quench that thirst best via the sacred hunt, as a hunt for the sacred, and the vision quest? Perhaps the problem lies in the culture of wildlife management itself, as anthropologist Stuart Marks says in his fascinating study of hunting traditions in the South,

> "My argument from ethnography is that discourse about wildlife is essentially about human relations. Biologists are on the wrong trail if they confine their scrutiny solely to the biological processes of organisms whose ecology increasingly bear the imprints of human providence. Even behind the loss of critical wildlife habitat lie the imprints of human incentives, conflictive rights, and 'benign' traditions. Our profound attempts to make nature useful have made the environment in which most Americans live a reflection of their own materialistic myths. Furthermore, this world has become structured and maintained by professionals… One source of the problem may lie in the limited professional and legal definitions of wildlife as resources. Wildlife species are not exclusively 'properties.'"

Wildlife management is founded largely on the vision of Aldo Leopold, and as such it is a patchwork of forager philosophy and agricultural control of nature. Leopold said that "Conservation is a state of harmony between men and land," but raising game "in the wild by manipulating its environment" has converted exploitation to cropping and become doctrine in wildlife management and among hunters as seen in this remark from outdoor writer Gene Wensel in *Traditional Bowhunter,*

> "Whitetail deer are now recognized as a crop. They are a manageable, harvestable natural resource that needs good farming practices as much as any valuable livestock or other resource."

Considered the property of the State, deer are equated to domestic livestock and a crop to be harvested. Nothing wild or numinous in that! Ben Peyton is a wildlife professor who, like me, grew up hunting in central Illinois. He toured a Texas hunting resort where he found windmills supplying water and stock feeders for game. "…each site looked to me much like a barnyard and not at all like a hunting opportunity. The situation required little knowledge about the land, the ecosystem, or the game animals – only that the hunter be proficient with the rifle or bow and could afford the trophy fees." Essentially what Peyton found was pastoralism disguised as big game hunting, a little like a Nevada brothel pretending to offer true love – for a price.

Out of this pastoral-farming devotion to produce a "harvestable surplus" Peyton sees the missing ingredient as the relationship of hunter to hunted and the environment they share. He believes that that relationship is essential to promoting an "effective and well-informed sense of ecological stewardship among the hunting community." In fact he sees the primary redeeming value of hunting to society as the development of stewardship among hunters of a healthy and diverse ecosystem "that provides for a variety of human values and needs." Peyton believes that an exhibition of stewardship by hunters is what will earn the respect of most of the non-hunting public, though it has not done so after decades as a central justification of hunting. Clearly he wants to save recreational hunting, but where he and his colleagues miss the mark is comprehension of what motivates a hunter to become a steward. What led Leopold to think like a mountain and plea for the humility that is necessary to preserve predators in a world dominated by pastoral-farming minded men?

The critical question is why isn't stewardship enough to sustain hunting? It is a necessary but insufficient justification for hunting. Stewardship is an outgrowth of "love and respect," to use Leopold's words. The feeling of love and attitude of respect towards things wild is precisely what identifies the spirit of hunting and differentiates it from pastoralism and farming. It is the difference between humility and arrogance, interdependence and independence. The aboriginal hunter depends on wild animals physically and spiritually, and the recreational hunter depends on wild animals spiritually. The eating of the animal is a ritual communion that honors it and the land and the hunter's bond with them.

As I read the reflections and concerns of Peyton and other wildlife biologists who are as I am deeply anxious about the decline of hunting, what is missing is the sacred dimension. The powerful influence that hunting wields in the lives of men is one of religious transformation. What a pity it is that professional wildlife management keeps beating around the scientific bush but missing the very heart of hunting. In terms of wildlife conservation, recreational hunting only needs more participants. In terms of human development and recovery of spiritual connection with the earth and creatures, hunting needs cultural mentoring.

Because wildlife management is largely an arm of the State and because it emulates the science of ecology, perhaps it has no room for the religious. Even so, where in Peyton's definition of the social values of hunting do we find the role that hunting serves in the initiation of boys to men? What do we find of character education, universal virtues or spiritual values? Where, exactly, are the psycho-spiritually redeeming benefits of hunting that are responsible for stewardship? It seems that there is little understanding of their role in male development.

Decline in Recreational Hunting

Wildlife biologists, John Organ and Erick Fritzell, anticipate a decline of recreational hunting and changing public policy that will tend to limit consumptive uses of wildlife to the purpose of management and subsistence. Fritzell is a hunter for whom hunting has religious significance, but they recognize that stable or declining hunting license sales "have forced agencies to explore alternative funding options and to address the needs of new constituencies." They discovered in a survey conducted of university programs in fisheries and wildlife that merely 25% of the students participate in hunting and 40% in fishing. A surprising number of students were opposed to hunting.

Changes in curricula of wildlife students reflect the changing public attitudes, with shifts toward fields that consider public perceptions, conservation biology, "human dimensions," and environmental ethics, which, in my opinion, are long overdue. At this point we might well ask how many wildlife professors dwell on Ortega y Gasset's discussions of the religious nature of hunting or on Paul Shepard's insights about hunting in terms of human ecology and development? Is there a university course anywhere that looks at hunting across time and space and its myriad effects and influences on human behavior, culture and spirituality?

Recently a state university asked me to teach a course on hunting for its graduate students in wildlife, about half of whom had no background in hunting or fishing. The more I pondered the approach the more I was convinced that the first requirement was to get the students out into the wilderness where they would have to forage for their food or go hungry. Vegetarians could pick berries, dig roots or gather nuts. Then, I told the chairman, we can talk about hunting, ethics, evolutionary theory and all the rest of it. He was cool to the idea and instead seemed to favor the comfortable menu of lecture and reading.

The declining rolls of hunting are ascribed to urbanization, lack of access to open lands, competing recreational pursuits, lack of hunting mentors, complex hunting regulations and climbing costs – when the State of Colorado cut the license fees for youngsters in half, recruitment of young hunters doubled in one year. According to surveys, Americans support legal hunting, but the perceived motivation of the hunter influences public acceptance. For example, Kellert's survey in 1978 reported that 60% of Americans did not approve of hunting for "sport" or recreation, but 80% approved of hunting for meat.

After reading Kellert's article and several of his books, I guessed that he was not a hunter because had he been a hunter he would have made it clear in his questionnaire that "sport" and recreational hunting normally encompass putting meat on the table. They are not mutually exclusive. I was right: Kellert took up hunting recently (1997). Most of his much quoted work suffers from categorical error, and while it certainly wasn't his intention I believe that his errors have harmed hunting by playing into the hands of anti-hunters who use his questionable results to justify their condemnations.

Within the field of wildlife management, sport and recreational hunting are synonymous, and both terms normally mean that animals are eaten. Hunting is not sport at all since sport is a form of play behavior with its own evolved drive system. In North America the term was adopted widely to separate re-creational hunting from market or commercial hunting. To separate meat hunting from re-creational hunting because the former is motivated to supply food is unjustifiable. The fact is that under the most economically austere conditions the costs of meat hunting – weapons, ammunition, licenses and fees, related equipment and costs plus loss of gainful income – far exceed the monetary value of meat gained from hunting. Hunters of meat prefer getting their meat by hunting. They are not simply seeking meat but also the hunt.

Kellert also failed to discriminate between trophy hunting solely for trophies versus hunting for trophies ***and*** meat, by far the more common motive. Kellert's exclusive categories certainly don't apply to me since I consider myself to be a nature hunter and a meat hunter and a re-creational (not sport) hunter and a trophy hunter, and I suspect that these same categories apply in varying degrees to nearly all hunters, which my questionnaire survey supports. I prefer re-creation as a term because modern hunting re-creates the age-old ritual of the hunt, a relationship of physical and spiritual interdependence with wild animals and nature. It helps to understand hunting from the inside, as a hunter, before conducting public opinion surveys about it which may in turn adversely influence public opinion and policy.

A lack of understanding of the psycho-spiritual dimensions of hunting in the wildlife field has meant that surveys of public attitude have overlooked the social and moral relevance of hunting, especially its role in youth development. Organ and Fritzell are correct that,

> "The wildlife profession has failed to communicate to hunters and society the cultural values of hunting. Hunting is typically marketed as an effective way to control wildlife populations and as an important source of revenues for conservation programs....It is understandable that 'wildlifers,' with their scientific training and focus on populations would construct a narrow message on hunting....this message may not suffice to justify hunting programs."

Among Organ and Fritzell's admirable recommendations are exposing wildlife students to experiential programs, i.e., hunting and fishing, and "the wildlife profession should develop a greater understanding of the cultural significance of hunting and communicate this to society." Emulating Leopold's lifepath, as a hunter and as a student of classical literature, would be a good start.

Biology, Culture and Stewardship

Robert Holsman takes a deeper look at environmental stewardship by hunters. He says that the connection between hunting and stewardship is "natural on an intuitive level. Though we ought not disregard such evidence completely, science demands more stringent proof that a connection exists." From a scientific perspective, the correlation between hunting experience and values, choices and actions of stewardship ought to speak well enough for hunting and it does. But of greater concern, it is precisely this kind of thinking that found professional wildlife with its back against the wall, unsure of how to save hunting. Wildlife management may employ population biology as a tool, but altogether is not a hard science nor should it be simply because it is, as Stuart Marks insists, not merely about the biology of wildlife but about culture, tradition, ritual and myth. Marks says,

"Hunting is not ephemera in a play world of little consequence. It is about life and death, about methods and means, about power and standing, about stories and myths... about people and the beasts within and without. The hunting cloth originates and connects with most other activities within the sorted continua of cultural behavior. Hunting is inseparable from the wider worlds of social and environmental realities, and its meanings entwine with them. Only by scanning both channels can we appropriately interpret the message." More succinctly, Marks says, "wild animals are not only good to pursue and to eat, they also give us distance to reflect upon ourselves," something wildlife biology has failed to communicate.

If all hunters do not measure up to the standards for environmental stewardship as set by Ducks Unlimited or Rocky Mountain Elk Foundation, then where does the weakness lie? In hunter education, which needs to encompass nature education and environmental ethics? Holsman does see a need for "more work to develop the theoretical basis for how stewardship develops among hunters and others," and he continues, "Though it is unrealistic to expect that all hunters will adopt Leopold's land ethic as their guiding worldview we should be striving to initiate hunters who embrace a holistic view of the environment and their personal role in maintaining its quality."

Jody Enck, Dan Decker and Tommy Brown recognize the overall importance of the social and cultural aspects of hunter initiation and the broader perspective of what it means to be a hunter. Perhaps hunter education should be radically revised to include most or all of what is recommended here for initiation of boys to manhood. If most hunters are to become environmental stewards perhaps they would profit much from subsistence hunting, vision quest and art, all with sound mentoring. The agencies would bemoan such a proposal, and I wonder if the State wants many men of heart anyway? Might they threaten its security, directly or indirectly? Would they be less dependent on the State, harder to control and manipulate – "man-age" – and might they lose interest in consumerism?

Animal Rights

In a thoughtful article about the future of hunting in light of the rising animal rights movement, Robert Muth and Wesley Jamison point first to anti-cruelty or the humane movement in the latter half of the 19th Century, then the 1942 Disney film "Bambi" as a dramatic event, a "major point of departure" for anti-hunting sentiment. To measure the sanity and goodness of the anti-vivisection/humane movement we need to compare it with virtues of hunting societies, virtually all of whom practice *ahisma*: avoiding unnecessary harm which for them means avoiding unnecessary cruelty to wild animals. Among traditional Native Americans at least, *ahisma* was practiced religiously regarding wildlife but not dogs to which there seemed to be no limit of cruelty. Here is a great paradox, but it suggests something fundamentally different in perception of wild and domestic animals among foraging cultures anyway. The wild animals on which hunters depend, and for whom nature is an analog of human society, receive admiration and respect, but the dog is perceived as something less worthy than a slave. Even though native hunters depend upon dogs in hunting and protection against predators and enemies, they are not numinous in contrast with their wild ancestor the wolf. Civilized Europeans also have been extremely cruel and insensitive to dogs which not so long ago were nailed to medical school walls, their cries excused as mere reflexes of machine-like animals, an explanation tendered by Cartesian philosophy and Newtonan mechanics. The anti-vivisectionists of England and America were right to protest against such foolishness.

Certainly, Muth and Jamison are right about the separation of urban humans from nature having an impact on growing concern about animal rights. They mention the critical effect of pets. Paul Shepard has written with depth about the radical influence of domestication on the perception of animals, nature and human society, even child development and human cognition, and it is here that wildlife biology might look to better understand the animal rights movement as an expression of modifications in human ecology. The real question is not "Bambi" itself but the shift in human attitudes and perceptions as a result of human "domestication," including the decline of the number of people who actually participate in the food chain and who confront death among animals and humans.

Elsewhere I have proposed that anti-hunting arose from anti-cruelty because of the equation of death with pain and suffering. Pain, suffering and death are inescapable for wildlife and domestic animals - with the possible exception of pain and suffering among fish. Avoiding unnecessary harm to domestic animals might be expected to evolve in modern civilization as an extension of Pleistocene ethics, but what is not clear is why hunting and killing of wild animals became branded as cruelty. Perhaps Bambiism reflects a shift from foraging, pastoralism and farming to urban living and its separation from the death of animals and humans. Vialles' study of *Animal to Edible* examines slaughterhouses in Western life as a mirror of urban distaste of killing and death, but the perception of food animals as "lesser brethren" can be traced back thousands of years to the origin of pastoralism itself. The ultimate consequences of the equation of cruelty with the death of wild animals is unthinkable, and yet it has come to that now that the animal rights people have sworn to accelerate the extinction or assimilation of all foraging societies and an end to all forms of hunting.

The inevitable next stage will surely include assignment of protection-wardens to prevent cougars from killing deer, coyotes from killing rabbits and dragonflies from catching insects! The bizarre attitudes represented by animal rights say something about how we have raised children apart from nature and the exaggerated influence of industrial education, i.e., schooling, as well as television on misunderstanding of life-and-death.

Muth and Jamison also consider the popularization of science as a contributor to the animal rights movement, and in this regard they go back to the Judeo-Christian view that humanity was created in God's image and was given dominion over animals. They hold this cosmology accountable for separation of humans from the nonhuman world, but I believe that Judeo-Christian cosmology is an outgrowth of pastoralism and ownership of animals. In another word, the shift to egoism and separation. Wildlife biology/management unknowingly perpetuates the same mythology today.

Then Muth and Jamison suggest that evolutionary theory and its popularization has dissolved the boundaries between humans and non-humans, thus contributing to the collapse of Judeo-Christian separation from animals and rights over them, as if to say that the genetic relatedness of humans and other species is in itself responsible for the animal rights movement There is a problem here: hunting societies consider wild animals to be closely related to humans; they also see them as intelligent and sentient, even superior to humans, and while they respect, admire and avoid causing unnecessary harm to them, they place wild animals and themselves in the same crucible of life-and-death.

In a broader social context, evolutionary theory may be seen as an extension of the myth of power born among pastoralists. It belongs to the subset of the historical myth of time as progress, but kept within a strictly scientific context, evolution does challenge the pastoral myth of human superiority and uniqueness so prevalent in humanism.

The difference between animal rightists and foraging peoples is the equation of cruelty with killing. Foragers and recreational hunters both know what modern life actively denies: death makes life possible. Hunting-gathering peoples see no difference between humans and the nonhuman world: all species participate in the same fundamental processes. As Gary Snyder says, we all sit at the same table: who eats today is eaten tomorrow. As an outgrowth of pastoralism and farming, wildlife management views animals as inferior, appropriately subjected to "management," "cropping," and "harvest." This principle applies to all animals, not merely the less defined, less intelligent domestic animal slaves, but also wild animals. Is it any surprise hunting peoples find these concepts offensive?

Does the collapse of distinctions between humans and animals irresistibly lead to anthropomorphism, another precursor to animal rights? Aside from the fact that the tabu on anthropomorphism is invalid, meaning that humans including scientists can only be anthropomorphic, hunting societies are extremely anthropomorphic toward wild animals, but they readily kill them, albeit according to strict rules of conduct. Among some foraging societies hunters feel that it is important to the animals that they be killed by deserving humans.

"So far we've seen that animals are experienced as members of the family, they are anthropomorphized as possessing human qualities, and a heavily interpreted and popularized science provides evidence that animals are truly like people. For many people, this raises a question,'Why don't animals deserve to be treated like people?'" We are most closely related to other humans, of course, but that has not kept millions of them from being slaughtered in wars in the past 100 years! We might just as well ask why don't people deserve to be treated like people?

The anthropomorphic tabu from behavioral science is part of the scientific myth of objectivity which may be traced back to the Cartesian duality of human ego separate from a mechanistic reality, itself an echo of the pastoral myth of human superiority over animals and nature. Contemporary physics' "observer effect" nullifies the possibility of objectivity because scientists interact with and necessarily influence whatever they observe. Though some biologists believe that Newtonian mechanics applies at the level of organization they observe, the separation of observer from world epitomized by biology is an expression of human egoism, which, from Ortega's philosophical perspective, does not hold up.

Animals do have the right to be treated like humans in the sense that who eats today will be eaten tomorrow, and in the chapter on "Buddhism, Hunting and Ethics," we emphasized that the First Precept, avoiding unnecessary harm, is a common ethic of hunting peoples and recreational hunters alike. Real ecology is about food chains, energy flow, which means that we all have the right to eat as well as an obligation to be eaten. We also said that the question of sentience needs re-thought in light of Bell's Theorem and other discoveries which suggest that sentience exists at every level of creation down to electrons at least.

If the animal rights movement is a moral crusade more about modern society and its discontents than it is about animals, then perhaps animals are the symbolic vehicles for reformation. Certainly that is a central message of Jim Swan's book, *In Defense of Hunting*, in which he shows that animal rightists care less about helping animals and more about harming hunters and other people they perceive as bad. The movement does reflect fear and disempowerment owing to loss of authentic society; in compensation, animals are adopted and identified as family members. The myth of Newtonian science, life as cause and effect, has disempowered people and led them to project their fear and anger at hunters. Discontent also comes from lack of proper development and deep, emotional bonding with mother, earth and cosmos, and a lack of meaningful rites of passage.

Of course it is true that unless we can 'fix' what millions of people see as wrong with contemporary Western life animal rights will continue to be a political issue. The premise of this book is that we must recover the Pleistocene man within if we are to find sanity and a sound environment without, thus the importance of bonding, play in nature, rites of passage, hunting as initiation and so on.

We agree with Muth and Jamison that the challenges presented by animal rights is a healthy thing for professionals in wildlife management and conservation, but only if the profession comes to an awareness of the social relevance of hunting, and that will mean a revision of wildlife biology from applied science to interdisciplinary study because hunting is the interaction between humans and the environment, which is to say it is as broad in scope and as deep in its significance as any discipline possibly can be. Such a revision will mean dialoguing with people outside wildlife biology. Individuals who have a broad understanding of the evolution of human nature and the origins of human culture, but also people who represent hunting in its primal form, namely members of hunting societies as well as anthropologists and ethnographers who study them, also psychologists of many stripes, philosophers, ethicists and cultural historians, and within this last group ought to be the spiritual leaders of foraging societies. If atomic physicists seek the insights of medicine people about the multi-dimensional nature of reality, it does not seem out of place for wildlife biologists to seek their counsel regarding human-wildlife relationships. An examination of recent wildlife journals indicates the insignificance of authorities outside the wildlife field, which is surprising considering the problems existing in the field today and Leopold's reliance on mythology and the classics. Subsistence hunting and vision quest should be core curriculum.

Psychology of Hunting

Nowhere in a recent professional wildlife publication about the future of hunting that examined anti-hunting sentiment was there any discussion of the psychology of hunting, which is surprising because anti-hunters have vehemently claimed that hunters are sadistic and psychopathic. Psychologist Jim Swan believes that one of the reasons that there has been a shift in attitudes about hunting is a lack of study of the motivations for hunting, but in any case he says, "Despite vitriolic accusations by some anti-hunters, there is no substantial psychological research or writing to conclude that hunting in general is in any way associated with mental disease. What evidence there is supports just the opposite position. Many of the best-respected behavioral scientists of our times, including Sigmund Freud, William James, Carl Jung, Erich Fromm, Marie-Louise van Franz and Karl Menninger, have agreed that hunting is a natural, healthy part of human nature..." It took many years for Swan to be invited to sit with the chiefs in wildlife management who want to save hunting.

Regarding the relationship between hunting and human aggression, professor of psychiatry and anthropology at Emory University, Melvin Konner says there is little if any evidence to indicate that predatory behavior has much in common with aggression between species. Some social scientists including Colin Turnbull have gone so far as to say that hunting peoples are especially happy and peaceful.

Because wildlife management effectively has become an arm of the State, its leaders see their role as serving society, which means that given enough dissent, hunting, fishing and trapping will be scuttled. In this crucial era of debate and dialogue within the profession, an eye must be kept on horizons far beyond the State and democratic process to the special role that hunting plays in human development. One wildlife biologist wrote a paper in 1998 on the public attitude problems created by the use of the word "sport" in reference to hunting, but the Ontario Federation of Anglers and Hunters, composed of hunters and fishers, voted to drop the term more than 30 years ago owing to its connotations. I have yet to find hunting referred to in the wildlife literature as an instinct that may be minimally mentored with unparalleled benefit for human development and the environment.

Wildlife management was founded on the vision of men whose lives were positively transformed and inspired by hunting. **Communication about the meaning of hunting as spiritual experience can no longer be relegated to the term "cultural benefits" nor to the intuitive, but must be experienced and studied cross-culturally and from a multi-disciplinary perspective as that which is at the very heart of human nature and life.** Re-creational hunting is an expression of the core of human nature, and its rewards and benefits must be measured not solely in terms of food or dollars or harvest or population regulation or science and the measurable, but the growth and health of the human soul, as spiritual ecology. That revision will in turn manifest as more extensive and effective environmental stewardship. Properly understood and mentored, hunting is a key both to human sanity and the realization of an authentic land ethic.

On a practical level, wildlife management has ignored the long-term influences of hunting on character and social behavior: I predict that men who have killed deer are less likely to kill another human. That prediction is in line with FBI/BATF studies of youth with legally owned firearms. What form of mentoring have eco-minded hunters, such as Leopold, Shepard, Swan, Peyton, Fritzell and myself received that may contribute to a better understanding of what hunter education and/or mentoring might accomplish? Averages and opinions are not our goal, but rather the ideal civilized hunter who personifies the values and virtues found among hunting societies. What can we learn from hunting societies that is applicable to hunter education? What can the wilderness/tracking schools teach us about mentoring young hunters? They are experts at mentoring people to nature because they learned from indigenous hunters.

If subsistence survival can have such a profound transformative effect on delinquents, might it also be good medicine for all boys? Isn't that marketable to society at large in a time when hundreds of millions of dollars are being spent to contain juvenile violence and incarcerate young criminals? If not, why not? When school shootings were at a high and much publicized, I contacted hundreds of wildlife biologists, university wildlife programs and wildlife agencies about lecturing on why hunting is good medicine for bad kids, but received not a single indication of interest, though several hunter groups invited me to speak. When I told a leading figure in hunter education about the benefit of subsistence hunting to delinquents he was quick to say that he doesn't want anyone to know about any connection between hunting and delinquency, as though some might blame hunting for youth crime. The antis and the media already have made such claims, without foundation, so isn't it appropriate to present evidence to the contrary, that hunting actually can reduce delinquency?

Hunter Education

Jim Posewitz has been for years a leading figure in hunter education. In an interview he did for "The Sacred Hunt" he explained why hunting is the ultimate relationship with the earth. For Posewitz, hunting is being a participant in nature and in life, and in the process of sustaining himself he has come to an understanding that he is a child of the earth. When an animal is taken he spends a reverent moment to think about what he's just done. He takes only the essential parts of the animal from the field, leaving some of the parts that are going to be disposed of right on the site. Not only does he recycle the nutrient content, with a notion of reverence, but he feels it is important to recycle an ethic that says because I have taken an animal that will sustain me I have a responsibility to sustain that species so I need to know what that sustenance requires and to meet that requirement. That is why, he adds, that associations of hunters come together to save the habitat, protect the environment and preserve wilderness.

Regarding the cultural history of hunting in North America Posewitz sees the hunters as heroes. They were first to stop the destruction of the environment and restore habitat for wildlife. Right up until the early 1970s, the hunters initiated every major piece of conservation legislation. Posewitz thinks that the hunting community needs to recover leadership once again in wilderness preservation and the continued restoration of wetlands, in which the hunters have an admirable history. He believes it is essential to teach the accomplishments of the hunting community to the rest of society, and to young people, and that once they are aware of the responsible activities engaged in by the hunting community the notion of being a part of that community will strengthen and grow.

Unfortunately, there is little indication that the message about the role hunting has played in conservation is winning hearts or recruiting youth.

Another leader in hunter education is David Knotts who directed the International Hunter Education Association, the 70,000 volunteer members of which teach hunter ed classes throughout North America. Knotts shared his thoughts about teaching hunting and religious values.

> "I have some very strong religious convictions, and those religious convictions I find are tied to the land. I find that young people that grow up in an agricultural or rural situation where they are dealing with the land, whether through the necessity of living or through a recreational type activity, seem to have a better level of self-confidence, a better understanding of their purpose in life, maybe acceptance of a being greater than they are. And I can honestly say we've kind of adopted the Indian method of thanking the Great Spirit for the life of the animal when we approach it, and then we treat it with dignity and respect even after it's been killed, and after we harvest it we process it. I grew up in a situation where basically everything I took I had to eat. I had to actually utilize the game I was after (for subsistence), and I taught the same things to my kids."

Environmental psychologist Jim Swan explains why hunting is especially relevant in the lives of young people today.

> "By being a hunter I feel it draws me more closely into nature than if I was just a wildlife watcher or a photographer. I've done those things and I've really enjoyed watching animals. I enjoy taking pictures, but the fact that the ultimate goal of that (hunting) experience is going to lead me to take the life of another creature instills in me a very deep respect for that animal. I have to feel connected to it in some way, and I have to own the fact that when I kill that animal I'm going to feel some sadness because this animal's life is gone as a result of what I've done. So what it does is force me to not be frivolous. It forces me to accept responsibility for my place in the food chain, and as a result that's what leads me to really love nature.
>
> "In the modern age of jet planes and computers and all the technology, it really is critical that we balance modern technology with things that keep us grounded in who we are and what we are and our place in nature. There's a great danger living in a technological society that we'll lose touch with who we are and what our place in the food chain is. And what life is all about. You discover yourself, you don't go finding it from a book, you discover yourself by becoming yourself, by following your own path and where your heart leads you. Hunting is like a mirror in that as you become a hunter you learn about yourself and it reflects back to you and your place in nature. I think if we could teach hunting, to show hunters as heroes, as they have been and should be in human cultures for thousands and thousands of years. What it (hunting) does is deepen your reverence for life, your respect for yourself and your respect for nature."

Hunter education in North America has been remarkably successful overall, especially in light of the fact that the front-line educators typically are volunteers. The state wildlife agency may employ a hunter education coordinator, but the actual courses are taught by unpaid men and women many of whom belong to the International Hunter Education Association, a private organization. The enthusiasm of volunteer teachers speaks to the power of hunting itself on a social level. The hunt has meant so much to the volunteers that they naturally want to be of service and pass it on. The basic course offered is usually 12 hours. It focuses on hunter safety, handling firearms, game laws, species identification and hunter ethics such as respecting the rights of land owners. Some states offer an advanced course.

Hunter education started with a primary focus on hunter safety, and that is still the emphasis in some states. There is a clear need for young hunters to learn about how to responsibly handle firearms, and no doubt hunter safety courses contribute to that need, to wit, hunting is the safest outdoor sport. As neuropsychologist Jim Rose said in his interview in the Foreword, firearm safety and use teach self-restraint, patience and responsibility to adolescent males.

Resource Management or Reciprocity?

I commend hunter ed instructors, but hunter education suffers because it is, effectively, an extension of the profession of wildlife management which is tailored to the precepts of the State. The doctrines of wildlife management shine through hunter education and reinforce the existing system of authority: we have hunter ed instructors teaching young hunters that hunting is justifiable because it controls and regulates populations of game species; if deer are not hunted they will overbrowse their food supply and starve. So, the anti-hunters say, let them starve! From their point of view starvation is a better alternative than cruelty exercised by hunters with weapons. The fact is that most deer herds are not controlled by human hunting anyway, but what if the antis come along with a satisfactory alternative to regulating deer herds, such as a chemical form of birth control that can be broadcast widely, as from the air?

As an arm of wildlife management hunter education justifies hunting in terms of "management of the resource," not in terms of our human relationship to wild things nor in terms of reciprocity between them and us nor in terms of why we actually hunt. Indigenous hunters despise the term "management," because they feel that is an expression of domination of wild animals and nature, upon whose generosity they depend. That generosity is earned through respectful thought, feeling and action, not by conceiving of deer as comparable to noxious weeds overcrowding the landscape. A genius in several fields, Rudolf Steiner is considered by many to be the foremost mystic of the modern world; he said that nature spirits are emissaries for holy spirits in which case the primal hunter's ethic of reciprocity makes sense.

Based on decades of field research, Fritz Berkes, Milton Freeman and others working with the Cree and Inuit of northern Canada convincingly demonstrate that these subsistence hunters effectively accomplish conservation of wildlife without the imposition of Euro-American wildlife management principles. Richard Nelson has claimed the same for Koyukon and Eskimo hunters, something the vast majority of wildlife biologists can't imagine. A leading figure in hunter education laughed at the possibility that Native Americans might have practiced conservation, and yet there are numerous indications in the ethnographic literature that foraging peoples around the world are conservationists. Anthropologist Colin Turnbull, for instance, documented decades ago that pygmies avoid killing pregnant elephants.

As the foremost defender of Inuit hunting rights, Milton Freeman has carefully documented abuses by government wildlife agencies that have deliberately falsified data to justify the need for them to manage wildlife resources. For all practical purposes, wildlife management in North America is vulnerable to the same abuses as government and big business.

Wildlife management in Europe has its problems, not the least of which is the extreme level of husbandry of "wild" animals, which, in many respects are managed as intensively as domestic livestock. Unfortunately, there are few hunters in Europe and extreme anti-hunting sentiment.

Wildlife management is modeled after domestic animal husbandry and forestry practices designed with maximization of production in mind. Though aimed at things wild it is industrial; for example, hunting is described by wild-life biologists as a "tool." But the fact is that we do not hunt to control game herds, and though a majority of recreational hunters may respond to questionnaire surveys that they hunt primarily for the meat, they could buy commercially ranch-raised elk, deer and pheasant at much less expense than what it cost to procure it by hunting. At least some of the real motives for re-creational hunting are psycho-spiritual and transcendent in nature. Wildlifers may doubt my conclusion, but what they cannot doubt is that the questionnaire surveys conducted of hunters on which they have relied much have been inadequately designed to account for the inner dimensions of hunting. As Stuart Marks, the anthropologist who studies both subsistence and recreational hunting said regarding these questionnaire surveys that are "a mile long and a foot deep," they haven't got a clue what culture means. They also know little about the immense potential hunting may serve as a rite of passage that develops responsible, caring young adults of virtue and character. Leopold's vision came from heart-intelligence, but like Western life generally, wildife biology has sunk to ego-intellect. It needs to be re-founded on Pleistocene wisdom, which is after all what inspired it.

Mine is a lover's quarrel: when it comes to admiration, I applaud the sincere conviction and dedication of the rank and file wildlife biologists, especially the elders who grew up fishing and hunting and for whom nature and wildlife are great teachers. Likewise, the hunter ed instructors who love hunting and fishing and care that the tradition is passed on, but are they presenting the truth of why we hunt and its meaning in our lives? In short, does wildlife management and hunter education fathom the social relevance or moral justification for hunting? Until they do, they may be destined to flounder amidst the ruins of wildlife husbandry rather than rise to the challenge of stewarding the soul of our youth. In this regard, prospects for the future are increasingly dismal because fewer wildlife biologists are hunters. If anyone in our culture requires initiation to the sacred hunt it is the wildlife biologist.

Hunter Recruitment

There are other problems. Hunting is under attack and recruitment is declining, but large influential organizations with enormous funding and support from the hunting and firearms industry are failing to communicate to the non-hunting public the meaning and value of hunting to our youth. They resist efforts to upgrade the quality and content of hunter education apparently because they fear that if hunter education is expanded it will take more hours and fewer young people are likely to enroll which would mean even lower hunter recruitment and lower sales by the hunting/shooting industry. Unless shooting sports and hunter-conservation groups fully comprehend and embrace the human justifications for hunting it may perish along with them.

Hunter groups like the Dallas Safari Club devote much of their effort to initiating boys and girls to shooting and hunting, and generally they do an excellent job; however, like wildlife professionals these groups have failed to articulate and communicate to the non-hunting community the value of hunting to youth. Equally serious, hunting organizations need to find ways to reach more kids. Big Brothers/Sisters for hunting, a program that is doing well in Kansas, should be widespread. Teen Anglers and Hooked on Fishing do a wonderful job initiating youth to fishing, and they have reached a huge audience by penetrating the schools, but schools would not be receptive to "Teen Hunters" owing to fear of firearms. Archery in the Schools has been very successful and is growing rapidly. Jay Macanich's survey suggests that many of the young archers are interested in pursuing bow hunting. Everything else being the same archery is a better choice of weaponry because it demands better hunting skills and offers more intimacy and communication between the animal and hunter.

Though fishing is more popular and acceptable in America than hunting, and while it offers much of value to our youth, it does not offer as much as hunting, in part because fish are so very different than us which means that we do not tend to identify with them, their suffering (they may not experience pain) or their death. Essentially, fishing doesn't have the emotional impact of hunting in terms of opening the heart and engendering compassion. Many hunters also are fishers and vice-versa, and while I would rate hunting above fishing as an initiatory path, it is better for kids to fish than not, just as it is better for a kid to shoot than not. The same applies to gathering and gardening.

Perhaps the ideal way to recruit more young people into the outdoors is for hunting groups to establish programs in which each member adopts a kid whom he/she mentors for at least one hunting season. The success of any broader-scale program that mentors hunting will rest upon effective communication about its benefits and values to society at large, and whether they realize it or not that means the hunting community must dig deep and embrace the hunt as ritual that pays homage to the mystery of life. Without bringing that awareness to the surface and accepting it, they will not be able to turn the tide for hunting, for youth, for nature-culture.

More Mentoring?

Hunter education is more about laws, regulations and safety, but mentoring refers to "lived experience," and while nearly all hunter education instructors have logged much experience outdoors, their volunteer work is undertaken mostly in classrooms with a little time given to actual shooting. Usually groups are too large to escort on actual hunts or nature explorations. Kids do need both hunter education **and** nature mentoring.

The outdoor industry is sponsoring experimental programs in mentoring youth to hunting, and I think they would do well to invite wilderness educators like Jon Young, interviewed in the Foreword, who have studied mentoring in indigenous peoples and perfected it over several decades. Natural history originates from and is part of hunting, and proper mentoring in hunting would be improved by encompassing principles used by tracking and wilderness awareness schools. The best primer for principles of mentoring is Young's *Coyote's Guide to Connecting with Nature.*

The core routines practiced in Coyote Mentoring will benefit all children and adults. They include Sit Spot, daily visitation, alone, to a natural place where a person can sit and quietly observe before playfully exploring beyond. The exercise expands the senses and develops an intimate connection with nature, similar to still hunting. Story of the Day consists of returning from nature and telling your story either to other people or by writing or drawing in a journal, not unlike what hunters do when they return to their village or camp. Questioning and Tracking involves becoming a detective and tracking everything as clues to be solved, asking questions until they yield answers.

Animal Forms encompasses the imitation of animals in their movements, behavior and personality, also fundamental to hunting. Mapping, Exploring Field Guides, Journaling, Survival Skills and Thanksgiving are other core routines which collectively connect people to nature, develop them on every level and often launch them into fishing and hunting.

With each passing day I grow more certain that civilization is collapsing, at least shifting, and I wonder what form human life may take. The imagination reels with the prospects of designing small communities sustained by permaculture, farming and foraging, but what hope is there for peace among societies when only a few cultures ever have achieved it? Isn't a post-apocalyptic world likely to resemble life as it was depicted in the Mad Max films? More of the same competition for resources, albeit on a smaller scale?

The Kalahari Bushman sought refuge in the desert from Bantu and later white oppression, and in that austere environment conflict between Bushman clans has been extremely rare. The density of pygmies is so low in the tropical forest that warfare is rare or non-existent. The Hopis deliberately chose to live in an environment so severe that there would be no cause for war.

Nomadic or not, the original human lifestyle of hunting and gathering does not entail long-term possession or accumulation of wealth and resources, and consequently it offers the greatest possibility for peace. Those who have shared the life of pygmies or Bushman are envious, finding there the genuine community, social security, nature connection, joy and laughter missing in other lifestyles.

I believe we owe it to ourselves and our children to learn how to survive in nature and enjoy doing it. Wilderness educator and tracker Josh Lane says that in some of the "environmental education" that public schools send kids to (for all of a week out of 12 years of schooling), nature is looked at but not interacted with in a dynamic way, the way of the hunter or gatherer. "It's such a different experience to learn about trees in the forest because you need to figure out which one will provide the best kindling to light your fire because you're COLD and HUNGRY and need to warm up and cook something. Live like that for a few days and you can figure out a lot about trees and how important they are. It's a lot different than hearing a teacher say 'this is a blahblah blah tree, and this is a blah....' Need produces interaction which produces a direct learning experience."

Learn to start a fire from scratch, meaning no matches or lighter, build a shelter to protect against a severe storm, make a rodent trap, build a bow and make arrows, and take time to identify poisonous and edible plants. The time for a new beginning may be closer than we think

Animals as Targets?

There are still other problems that cannot be ignored. What do you think Leopold would say about "hunting" varmints? Would he cringe to think that state wildlife agencies, hunter education and the outdoor industry condone the killing of gophers, coyotes and jack rabbits as legitimate hunting? Is it a measure of how far off center we have become and how little professional wildlife management has done to bring us back? Jimmy Carter's "Daddy" had it right when he said if you don't intend to eat it don't kill it. It is one thing to kill a coyote or bobcat that threatens your chickens or lambs or a cougar that stalks deer close to where your child plays; it is quite another to go out and shoot them simply as live targets, excusing it because the animals are numerous or unpopular. From an ecological perspective, are varmint shooters merely thinning the population enough to encourage more reproduction? I could never take a young person out to "hunt" varmints unless we did so for food or clothing. Woe be to anyone who is critical of any form of "hunting." They are apt to be perceived as a threat to all hunting and shooting, so the industry limps along refusing to question practices in fear that it will mean losing a war with the antis, and in the end this lack of self-criticism weakens its position altogether.

I am not necessarily against hunting big predators such as cougar and black bear. Having spent years studying interactions between larger carnivores and humans I can safely say that without hunting these species with dogs, as they were for millennia by natives before colonization, they will increasingly threaten human life, which eventually could precipitate a zealous backlash. It's a matter of boundaries, like Gary Snyder killing a raccoon every few years.

Hunting is literally and metaphorically the original, fundamental and most potent bond between men and nature. It is the medicine boys need to become men of respect, responsibility and spiritual power. It is socially relevant and morally justifiable, and if I am right it is among the last hopes for civilized humanity to recover sanity and save itself and the earth. In the closing words of "The Sacred Hunt," "People who would stop others from hunting do not participate in the most fundamental processes of life: their food. Someone else grows their vegetables, and kills the chickens and cows they eat and wear on their bodies...Like the primal hunter, the re-creational hunter loves animals and nature. Like the primal hunter, the re-creational hunter also knows that animals are intelligent and conscious, worthy of his respect and admiration. Hunters do not question the value of wilderness and wild things or the need for preserving them. And if most men had been properly initiated into the sacred traditions of hunting, there would be none of the environmental problems presently facing us, wildlife and the earth. The great mystery into which every true hunter enters teaches him that a man thinks with his heart, not his head. That is the secret of hunting."

Perpetuating Hunter Tradition

The keynote address I gave at Ontario Federation of Anglers & Hunters was entitled, "Why hunting is good medicine for ***bad*** kids." The insertion of the word "bad" generated enormous, international publicity which included press releases being carried by the Canadian wire service, an appearance on "Canada AM," largest audience TV program in the country, interviews in the major Toronto papers and two radio stations there, an interview on CBC, some newspaper coverage in the northeast and northwest US, and a live interview on BBC Radio to its worldwide audience of several hundred million people, all with a positive message about youth hunting.

I spoke about the program for delinquent boys who had to survive in the wilderness for two weeks on whatever they could catch or kill, the most successful program to date ever launched for troubled teens – see interview of Dr. Wade Brackenbury in the Foreword. My conclusion was that hunting is good for bad kids because it is good for all kids; moreover, I was inundated for weeks by single moms wanting to know how to get their teen boys involved in hunting.

It would be wise for the hunting community to promote hunting as authentic rite of passage for boys to manhood. Properly publicized, the theme of this book could have a huge impact on youth recruitment and the public image of hunting.

The conservation message is not bringing more young people to our door, nor will it. That traditional outdoor recreation develops youth into better adults will get the attention of parents, teachers, politicians, judges, the press and media. In focusing on conservation, a very significant byproduct of hunting, we have overlooked the human in the center.

"What we have here," the Warden in Cool Hand Luke said, "is a failure to communicate."

It is imperative that we rise to the challenge of attracting more people to hunting for the benefit of our youth, society and the environment. We are launching production of a general audience documentary about "The Next Kid in the Woods" which will show that the appropriate medicine for "nature deficit disorder" is traditional outdoor recreation. We also are promoting a DVD workshop for conservation professionals and the outdoor industry about how to be a better evangelist for hunting – we need to educate our ranks.

We must explore ways to elevate the image of hunting, fishing and shooting, such as an "Outdoor Celebrity Hall of Fame," which honors and inducts leading outdoors men and women. There could be two divisions: outdoor celebrities; outdoor leaders and conservationists. I envision celebrities promoting the outdoors to kids and parents alike; the celebrity division could include extremely high profile individuals like Morgan Freeman, Kurt Russell, Shaq O'Neal, pro athletes, country singers, Nascar drivers and so on, who already are acceptable role models. To get these same people to advertise the outdoors would cost megamillions annually, but by honoring them they will come for an airticket and lodging, and what they say in their acceptance speech is perfect copy for publicity at the time but also later in PSA campaigns on radio/TV across the continent. "Build it and they will come."

Why not an annual contest for best screen play with an outdoor theme – "A River Runs Through It" did wonders for fly fishing not to mention wilderness and trout!

Reforms can base K12 education on hunting, fishing, shooting/archery, wilderness awareness, nature study and tracking: an entire curriculum can be delivered in the outdoors which would be infinitely more effective, attractive and fun for students of all ages.

We need a short booklet on, "Should Your Child Hunt?" which explains to parents all the ways that hunting can develop children into better, healthier, happier and responsible adults who take care of the environment.

It is imperative that larger hunter/shooting sports organizations begin to utilize creative communications and the assistance of publicists to cover newsworthy speakers, projects and events. Publicity properly planned and placed can reach the choir and beyond and elevate the image of hunting as well as promote youth recruitment.

"Silence is the absolute poise or balance of body, mind and spirit."

~ CHARLES A. EASTMAN (Ohiyesa), Santee Sioux

Chapter 15

The Vision Quest

"Each of us must find out for himself or herself what their gift is, so that they can use it in their life. The old people say everyone has a song to sing. This song is the reason we are on this earth. When we are doing what we came on this earth to do, we know true happiness. How will we know our song? Pray. Ask the Great Mystery... He will tell you. He will even help you develop yourself to accomplish His mission."

~ JIMMY JACKSON, Ojibway

Around the world over time numerous cultures have given young men rituals that initiate them into the life of the spirit. The rites take many forms but the essential experience is the same – discovery that there is more to life than what meets the eye.

The classical vision quest associated with the natives of Turtle Island consists of solitude and fasting. The quest may be for a dream-vision, as among the Ojibwe described by Kohl, above, or it may be for a waking vision as sought by the Lakota. The vision quest fits the model of a full rite of passage because it includes separation from society, transformation and return or reincorporation. The young man dies to his boyhood past and is reborn a man. He undergoes deprivation of food and water for several days, ranging from three or four up to ten or more, and he must be brave enough to give up the usual comfort and the security of his familiar world for solitude in the wilderness. In addition to enduring hardship, which prepares him for adult life, the young man has much time to contemplate the meaning of life and to "cry for a vision," as Black Elk said, about his life's mission and purpose.

Fasting has been associated universally with spiritual guidance aimed at solving problems in the real world. When the body is starved, the pineal gland is activated. It is a center for metabolism, and in birds regulates storage of fat as well as migration. The bird's pineal is light sensitive, actually detecting photo-period, length of day, a trigger for migration. It is a vestigial eye, the "third eye" employed by Hindus for spiritual sight. Fasting activates the pineal and induces it to secrete neurohormones, which activate inner vision.

The entire process is creative in nature. If the body is starving, then there must be something wrong with life as usual so the pineal gland kicks into action and activates creative solutions. Descartes considerd it the site of the soul, where we "see the light." So fasting is not merely about enduring hardship to prove oneself worthy, but about activating higher awareness and accessing the spiritual realm.

In my initial vision quest at the age of 32, my vision came in the form of vivid coherent dreams about the nature of masculinity and my own need to recover my heart and soul, i.e., to temper the masculine with the feminine. The writing I did during the quest was peculiar and reflected spiritual influence: page after page I wrote, "I AM that I AM that I AM!" At that time I had no knowledge of this passage in the Bible, though intuitively I understood.

My sensitivity to nature and my own body and mind reached a zenith. I felt a sense of unity with other living things, plant and animal, that I had known only while hunting. After three days and nights I walked out of the mountain wilderness, and as I descended on a logging road heard a deafening sound that became louder. For the life of me I could not identify the nature of the sound, but it pierced and disturbed my entire being as no sound ever had. I thought for a while that it must be the sound from a giant saw cutting logs in a mill. Finally, as I drew near to a state highway, I recognized the sound as cars driving by on the road. The quest had meant a recovery of primal awareness which is normally suppressed in civilized life.

Twenty-two years later I began a pilgrimage over several years in "Mayup," the land of the Maya, in Mexico's Yucatan. I was there to learn about the sacred traditions of the Maya, who to this day are forager-farmers who hunt and grow crops in the dry tropical forest. The traditional initiation rites of Mayan men were the most advanced I've encountered anywhere on earth.

The seven temples found in ancient sites such as Chichen Itza were for seven initiations. The elaborate series of initiations corresponds with the seven main charkas or energy centers of the body, starting with the lowest chakra at the base of the spine which receives what the Hindus call *kundalini* energy. The first initiation was in the ball court, but contrary to tour guides of Aztec descent, the winning team did not have their heads cut off! If they won they successfully completed the first initiation: mastery of the body. Then they were allowed to move onto the next initiation, associated with the second chakra located below the navel. The stone base of the second temple, immediately next to the ball court, is covered with the etchings of skulls, which has led to the popular notion of the winning team's decapitation. Each skull represents one young man's successful completion of the second initiation. Meditation was used to induce an out-of-body experience, but if meditation failed, psychotropic plants were used to achieve the same end. To leave the body is to experience death, and what one discovers, of course, is that there is life beyond the body, i.e., that one's spirit survives the body, which deflates trust in ego and promotes heart-intelligence.

Like the vision quest, the second initiation of the Maya teaches a young man that his true nature is spiritual. In both there is death and rebirth.

For successful initiates, the initiations continue, chakra by chakra, temple by temple. The sixth initiation is associated with the third eye or pineal, and occurs in the temple of the Chacmul. The young man lies down on a stone altar supported by columns with carvings of adult men of the known races of the world (including Semitic, Polynesian and African). The purpose of the initiation is death of the ego which activates spiritual vision. Each one of the columns outside the temple stands for a man who graduated from the Chacmul temple to the final initiation in the solar temple, associated with the crown chakra and enlightenment, which I had experienced a few months after my first vision quest.

Unlike the warring Aztecs, for whom the jaguar is a symbol of powerful manhood, the goal of Mayan males was to transcend the body or ego, represented by the jaguar, and connect via the snake with the eagle, as depicted on temples and ruins throughout Mayup. The snake symbolizes the spirit and the eagle represents the heavenly Creator. Essentially, the Mayan religious symbols of jaguar, snake and eagle are comparable to the Christian symbols of Son (physical creation, body, ego), Holy Spirit and Father.

The point is that whatever form a vision quest may take its purpose is to integrate the lower with the higher, to temper the masculine with the heart. That is the path to self-mastery.

Vision quest programs are offered at a few high schools and colleges for both males and females. Steven Foster and Meredith Little direct the School of Lost Borders, a ceremonial center for wilderness initiation which sponsors vision quests. They see the vision quest as re-creation of "an ancient rite of dying, passing through, and being reborn." Foster's first vision quest, undertaken as an adult gave him this guidance: "You must look within your heart and see what you have to give to your people. Then you must go back and give it away."

Foster and Little share an account from Wendell Berry who writes about the death of a friend's friend.

> "She was trying to get from one phase of her life to the next and could not make it so she destroyed herself. How does a person pass from youth to maturity without breaking down? Rites of passage are needed at the most difficult times. A rite of passage is the traditional cultural answer to a personal crisis of meaning. Through the rite of passage, individuals and groups make themselves receptive to spiritual meaning. Contact with this spiritual meaning (God, The Great Spirit, the Life Force, higher consciousness) resolves the crisis, and the transition is completed."

The vision quest, like all rites of passage, includes a severance from the usual temporal world, being taken away to a place apart to prepare for the second phase, the threshold, a direct existential experience of the meaning of a life transition,

> "The participant steps across the threshold into the unknown, armed with symbolic tools of self-birth, and enters a universal order that is sacred and immortal. During this threshold period, secret knowledge and power are transmitted and confer on the individual new rights, privileges and responsibilities upon returning."

Reincorporation involves the return of the seeker from the spiritual realm of knowing and power to the mortal realm of community. Hopefully, the individual is supported in living out the internal changes that occurred during the rite of passage.

In Foster and Little's program, the person attends some classes that help them prepare for the severance or separation. They study native and archaic rites of passage and talk about their own deaths and rebirths, the world they are leaving behind and the one to which they will be retuning. Participants learn basic emergency survival skills and what to take along: back pack; sleeping bag and pad; ground cloth or rain tarp; rope; pocketknife or universal tool; matches; bandanna; two gallons of water if none is available; journal and pencil; toilet paper; warm clothes, stout boots and wool cap; cup and spoon; change of warm clothes.

The seeker(s) travels with a mentor to an appropriate wilderness site where they prepare for the vision quest. The seeker locates his place, selecting it according to his inner sensitivity, then confirms its location with a mentor and the path between it and the base camp occupied by the mentor. The seeker prepares himself to face adversity: nature is unpredictable and he may never have spent time alone or in the wilderness. "Risk and fear are the Earth Mother's handmaidens. They strip one of pride, rip off the habitual blinders, awaken the sleeping senses."

Seekers feast before and after questing, but for three days and nights they fast. No music or tape players are allowed: one must make music or hear it from the earth, creatures or sky. The seeker must know the symptoms of heat exhaustion, dehydration, sunburn and exposure and how to avoid or treat them. Caution must be taken to avoid talus slopes and cliffs, flashfloods, etc., and the person must be able to build a fire and construct a temporary shelter. He will need to know the habits of poisonous snakes and stinging insects and what to do if bitten or stung.

When several seekers go out together, they establish an intersection of trails that lead off to their questing spots and each day walk to that intersection at different times where they place a stone to indicate to one another or to a mentor(s) that they are okay.

Threshold

The quest itself introduces a seeker to the eternity of nature and the infinity of creation outside himself. The mountains and rocks hundreds of millions of years old and the galaxy of millions upon millions of stars belittles and humbles him with its grandeur, and it also mirrors his own internal eternity-infinity. The absence of familiar sights and sounds, the dropout of endless chores, tasks and distractions leaves the young man's conditioned mind lost and feeble. Another awareness begins to emerge from the great silence and time is measured not by clocks but by bird and insect song, the scuffle of a lizard, the beating of the heart, the passing of the sun.

The place that called you to it holds something of value. It is the medium between you and nature, the place where you learn to touch the earth and caress stones, your sacred altar, where you may speak aloud to the spirit of life, walk barefoot and nude, listen to the wind's voice and dream the dreams of the creatures who share the place with you.

The fast will purify the body and fill the spirit. You may go weeks without food but only a few days without water so drink. Going without earthly food is a sacrifice that prepares you to receive spiritual food. It prepares you to ask the Great Spirit for mercy and satisfy the hunger of your soul.

The young man may construct a circle of stones around his place to create a ritual space. He may designate the four directions and offer some of his water or tobacco to the earth and to the grandfathers from which he seeks guidance. He may build a fire, not for warmth and protection but as a ritual that honors the light and warmth of the sun and his own heart. The fire may speak to him.

This is the time for the young man to identify his emergent self with a new name. It may come in dreamtime or vision or on the wings of a raptor, but it will come. This is the special time and place to ask earth, the spirits and the Creator for the guidance he seeks. While falling asleep he may pray as I pray, "Master Power (or God, Creator, Holy Spirit), please show me the images with sounds I can hear in dreamtime that will resolve_______________(my purpose in life, my spirit name, the lessons you hold for me, etc.) for the good of all." Record your dreams and your reflections on them. The journal you keep of this transitional experience will provide valuable reference for years to come.

This also is the time to descend shamelessly into your wounds and grieve them outloud. Here is the place to release and heal. The bosom of the earth mother welcomes your tears. Now you may forgive yourself and all those whom have transgressed against you – and bless them. You may invite them to dance around the fire with you. Howling at the sky is not reserved for coyote.

Your vision may come in the form of wisdom, the knowing of the heart. It may appear as an insight or a deep feeling of connection or a dream or creative energy or as the meaning of life, your life. Whatever form it takes you will be ready for your new journey as an adult.

Reincorporation

Ideally, the initiated quester's return to the world he knew finds him in the company of other questers and/or a mentor at a base camp in or next to wilderness where he can recount his adventure and hear those of others. The mentor may help him interpret his dreams. Feasting is in order, also song and dance around a ceremonial fire and another night spent sleeping on the earth.

Then it's back to civilization and its humdrum ruts where little sympathy is found for vision questers. The young man may recoil from the insensitivity and pace of it all. It may frighten him to think he ever accepted life in this world. It has not changed but he has. Solace may be found in a return to solitude, if only for an hour in the late afternoon or early evening, perhaps in a park or the edge of town.

The initiate may experience a "healing crisis," and waver between elation and depression. Talking with a mentor or fellow quester can be good medicine. The trick is carrying the fruits of the vision quest as he moves through the world as an ambassador between the realm of spirit and nature and the realm of human life. His very presence, peace of mind and solid connection to what is real is a gift to the world. There will be those who sense his change and ask him about it, and he will be able to offer them "little bits of wisdom," and some will seek his assistance in making their own vision quest.

The decision to make a vision quest may prove more significant than the vision quest itself because in making that decision a young man is committing himself to the "hero's journey," but it may come when he least expects it.

In 1975, about a month after my first vision quest in the foothills of the Cascades, I unexpectedly took the hero's journey in the midst of the civilized world. In the middle of the afternoon I sat on a couch talking with a friend in Bellevue about the art of becoming a detached observer of self and the world. I told her that, "I feel like I've been climbing stairs and when I get to the top there is a doorway, and on the other side of the doorway is the answer, but the moment I try stepping over the threshold..." And at that very moment I was gone, taken from this body and world into other dimensions. At one "stop" I was shown the history of the universe and from outside observed it contract and expand repeatedly like a beating heart. That was four years before the "long view" theory was proposed in scientific literature: that there was not simply one big bang but a series of big bangs followed by an expanding universe that then contracts and explodes again. Turns out that the ancient Hindus also held the long view, but they were not recognized in the scientific article.

My ultimate "stop" was an experience of "eternity-infinity," in which I was "everywhere at once beyond time." Words do not suffice, but somehow I experienced all of what lies beyond space and time and was virtually identical with it. There was perfect knowledge and peace in my true being, one with Divinity, one with all. And during my "return" there was another stop where I was shown a shimmering gold sine wave of infinite extension with six crests. I knew that this was the prototype of creation, the interface of the Great Void or Godhead I had been one with and manifest creation. I described it later as fluxion of energy upon itself, essentially the will of God to create. The sine wave is the boundary between the unmanifest or Creator and the manifest Creation, God and the Son of God. I also knew that each of us exists simultaneously at each and every one of these levels or dimensions, and that we come into the world from the Great Void, through the sine wave, and that eventually we return to it – I sometimes call it Home. We are here and at Home even now because we are multi-dimensional beings, who, owing to extreme conditioning in an egoic world spend most of our lives at the 3D level falsely believing it is all there is.

As I began to return to my body, feeling every cell in it pulling me into the earthly dimension, I was reluctant and wanted to stay where I was. But I also sensed that there was more for me to do in the body and that I needed to bring the gifts of my momentous journey back into the world and share them with others. When I collided with my body and it lurched back against the couch I immediately began to laugh the happiest laughter of my life that I had ever feared death or anything.

For six months I was in a state of "samadhi," perfect bliss and knowledge. I knew when someone was about to phone me and what they wanted. I knew where to drive in Seattle to provide assistance to someone in need. During these six months I was never angry, jealous, envious, doubtful, skeptical, afraid or anxious, not for a single second. I returned a very different person than when I left, and as I was filled with light and buoyed by love, able to see only goodness, humor and beauty, I attracted but also frightened many people. I encountered blank faces among family, friends and colleagues when I attempted to explain to them my experience and the truth about who and what we really are. They saw and felt the change in me but for the most part they were frightened by the temptation that I might be right, in which case their ego defenses would be useless and they might fail here in this competitive, fearful world.

Was my ultimate vision quest a near-death experience? When it happened there had been no books written about them, no interviews on TV talk shows. I had never heard of anyone having an experience like I had had, nor did I encounter anyone for many years after who had had a similar experience. The subsequent books on death and dying did provide accounts but the descriptions were not like my own.

When I refused to accept that I could not help my wife make the same leap I had made, I crashed into my own ego and found myself back in the world of fear and desire. Refusal to accept was an egoic act that closed the curtain on enlightenment. I had forgotten the truth of that little book, *The Lazy Man's Guide to Enlightenment*, which contains one lesson throughout: no resistance. I spent years trying to find my way back to Samadhi, and in that quest I once sat and told my story to a Rimpoche at a Tibetan Buddhist temple south of Ashland, Oregon. He listened intently and when I finished he reflected for a minute then said, "You are telling me that you found enlightenment and lost it?" I said yes. Then he shook his head violently sideways and raised his hands, exclaiming, "and I haven't even found it!" I took his comment to mean, "Oh my God, does this mean I might find enlightenment then lose it?"

Finally I realized that I had been given a gift and that I still carried the jewel within me, and that the challenge is to keep polishing it as I move through this life. The Zen Buddhists refer to the process as polishing the mirror. In short, the gift of vision is a continual reminder of who we are and the level we can attain in this world if we continue to work at it. The yogi says, "After Samadhi we sweep the floor." The Buddha said, "Before enlightenment, cut wood and carry water. After enlightenment, cut wood and carry water." I'm still cutting wood and carrying water.

The unexpected, unexplainable out-of-body experience a month after my formal vision quest was for me an actual rite of passage with separation-transformation-return that encompassed death and rebirth. The most important step we make is the first step and that is the choice, our intent.

Over the following five years I had three out-of-body or "near death" experiences, but they consisted simply of leaving the body and remaining nearby in this dimension, fully aware of everyone in the room and what they said and did as well as my lifeless body on the floor. In one of these I experienced a gold cord of energy running lengthwise through my body and knew that the cord could break and I would be unable to return to my body, in a word, die, but through concentration on the cord I returned to it.

Finally I came to understand my journey to the Godhead as revelation.

Steven Foster and Meredith Little offer some sound advise in their book, *Vision Quest*:

> "The hero/ine learns to live in two worlds...perhaps the most important teaching of the Vision Quest. One world is sacred, spiritual, eternal. It is the world you stepped into when you crossed the threshold. The other world is mortal, material and subject to change. It is the worlds you stepped into when you recrossed the threshold. The first world is where your vision is conceived; the second world is where you give birth to your vision."

A vision quest can be done at any age from about 15 on, though in our culture I think it might make good sense to connect it with graduation from high school, either in the last term or soon after commencement ceremony, since that event corresponds with leaving childhood and home for a new life. Once a person has sought a vision, he or she can do it again whenever it feels appropriate, as during life transitions or crises. At the end of the book are resources that include individuals and organizations that offer formal vision quest programs for young (and older) people.

Dreamtime as Vision and Rite of Passage

"The interpretation and understanding of a dream can become a form of inner rite of passage. The dream teaches the dreamer to relate to her/his own symbols. They are themselves thresholds to be crossed as the dreamer takes a journey to individuation," says Louise Mahdi.

Vision may be born by dreams, as for the Ojibwe and certainly myself: a Lakota medicine man described me as a "dream shaman." There are people who insist that they do not dream, but all research to date suggests that in fact everyone does. "Knock and the door will open" applies to conscious dreaming. All one needs to do is seek a dream, i.e., to will awareness of their dreams. The dream prayer I offered above also has worked well for many people. Keeping a journal handy at night is recommended. When you awaken during the night and in the morning your dreams are more likely to be vivid so that's a good time to be still, recollect, record and reflect on them.

A common theme in my dreams has been of dead wild animals, especially deer and elk (I have never killed either of these species), rising from the earth, from gutters and graves and bone heaps to resume life and follow me down a path at night. The first few times I had one of these dreams I was amazed and ecstatic, but at the same time perplexed as to how I was going to tell other people that the spirits of the animals we kill live on, an ominous difficulty owing to the influence of three centuries of mechanistic science.

I also have had similar dreams about my Paleolithic ancestors as skeletons under my bed who arose with full body and mind to greet me. I recognized them as my kin and celebrated our reunion, even introducing them to friends as my brothers from long ago.

Though it has taken many kinds of experiences to reawaken my awareness of the nature of life after being indoctrinated in the scientific tradition of the West, I now know that every living thing has a spirit that survives the body, and we need to recognize that and pay respect and give thanks to the countless creatures who have died that we might live. I have come to believe that the spirits of our ancestors also survive the death of the body, and rather than store them under our beds as sleeping old bones, they, too, can come to life and participate in it with us. They want to be invited. The Old Ways are knocking at the door.

The Kalahari Bushman dance nightly, enter trance and leave their bodies and travel to visit with their deceased ancestors to receive their guidance. See Bradford Keeney's *Bushman Shaman.*

Once we accept dreamtime as a legitimate form of communication between the conscious and unconscious, sleep may become a setting for receipt of higher guidance regarding our everyday waking life, a form of healing for the body, mind and soul, and a means of spiritual communication. Dreams may be highly symbolic but they also can be literal, even clairvoyant. While a teenager, a well-known rocket scientist received detailed instructions each night for three years about the design and construction of a rocket which his father built. The design was completely novel, though he was shown one like it at Area 51 which had come to earth from outer space.

Once I dreamed about a young woman whose name was Cindy, and the next morning when I arrived at my university office there was the young woman whom I had seen in the dream. She had made no appointment to see me, nor had I ever seen her prior to the dream. I walked up to her and said, "You must be Cindy." Discussions with hundreds of students in classes I taught over the years indicated that it is common for people to encounter and communicate with a dead relative in a dream during the evening in which that relative died, though the dreamer was not yet aware of their death. There were several cases in which the relative communicated to the dreamer that they were okay.

Three years ago I received the same dream instruction over and over throughout the night, "Remember, N.A.T.U.R.E. means North American Teachers for the Understanding and Respect of the Earth." Perhaps I am one of those teachers and the sacred hunt is the path that young men need to walk to become members of the oldest fraternity on earth, a fraternity of mentors who understand and respect the earth. We are forming a non-profit organization known as N.A.T.U.R.E., one of the functions of which is to mentor young people's rites of passage according to the formula I've outlined in this book. It was in a dream that I received the vision of how to initiate boys into manhood: vision quest; subsistence survival/ hunting; and, art. I had used the dream prayer and asked what is the ideal way to initiate boys.

MOONdreamer

My food is the cactus, grasshoppers
Wombparts left by antelope
Eggs along the river in spring
Grandmother gives me food, shelter, everything
This place is my home until I die and after
I come from this land
I stay to make life for the creatures
My dream is for the living
The moon is my dream tonight
And Grandfather sun tomorrow
My spirit name is MOONdreamer
I am the keeper of the spirit world
My tribe is the spirits of the dead
This sacred place is my home

He placed his right hand on her left knee
And pointed to the moon
"This is the wish of Her
Who rules our night
We are her children now
She brought you here and me to your camp
You are like me
Moon is our spirit guide
We are the same
This time you brought old man and moon
To be your secret lovers
This time you make sacred love
The spirits are happy"

He raised his head to the sky
Whooped twice at the moon
And cried like a red-railed hawk
His eyes closed and he leaned toward her
As though to give her a kiss
She moved her head towards his and they touched
Her brow pressed lightly against his and they sat that way
She placed her palms on his rough knees and let her breath go
Her head lit up with bright light
She reeled back with open eyes
To see the moon which shined on his forehead
He patted her on the knees and said
"It's spirit light
The moon inside has light"

His gentleness swayed her
She closed her eyes and leaned forward again to touch his forehead
The light returned changing from bright white to blue-white
Rings of pulsating tingles engulfed her skin
Then all at once she was connected to the Earth
Energy flowed upward through her back
And made her heart glow golden yellow
It flowed outward in every direction
As purple light shimmered on her skull
Suddenly there was dancing and music
The stars shot colored arrows through her
And she was everywhere at once beyond time

As the sun rose over the rocks across the river
She awoke under her blanket in front of the van
With the coydog curled up beside her
She scanned the horizon looking for the old Indian
She felt the sand where he had sat
But there were no signs

Magpies quarreled by the river bed
As her eye caught sight of a solitary eagle rising
On a thermal above the rocks
It spiraled upward higher and higher
Until a mere speck against the sun
The eagle folded its wings
Swooped down at great speed over her head

As it rose screaming a feather fell to the earth
She picked it up and held it to her forehead

~ Randall L. Eaton

"Our true enemies, as well as our true sources of strength, lie within."

~ Willaru Huayta, Quechua Nation, Peru

Chapter 16

Art as Rite of Passage

"Earth teach me kindness, as dry fields weep with rain"

~ Ute Prayer

An Owl Who Wouldn't Die

I hadn't been back to Illinois during fall in many years, and I was eager to hunt pheasants and quail in the brisk climate of fading November. Cold mornings, gray forests with straggling clumps of red and yellow, skeins of honking geese and immense solitude made the farm on the Sangamon River well worth coming home.

Though poachers and a lawyer who paid to hunt had already scoured the ditch banks, pond edges and overgrown soil bank along the river itself, we managed to flush dozens of birds without a dog. There was but one way to hunt the bottomland, so rich that horseweeds grow ten feet tall, and that was by brute force, pushing our way through. The moist soil, a black clay called gumbo stuck to our boots adding several pounds to each step. The blackberry and sharp sedges pricked and sliced our faces and hands, but the bulldozing strategy got the birds out.

Kathy was a fine shot but she had no field experience and it showed. By the time I'd flushed a cock pheasant, wheeled in its direction and shot it, she still didn't have her gun up to her shoulder.

She was starting to understand why I had always shot skeet by waiting until the clay pigeon was airborne before I lifted my gun to fire. The highly specialized style used by skeet shooters, guns held up and ready before the clay bird appears, isn't the best preparation for hunting the Sangamon jungle or anywhere else. She was miffed at me for shooting the birds before she had a chance to fire so I started "pushing" for her: driving birds in her direction, telling her to get ready when I thought they were about to flush, but the skeet syndrome proved her too slow.

Between outings we returned to the car where I threw clay pigeons with a hand-trap so she could practice shooting by getting on aim after the bird was airborne. She quickly got the hang of it. Towards the end of our third day out, she had yet to fire at a pheasant or quail. Determined to make a hunter of her yet, I headed us down to the Chain of Lakes, a series of ponds surrounded by willow, millet and rushes. The fields on both sides of the ponds were recently plowed, but the amount of natural food right around them was enormous and there always had been pheasants and quail there.

At the overgrown ditch between the first two ponds, I tromped into the center of the short willows hoping to flush birds out towards her on the side next to the field. "You move on ahead of me, along the edge of the brush. That's right, now don't shoot back towards me," I instructed her, anticipating that birds would fly out straight ahead of me in range of her. Just then my eye caught a covey of quail running ahead through the willows. "Get ready, quail. They'll fly out in front of me."

Wings buzzed and small brown blurs exploded in flight. Bang! "Did you get one?" "Yes," she said, "I think so, I saw something fall." "Right about there?" She nodded yes. I saw a brown feather on the ground and then the bird, and knelt to pick it up, finding it to be a short-eared owl, similar in color but larger than a quail. It must have been roosting in the willows in front of me, and when the quail flushed, it flushed, too.

I yelled to Kathy that it was an owl. Both of us were surprised, and she felt terrible about shooting it. Not only are owls protected, as they should be, both of us were especially fond of owls.

It was dead or dying. Its head was covered with spots of blood, one eye looked ruined, and its feathers were ruffled as though it had been squarely hit. I held it in my hands as Kathy inspected the lifeless body and said, "Poor owl, poor little owl."

Since I had to pay a visit to my undergraduate college before returning to Georgia, I stuck the owl in my hunting coat so its skin could be salvaged for a museum specimen. To preserve the feathers, I placed the owl carefully in the game bag where it couldn't be sat on or twisted.

That evening when I grabbed my coat to remove the pheasants and quail to dress them for dinner, I took out the owl to put it in the freezer. It was alive, popping its beak at me, and blinking its one good eye while flapping its wings and clawing me with its talons. It must have experienced much stress being jostled every which way inside the coat, and being handled could only worsen matters, so I quickly released it on the back porch. It fell to the floor then turned to face me and pop its beak some more.

"Hey, the owl's alive. Do you believe it? It's alive after all that," I shouted to Kathy as she trotted in from the living room. Seeing the owl standing on the porch, she jumped up and down with joy. "God, I can't believe it," I said, shaking my head. "Will he be all right? Will he live?" she asked. "I don't know. Looks like he's lost an eye, and his wing might be broken. Hard to say." "Isn't there any-thing we can do?" she wondered. "Not right now, but if he's not better by morning, we'll find a decent veterinarian even if that means driving to Peoria."

Early next morning I came downstairs to eat breakfast and go to the farm to hunt one more day. After shooting the owl, Kathy had lost her enthusiasm for hunting; her heart wasn't in it. I expected the owl to be dead from internal wounds, but when I opened the door to the porch I was greeted by the pop, pop, pop of its beak. The owl flew from the window sill to the screen on the opposite wall. Obviously it could fly, and most surprising, its bad eye was open and bright. I caught the owl, tucked it securely in my coat, making sure it could breath and headed for the farm. I drove straight to where the dirt road crosses the Chain of Lakes drainage, about 400 yards from where it had been shot, got out and lifted the owl high and said, "Okay, this is your home. Fly well and stay safe." My fingers loosened and it flew off through the dimly lit sky toward yesterday's roost.

The last couple of hours that day I set out duck decoys on the third pond in the chain. It had been a crystal clear afternoon, without wind and no sign of waterfowl, and though I was fairly certain that there wouldn't be a single duck until well after sundown, just the same this pond was so much a part of me that the hunting prospects didn't matter. Being all alone on the marsh as the day yields to night, listening to the scoldings of a kingfisher and marsh wrens was reward aplenty. At dark I picked up the decoys, set them down in the blind, and sat there, eyes closed smelling the sweet willow. The air was cold and the stars were shining as the last light loomed in the southwest. Visions reeled of building blinds, sewing millet, the huge honker I missed three times. A continuous image of Novembers had brought me home. Once again I was connected.

I lit my corncob pipe, threw the sack of decoys over one shoulder, my gun over the other, and leaned down to pass under the rim of willows behind the pond. Twenty yards out into the field, I paused to take deep breaths and gaze at the stars when something caught my eye. I strained to see as it circled around only five feet above my head. Around and around, again and again...it was the short-eared owl.

My head craned to follow its slow flight, but I was leary about moving any part of my body or speaking since that might frighten the owl. My mind was inundated with questions: since when do owls fly around people's heads? Great horned owls sometimes confuse bald heads in the moonlight with reflections off rabbits, but I was not bald, there was no moon and this was no great horned owl. Why would this owl fly around me? After we shot it and put it through so much? As my thoughts melted away I set the decoys down with the gun, removed my hat and spoke to the owl, telling it that I was glad it was okay, and thanked it for letting me know. Unfrightened, it kept circling several times and then flew back toward the willows.

On the drive home I thought about how many magical experiences the farm had given me, and was eager to tell Kathy that the owl had made it. Even now, I wonder how to tell a scientist that a wild owl knows how to say thank you.

~ RANDALL L. EATON, *The Sacred Hunt*

The Stories We Tell

The stories we tell our youth much influence them and their lives. The stories we tell our boys as they make a transition from childhood to manhood are especially important in helping them to redefine their new life as adults. These stories provide models for their own transformation and give them a matrix in which to factor their own personal journey.

As these pages document, the chasm between academic doctrine and what many of us feel "deep down" is enormous. The "story"of science, does not and cannot sustain us at a soul level. Now that we face the prospect of annihilation, empowered directly or indirectly by science and technology - nuclear weapons, bio-warfare, global warming or destruction of our atmosphere - we are compelled to look inward and also backward to our original teachers.

Denny Olson whose boots were systematically "marked" by a beaver he was observing "objectively" had similar experiences, such as imitating bird calls so birds would land on his head or watching coyotes kill a deer by means of an elaborate ruse. He began to see animals' actions as "talk" and his observations as "listening" to their language. Which in turn led him to Native American elders whose ancient and perfected traditions were made from millennia of nature observation.

Olson is right that we humans are story-tellers. And as Fred Wolfe discovered, each of our lives is a story we write, a play we direct and star in. Science itself is a story. I especially like what Olson says about story, "...we are transcended by the stories we carry and pass to others, and by the risks we take in that process. We are not important. We are vessels carrying water in a desert and fire through a blizzard. Our importance lies in the thoughts we carry, and the sharing of water and fire with those who follow."

In western life, stories are seen as entertainment, a way to pass time until something really important needs to be done. The stories of native peoples are seen as cute tales of animals for the amusement of young people. But in the native world, there are only participants. The act of observing is a form of participation, which is what quantum physics terms the observer effect, meaning that the observer influences what he observes. From the Native perspective, there is no framework since everything from thoughts, feelings, actions and stories are interwoven in nature, and as Olson says, "everything, even the darkest secret feelings we tell no one else, has a set of consequences connected to it. It is no wonder that traditional Native people acted with such a sense of responsibility toward the land. They saw no difference between the land and themselves."

In the native view, we are not only hitched to everything else, we are made of everything else. As Chopra reminds us again and again in his writings, each of us now has in our body hundreds of atoms that were once in the body of Hitler or Stalin. Separation? The view of native peoples that life is interpenetrating and intercommunicative is closely aligned with that of contemporary physics. The illusion of separation prevents us from seeing that each species holds gifts for us; moreover, that we are the very thing we wish to dominate. Perhaps master would be a better word.

Traditional peoples did not learn about animals in a scientific sense, but instead learned from them how to live. Each species had its unique character or ability which humans needed to learn. Animals were not considered inferior. There were bear people, plant people, stone people, all gifted with their particular view of the world. As Olson says, "They all reflected the future, fed each other, and taught each other." In an age that is struggling to regain proper relationship with nature there are bizarre standards and codes being promoted. It is one thing to know we all deserve to be here and we are equal participants in life. It is another to pretend that life does not live on life. The animals have been giving us their bodies and spirits forever, and despite all our efforts to the contrary, we also feed them when our bodies die.

We are struggling with serious environmental problems we created from a lifestyle of arrogance and hubris. Our men grow up devoted to the dark side of the masculine – possessiveness, violence and brutality – because we have forgotten that each generation needs careful initiation that centers on tempering the masculine with the feminine, ego with heart. Perhaps it is time to listen to the oldest teachers on earth. The native peoples are not the original teachers, they simply listened closely to the rest of the earth with open heart, "giving voice to bear, eagle, raven and stone, and carried the water through the desert, to us...perhaps we can take a sip or two."

So the reader may take a sip or two of sacred water, I touch briefly on some of Olson's stories and the lessons different species have for us.

I AM LIKE A BEAR
I HOLD UP MY HANDS
WAITING FOR THE SUN TO RISE

~ Northern Ute Song

Bears are us. Like bears we are omnivorous, and like bears we are a high-ranking species, dominating all other lifeforms except one another. They stand on their hind legs, like us, and also like us they have a dark side, potentially a very ferocious dark side. Because bears are solitary and spend half the year in a den or cave, they are for many native societies keepers of the west in the great medicine wheel. The west is where the sun disappears and yields to darkness. West is the place of introspection, and so the bear is the "model for knowledge of self as a source of power."

Bear conducts an extensive vision quest every winter. The kiva of the southwest natives is like a bear den, and people who emerge from them after a few days of reflection are transformed as a result of their isolation and self-inspection. By becoming aware of the inner landscape we better understand the outer world and how to relate to it. Bear shows us how to operate from the center of our being.

Olson shares with us an Ojibwe story about a couple who took each other for granted. They both wanted more passion in their marriage. The husband was more interested in hunting than his wife, and though they had plenty of dried meat for the winter he kept going hunting. His wife who was bored decided to take baskets into the forest to pick blackberries. After filling her baskets the woman took a nap and dreamed about meeting a powerful young man with black hair. He reached out to touch her and her clothes fell off. They made passionate love.

When she awoke she had a strange feeling. The blackberries had become soft and juicy. As she walked home she met a bear on the path so she put the baskets down on the ground, but the bear wanted her, not the berries. She was afraid and did not want to be eaten so she sang a beautiful song of praise to the bear. The bear relaxed but each time she got closer to edge around him he became alert. So she used her song to get closer and closer, finally reaching out and touching the bear on its fur. When the bear reached out and touched her gently her clothes fell away and they made love just like in her dream. She gave the berries to the bear and walked home.

Every day the woman went back up the mountain to gather more berries or so she told her husband, though each night when she returned there were few berries in her basket. Since she became more content and graceful her husband became suspicious and followed her on the path one day. He became angry when he witnessed the bear and his wife together, so the next day he told his wife he was sick and asked her to fetch something far from the house. While she was gone he dressed up like a woman and met the bear and killed it after a great fight. The man was wounded but managed to eat the bear's genitals before he crawled home. When his wife returned home she washed his wounds carefully. He touched her and her clothes fell away and they made love with more fire than ever.

The man was still angry so he took his wife to see what was left of the bear. She screamed and grieved and turned into a bear and ran into the forest. Four nights she returned to the lodge but each night turned back to the forest. On some evenings there are beings who walk the edge of the camp, just beyond the fire light. They are called bearwalkers. Sometimes they wear fur, sometimes smooth skin.

When Ojibwe women meet a bear in the woods they protect themselves by opening their dresses and showing their bodies, saying to the bear, "It is only me, my husband." Tagish women call bears they meet brother believing that the incest taboo will keep them safe.

Is this inter-mixing of humans and bears merely the confusion of primitive, superstitious minds? Olson explains that "it is acknowledgement that there are no 'objective observers' in this world, only participants. We eat the bear, and we are the bear. The bear eats us, and the bear is us. We watch the bear in an 'objective' way, and the bear still teaches us, and its spirit is part of us. The real illusion is the one that says we are somehow separate from each other." Olson says,

> "In us, that which is Bear remains, reminding us of our relationship with nature, our emotional and spiritual side, our ability to look within ourselves and find a balance, a center, within the great circles spinning around us every second of our lives. Without the acknowledgement of our dark, wild side, the center will remain elusive. A case could be made that without the Bear, our culture will continue to suffer the confusion that lies just behind our arrogance."

As citizens of the earth, we humans are equal participants in the Great Mystery. We may be physically superior to many lifeforms, but in no way better. While books have been written about the role that animals and nature play in the story traditions of many peoples, suffice it to say that like Native Americans the ancestors of European Americans and Afro-Americans taught their young about life by attending to the behavior, habits and disposition of animals. In this sense, animals and nature have been primary teachers for humanity throughout the ages and they still are.

> New light. Earth teach me suffering, as old stones suffer with memory. Earth teach me humility, as blossoms are humble with beginning. Earth teach me caring, as mothers nurture their young. Earth teach me courage, as the tree which stands alone. Earth teach me limitation, as the ant which crawls on the ground. Earth teach me freedom, as the eagle which soars in the sky. Earth teach me acceptance, as the leaves which die in the fall. Earth teach

ME RENEWAL, AS THE SEED WHICH RISES IN THE SPRING. EARTH TEACH ME TO FORGET MYSELF, AS MELTED SNOW FORGETS ITS LIFE. EARTH TEACH ME TO REMEMBER KINDNESS, AS DRY FIELDS WEEP WITH RAIN.

~ UTE PRAYER

If there are two forms of human behavior that are so much a part of men that they are transparent to their eyes, they are the hunt and story-telling. Story is the very glue that gives coherence and meaning to life for individuals and society and to young men undergoing initiation rites. Elaine Wynne reminds us that hearing of tales and the telling of them is itself an initiatory process, and that as members of the community, storytellers express the yearnings, noble deeds and mythical memories of the society. Because initiation to adulthood is a change in our life, it must of necessity involve a change in our stories.

Wynne wondered if she might be able to construct a ritual strong enough to symbolize her children's passage from childhood to adulthood. On each child's 18th birthday, a rite of passage was conducted with both parents and a male and female guide. The purpose of the guides was to keep the ritual moving and to encourage the parents and child to express themselves. The rite itself is a process of storytelling from the child's conception through childhood to the moment of passage into adulthood. After several hours, completion of adulthood is achieved and a new relationship with the parents is acknowledged. Gifts are given and the initiate expresses his or her dreams and visions for life.

At rites of passage structured around stories, Wynne often reads Iron Hans (also known as Iron John) for boys.

Of course television has become the major storyteller in the civilized world, and it is the primary tool for marketing in the industrial world. It is not devoted to the values needed to sustain culture nor to stories that help an adolescent understand his changing life or to define adulthood. If anything, television infantilizes viewers, not only by preventing development of imagination, but also by fixing the immature person's identity on material things and superficial images. We can not afford to stop telling stories to our children, and it is imperative that we recognize the critical role storytelling has during adolescence.

Some may disagree with Wynne's choice to include parents in a rite of passage for a young man because he cannot die to his childhood and embrace a new adult life without separating from his parents. Boys need mentors to become men.

An alternative rite of passage for boys is writing their own story, a story that encompasses their childhood and which visualizes their future. It is another way of creatively tapping the unconscious for symbols that have soulful meaning, and, like The Journey, often will include a descent into wounds, a symbolic healing and gifts for the community. In fact, many creative writers feel that their work amounts to rites of passage. For me personally, writing has become a satisfying path of mentorship. Every kind of art that can be used to facilitate rites of passage – or as a rite of passage itself – is also a form of healing. As we move from one stage of life we need to heal its wounds so we can put it to rest and move on reborn and renewed into the next.

Art and The Inner Journey

In the internal rite of passage known as "The Journey," David Oldfield asks groups of adolescents what issues they need to face in their lives and how they propose dealing with them. They are encouraged to look for answers by examining the images that come to them spontaneously. Often the young people represent their entry into adulthood as a movement downward. Oldfield says, "One must go 'down and in' before one can come 'up and out again,' as a transformed human being," which sounds much like Bly's description of a boy's descent into his wounds as part of initiation. Parents may become worried over a child who becomes quiet and withdrawn, fearful that the child is depressed, but he/she simply may be going down and in to mine new sources of creative energy.

Wounding and scarification frequently enter into traditional rites of passage, but Oldfield says that, "Today, youngsters often feel an inner wounding, typified in terms of imagery as, for example, a bird whose wing has been broken or some other wounded animal. Adolescents often feel like wounded animals, and like them, often are dangerous because they are scared…" The images that young people present may be vulgar and offensive, but they are valid and should not be questioned or doubted. Oldfield says, "…these images accurately express how the youngster feels at that moment, and we need to work with those feelings exactly as they are." In an example Oldfield gives, a boy saw himself literally as shit, a mirror of his feeling of absolute worthlessness, but as the boy continued to work with images his story changed until he saw himself surviving a forest fire that destroyed his home and everything around it except himself, which Oldfield interprets as a metaphor for the devastation that had taken place in his family life. The boy was the only organic thing to survive the fire and he spread himself all over the ground as fertilizer! In his final drawing, new shoots of grass grew up through him, and with the help of a social worker was able to help his entire family grow into a healthier way of relating to one another.

The Journey confronts death. Oldfield considers it central to his work because it has a central place in rites of passage. He is right that death is taboo in America, that it is neglected in our educational system, and that exposure to death in the media is bizarre and fantastic. "But our children are given no opportunities to learn about death as a meaningful part of real life. As a result, our children are at once terrified of death yet naively unmindful of the value of human life," he says. The symbolic death marks the end of one phase of life and the initiation of another, and this, too, can be expressed artistically.

Oldield instructs the youngsters to focus on the inner discoveries they've made in their journey and to translate them into actions and contributions to the world, again, not unlike Bly's prescription for a young man to transmute his wounds into gifts for the community. The new vision of life that a young person distills from their inner quest is unique to themselves, just as the dream-vision was to the Ojibwe or the vision quest to the Lakota.

Now the youth faces the challenge of expressing their vision in the best way to be understood by the community. "Telling a story, writing a song, painting the vision on a shield, dancing the vision – these were the common ways to share the uniqueness of one's vision with others. Now the challenge is to bring this into life. A vision is the beginning."

The final phase of The Journey is an actual ceremony that honors the young person's passage. Oldfield invites the adolescents to design a ceremony or celebration that honors the insights and knowledge they have gleaned along the way. Ritual time and space are created with adornments, changes in language, symbolic stories, enactment of symbolic dramas, eating symbolic foods, all to honor the unseen world felt within.

The Journey is much like a vision quest, though it relies more upon depiction of inner images and symbols. Like the vision quest, The Journey includes a reincorporation or return to mentors or the community with whom the initiate expresses his inner journey and guidance.

The arts are important in helping us find our identity, a primary function of rites of passage to adulthood. Drawing, painting and carving can express a vision of our new life as an adult. Kaye Passmore encourages adolescents to draw or paint personal shields. She also promotes an integration of arts in school programs that combines Native American art with writing and symbolism.

Real shields are used for protection against danger. Symbolic shields pronounce and protect the new identity that comes from the psychic reintegration of rites of passage. Shields are especially appropriate for young men. In dreamtime my personal shield was shown to me as a heart-shaped shield, red on one side, black on the other with a white eagle's skull at the top. These are the symbolic colors of male initiation: red for blood, life-force and masculine passion; black for the dark-side and the deep waters of feminine compassion; and white for the spiritual wisdom that comes out of balancing red and black (outer and inner, male and female). The eagle's skull is an archetypal symbol of spiritual vision, and the shape of the shield stands for integration within the encompassing heart.

The genius and mystic, Rudolf Steiner, said that a real artist knows that when he/she is in the process of being creative, a higher spirituality is definitely present.

Art as Transcendence

Art, ritual, scripture and meditation reveal what normally is hidden, but which the heart is ready, even eager, to recognize. Art carries us beyond the two sides of ego, desire and fear, to awareness of infinity in a grain of sand, and to the rapture of seeing in a solitary hair a thousand golden lions. To penetrate the mystery of anything is to unveil the same mystery of the being of the universe and of ourself. Art is transforming because it reveals the radiance that shines through all things, giving us a momentary sense of existence that cannot be found in the empirical. Art evokes, Joseph Campbell suggests, like a shaman's drum, not like a formula of Einstein. He believes that the goal of life is rapture, and that art is the way we experience it.

In *A Portait of the Artist as a Young Man*, James Joyce distinguishes between proper art, which induces esthetic arrest or awe, and improper art, which moves us to desire or fear and loathing. Referring to Aquinas, Joyce says that proper art renders three moments: wholeness; harmony; and radiance. The mind is arrested and raised above desire and loathing, ego and survival, and the world, beheld without judgement of its relevance to the well-being of the observer, is seen as a revelation sufficient in itself. He is saying that the experience of art goes beyond morality to a sacred field where we no longer have to know the name of a thing or its utility. A case of pure subject beholding pure object.

The artist Cezanne said that art is a harmony parallel to nature. There are two natures: the world out there and the world of nature within. Art generates a harmony parallel to nature that resonates with something inside us evoking esthetic arrest or an "aha" experience. Art opens the tangible, visible world, revealing its radiance as the same radiance within us.

Joseph Campbell much admired Japanese gardens where it is impossible to tell where nature ends and art begins. Nature is harmonized with the nature within.

The biological urge of desire and fear and the social urge to judge and evaluate good or evil fall away in the presence of art, and rapture emerges releasing the mind for a moment from all anxieties. Ego dissolves, what is meant by "no mind," release or enlightenment, nirvana. The point of stillness is pure joy, experience of the Divine. Art brings us to transcendence of ego, and it evokes compassion for the suffering of the world.

As a set of wings that liberates us from our own entanglements, art brings us back to peace and joy. At the deepest level, Campbell proposed, all we really want to do is dance. The sacred dance brings us to the Divine within us, and in so doing art invites us to participate joyfully in the sorrows of the world. We cannot end the suffering of the world, but we can choose to be joyous.

"But the Kingdom is within you and it is without you. If you will know yourselves, then you will be known and you will know that you are the sons of the Living Father. But if you do not know yourselves, then you are in poverty and you are poverty," said Jesus Christ.

It is possible for us to embrace the Divine bliss within and bring it into our life and world. When the disciples asked when the Kingdom will come, He replied, "But the Kingdom of the Father is spread upon the earth and men do not see it."

Men do not see the radiance everywhere. They are not aware of the harmony between their Divine nature and Nature out there, which brings us back full circle to the heart of the hunter which is one with all. The hunter is a model for sustainability because his heart is harmonized with nature.

> *"Love is something that you can leave behind you when you die. It's that powerful... The Old Ones say, love is all anyone needs. Love doesn't go away nor can love be divided....Every love act or love thought has an affect on each person as well as touching the whole world. If you live a life filled with love, the results will affect your friends, relatives and other people, even after you go to the other side. So...Love."*
>
> ~ John (Fire) Lame Deer, Rosebud Lakota

Chapter 17

On the Initiation of Boys and the Sanity of Men

"But the Kingdom of the Father is spread upon the earth and men do not see it."

~ Jesus Christ

"Thus in the heart of man, and above all, within this turbulent century, the Odyssean voyage stands as a symbol of both man's homelessness and his power... Plotinus wrote of the soul's journey, 'It shall come not to another, but to itself.' It is possible to add that for the soul to come to its true self it needs the help and recognition of the dog Argos. It craves that empathy clinging between man and beast, that nagging shadow of remembrance, which, try as we may to deny it, asserts our unity with life and does more. Paradoxically, it establishes in the end, our own humanity. One does not meet oneself until one catches the reflection from an eye other than human... The surprising thing about the story's descent through the millennia is that it comes from a fierce and violent era, yet it bespeaks some recognized bond between man and beast. The tie runs beyond the cities into some remote glade in a far forest where man willingly accepted the help of his animal kin. Though men in the mass forget the origins of their need, they will bring wolfhounds into city apartments, where dog and man both sit brooding in wistful discomfort...The magic that gleams an instant between Argos and Odysseus is both the recognition of diversity and the need for affection across the illusion of form. It is nature's cry to homeless, far-wandering, insatiable man: Do not forget your brethren, nor the green wood from which you sprang. To do so is to invite disaster."

~ Loren Eiseley, *The Unexpected Universe*

The biological dimensions of masculinity other than the hunt - war, sex and sport – either stem from hunting or are dependent upon it. War with predators over meat became an adjunct to successful big game hunting. Originally as a form of play among adolescent and adult males, sport evolved from hunting animals for food and making war against predators. It acquired its own motivation and intrinsic rewards with benefits of many kinds including enhanced performance in hunting and warring. Though sex precedes hunting, it became subordinate to hunting when successful big game hunting became a requirement for male reproduction. To this day, courtship by young adult males is enhanced by juicy steaks, no mere coincidence.

Like meditation, vision quest has its origins in the hunt, which often places males in stillness and solitude for hours, even days. It is not uncommon today for boys who are hunting to sit quietly, unable to move around, for twelve or more hours in a tree stand – without Ipods - enough to rival Buddhist monks! I suspect that a lot of boys diagnosed with ADD at school would not indicate their symptoms in the field. The unparalleled alertness associated with hunting combined with extended periods of quiet sitting often is transcendent. Esthetic arrest, awe and awareness of existence come from the hunt which also has given rise to artistic expression ranging from dance, music and song to mime, drama, language, story-telling, etching, painting and sculpture.

If there is a war against the human imagination, the one front where we are winning is the hunt, which relies on imagination: what if the animal bolts in that direction? What do I do if it walks up behind me? Where are the geese likely to appear? Many hunters also learn that as a key component of hypothesis and prayer, imagination is a creative faculty, that, "what you can imagine you can create." Which is what I did on a hunt when I marveled at an elk offering itself to me rather than kill it. Imagination coupled with exuberance is the creative wild in each of us.

Ritual life is as fundamental to aboriginal and recreational hunting as weaponry. As Joseph Campbell said, hunting is a ritual; as Ortega said, the hunt is religious.

Like civilization, the medicine boys need to become sane men of heart must be founded on nature-culture, meaning culture that is nature-based, and what is nature-based, as Michael Gurian said, is spiritual.

To illustrate just how far away we are from revival of nature-culture, allow me to share with you a conversation I held yesterday with a Scout leader who lives in a rural ranching and farming area. So some of his Scouts could undertake "wilderness survival," he said he would plant chickens like Easter eggs so the boys would have to "hunt" for them. The Council ruled against his proposal because, "They didn't want the kids to be getting any ideas about killing. Then there was all the mess," meaning the blood and guts encountered in butchering.

A leader of the animal rights/anti-hunting movement is moral philosopher, Tom Regan. He proposes the most unusual thing: man is moral, nature is amoral, and man is separate from nature. How exactly can any human be separate from nature? From where comes his air, food, water? To where goes his sewage and garbage, his bones? That many species make moral decisions is abundantly clear from decades of research on wild animal behavior. Isn't separation from nature a new version of Cartesian philosophy? From where does this man come? Brooklyn! The leaders of the animal rights/anti-hunting movement have for years been based in New York City and Los Angeles. When I shared Regan's views with some Western Shoshone friends they exclaimed, "He's crazy!" The only negative comment I ever heard them make about anyone or anything including the US Government which they have been fighting in court for decades.

Consciousness is the content of consciousness. Evolution "assumed" that we'd all find ourselves growing up in nature living close to the earth, dependent upon it. And our conscious minds would be overflowing day and night with the resplendent glory, beauty and intelligence of the nonhuman other. Compare the content of consciousness of a Kalahari Bushman with that of a typical U.S. farmer or rancher and theirs with that of a city person. The Bushman accurately imitates the sounds of more than 300 mammals, birds and insects, a reflection of the quality and quantity of otherness in his life. Perhaps a farmer can imitate the sounds of fifteen different species, some of them domestic animals. The city person might imitate dogs, cats, pidgeons and zoo lions.

It is not difficult to fathom why a hunter's mind is like his world: so much more vibrant, exciting, diverse and numinous, nor should it be too surprising perhaps that Brooklyn-born Regan thinks that man is separate from nature. The same principle applies to a recreational hunter compared to a nonhunter, not simply because of any difference in natural diversity of their worlds, but because the hunter's affection and attention to nonhumans are so much greater. The same is true for graduates of wilderness/tracking schools.

I believe that the soul is voraciously hungry to encounter and experience other versions of itself. Its growth is dependent on the quality and quantity of otherness because, in truth, all is One. Behind the illusion of form is an essential unity. When a man hunts he studies nature and in it he discovers the many faces of God. The hunter who imitates the animal so well identifies with it and discovers that he is one with the animal he kills: a young man's most significant surprise in life is that he and the other are essentially the same.

My first observation of nature, while crawling in the back yard, thrilled me to no end. And years later I wrote that, "The robin pulling worms from the earth is naught but God eating himself." The hunt is a conscious and deliberate acquiesence to death as the fact of life. It is a ritual conducted by civilized men who refuse to forget their brethren or the green wood from which they sprang.

Boys who are properly initiated into manhood by the sacred hunt, vision quest or artistic expression – preferably all three – embody the awareness capable of recovering sanity in an insane world. They are the holders of the archetypal nature-culture that connects us to the environment, to one another and to the divine.

These are some of the pathologies of contemporary civilized life that proper initiation may help heal:

- fear of death;
- denial of the pain and suffering inherent in living;
- denial of the spiritual;
- fear of the body;
- belief in the normality of living alone, i.e., without family and/or society;
- separation from nature, particularly throughout childhood;
- identification with and worship of the ego;
- failure to discriminate between ego-intellect and intelligence or wisdom (knowing what is appropriate);
- greed, selfishness, materialism and possessiveness;
- addiction and obsession;
- violence, aggression and brutality;
- failure to love and respect the creatures and earth;

- belief in life as competition;
- lack of meaning and purpose in life;
- alienation;
- lack of meaningful rites of passage and the critical value of ritual and ceremony;
- separating infants and small children from their mothers (includes bottle-feeding);
- broken homes and the growing belief that one parent is enough to successfully raise children;
- belief that the nuclear family is sufficient to meet the developmental needs of children and the social needs of adults;
- lack of respect for elders and the practice of separating elders from the family/society;
- the belief in unlimited human freedom and potential;
- failure to recognize that the glue of society is the sharing of fundamental beliefs about the nature and meaning of life;
- failure to perceive life, nature and the earth as sacred;
- absence of belief in a higher power;
- reduction of the carrying capacity of the land, earth and sea;
- the pollution and destruction of the viability and diversity of the food chain and the environment;
- the pursuit of power over other humans and nature;
- impatience and lack of presence;
- lack of empathy;
- failure to view life as renewal (compared to history and progress);
- inability to identify with creation;
- inability to sense the unity of life;
- self-doubt and distrust.

"The fantasies, anxieties, and hostilities of unresolved immaturity are acted on or repressed and redirected in many ways. In this dark shadow of adult youthfulness is an enduring grief, a tentative feeling about the universe as though it were an incompetent parent, and a thin love of nature over deep fears," says Paul Shepard in *Nature and Madness*. Agriculture discovered that plants and animals could be enslaved and subordinated, but that masses of men could be controlled by manipulating these anxieties and perpetuating their search for protection, their dependence, their helplessness, irrational surges of hate and adulation, submission to authority and fear of the strange.

Western humanity has broken bonds with the earth, nature and the land and separated the human spirit from the seasons and cycles of renewal. So awakened fear of the body and world and a glorification of separation anxiety. Adolescent rites of passage are a cultural response to an inherent need. The desire to prove oneself worthy, infantilisms, poeticism, idealism and a search for an enlarged identity are inherited traits of adolescence. Initiation ceremonies serve an ecological function by completing a critical stage of the life cycle, as Shepard says, "The natural world can become, in retrospect, an object of veneration if it is first an object of thought, as the prototype of coherence – and it is that because of the quality of early maternal care."

The psychotic conviction of modern humanity that it can change the world to meet its needs has launched us on a crisis course. The only way we can change our trajectory is to move adolescents from the infantile regression they've been stuck with for so long to the new ideal of saving humanity from its own nonhuman status. The difficulty for us today is a shortage of elders who are adequately equipped to mentor that transition.

So in this time the members of industrial society are stuck ontogenetically and adhering to the past and its shortcomings. We no longer remember the simple wisdom of small group nomadic life, limited possessions and consensuality, initiation rituals, the study of nature as everyone's joyful vocation, the total immersion in other-than-human with its intellectual, poetic and spiritual meaning, nor the natural bond between infant and mother. The question of our age is whether we can recover the competence to live these? Shepard's answer is that each of us holds the potential competence within ourselves.

Normal, healthy growth is within our reach if we emulate hunter-gatherers. Living in a small group in a spacious natural setting is feasible, as is limited foraging and ritual life. Beneath the "veneer of civilization," does not lie the savage or barbaric, but the human who knows the goodness of gentle birthing, the importance of an environment rich with the nonhuman, the ritual expression of receiving food as a gift, the cultivation of "metaphorical significance of natural phenomena of all kinds," membership in small clans and the overwhelming significance of ritual initiation and the adult stage of mentorship. Is there an undamaged secret person in all but the most unbonded and abused of us who adheres to heart-intelligence? Cliff Richards' song says, "It's in every one of us to be wise/Open your heart, open up both your eyes/We can all know everything without ever knowing why/It's in every one of us bye and bye."

The road to recovery starts with the genuine expression of the heart in the simple things of life, such as hunting and gathering, vision quest and making sacred, pausing to watch and listen to a redtail hawk, sleeping on the earth, reflecting on a dream, writing a poem, observing the tension in our body, forgiving, giving thanks, seeing someone else as another version of ourself, telling stories by a fire, walking the path of joy and peace, being present, singing and dancing.

Mel Gibson's recent film, Apocalypto, has a pressing message**: it is time to return to nature and make a new beginning.** The world he portrayed symbolizes the insanity of contemporary civilization which already is undergoing apocalypse. Now is the time for us to plant seeds for that new beginning. Teaching our boys how to hunt is the practical side of connecting our children to nature.

Now is also the time to plan self-sustaining, self-replicating communities which at every level are founded on interdependence. These communities will need olders to be elders who can mentor youth. I am working with Jon Young and the Regenerative Design Institute to promote regenerative community life.

For those who imagine it is too late for the recovery of sanity and proper relationship, remember the Hopi who deliberately chose the most austere location on which to found their life in North America. A place where no rivers flow and rain is rare they have lived and grown corn for millennia. They chose their home because living and growing corn there would require that they never let their spiritual traditions die. Each year their life depends upon the success of rainmakers who invoke the blessings of nature spirits. A failure in any one year would mean the end of their people and culture, but they are still here, their corn still grows, their boys still undertake traditional rites of passage overseen by elders, and the entire community faithfully devotes much of its life to sacred ritual. And more of us are heeding their teachings about life in balance.

If the Hopi civilization can maintain Pleistocene values in the desert, there is hope for us, too. We are weary of the artificial, of war, anxiety and life without meaning. We prefer love over fear, spirit over ego, wisdom over intellect, community over separation.

Where Rites of Passage Lead

The date is March 9, 2003. The politicians are heating up for a war. The impression I get from the news casters and commentators goes beyond their excitement over more attentive audiences in the days ahead to celebration of a grand spectacle rivaled only by the Super Bowl. One man declares that Jimmy Carter is no less than a traitor for advocating a peaceful solution. I cannot help but wonder what they would be saying if ever they had killed a deer and watched it bleed and die? I say to my wife, "If most of the men in our country had hunted and killed even one of the many animals that have fed and clothed them they would not debate the outcome of a war as if it were a sporting event."

When the Kalahari Bushman were interviewed repeatedly over many years about an old battle, they shook their heads in shame saying how terrible it was. Finally, it came out that one man was killed. Hunters know from actual experience the seriousness of killing and death. To Fox News and CBS, a war in Iraq might as well be a video game with the promise of higher ratings.

As for me, Jimmy Carter is far more than an American hero; he is a model man of heart. Far from being a traitor, he is utterly honest when others before and since were liars and deceivers, like pastoral chiefs devoted to slaying lions, building herds and amassing power. Though I did not agree with all his decisions, I never doubted that Carter spoke from his heart. We may be sure that he bonded deeply with his mother, and that during his adolescence hunting bonded him firmly to society, nature and God. Carter is a deeply spiritual man who stands for peace and human rights and who champions the environment. By his own choice he lives a remarkably austere life.

How we raise our boys has real consequences.

The recovery of rites of passage aimed at opening the male heart will mean a reduction in juvenile violence, gangs, and in a short time, all crime including child abuse. It will reduce teen suicide. It also will mean more secure marriage and more stable families, lower addiction of all kinds including consumerism Stress and related diseases will decline and health will improve. There will be more cooperation and generosity, less competition. Older people will finally regain the importance and value they deserve as elders. Creativity will soar as will citizenship, and spiritual life will flourish. Pollution will decline along with war. There will be no more unsustainable economy, and stewardship of the environment will prevail over degradation.

The recovery of rites of passage must be undertaken with humility. Though sexual instinct awakens in all boys, as adults some men may choose a life of celibacy. The same principle applies to hunting. A single hunt may be all a young man needs to reap its benefits. Others may not need even one, though I believe that any boy who eats meat should actually kill one animal, wild or domestic. In the rational, scientific world in which meaning has become equated with the empirical, external or measurable we have forgotten that the soul calls each of us to certain paths and experiences so we can grow. Like the hunt, vision quest is an experience that prepares us for a life founded on spiritual guidance , i.e., "vocation," which means "inner voice." It teaches us that Spirit was made flesh and it survives flesh. The more men follow their hearts the better off they will be in a world that wants uniform worker-consumers who are easy to manipulate because they live in a controlled state of fear from identification with the body.

Identification with Spirit and love as opposed to ego and fear is promoted by every aspect of adult initiation including art and ritual. Men make war because they are afraid of death, and they are afraid of death because they believe they are vulnerable, so they attack and kill those whom they fear may attack and kill them. Nearly every form of human suffering has its origin in the belief in vulnerability, which is a reflection of ignorance about who and what we truly are. The truth is that we are spiritual and so we are invulnerable. "What is real cannot be threatened. What is unreal does not exist." Without proper bonding throughout development we may never achieve the presence needed to discover who and what we really are. Significantly less negative enculturation – fear, shame, guilt, punishment, doubt – may help us achieve and maintain transcendence.

Every rite of passage recommended here promotes peace: only inner peace allows us to be of greater service to others. Over 90% of the recreational hunters I've surveyed consider hunting to be extremely important to their sense of inner peace. Without forgiveness of others and ourselves there can be no inner peace. Christians believe this even if few practice it, and so do many indigenous peoples. The first inquiry a Kahuna makes in caring for a sick person is whom he has not forgiven. Mentors of boys and their models need to teach forgiveness as an essential path to liberation from the ego. Without applying the keen awareness of hunting to ourselves we cannot know whom we need to forgive or the negative emotional attachments and blocks we need to dissolve. Wilderness awareness, vision quest, hunting, artistic expression and ritual life all help us expand self-awareness so we can clear the cobwebs from the subconscious which, without grieving and forgiveness, fester and block health, intelligence, creativity, wisdom and enthusiasm. The inner hunt begins when we identify with the observer. The sacred hunt is a hunt for the sacred.

The virtues drawn out by hunting – patience, generosity, courage, fortitude, humility, compassion, inner peace – are reinforced by other forms of initiation. I keep emphasizing that education means to draw out what already is in us. Each of us knows what we are meant to experience, and we learn from those experiences by following what attracts us. Children learn what they are supposed to learn by playing, the only experience they pursue relentlessly with unparalleled enthusiasm If we were spiritual rather than egotistical and frightened, we would let them play and play, and we would hold faith in the outcome, i.e., what comes out of them in way of growth as a result of their experience. Instead we serve the gods of ego and fear and wonder why "education" isn't working. What if we stop proposing more of the same, and instead revamp schooling immediately, get kids outdoors, make learning fun and design curricula around nature? Our kids, our society and our environment all would benefit enormously.

Is it in the interest of corporate profits and government power that we are spiritually retarded? Do you suppose the last thing they want is a population of fearless people? The recovery of sanity calls for a program of human development that aims at bonding and ego transcendence. We do not advocate asceticism or ascension, but a life of vigorous activity and relationship guided from within rather than by the facile, materialistic values of a world plagued by fear. Spiritual life begins with awareness, and awareness depends upon presence, keen attentiveness in the moment to what is. Wilderness awareness, vision quest, hunting, artistic expression and ritual life heighten our awareness and bring us into the present. Ultimately, they teach us our interdependence, that we are the world and the world is us. Without that realization there can be no compassion, no trust, no love, no morality, only the egotistical illusion of separation that underlies the suffering of the world. In this sense, wilderness education and the sacred hunt amount to therapy.

Given proper developmental bonding from birth through adolescent rites of passage, a boy becomes a man endowed with the virtues necessary to protect and provide. By applying the attentive awareness of the hunt and the keen introspection of the vision quest to his own psychic wilderness he may master the negative emotions of pride, greed/addiction, deception/manipulation and anger and thus grow in consciousness and capacity to serve other souls. The treasures of the inner hunt are peace, joy, love, a deep sense of connection, trust and wisdom.

People who are deeply connected to nature exhibit inner peace and self-awareness. Studies on the effect of meditation on crime rates in large cities indicate that when one in a thousand people meditates on peace the world is changed. A spiritually empowered man looks to himself and by doing so saves the world.

Na Nin Da Hey. I speak from the heart!

Epilogue

Nature, the Heart and Spiritual Knowledge

"Seek ye the old path and follow it."

~ Holy Bible

Michael Meade tells a story about how this current creation was made by two bird-like beings who were flying over the world when it last ended. There was nothing left over the whole earth except ashes. They flew with their hands out in front of them, and where their longest fingers pointed down, they landed.

First, one picked up a cinder and started to drum while the other danced. They did this one time – nothing happened. They did this a second time – again nothing. They did this a third time and a small sprout came up out of the earth. They drummed and danced more as the sprout became a tree, then they threw rocks up into the branches and when the rocks came back down to Earth they sprouted up all kinds of new life.

It was in this way that two beings drumming on cinder and dancing on ashes brought this creation that we now live in into existence. This is a time to rise out of the ashes.

I interpret the global crisis as a case of mistaken identity. The solution lies not in who we are but what we are. The who is ego which rose to chairman of the board when we identified with the body. As difficult as it may be to grasp, identification with the body lies behind all human suffering and keeps us in a state of relentless insecurity and perpetual defensiveness. It is responsible for fear and its many faces, including greed, hate, anger, anxiety, stress, jealousy. It lies behind pollution, war, conflict, competition, unsustainability. What we are is Spirit. Whatever transcends ego opens us to our true nature.

The Kalahari Bushman say there is a dream dreaming us. When the Buddha found enlightenment someone asked him if he is God. He replied, " I am awake." Ego has created a nightmare on earth, but it is possible through a profound emotional education for us to awaken.

Anyone who sincerely strives will achieve knowledge and abilities in the higher worlds of spirit. The path begins with a basic mood or attitude of reverence and devotion. The young person's devotion may begin with nature or a person. Their feelings of devotion do not lead to subservience or slavery, but rather to a reverence for what flows freely from their heart. We find the inner strength to evolve to a higher level when we develop an inner feeling that there is something higher than ourselves. Only if we pass through the door of humility may we ascend to the lofty level of spirit, and for boys that doorway often is nature, and for adolescent boys, hunting.

Rudolf Steiner preceded Joe Pearce in recognizing the negative enculturation young people receive in civilization. Steiner saw that our civilization is more prone to criticize, judge and condemn rather than feel devotion or veneration. Like us, our youth criticize more than they revere or respect. Just as each feeling of reverence and devotion empowers the soul's striving for higher knowledge, each act of judgment and criticism sets the soul's journey back. What Western man has gained in science, technology, industry and commerce has meant corresponding losses in spiritual life, another way of stating that our master has been ego and fear, not spirit and love.

In primal settings in which material concerns were simpler, it was easier to make spiritual progress. There the sacred and revered stood out more clearly from the rest of life. But in this age of criticism, judgment and egoism, ideals are degraded. Reverence, wonder, awe, adoration and respect are replaced by other feelings; however, recreational and indigenous hunters describe their primary attitude toward wild animals and nature as admiration, respect and reverence. Hunters epitomize the esoteric path because their mood of devotion to nature arouses admiration and respect. They are not critical of the weaknesses of wild animals, but instead enter deeply and lovingly into their good qualities and in so doing gather in their power and grace. They are immersed in the living strength that comes from seeing the good and withholding critical judgment. Because their consciousness is filled with admiration, respect and reverence for life and the world, they advance more quickly towards higher spiritual knowledge. Consequently, they come to see their fellow humans in a new light and also assume moral responsibility for the environment.

Perhaps at first glance it is not obvious that the basic mood of devotion and reverence are fundamentally linked to knowledge, but that is because we tend to think that cognition is in no way connected to our souls. We forget, Steiner says, that it is the soul that cognizes. Food is to the body as feelings are to the soul, which is nourished with reverence and respect. These make the soul strong, especially for knowing. Antipathy and disrespect, on the other hand, slay and paralyze cognition.

Because hunters actively seek and temporarily recover the essence of primal life, they become people whose souls are rich in feeling. Thus, their inner experience is the key to beholding the beauty of the outer world. One sees God in nature because God is in one's mind. The world of hunters is filled with the glory of God precisely because they have experienced the divine within their souls. Like spiritual masters, they actively seek and create the silence and solitude of nature so they may withdraw into themselves. Remember that in the surveys I conducted, hunters chose "inner peace" and "patience" as the most important virtues they acquired from hunting. It is the moments of inner peace that allow us to distinguish the essential from the unessential. Hunting actually prepares us to look upon the world with new eyes, so that every animal, each flower and action reveal mysteries never dreamed of. Which is why Ortega said the hunter is the truly alert man. A man discovers in nature his true nature, and that leads him to his heart.

Let us remember well that love is the most renewable resource of which there is an inexhaustible supply: the more we give away the more we have to give. More than knowledge, technology and survival strategies, a sustainable earth requires sustainable hearts.

> *"Peace…comes within the souls of men when they realize their relationship, their oneness, with the universe and all its powers, and when they realize that at the center of the Universe dwells Wakan-Tanka, and that this center is really everywhere, it is within each of us."*
>
> ~ Black Elk, Oglala Sioux

Afterword

"There's A Better Way"

Where I was teaching temporarily at a college in Wyoming it got down to 50 below, cold enough to sneak my golden retrievers, Jake and Luna, from my car into the dormitory apartment. I waited until dark so no one would see the dogs coming inside with me, but in the dimly lit parking lot I saw a man standing behind my car with something in his hand.

As I walked toward the car and he moved on down the lot out of sight, I recalled someone in the dorm saying that gas was being stolen from cars. Immediately I knew I should do what John Wayne would do. I'd get my rifle out of the trunk, apprehend the thief and march him into the dorm at gun point, call the sheriff and be a hero.

The moment I reached for the rifle a voice in my head said, "There's a better way." I set the rifle down, closed the trunk and headed after the man who now was coming back towards me. I could see a gas can in one hand, a hose in the other, but when he saw me approaching he tossed the can to his right, the hose to his left. The can clanged loudly on the pavement, and he kept on walking straight ahead as though he heard nothing. We met under a light.

"Are you looking for gas?" "What do you mean? Looking for gas?"

Suddenly a man walked briskly down the hill overlooking the lot and asked the other guy,

"Hey, man, is this guy giving you a hard time?"

I sensed that they were about to attack me and make a run for it so I raised both hands, palms up.

"Now just take it easy. I saw this guy with a gas can and asked him if he was looking for gas."

They paused, looked at one another for a moment then back at me, and one of them asked,

"Hey, man, you got any beer?"

The other quickly followed with,

"Yeah, man you got any dope?"

"No, I don't have any beer and I don't have any dope, but if you want some gas you can come down to my car and get some."

They hesitated, then one of them went back up the hill, probably to a vehicle he had been using as a lookout. The other picked up the gas can and hose and followed me to my car where he proceeded to siphon gas, but he swallowed a mouthful and coughed and gagged repeatedly.

When he had filled the can with maybe a gallon of gas he capped it off, stood erect with a grin and reached out his hand to me,

"Hey, man, thanks a lot."

"You're welcome."

As he walked away I let Jake and Luna out so they could run through the sagebrush before coming inside for the night. I stood there wondering if three men might have died tonight over a gallon of gas? The next morning the topic of my lecture was, "Do real men listen to the heart?"

There were no more reports of gas theft.

They also learned, and perhaps this was the most important thing, how to look at things through the eyes of the Higher Powers."

~ FOOLS CROW, Lakota

Our eyes can only see our beliefs. Our beliefs cause us to make assumptions, draw conclusions, and cause confusion. Our five senses are very limiting. The Creator has a way of allowing us to see or know in the spiritual world. This is called the Sixth Sense. The Sixth Sense is like a radar system; our personal radar system. It will help us "see" opportunities and help us avoid disaster. This Sixth Sense is controlled by God. We must learn to listen to it. We must learn to trust it. We must learn to act on it even if our head says differently. We must learn to look at things through the eyes of God.

My Creator, guide me today. If my eyes cause confusion, let me close them and see through Your eyes. If my ears hear confusion, let me listen to my heart. Let me let You guide me.

Notes & References

FOREWORD

Brackenbury, Wade. 1998. Interview in Randall Eaton's production, "The Sacred Hunt II: Rite of Passage. Sacred Productions, Ashland, Or. 60 minutes.

Campbell, Joseph. See D. K. Osbone's 1991 book, *A Joseph Campbell Companion.* Harper Collins, New York.

Cutting, Scott. Personal communications from interview in Raleigh, N.C. in 2000.

Gurian, Michael. 2004. Interview in Randall L. Eaton's production, "Respect and Responsibility: The Truth About Kids Who Hunt." Enterprise, Or. 45 minutes.

Gurian, Michael. 1996. *The Wonder of Boys.* Tarcher.

Gurian, Michael. 1998. *A Fine Young Man.* Tarcher.

Gurian, Michael. 1999. *The Good Son.* Tarcher.

Jacobs, Don Trent and Jessica Trent-Spencer. 2001. *Teaching Virtues.* Rowman.

Jacobs, Don T. 1998. *Primal Awareness.* Inner Traditions, Rochester, Vt.

Olson, Dennis. 1999. *Shared Spirits.* Northwood Press, Minocqua, Wi.

Parsons, Herb. Among the greatest shooters who ever lived, his feats with a shotgun are inspiring. Herb has been featured on the History Channel and in numerous documentaries. He knew that boys needed to have their instincts mentored to develop well.

Rose, Jim. 2004. Interview in Randall L. Eaton's production, "Respect ad Responsibility: The Truth About Kids Who Hunt." Randall Eaton Productions, Enterprise, Or. 45 minutes.

Young, Jon. 2004. Interview in Randall L. Eaton's production, "Respect and Responsibility: The Truth About Kids Who Hunt." Randall Eaton Productions, Enterprise, Or. 45 minutes.

Young, Jon and Tiffany Morgan. 2007. *Animal Tracking Basics.* Stackpole, Mechanicsburg, PA

Young, Jon, Ellen Haas and Evan McGown. 2008. *Coyote's Guide to Connecting with Nature.* OWLink Media, Shelton, WA.

OVERVIEW

Bly, Robert. 1992. *Iron John.* Vintage, New York.

Levi Carson is a Nez Perce who was interviewed in "The Sacred Hunt II: Rite of Passage," Sacred Productions, 1998.

Dolph, Tom. 2002. *Book of the Hunt.* Writer's Club Press.

Eaton, Randall L. 1979. Interference competition between carnivores: a model for the evolution of social behavior. *Carnivore* II (l).

Eaton, Randall L. 1978. Evolution of trophy hunting. *Carnivore* I (l).

Gurian, Michael. See interview of Michael Gurian in Chapter 11 or "Respect and Responsibility: The Truth About Kids Who Hunt," Randall Eaton Productions, 2004. Or visit Michael Gurian's website to learn about several books he's authored about raising boys.

Jacobs, Don T. See interview in Foreword or "Respect and Responsibility: The Truth About Kids Who Hunt," Randall Eaton Productions, 2004.

John, Peter. An Athabascan elder interviewed in "The Sacred Hunt: Hunting as a Spiritual Path," Sacred Hunt Productions, 1997.

Leopold, Aldo. 1948. *A Sand County Almanac.* Oxford.

Meade, Michael. 2003. "Holding the thread of life." Audiobook. Mosaic, Seattle.

Ortega y Gasset, Jose. 1964. *Meditations On Love.* Meridian.

Osborn, D. K. 1991. *A Joseph Campbell Companion.* Harper Collins, New York.

Pearce, Joseph Chilton. 1977. *Magical Child.* Dutton, New York.

Pearce, Joseph Chilton. 2002. *The Biology of Transcendence.* Park Street Press, Rochester, VT

Rose, Jim. See interview in Foreword, also "Respect and Responsibility: The Truth About Kids Who Hunt," Randall Eaton Productions, 2004.

"The Sacred Hunt" was released in 1997. The Western Shoshone interviewed was Felix Ike.

Shepard, Paul. 1996.. *The Others: How Animals Made Us Human.* Island Press, Washington, D.C.

Van der Post, Laurens. 1961. *Heart of the Hunter.* Harcourt Brace & Co., New York.

CHAPTER 1

Anonymous. 1975. *A Course in Miracles*. Foundation Inner Peace, Tiburon, Ca.

Bly, Robert. 1992. *Iron John*. Vintage, New York

Bly, Robert. 1996. *Sibling Society*. Perseus Books, New York.

Cohen, Leonard. Wrote and sang "Suzanne," probably his best known song, which refers to sinking beneath her wisdom like a stone.

Coon, Carleton . 1971. *The Hunting Peoples*. Little, Brown. Atlanta.

Eaton, Randall L. 1998. *The Sacred Hunt: An Anthology*. Sacred Press, Ashland, Or.

Eaton, Randall L. 1985. The hunter as alert man: an overview of the history of the human/animal connection. In: Randall L. Eaton (Editor), *The Human/Animal Connection*. Carnivore Press.

Fromm, Erich. 1955. *The Sane Society*. Fawcett.

Lomborg, D. 2001. *The Skeptical Environmentalist*. Cambridge University Press.

Meade, Michael. 1993. *Men and the Water of Life*. Harper, San Francisco.

Olson, Dennis. 1999. *Shared Spirits*. Northwood Press, Minocqua, WI

Pearce, Joseph Chilton. 1995. *Magical Child Matures*. Dutton, New York.

Pearce, Joseph Chilton. 2002. *The Biology of Transcendence*. Park Street, Rochester, VT

Reisner, Zac. The Zen Cowboy used to live near Pinedale, Wyoming, which he described as "the last place." A hunter who did sweat lodges and painted, Zac was a cowboy who thought with his heart. Turns out he and the poet Gary Snyder were old friends.

Shepard, Paul. 1982. *Nature and Madness*. University Georgia Press, Athens.

Shepard, Paul. 1998. *Coming Home to the Pleistocene*. Island Press, Washington, D.C.

Shepard, Paul. 1978. *Thinking Animals*. Viking, New York.

Stalking Wolf was an Apache shaman and mentor of Tom Brown, Jr. See Brown's book, *Awakening Spirits*, 1994, Berkeley Books, New York, for a description of Stalking Wolf's visions.

Upton, Bruce. 2005. *The Biology of Belief*. Mountain of Love, Santa Rosa, CA Bruce Upton is a cell biologist who has produced videos that popularize the new Lamarkian inheritance and its implications which are empowering for human life.

Wolf, Fred. 1991. *The Eagle's Quest*. Simon & Shuster, New York.

CHAPTER 2

Anonymous. 1975. *A Course in Miracles*. Foundation Inner Peace, Tiburon, Ca.

Capra, Fritov. 1975. *The Tao of Physics*.

Kammer, Carole and Judi Gold.1998. *Call to* Connection*: Bringing Sacred Tribal Values into Modern Life*. Commune-A-Key, Salt Lake City.

McLuhan, T.C. 1971. *Touch the Earth*. Promonotory Press, New York.

Ortega y Gasset, Jose. 1969. *Some Lessons in Metaphysics*. Norton, New York. Ortega's philosophy of co-existence or interdependence points to a third party, the observer of ego and its relationship with circumstance, which implies that the real "I" is not ego itself, which agrees with the great teacher Krishnamurti who refers often to the observer. The quiet, inner observer is nothing less than spirit which ego would belittle to maintain its autocracy of fear. In fact, Mary Ann Williamson was right when she said, "Our greatest fear is that we are powerful beyond measure," meaning that ego's greatest fear is of the indwelling spirit.

Ortega y Gasset, Jose. 1960 *What Is Philosophy*? Norton, New York. Which could have been entitled, "What science is not." Highly recommended for readers who want a clear demarcation between philosophy as truth and science as contingent knowledge.

Ortega y Gasset, Jose. 1958. *Man and Crisis*. Norton, New York.

Pearce, Joseph Chilton. 2002. *The Biology of Transcendence*. Park Street, Rochester, VT

Quinn, Daniel. 1999. *Beyond Civilization*. Three Rivers Press, New York.

CHAPTER 3

Brown, Tom Jr. 1979. *The Tracker*. Berkley.

Byrne, Rhonda. 2006. *The Secret*. Atria Books, New York.

Eaton, Randall L. 1997 – 2004. "Sacred Hunt," "Sacred Hunt II: Rite of Passage," and "Respect and Responsibility: The Truth About Kids Who Hunt," Sacred Productions and Randall Eaton Productions. Order at www.randalleaton.com.

Eaton, Randall L. 1998. *The Sacred Hunt: An Anthology*. Sacred Press, Ashland, Or.

Fritzell is quoted in Jim Swan's 1999 book, *The Sacred Art of Hunting*, Willow Creek Press.

Heinz, J.J. 1977. The Bushman's story of scientific knowledge. Pp 148-161 In: P.V.Tobias (Editor), *The Bushmen*. Human and Rousseau, Cape Town and Pretoria.

Keeney, Bradford. 2005. *Bushman Shaman*. Destiny Books, Rochester, Vt.

Keeney, Bradford. 2003. *Ropes to God*. Ringing Rocks Press, Philadelphia.

Krishnamurti, Jidu. Numerous collections of his verbal teachings are available from Amazon or Abebooks. He wrote only one book, *Education and the Significance of Living.*

Long, Max Freedom. 1975. *Introduction to Huna.* Luminary Press. Readers interested in Huna beware that Long didn't get it all right. Huna was banned by the Church then outlawed, so it went underground. The truth about the original and impressive Polynesian religion/healing system is emerging now from the people who know and practice it.

MacLuhan, T.C. 1971. *Touch the Earth.* Promonotory Press, New York.

Ortega y Gasset, Jose. 1972. *Meditations On Hunting.* Scribners, New York.

Pearce, Joseph Chilton. *The Biology of Transcendence.* Park Street, Rochester, VT

Regan, Tom. 1985. *The Case for Animal Rights.* University California Press, Berkeley.

Swan, James A. 1999. *The Sacred Art of Hunting.* Willow Creek Press.

Turnbull, Colin. 1961. *The Forest People.* Simon and Shuster, New York.

Van der Post, Laurens. 1961. *Heart of the Hunter.* Harcourt Brace & Co., New York. Also see his *Lost World of the Kalahari.*

Zencey, Eric. 1998. *Virgin Forest.* U. Georgia Press, Athens.

CHAPTER 4

Baynes, Wilhelm (translator). 1963. *I Ching* (Book of Changes). Bollingen Foundation, New York.

Bookchin, M. 1987. *The Rise of Urbanization and the Decline of Citizenship.* Sierra Club Books, San Francisco.

Cameron, Charles. 1985. Creature spirits everywhere about us: a voice for the black elk nation. Pp. 30 -41 In: Randall L. Eaton (Editor). *The Human/ Animal Connection*, Carnivore Press.

Eldredge, John. 2001. *Wild at Heart.* Nelson Books, Nashville, TN. Regarding Christians in America, it would be illuminating for them to take time to read the Patriot Act I and II, pushed through by "born-again" President Bush since these laws of the land stipulate that in a national emergency the three groups to be contained are gun owners, Christians and constitutionalists. The record in the U.S. shows that national emergencies can be generated by government to serve its own purposes, which also was the case of the Nazi Party burning the Reichstag and blaming it on the communists. See www.infowars.com.

Krishnamurti, J. 1973. *The Awakening of Intelligence.* Avon, New York.

Krishnamurti, J. 1960. *Commentaries On Living.* Quest Books, Wheaton, Il.

Lee, Richard and Irwin DeVore (Editors). 1976. *Kalahari Hunter-Gatherers.* Harvard University Press, Cambridge, Ma.

Lee. Richard B. 1979. *The !Kung San.* Cambridge University Press, New York.

Jacobs, Don T. 1998. *Primal Awareness.* Inner Traditions. Rochester, Vt.

Lee, Richard and Richard Daly (Editors). 1999. *The Cambridge Encyclopedia of Hunters* and *Gatherers.* Cambridge University Press, Cambridge.

Nelson, Richard. 1993. Searching for the lost arrow. Pp. 201-228 In: S. Kellert and E. O. Wilson (Editors), *The Biophilia Hypothesis.* Island Press, Washington, D.C.

Nelson, Richard. 1997. *Heart and Blood.* Knopf, Westminster, Md.

Pearce, Joseph Chilton. 2002. *The Biology of Transcendence.* Park Street, Rochester, VT

Sandburg, Carl. 2001. "To a contemporary bunkshooter." *Selected Poems.* Grammery.

Service, Elman. 1979. *The Hunters.* Prentice Hall Englewood. Clifton, N.J.

Shepard, Paul. 1998. *Coming Home to the Pleistocene.* Island Press, Washington, D.C.

Shepard, Paul. 1973. *Tender Carnivore, Sacred Game.* U. Georgia Press, Athens.

Thompson, William Irwin. 1981. *The Time Falling Bodies Take to Light.* St. Martin's Press, New York.

Tolle, E. 2004. *The Power of Now.* New World Library.

Turnbull, Colin. 1983. *The Human Cycle.* Simon and Shuster, New York.

Van der Post, Lauren. 1985. Wilderness – a way of truth. Pp. 45-58, In: C.A. Meier (Editor). *A Testament to the Wilderness.* Lapis Press, Santa Monica.

Van der Post, Laurens. 1978. *Jung and the Story of Our Time.* Random House, New York.

Wilber, Ken. 1981. *Up From Eden.* Doubleday, New York.

On Romancing the Cow. I am aware that Jerad Dimond has written at length about domestication of livestock and civilization; however, I did not read beyond his first book about human evolution, *The Second Chimpanzee*, in which he saw the people of New Guinea as a model for human foraging societies, when in fact they are farmer-pastoralist-foragers, not merely foragers, and it is abundantly clear that their possession of livestock and farming has had immense influence on their perceptions, values and relationships within and among societies and to the environment, as I have been saying since 1985 and which Paul Shepard has been saying since 1973.

CHAPTER 5

Anonymous. 1975. *A Course in Miracles*. Inner Peace Fndt'n., Tiburon, CA

Coon, Carleton. 1971. *The Hunting Peoples*. Little, Brown. Atlanta.

Harry F. Harlow was a psychologist at University of Wisconsin who explored bonding between infant and mother monkeys and the influence of bonding on their behavior as adults. His work had important implications for the importance of maternal bonding in humans. His popular 1971 book, *Learning to Love*, published by Fawcett, is available from www.abebooks.com.

Louv, Richard. 2005. *The Last Child in the Woods*. Algonquin Press, Chapel Hill.

MacLean, Paul. 1990. *The Triune Brain in Evolution*. Plenum, New York.

Pearce, Joseph Chilton. 1977. *The Magical Child*. Dutton, New York.

Pearce, Joseph Chilton. 1995. *Magical Child Matures*. Dutton, New York.

Pearce, Joseph Chilton. 2002. *The Biology of Transcendence*. Park Street, Rochester, VT

Pearce, Joseph Chilton. 1991. *Evolution's End*. Harper, San Francisco. Commentary on Pearce. I could not say enough about the brilliant insights that Pearce has brought into human development, creativity and intelligence. More than a master synthesizer, Pearce is nothing less than a prophet with a grand vision of human potential and why it is falling short. He has written a number of books, but his Magical Child books are the best known and are directly responsible for reversing horrendous child-birthing and infant care practices in the civilized world which have elevated the development and life prospects for millions of people. If anyone deserves the Nobel prize in medicine it is Pearce. Beyond his significant contribution to human development lies an even more profound message about the grave danger of untempered ego-intellect and its arrogance.

Shepard, Paul. 1978. *Thinking Animals*. Viking, New York.

Shepard, Paul. 1982. *Nature and Madness*. University of Georgia Press, Athens.

Turnbull, Colin. 1983. *The Human Cycle*. Simon and Shuster, New York.

Ventura, Michael. 1987. *The Whole Earth Review*.

CHAPTER 6

Bettelheim, Bruno. 1975.. *The Uses of Enchantment*. Knopf, New York.

Bly, Robert. 1992. *Iron John*. Vintage, New York.

Boscher, Adrian. His incredible life and discoveries in Africa were documented in Lyall Watson's 1983 book *Lightning Bird*, a Touchstone book.

Bronowski, Jacob. 1976. *Ascent of Man*. Little Brown, New York.

Cordain, Loren. 2005. *The Paleo Diet for Athletes*. Rodale.

Eaton, Randall L. 1979. Meditations on the origin of Art. *Carnivore* II(l).

Eaton, Randall L. 1998. *The Orca Project: A Meeting of Nations*. Sacred Press, Ashland, Or.

Eaton, Randall L. 1998. "Orca: The Sacred Whale." 52 minutes. Sacred Productions, Ashland, Or.

Eaton, Randall L. *The Cheetah*. Van Nostrand Reinhold Co., New York.

Eaton, Randall L 1978. The evolution of trophy hunting. *Carnivore* I (l).

Eaton, Randall L. 1979. Interference competition between carnivores: a model for social evolution. *Carnivore* II(l).

Fromm, Erich. 1973. *The Anatomy of Human Destructiveness*. Holt Rinehart Winston, New York

Hoyt, Erich. 1974. *Orca: A Whale Named Killer*.

Hrdy, Sarah. 1983. *The Woman That Never Evolved*. Harvard University Press, Cambridge, Ma.

Isaacs, Glynn and Richard B. Leaky. 1979. *Human Ancestors*. W.H. Freeman.

Keen, Sam. 1991. *Fire in the Belly*. Bantam, New York.

Kropotkin, Prince. 1947. *Ethics: Origin and Development*. Tudor.

Lee, Richard B. 1993. Art, science or politics: The crisis in hunter-gatherer studies. *American Anthropologist* 94: 31-54.

Lyons, Oren B. 2007. Published on the internet by White Bison.

Stange, Mary Zeiss. 1997. *Woman the Hunter*. Beacon Press.

CHAPTER 7

Anderson, J. K. 1985. *Hunting in the Ancient World*. University of California Press, Berkeley.

Bergman, Charles 1997. *Orion's Legacy*. Plume.

Bly, Robert. 1992. *Iron John*. Vintage, New York.

Cartmill, Matt. 1993. *A View to a Death in the Morning*. Harvard University Press, Cambridge, Ma.

Dolph, Tom. 2002. *Book of the Hunt: Initiations into the Life of Honor*. Writer's Club Press, New York.

Giegerich, Wolfgang. 1993. Killings: Psychology's Platonism and the Missing Link To Reality. *Spring Journal* 54: 5 – 18.

Golding, Richard. 1959. *Lord of the Flies*. Perigee Trade.

Henderson, J. L. 1979. *Thresholds of Initiation.* Wesleyan University Press.

Jung, C. G. 1972. *Psychological Reflections*. Bollingen Foundation.

Moore, David and Douglas Gillette. 1990. *King, Warrior, Magician,* Lover. Harper Collins.

Sandburg, Carl. 1957. "Chicago." In: N. Foerster (Editor), *American Poetry and Prose*. Houghton Mifflin, Boston.

Sri Chin Moy died in 2008. He came to Flushing New York as a young yogi who wrote poetry, made music and taught meditation until inspired in his 50s to take up weight lifting. Information about him and his uncanny feats of "unconflicted" behavior are on the internet.

Xenophon. 1925. *On Hunting*. Loeb Classical Library.

CHAPTER 8

Eaton, Randall L. In progress. The Greatest Things I Never Did.

Eliade, M. 1965. *Ritual Symbols of Initiation*. Harper & Row, San Francisco.

Meade, Michael. 1993. *Men and the Water of Life*. Harper, San Fransisco.

Thomas, E. M. 1958. *The Harmless People*. Vintage, New York.

Turnbull, Colin. 1983. *The Human Cycle*. Simon & Shuster.

Van Gennep, Arnold. 1969. *Rites of Passage*. Johnson Reprint Co., New York.

CHAPTER 9

Axtell, Horace and Margo Aragon. 2000. *A Little Bit of Wisdom*. U. Oklahoma Press, Norman.

Bassom, Nauk. 1996. "Baskets at the crossroads," In: L. C. Madhi, N.G. Christopher and M. Meade (Editors), *Crossroads: The Quest for Contemporary Rites of Passage*. Open Court, Chicago.

Black Elk, Wallace. 1985. See Charles Cameron's "Creature spirits everywhere about us: A voice of the black elk nation," In: Randall L. Eaton (Editor), *The Human /Animal* Connection. Carnivore Press, Incline Village, NV.

Chopra, Deepak. 1994. *Ageless Body, Timeless Mind.* Harmony.

Dolph, Tom. 2002. *Book of the Hunt: Initiations into the Life of Honor*. Writers Club Press, New York.

Ingwe. See M. Norman Powell. 1995. *Ingwe*. OWLink Media, Shelton, Wa.

Katz, P. 1982. *Boiling Energy*. Harvard University Press, Cambridge, Ma. But also see Bradford Keeney's *Bushman Shaman* and *Ropes to God*, which for the first time reveal how the Bushman actually are healing one another when they dance into trance and place hands on one another.

Kohl, Johann G. 1965. *Kitchi-Gami*. Minnesota Historical Society Press, St. Paul.

La Fountain, John. 1998. Transcribed interview in "The Sacred Hunt II: Rite of Passage," produced by Randall L. Eaton. Sacred Productions. 60 minutes.

Lee, Richard B. 1993. *The Dobe Ju/'hoansi*. Harcourt Brace, New York.

Leopold, Aldo. 1948. *A Sand County Almanac*. Oxford University Press.

Marks, Stuart.1976. *Large Mammals and a Brave People*. University Washington Press, Seattle.

Meade, Michael. 1993. *Men and the Water of Life*. Harpers, San Francisco.

Moy, Sri Chin. See website and numerous booklets written by Sri Chin Moy whose incredible feats of strength have been officially verified by the British Weightlifting Association. Mr. Olympia, Frank Zane, and Mr. Universe/America, Bill Pearl both knew Moy well and vouched for his authenticity. So do hundreds of American orthopedic surgeons who invited Moy to their annual conference and scrutinized his lifts.

Moyers, Bill. 1992. " Health and the Mind." A 3-part series. PBS TV, Boston.

Ohnuki-Tierney. 1974. *Ainu of the Northwest Coast of southern Sakhalin*. Holt Rinehart Winston.

Pearce, Joseph Chilton. 2002. *The Biology of Transcendence*. Park Street, Rochester, VT

Rael, Tom. 1998. "Saved by a killer elk," chapter in Randall L. Eaton's *The Sacred Hunt: An Anthology*, Ashland, Or.

Saitoti, Tepalit Ole. 1988. *Worlds of a Maasai Warrior*. U. California Press, Berkeley.

Schwartz, Jack. 1992. *I Know from My Heart*. Celestial Arts, Berekely.

Schwartz, Jack 1988. *It's Not What You Eat, It's What's Eating You*. Celestial Arts, Berkeley.

Swan, James A. 1998. Interview in Randall L. Eaton's production, "The Sacred Hunt II" Rite of Passage." Sacred Productions, Ashland, Or.

Swan, James A. 1990. *Sacred Places*. Bear & Co., Sante Fe.

Swan, James A. 1992. *Nature as Teacher and Healer*. Villard.

Swan, James A. 1995. *In Defense of Hunting*. Harper One, San Francisco.

Swan, James A. 1999. *The Sacred Art of Hunting*. Willow Creek Press.

Watson, Dave. 1998. Interview in Randall L. Eaton's "The Sacred Hunt II: Rite of Passage." Sacred Productions, Ashland, Or. 60 minutes.

CHAPTER 10

Babbit, I. 1936. *The Dhammapada*. New Directions, New York.

Campbell, Joseph 1991. See D.K.Osborne's book,

A Joseph Campbell Companion. Harper Collins, New York.

Carnivore: Carnivorous Mammals Including Humans was edited and published by Randall Eaton's "Carnivore Research Institute," from 1978-1987.

Crook, John. 1980. *The Evolution of Consciousness*. Oxford University Press.

Eaton, Randall L. l985. *The Human/Animal Connection*. Carnivore Press, Incline Village, NV.

Eaton, Randall L. 1998. *The Sacred Hunt*. Sacred Press, Ashland, Or.

Jampolsky, Gerald. 1984. *Love Is Letting Go of Fear*. Bantam, New York.

Keen, Sam. 1991. *Fire in the Belly*. Bantam, New York.

Kellert, Stephen R. and Edward O. Wilson (Editors). 1993. *The Biophilia Hypothesis*. Island Press, Washington, D.C.

Kruishnamurti, J. 1960. *The Awakening of Intellligence*. Theosophical Press, Wheaton, Il.

Lao Tzu. 1955. *The Tao Teh Ching*. R. B. Blackney, translator. Mentor, New York. .

Maslow, Abraham H. 1976. *Religions, Values and Peak Experie*nces. Penguin, New York.

Meade, Michael. 1993. *Men and the Water of Life*. Harpers, San Francisco.

Meier, C. A. 1985. Wilderness and the search for the soul of modern man. In: C. A, Meier (Editor), *A Testament to the Wilderness*. Lapis Press, Santa Monica.

Miyuki, M. 1985. "The arts of Mr. Hun Tun." In: C. A. Meier (Editor), *A Testament to the Wilderness.* Lapis Press, Santa Monica.

Nelson, Richard. 1983. *Make Prayers to the Raven*. U. Chicago Press.

Nelson. Richard. 1965. *Hunters of the Northern Ice*. U. Chicago Press.

Olson, Dennis. 1999. *Shared Spirits*. Northwood Press, Minoqua, Wi.

Ortega y Gasset, Jose. 1972. *Meditations On Hunting*. Scribner's, New York.

Sociobiology. Edward O. Wlson's l975 book *Sociobiology* and Richard Dawkins' 1976 book *The Selfish Gene* are perhaps the best-known references to sociobiology as Neo-Darwinism, the mechanistic reduction of animal and human behavior to selfish genes, a term which in itself is an oxymoron because genes cannot be selfish though organisms can. Even if sociobiology applies at the level of biology, instinct and ego, thank God we are also spiritual and that our choices are not at the mercy of genes; moreover, the course of proper development/bonding has a huge influence which expands our interests to the other and to our world.

Snyder, Gary.1995. *A Place in Space*. Counterpoint, Washington, D.C.

Snyder, Gary. 1990. *The Practice of the Wild*. North Point Press, Berkeley.

Snyder, Gary. 1975. *Turtle Island*. North Point Press, Berkeley.

Weiner, Norbert. 1950. *The Human Use of Human Beings*. London.

CHAPTER 11

Eaton, Randall L. 1985. They put people to sleep don't they? In: Randall L. Eaton (Editor), *The Human/Animal Connection*. Carnivore Press, Incline Village, NV.

Eaton, Randall L. 1998. *The Orca Project: A Meeting of Nations*. Sacred Press, Ashland, Or.

Eliade, M. 1958. *Rites and Symbols of Initiation*. Harper, New York.

Fulghum, Robert. 1988. *All I Ever Needed to Know I Learned in Kindergarten*. Random House, New York.

Ishi. See Theodora Kroeber's 1973 book entitled *Ishi, the Last of His Tribe*. Bantam Starfire Books.

Keeney, Bradford. 2005. *Bushman Shaman*. Destiny Books, Rochester, Vt.

Krishnamurti, J. 1960. *Commentaries On Living*. Theosophical Press, Wheaton,Il.

Meade, Michael. 1993. *Men and the Water of Life*. Harpers, San Francisco.

Some', Malidoma. 1996. "Ritual, the sacred and the community." In: L.C. Madhi, N.G. Christopher and M. Meade (Editors), *Crossroads: The Quest for Contemporary Rites of Passage*. Open Court, Chicago.

CHAPTER 12

Adamson, Joy. 1967. *The Peoples of Kenya*. Harcourt Brace and World, New York.

Boas, C. V. and C. V. Boas. 1970. *Xingu: The Indians, Their Myths*. Farrar, Straus and Giroux, New York.

Carson, Levi. 1998. Interviewed in Randall L. Eaton's production, "The Sacred Hunt II: Rite of Passage," Sacred Productions, Ashland, Or 60 minutes.

Guggisberg, C. A. W. 1962. *Simba*. Chilton Books, Philadelphia..

Guggisberg, C. A. W. 1970. *Man and Wildlife*. Arco, New York.

Howell, F. C. 1965. *Man*. Time-Life Books, New York.

Jensen, A. E. 1961. *Myth and Cult Among Primitive Peoples*. University California Press.

Keeney, Bradford. 2006. *Bushman Shaman*. Destiny Books, Rochester, Vt.

Lantis, M. 1966. *Alaskan Eskimo Ceremonialism.* University Washington Press, Seattle.

Leopold, Aldo. 1948. *A Sand County Almanac.* Oxford University Press.

Marks, Stuart. 1976. *Large Mammals and a Brave People.* University of Washington Press, Seattle.

Marshall, J. 1957. "The Hunters." McGraw Hill, New York.

Meggers, B. J. 1971. *Amazonia: Man and Culture – A Counterfeit Paradise.* Aldine, Chicago

Nelson, Richard. 1969. *Hunters of the Northern Ice.* U. Chicago Press.

Posewitz, Jim. 1994. *Beyond Fair Chase.* Falcon Press.

Summers, M. 1946. *The Werewolf.* Bell Publishing, New York.

Thomas, E. M. 1958. *The Harmless People.* Vintage, New York.

Turnbull, Colin. 1961. *The Forest People.* Simon and Shuster, New York.

Wagley, C. 1977. *A Welcome of Tears.* Oxford University Press.

Weyer, E. M. 1932. *The Eskimos: Their Environment and Folkways.* Yale University Press, New Haven, Ct.

CHAPTER 13

Amory, Cleveland. 1997. *Ranch of Dreams.* Viking, New York.

Bly, Robert. 1992. *Iron John.* Vintage, New York.

Bradshaw, John. 1990 *Homecoming.* Bantam, New York,

Carter, Jimmy. 1988. *Outdoor Journal.* Bantam, New York.

Eaton, Randall L. 1998. "A forest for life," In: *The Sacred Hunt.* Sacred Press, Ashland, Or.

John, Peter. 1997. Interviewed in Randall Eaton's production, "The Sacred Hunt." Sacred Productions, Ashland, Or. 90 minutes.

Marshall, J. 1955. "The Hunters."

Pearce, Joseph Chilton. 1995. *Magical Child Matures.* Dutton, New York.

Smith, Helen. 2004. Interview in Randall Eaton's production, "Respect and Responsibility: The Truth About Kids Who Hunt." Randall Eaton Productions, Enterprise, Or. 45 minutes.

Smith, Helen. 2000. *Scarred Hearts.* Calisto, Knoxville.

Shepard, Paul. 1978. *Thinking Animals.* Viking, New York.

Snyder, Gary. 1974. *Turtle Island.* New Directions.

Watson, Dave. 1998. Interview in Randall Eaton's production, "The Sacred Hunt II: Rite of Passage." Sacred Productions, Ashland, Or. 90 minutes.

CHAPTER 14

Berkes, F. 1999. *Sacred Ecology.* Taylor & Francis, Philadelphia.

Eaton, Randall L. 1997. "The Sacred Hunt." Sacred Productions, Ashland, Or 90 minutes.

Enck, Jody W., Dan T. Decker and Tommy L. Brown. 2000. Status of hunter recruitment and retention in the United States. *Wildlife Society Bulletin* 28(4): 817-824.

Freeman, Milton M. R. and L. N. Carbyn (Editors). 1988. *Traditional Knowledge and Resource Management in Northern Regions.* IUCN Report.

Freeman, Milton M. R. 2000. *Endangered People of the Arctic.* Greenwood Press.

Holsman, Robert. 2000. Goodwill hunting? *Wildlife Society Bulletin* (4): 800-816.

Iroquois Confederation. See Jerry Mander's 1992 book, *In the Absence of the Sacred: The Failure of Technology and Survival of the Indian Nations,* Sierra Club Books. Also see his book on ten reasons not to watch TV as well as his most recent treatise on why global economy is failing and why we need to look to local economy. Many of Mander's messages are similar to mine and those of Joe Pearce, Paul Shepard, Gary Snyder and others, meaning that he comprehends the failure of techno-civilization at every level and he favors recovery of the Old Ways in human society and our relationship to the earth.

Knotts, Dave. 1998. Interview in Randall Eaton's production, 'The Sacred Hunt: Rite of Passage," Sacred Productions, Ashland, Or. 60 minutes.

Konner, Melvin. 1982. *The Tangled Wing.* Henry Holt, New York.

Leopold, Aldo. 1948. *A Sand County Almanac.* Oxford University Press.

Marks, Stuart. 1991. *Southern Hunting in Black and White.* Princeton University Press, Princeton, N.J.

Norton, Bob. 2007. *The Hunter:Developmental Stages andEthics.* Riverbend Press.

Organ, John and E.K. Fritzell. 2000. Trends in consumptive recreation and the wildlife profession. *Wildlife Society Bulletin* 28(4): 780-797.

Pearce, Joseph Chilton. 2002. *The Biology of Transcendence.* Park Street, Rochester, Vt

Peyton, R. Ben. 2000. Wildlife Management: cropping to manage or managing to crop? *Wildlife Society Bulletin* 28(4): 774-779.

Posewitz, Jim. 2004. Interview in "Respect and Responsibility: The Truth About Kids Who Hunt." Randall Eaton Productions, Enterprise, Or. 45 minutes.

Shepard, Paul. 1996. *The Others: How Animals Made Us Human.* Island Press, Washington, D.C.

Shepard, Paul. 1978. *Thinking Animals.* Viking, New York.

Vialles, N. 1994. *Animal to Edible.* Cambridge University Press.

Swan, James A. 1995. *In Defense of Hunting.* Harper One, San Franscisco.

Swan, James A. 1999. *The Sacred Art of Hunting.* Willow Creek Press.

Wensel, Gene. 2000. Update. *Traditional Bowhunter* 3: 107-108.

Young, Jon, Ellen Haas and Evan McGown. 2008. *Coyote's Guide to Connecting to Nature.* OWLink Media, Shelton, WA.

CHAPTER 15

Foster, Steven and Meredith Little. 1987. *Book of the Vision Quest.* Prentice Hall, New York.

Foster, Steven and Meredith Little. 1989. *Roaring of the Sacred River.* Simon and Shuster, Riverside, N. J.

Golas, Thaddeus. 1981. *The Lazy Man's Guide to Enlightenment.* Bantam, New York.

Keeney, Bradford. 2005. *Bushman Shaman.* Destiny Books, Rochester, VT

Mahdi, Louise, Steven Foster and Meredith Little. 1987. *Betwixt and Between: Patterns of Masculine and Feminine Initiation.* Open Court, Chicago.

Niehardt, J. G. 1959. *Black Elk Speaks.* Washigton Square Press, New York.

CHAPTER 16

Oldfield, David.1996. "The journey," In: Louise C. Mahdi et al (Editors). *Crossroads*, Open Court, Chicago.

Olson, Dennis. 1999. *Shared Spirits.* Northwood Press, Minoqua, Wi.

Passmore, Kay. 1996. "Personal shields," In: Louise C. Mahdi et al (Editors). *Crossroads*, Open Court, Chicago.

Steiner, Rudolf. 2000. *Guardian Angels.* Rudolf Steiner Press, London.

Wynne, Elaine. 1987. "Storytelling," In: Louise C. Mahdi et al (Editors), *Betwixt and Between,* Crossroads, Chicago.

CHAPTER 17

Bly, Robert and Michael Meade (Editors). 1992. "Old Song." In: *The Rag and Bone Shop of the Heart.* Harper, New York.

Campbell, Joseph. 1988. *Historical Atlas of the World Pt 1.* Harper Collins, New York.

Eaton, Randall L. 1998. *The Sacred Hunt.* Sacred Press, Ashland, Or.

Eiseley, Loren. 1969. *The Unexpected Universe.* Harvest Books, New York.

Gibson, Mel. 2006. "Apocalypto." DVD.

Ortega y Gasset, Jose. 1972. *Meditations On Hunting.* Scribners, New York

Regan, Tom. 1985. *The Case for Animal Rights.* University California Press, Berkeley.

Richard, Cliff. 1985. "It's in Every One of Us." LP.

Shepard, Paul. 1982. *Nature and Madness.* University Georgia Press, Athens.

EPILOGUE

Steiner, Rudolf. 1994. *How to Know Higher Worlds.* Anthroposophic Press, Hudson, New York.

Bibliography

Adamson, Joy. 1967. *The Peoples of Kenya*. Harcourt Brace and World, New York.

Amory, Cleveland. 1997. *Ranch of Dreams*. Viking, New York.

Anderson, J. K. 1985. *Hunting in the Ancient World*. University of California Press, Berkeley.

Anonymous. 1975. *A Course in Miracles*. Foundation Inner Peace, Tiburon, Ca.

Axtell, Horace and Margo Aragon. 2000. *A Little Bit of Wisdom*. U. Oklahoma Press, Norman.

Babbit, I. 1936. *The Dhammapada*. New Directions, New York.

Bassom, Nauk. 1996. "Baskets at the crossroads," In: L. C. Madhi, N.G. Christopher and M. Meade (Editors), *Crossroads: The Quest for Contemporary Rites of Passage*. Open Court, Chicago.

Baynes, Wilhelm (translator). 1963. *I Ching* (Book of Changes). Bollingen Foundation, New York.

Bergman, Charles 1997. *Orion's Legacy*. Plume.

Berkes, F. 1999. *Sacred Ecology*. Taylor & Francis, Philadelphia.

Bettelheim, Bruno. 1975. *The Uses of Enchantment*. Knopf, New York.

Bly, Robert. 1992. *Iron John*. Vintage, New York.

Bly, Robert. 1996. *Sibling Society*. Perseus Books, New York.

Bly, Robert and Michael Meade (Editors). 1992. "Old Song." In: *The Rag and Bone Shop of the Heart* Harper, New York.

Boas, C. V. and C. V. Boas. 1970. *Xingu: The Indians, Their Myths*. Farrar, Straus and Giroux, New York.

Bookchin, M. 1987. *The Rise of Urbanization and the Decline of Citizenship*. Sierra Club Books, San Francisco.

Bradshaw, John. 1990 *Homecoming*. Bantam, New York,

Bronowski, Jacob. 1976. *Ascent of Man*. Little Brown, New York.

Brown, Tom Jr. 1979. *The Tracker*. Berkley.

Byrne, Rhonda. 2006. *The Secret*. Atria Books, New York.

Cameron, Charles. 1985. Creature spirits everywhere about us: a voice for the black elk nation. Pp. 30 -41 In: Randall L. Eaton (Editor). *The Human/ Animal Connection*, Carnivore Press.

Campbell, Joseph. 1988. *Historical Atlas of the World Pt 1*. Harper Collins, New York.

Capra, Fritov. 1975. *The Tao of Physics*. Bantam, New York.

Carter, Jimmy. 1988. *Outdoor Journal*. Bantam, New York.

Cartmill, Matt. 1993. *A View to a Death in the Morning*. Harvard University Press, Cambridge, Ma.

Chopra, Deepak. 1994. *Ageless Body, Timeless Mind*. Harmony.

Coon, Carleton . 1971. *The Hunting Peoples*. Little, Brown. Atlanta

Cordain, Loren. 2005. *The Paleo Diet for Athletes*. Rodale.

Crook, John. 1980. *The Evolution of Consciousness*. Oxford University Press.

Dawkins, Richard. 1976. *The Selfish Gene*. Oxford U. Press

Dolph, Tom. 2002. *Book of the Hunt*. Writer's Club Press.

Eaton, Randall L. 1979. Interference competition between carnivores: a model for the evolution of social behavior. *Carnivore* II (l).

Eaton, Randall L. 1978. Evolution of trophy hunting. *Carnivore* I (1).

Eaton, Randall L. 1998. *The Sacred Hunt: An Anthology*. Sacred Press, Ashland, Or.

Eaton, Randall L. 1985. The hunter as alert man: an overview of the history of the human/animal connection. In: Randall L. Eaton (Editor), *The Human/Animal Connection*. Carnivore Press.

Eaton, Randall L. 1997 – 2004. "Sacred Hunt," "Sacred Hunt II: Rite of Passage," and "Respect and Responsibility: The Truth About Kids Who Hunt," Sacred Productions and Randall Eaton Productions.

Eaton, Randall L. 1979. Meditations on the origin of Art. *Carnivore* II(l).

Eaton, Randall L. 1998. *The Orca Project: A Meeting of Nations*. Sacred Press, Ashland, Or.

Eaton, Randall L. 1998. "Orca: The Sacred Whale." 52 minutes. Sacred Productions, Ashland, Or.

Eaton, Randall L. *The Cheetah*. Van Nostrand Reinhold Co., New York.

Eaton, Randall L. 1985. They put people to sleep don't they? In: Randall L. Eaton (Editor),

The Human/Animal Connection. Carnivore Press, Incline Village, NV.

Eaton, Randall L. 1998. "A forest for life," In: *The Sacred Hunt*. Sacred Press, Ashland,

Eiseley, Loren. 1969. *The Unexpected Universe*. Harvest Books, New York.

Eliade, M. 1965. *Ritual Symbols of Initiation*. Harper & Row, San Francisco.

Eldredge, John. 2001. *Wild at Heart*. Nelson Books, Nashville, TN.

Enck, Jody W., Dan T. Decker and Tommy L. Brown. 2000. Status of hunter recruitment and retention in the United States. *Wildlife Society Bulletin* 28(4): 817-824.

Foster, Steven and Meredith Little. 1987. *Book of the Vision Quest*. Prentice Hall, New York.

Foster, Steven and Meredith Little. 1989. *Roaring of the Sacred River*. Simon and Shuster, Riverside, N. J.

Freeman, Milton M. R. and L. N. Carbyn (Editors). 1988. *Traditional Knowledge and Resource Management in Northern Regions*. IUCN Report.

Freeman, Milton M. R. 2000. *Endangered People of the Arctic*. Greenwood Press.

Fromm, Erich. 1955. *The Sane Society*. Fawcett.

Fromm, Erich. 1973. *The Anatomy of Human Destructiveness*. Holt Rinehart Winston, New York

Fulghum, Robert. 1988. *All I Ever Needed to Know I Learned in Kindergarten*. Random House, New York.

Golas, Thaddeus. 1981. *The Lazy Man's Guide to Enlightenment*. Bantam, New York.

Golding, Richard. 1959. *Lord of the Flies*. Perigee Trade.

Guggisberg, C. A. W. 1962. *Simba*. Chilton Books, Philadelphia..

Guggisberg, C. A. W. 1970. *Man and Wildlife*. Arco, New York.

Gurian, Michael. 1996. *The Wonder of Boys*. Tarcher.

Gurian, Michael. 1998. *A Fine Young Man*. Tarcher.

Gurian, Michael. 1999. *The Good Son*. Tarcher.

Henderson, J. L. 1979. *Thresholds of Initiation*. Wesleyan University Press.

Heinz, J.J. 1977. The Bushman's story of scientific knowledge. Pp 148-161 In: P.V.Tobias (Editor), *The Bushmen*. Human and Rousseau, Cape Town and Pretoria.

Holsman, Robert. 2000. Goodwill hunting? *Wildlife Society Bulletin* (4): 800-816.

Howell, F. C. 1965. *Man*. Time-Life Books, New York.

Hoyt, Erich. 1974. *Orca: A Whale Named Killer*. Firefly.

Hrdy, Sarah. 1983. *The Woman That Never Evolved*. Harvard University Press, Cambridge, Ma.

Isaacs, Glynn and Richard B. Leaky. 1979. *Human Ancestors*. W.H. Freeman.

Jacobs, Don T. 1998. *Primal Awareness*. Inner Traditions. Rochester, Vt.

Jacobs, Don Trent and Jessica Trent-Spencer. 2001. *Teaching Virtues*. Rowman.

Jacobs, Don T. See interview in Chapter11 or "Respect and Responsibility: The Truth About Kids Who Hunt," Randall Eaton Productions, 2004.

Jampolsky, Gerald. 1984. *Love Is Letting Go of Fear*. Bantam, New York.

Jensen, A. E. 1961. *Myth and Cult Among Primitive Peoples*. University California Press.

John, Peter. An Athabascan elder interviewed in "The Sacred Hunt: Hunting as a Spiritual Path," Sacred Hunt Productions, 1997.

Jung, C. G. 1972. *Psychological Reflections*. Bollingen Foundation.

Kammer, Carole and Judi Gold.1998. *Call to* Connection*: Bringing Sacred Tribal Values into Modern Life*. Commune-A-Key, Salt Lake City.

Katz, P. 1982. *Boiling Energy*. Harvard University Press, Cambridge, Ma.

Keen, Sam. 1991. *Fire in the Belly*. Bantam, New York.

Keeney, Bradford. 2005. *Bushman Shaman*. Destiny Books, Rochester, Vt.

Keeney, Bradford. 2003. *Ropes to God*. Ringing Rocks Press, Philadelphia.

Kellert, Stephen R. and Edward O. Wilson (Editors). 1993. *The Biophilia Hypothesis*. Island Press, Washington, D.C.

Kohl, Johann G. 1965. *Kitchi-Gami*. Minnesota Historical Society Press, St. Paul.

Konner, Melvin. 1982. *The Tangled Wing*. Henry Holt, New York.

Krishnamurti, J. 1973. *The Awakening of Intelligence*. Avon, New York.

Krishnamurti, J. 1960. *Commentaries On Living*. Theosophical Press, Wheaton,Il.

Kroeber, Theodora. 1973. *Ishi, the Last of His Tribe*. Bantam Starfire Books.

Lantis, M. 1966. *Alaskan Eskimo Ceremonialism*. University Washington Press, Seattle.

Lao Tzu. 1955. *The Tao Teh Ching*. R. B. Blackney, translator. Mentor, New York. .

Lee, Richard and Irwin DeVore (Editors). 1976. *Kalahari Hunter-Gatherers*. Harvard University Press, Cambridge, Ma.

Lee. Richard B. 1979. *The !Kung San*. Cambridge University Press, New York.

Lee, Richard and Richard Daly (Editors). 1999. *The Cambridge Encyclopedia of Hunters* and *Gatherers*. Cambridge University Press, Cambridge.

Lee, Richard B. 1993. Art, science or politics: The crisis in hunter-gatherer studies. *American Anthropologist* 94: 31-54.

Lee, Richard B. 1993. *The Dobe Ju/'hoansi*. Harcourt Brace, New York.

Leopold, Aldo. 1948. *A Sand County Almanac*. Oxford.

Lomborg, D. 2001. *The Skeptical Environmentalist*. Cambridge University Press.

Long, Max Freedom. 1975. *Introduction to Huna*. Luminary Press.

Louv, Richard. 2005. *The Last Child in the Woods*. Algonquin Press, Chapel Hill.

MacLean, Paul. 1990. *The Triune Brain in Evolution*. Plenum, New York.

Mahdi, Louise, Steven Foster and Meredith Little. 1987. *Betwixt and Between: Patterns of Masculine and Feminine Initiation*. Open Court, Chicago.

Mander, J. 1992. *In the Absence of the Sacred: The Failure of Technology and Survival of the Indian Nations*, Sierra Club Books.

Marks, Stuart.1976. *Large Mammals and a Brave People*. University Washington Press, Seattle.

Marks, Stuart. 1991. *Southern Hunting in Black and White*. Princeton University Press, Princeton, N.J.

Marks, Stuart. 2008. *On the Ground and in the Villages*. Mipashi Associates.

Marshall, J. 1957. "The Hunters." McGraw Hill, New York.

Maslow, Abraham H. 1976. *Religions, Values and Peak Experie*nces. Penguin, New York.

Meade, Michael. 1993. *Men and the Water of Life*. Harper, San Fransisco.

Meade, Michael. 2003. "Holding the thread of life." Audiobook. Mosaic, Seattle.

Meggers, B. J. 1971. *Amazonia: Man and Culture – A Counterfeit Paradise*. Aldine, Chicago

Meier, C. A. 1985. Wilderness and the search for the soul of modern man. In: C. A, Meier (Editor), *A Testament to the Wilderness*. Lapis Press, Santa Monica.

McLuhan, T.C. 1971. *Touch the Earth*. Promonotory Press, New York.

Miyuki, M. 1985. "The arts of Mr. Hun Tun." In: C. A. Meier (Editor), *A Testament to the Wilderness*. Lapis Press, Santa Monica.

Moore, David and Douglas Gillette. 1990. *King, Warrior, Magician, L*over. Harper Collins.

Moyers, Bill. 1992. " Health and the Mind." A 3-part series. PBS TV, Boston.

Nelson, Richard. 1993. Searching for the lost arrow. Pp. 201-228 In: S. Kellert and E. O. Wilson (Editors), *The Biophilia Hypothesis*. Island Press, Washington, D.C.

Nelson, Richard. 1997. *Heart and Blood*. Knopf, Westminster, Md

Nelson. Richard. 1965. *Hunters of the Northern Ice*. U. Chicago Press.

Nelson, Richard. 1983. *Make Prayers to the Raven*. U. Chicago Press.

Niehardt, J. G. 1959. *Black Elk Speaks*. Washington Square Press, New York.

Norton, Bob. 2007. *The Hunter: Developmental Stages and Ethics.*. Riverbend Press.

Ohnuki-Tierney. 1974. *Ainu of the Northwest Coast of Southern Sakhalin*. Holt Rinehart Winston.

Oldfield, David.1996. "The journey," In: Louise C. Mahdi et al (Editors). *Crossroads*, Open Court, Chicago.

Olson, Dennis. 1999. *Shared Spirits*. Northwood Press, Minocqua, WI

Organ, John and E.K. Fritzell. 2000. Trends in consumptive recreation and the wildlife profession. *Wildlife Society Bulletin* 28(4): 780-797.

Ortega y Gasset, Jose. 1964. *Meditations On Love*. Meridian.

Ortega y Gasset, Jose. 1969. *Some Lessons in Metaphysics*. Norton, New York.

Ortega y Gasset, Jose. 1960 *What Is Philosophy*? Norton, New York. Ortega y Gasset, Jose. 1958. *Man and Crisis*. Norton, New York.

Ortega y Gasset, Jose. 1972. *Meditations On Hunting*. Scribners, New York.

Osbon, D. K. 1991. *A Joseph Campbell Companion*. Harper Collins, New York.

Passmore, Kay. 1996. "Personal shields," In: Louise C. Mahdi et al (Editors). *Crossroads*, Open Court, Chicago.

Pearce, Joseph Chilton. 1977. *Magical Child*. Dutton, New York.

Pearce, Joseph Chilton. 1995. *Magical Child Matures*. Dutton, New York.

Pearce, Joseph Chilton. 2002. *The Biology of Transcendence*. Park Street Press, Rochester, VT

Pearce, Joseph Chilton. 1991. *Evolution's End*. Harper, San Francisco.

Peyton, R. Ben. 2000. Wildlife Management: cropping to manage or managing to crop? *Wildlife Society Bulletin* 28(4): 774-779.

Poole, R. M. 2007. Hunters: for love of the land. *National Geographic* November.

Posewitz, Jim. 1994. *Beyond Fair Chase*. Falcon Press.

Powell, M. Norman. 1995. *Ingwe*. OWLink Media, Shelton, Wa.

Quinn, Daniel. 1999. *Beyond Civilization*. Three Rivers Press, New York.

Regan, Tom. 1985. *The Case for Animal Rights*. University California Press, Berkeley..

Richards, Cliff. 1985. "It's in Every One of Us." LP.

Saitoti, Tepalit Ole. 1988. *Worlds of a Maasai Warrior*. U. California Press, Berkeley.

Sandburg, Carl. 1957. "Chicago." In: N. Foerster (Editor), *American Poetry and Prose*. Houghton Mifflin, Boston.

Schwartz, Jack. 1992. *I Know from My Heart*. Celestial Arts, Berekely.

Schwartz, Jack 1988. *It's Not What You Eat, It's What's Eating You*. Celestial Arts, Berkeley.

Service, Elman. 1979. *The Hunters*. Prentice Hall Englewood. Clifton, N.J.

Shepard, Paul. 1982. *Nature and Madness*. University Georgia Press, Athens.

Shepard, Paul. 1978. *Thinking Animals*. Viking, New York.

Shepard, Paul. 1998. *Coming Home to the Pleistocene*. Island Press, Washington, D.C.

Shepard, Paul. 1973. *Tender Carnivore, Sacred Game*. U. Georgia Press, Athens.

Shepard, Paul. 1996. *The Others: How Animals Made Us Human*. Island Press, Washington, D.C.

Smith, Helen. 2000. *Scarred Hearts*. Calisto, Knoxville.

Snyder, Gary.1995. *A Place in Space*. Counterpoint, Washington, D.C.

Snyder, Gary. 1990. *The Practice of the Wild*. North Point Press, Berkeley.

Snyder, Gary. 1975. *Turtle Island*. North Point Press, Berkeley.

Some', Malidoma. 1996. "Ritual, the sacred and the community." In: L.C. Madhi, N.G. Christopher and M. Meade (Editors), *Crossroads: The Quest for Contemporary Rites of Passage*. Open Court, Chicago.

Stange, Mary Zeiss. 1997. *Woman the Hunter*. Beacon Press.

Steiner, Rudolf. 2000. *Guardian Angels*. Rudolf Steiner Press, London.

Steiner, Rudolf. 1994. *How to Know Higher Worlds*. Anthroposophic Press, Hudson, N.Y.

Summers, M. 1946. *The Werewolf*. Bell Publishing, New York.

Swan, James A. 1990. *Sacred Places*. Bear & Co., Sante Fe.

Swan, James A. 1992. *Nature as Teacher and Healer*. Villard.

Swan, James A. 1995. *In Defense of Hunting*. Harper One, San Francisco.

Swan, James A. 1999. *The Sacred Art of Hunting*. Willow Creek Press.

Thomas, E. M. 1958. *The Harmless People*. Vintage, New York.

Thompson, William Irwin. 1981. *The Time Falling Bodies Take to Light*. St. Martin's Press, New York.

Tolle, E. 2004. *The Power of Now*. New World Library.

Turnbull, Colin. 1961. *The Forest People*. Simon and Shuster, New York.

Turnbull, Colin. 1983. *The Human Cycle*. Simon and Shuster, New York.

Upton, Bruce. 2005. *The Biology of Belief*. Mountain of Love, Santa Rosa, CA

Van der Post, Lauren. 1985. Wilderness – a way of truth. Pp. 45-58, In: C.A. Meier (Editor). *A Testament to the Wilderness*. Lapis Press, Santa Monica.

Van der Post, Laurens. 1978. *Jung and the Story of Our Time*. Random House, New York.

Van Gennep, Arnold. 1969. *Rites of Passage*. Johnson Reprint Co., New York.

Ventura, Michael. 1989. *The Whole Earth Review*, Winter.

Vialles, N. 1994. *Animal to Edible*. Cambridge University Press.

Wagley, C. 1977. *A Welcome of Tears*. Oxford University Press.

Watson, Lyall. 1983. *Lightning Bird*. Touchstone Books, New York.

Weiner, Norbert. 1950. *The Human Use of Human Beings*. London.

Wensel, Gene. 2000. Update. *Traditional Bowhunter* 3: 107-108.

Weyer, E. M. 1932. *The Eskimos: Their Environment and Folkways*. Yale University Press, New Haven, Ct.

Wilber, Ken. 1981. *Up From Eden*. Doubleday, New York.

Wilson, E. O. l975. *Sociobiology*. Harvard University Press, Cambridge, Ma.

Wynne, Elaine. 1987. "Storytelling," In: Louise C. Mahdi et al (Editors), *Betwixt and Between*, Crossroads, Chicago.

Xenophon. 1925. *On Hunting*. Loeb Classical Library.

Young, Jon and Tiffany Morgan. 2007. *Animal Tracking Basics*. Stackpole, Mechanicsburg, PA

Young, Jon, Ellen Haas and Evan_McGown. 2008. *Coyote's Guide to Connecting with Nature*. OLWlink Media, Shelton, Wa

Zencey, Eric. 1998. *Virgin Forest*. U. Georgia Press, Athens.

Appendix I
Resources

Wilderness Education/Tracking Schools and Classes

SACRED GROUND INTERNATIONAL
Contact: Tana Blackmore
Box 78
Pryor, MT 59066
406-245-6060

COYOTE TRAILS SCHOOL NATURE
Contact: Joe Kreuzman
P.O. Box 3557
Ashland, OR 97520

EARTH SKILLS
Contact: Jim Lowery
1113 Cougar Ct.
Frazier Park, CA 93225
661-245-0318
www.earthskills.com

KEEPING TRACK
Contact: Sue Morse
P. O. Box 444
Huntington, Vt 05462
802-434-7000
www.keepingtrack.org

A NATURALIST'S WORLD
Contact: Dr. Jim Halfpenny
P. O. Box 989
Gardiner, MT 59030
406-848-9458
www.tracknature.com

NATURE MAPPING
Contact: Karen Dvornich
University of Washington
Fish & Wildlife Unit
Box 357980
Seattle, WA 98195
206-543-6475

PRESCOTT COLLEGE
220 Grove Avenue
Prescott, AZ 86301
928-350-1102
www.prescott.edu

QUAIL SPRINGS
Contact: Warren Brush
P. O. Box 417
New Cuyama, CA 93245

REGENERATIVE DESIGN INSTITUTE
Integral Awareness Training Series
P. O. Box 923
Bolinas, CA 94924
415-868-9681
www.regenerativedesign.org

RIEKES CENTER
Bay Area Tracking Club
Contact: Ken Clarkson
3455 Edison Way
Menlo Park, CA 94025
650-364-2509
www.riekes.com

SAN DIEGO TRACKING TEAM
Contact: Barry Martin
P. O. Box 502345
San Diego, CA 92150-2345
760-715-4102
www.sdtt.org

SHIKARI TRACKING GUILD
80 N. Cabrillo Hwy
Box 150, Ste 2
Half Moon Bay, CA 94019
www.shikari.org

TATANKA MANI CAMP
Contact: Diane Marie
26971 SD HWY 89
Hot Springs, SD 57747
605-745-4119
www.tatankamani.org

TOM BROWN'S TRACKING SCHOOL
Contact: Tom Brown Jr.
P. O. Box 927
Watertown, NJ 08758
609-242-0350
www.trackerschool.com

TREE OF PEACE SOCIETY
326 Cook Road
Hogansburg, NY 13655
518-358-2641
treeofpeace@earthlink.net

VERMONT WILDERNESS SCHOOL
3 University Way Ste 5
Brattleboro, Vt 05301
802-257-8570
www.vermontwildernessschool.org

VICTOR WOOTENT
Bass/Nature Camp
Skyline Music
Lancaster, NH
603-586-7171
www.victorwooten.com

WHITE PINE PROGRAMS
Contact: Dan Gardoqui
330 Mountain Road
Cape Neddick, ME 03902
www.whitepineprograms.org

WILDERNESS AWARENESS SCHOOL
P. O. Box 5000, PMB-137
Duvall, WA 98019
425-788-1301
www.natureoutlet.com

WILDERNESS YOUTH PROJECT
5386 Hollister Ste D
Santa Barbara, CA 93111
805-964-8096
www.wyp.org

Tracking Organizations

CYBER TRACKER CONSERVATION
Contact: Louis Leibenberg
P. O. Box 1211
Noordhoek, Cape Town 7985
South Africa
www.cybertracker.org

INTERNATIONAL SOCIETY OF PROFESSIONAL TRACKERS
Contact: Del Morris
288 Brand Rd.
Santa Rosa, CA 95409
www.ispt.org

NATIONAL WILDLIFE FEDERATION
11100 Wildlife Center Drive
Reston, VA 20190-5362
1-800-822-9919
www.nwf.org

Mentoring and Rites of Passage

SCHOOL OF LOST BORDERS
P. O. Box 55
Big Pine, CA 93513
www.schooloflostborders.com

SACRED GROUND INTERNATIONAL
Contact: Tana Blackmore
406-245-6070

N.A.T.U.R.E.
Contact: Randall Eaton
www.randalleaton.com
513-244-2826

Hunter and Conservation Organizations

Those organizations with an asterisk have numerous chapters and affiliates, many with youth programs. Information is available at their websites on the internet.

- BUCKMASTERS AMERICAN DEER FOUNDATION*
- CAMP FIRE CLUB*
- DALLAS SAFARI CLUB
- DUCKS UNLIMITED *
- FOUNDATION FOR NORTH AMERICAN WILD SHEEP *
- HOUSTON SAFARI CLUB
- IZAAK WALTON LEAGUE OF AMERICA*
- MULE DEER FOUNDATION*
- NATIONAL RIFLE ASSOCIATION *
- NATIONAL TRAPPERS ASSOCIATION
- NATIONAL WILD TURKEY FEDERATION*
- NORTH AMERICAN GROUSE PARTNERSHIP*
- PHEASANTS FOREVER *
- QUAIL UNLIMITED
- ROCKY MOUNTAIN ELK FOUNDATION*
- RUFFED GROUSE SOCIETY*
- SAFARI CLUB INTERNATIONAL *
- SHIKAR SAFARI CLUB
- TEXAS WILDLIFE ASSOCIATION
- WHITETAILS UNLIMITED*
- WILDLIFE FOREVER
- WILDLIFE HABITAT COUNCIL

Other Hunting and Conservation Organizations

National Wildlife Federation has state affiliate organizations which typically include most of the hunting, fishing and conservation groups of the state. To locate affiliate offices, contact NWF at 1-800-822-9919 or visit their website at www.nwf.org. In Canada, contact Canadian Wildlife Federation for provincial affiliates at 1-800-563-WILD or visit www.cwf-fcf.org.

Hunter Education Classes

DIRECTORY OF ADMINISTRATORS OF HUNTER EDUCATION
These Are Employees of State/Provincial Wildlife Departments. They can direct youth to hunting organizations and provide information about hunter education classes as well as places to hunt. Visit the website of the International Hunter Education Association, www.ihea.org, for current Contact information.

Bowhunting Education

DELTA WATERFOWL FOUNDATION*
www.deltawaterfowl.org
1-888-987-3695 (US)
1-877-667-5656 (Canada)

WILD SHEEP FOUNDATION (FNAWS)*
www.wildsheepfoundation.org
307-527-6261

NORTH AMERICAN BOWHUNTING COALITION
www.nabowhuntingcoalition

POPE AND YOUNG CLUB
www.pope-young.org

CHRISTIAN BOWHUNTERS OF AMERICA*
www.christianbowhunters.org

NEW YORK BOWHUNTERS
www.newyorkbowhunters.com

WASHINGTON STATE BOWHUNTERS
www.wabowhunters.org

MICHIGAN TRADITIONAL BOWHUNTERS
www.mitradionalbow.com

MONTANA BOWHUNTERS
www.mtba.org

TRADITIONAL BOWHUNTERS OF BRITISH COLUMBIA
www.kics.bc.ca

INTERNATIONAL BOWHUNTERS ORGANIZATION*
www.ibo.net

BRITISH COLUMBIA WILDLIFE FEDERATION (BCWF)*
officeinfo@bcwf.bc.ca
604-291-9990

ONTARIO FEDERATION ANGLERS & HUNTERS*
ofah@ofah.org
705-748-6324

NATIONAL BOWHUNTING EDUCATION FOUNDATION
www.nbef.org

Gun Safety Courses

In Canada contact National Firearms Association at 780-439-1394 or visit www.nfa.ca. In the U.S., National Rifle Association teaches a number of approved courses in gun and hunter safety via their many affiliate groups throughout the country: 1-800-672-3888 or visit www.nra.org.

Permissions

Thanks to White Bison for permission to reprint several Meditations of the Elders. Anyone may subscribe to their daily meditations at www.whitebison.org.

Jimmy Carter, excerpts from *An Outdoor Journal.* Copyright © 1988 by Jimmy Carter. Reprinted with the permission of the University of Arkansas Press, www.uapress.com.

Copyright © 1996 by Gary Snyder from *A Place in Space: Ethics, Aesthetics, and Watersheds.* Reprinted by permission of the publisher.

By permission of Oxford University Press, Inc. excerpt from *A Sand County Almanac* by Aldo Leopold, copyright ©1948.

Excerpts from *A Testament to the Wilderness*, reprinted by permission of Daimon Zurich.

WILHELM, RICHARD; THE I CHING, OR BOOK OF CHANGES (THIRD EDITION). Copyright © 1950 by Bollingen Foundation Inc. New material copyright © 1967 by Bollingen Foundation. Copyright ©renewed 1977 by Princeton University Press. Reprinted by permission of Princeton University Press.

Excerpts from *Book of the Hunt: Initiations into Life of Honor*, reprinted by permission of Tom Dolph .

Excerpts from *Bushman Shaman,* reprinted by permission of Inner Traditions.

Excerpt from *Ceremony and Other Poems,* reprinted by permission of Houghton Mifflin.

Excerpt from "To a Contemporary Buckshooter" in CHICAGO POEMS by Carl Sandburg, copyright 1916 by Holt, Rinehart and Winston and renewed 1944 by Carl Sandburg, reprinted by permission of Houghton Mifflin Harcourt Publishing Company.

Excerpts from *Coming Home in the Pleistocene,* reprinted by permission of Island Press.

Cover Illustration by Jodi Bergsma, reprinted by permission of Bergsma Gallery

Excerpts from *Crossroads: The Quest for Contemporary Rites of Passage,*

Reprinted by permission of Open Court Publishing Company, a division of Carus Publishing Company, Peru, IL from *Crossroads: The Quest for Contemporary Rites of Passage* Edited by Louise Carus Mahdi, Nancy Gever Christopher, and Michael Meade, © 1996, Carus Publishing.

Excerpts from *Ingwe,* reprinted by permission of Elizabeth Powell

Excerpts from *Iron John,* Copyright © 1991 by Robert Bly from *Iron John.* Reprinted by permission of Robert Bly.

Excerpts from *King Warrior, Magician, Lover,* reprinted by permission of Dr. Robert Moore.

Excerpts from *Magical Child Matures, The Biology of Transcendence and Evolution's End* reprinted by permission of Joseph Chilton Pearce

Excerpts from *Men & the Water of Life,* reprinted by permission *of* Michael Meade

Permission to use granted by The University of Georgia Press from *Nature Madness* by Paul Shepard, copyright ©1982, Paul Shepard.

Excerpts from *Orion's Legacy*, reprinted by permission *of* Charles Bergman.

Excerpts from *Respect & Responsibility,* reprinted by permission of Helen Smith

Excerpts from *The Sacred Art of Hunting* permission granted by Willow Creek Press.

Excerpts from *Shared Spirits,* reprinted by permission of Dennis Olson.

Excerpts from *Southern Hunting in Black and White,* reprinted by permission of Princeton U Press

Excerpts from *Wild America interview of Peter John,* reprinted by permission of Marty Stouffer.

"The Earth is crying out for more young men to fall in love with her."

~ Randall L. Eaton, *The Sacred Hunt*

About the Author

DR. RANDALL L. EATON holds an international reputation in animal behavior, human evolution and wildlife conservation. He also has made contributions to history of science, philosophy, environmental ethics, mythology, men's studies and prehistoric art. He has held faculty positions in zoology, psychology, wildlife and humanities at several universities including U. Washington and U. Georgia, and held adjunct appointments at Evergreen State, UCLA, Oregon State and U. Alberta. He has published 115 articles in refereed journals including *Science, Evolution* and *J. Wildlife Management,* and his popular communications have appeared in *Sports Illustrated, Magical Blend* and *Utne Reader.* He has authored or edited 14 books, two of which received national awards. His film, "The Sacred Hunt," received 11 awards, and another of his productions, "Orca: The Sacred Whale," won first place among natural history broadcasts in 2000. Randall befriended wild orca whales in British Columbia, and discovered the first "talking" whale, a beluga who accurately imitated human speech and made every possible effort to communicate with humans. He carries a Sacred Pipe in the Cherokee Tradition.

Randall was a leader in the protection of spotted cats from illict poaching for the fur trade, and in the global protection of whales. He was at the center of a revision in zoo philosophy and goals to naturalism. He founded and edited an interdisciplinary journal, *Carnivore*, the editorial board of which included Nobel laureate Niko Tinbergen and Harvard's Edward O. Wilson. He has conducted programs and published with Pulitzer prize-winning poet Gary Snyder, Paul Shepard and Richard Nelson. In 2000, he was Conservationist Lecturer of the Year at North Carolina State, in 2002 the "Distinguished Visiting Scholar" at U. Alberta, and in 2007 the annual "Brooks Lecturer" at West Virginia University. He has lectured on sixty campuses in North America and delivered keynote addresses at major conservation conferences throughout North America and Europe.

A speech he gave was broadcast by CBS TV National News, and he has been interviewed on Fox TV National News, PBS TV's NOVA, CBS Radio National News, NPR, CBC and BBC Radio News worldwide. A frequent guest on radio and TV programs, Randall has been interviewed in the *Washington Post, LA Times, NY Times, Sports Illustrated and Saturday Review* among others.

Randall lectures widely, teaches workshops on the sacred hunt, and he mentors teens and adults in hunting. He is an Advisor to Conservation Force, Founder of The Sacred Hunt Society. He has two sons, Robb and Drake. The pine forest he planted as a boy in central Illinois prospers. He likes people.

Learn more at www.randalleaton.com.

Books and Audio Products from OWLink

These and other original titles are available for sale online at: http://owlinkmedia.com

Books

Coyote's Guide to Connecting with Nature
by Jon Young, Ellen Haas, and Evan McGown.
The essential guide for anyone seeking practical ways to build a dynamic relationship with nature. Forward by Richard Louv, author of *Last Child in the Woods*. This book offers the solution to nature deficit disorder!

Animal Tracking Basics by Jon Young and Tiffany Morgan. Stackpole Press.
Learn tried and true techniques that will immerse your senses in the natural world. Tracking opens a window into the ways of the animals and the stories of the landscape.

Exploring Natural Mystery by Jon Young.
An introduction to the essential foundational skills of the naturalist. Many people have called this a "life-changing" course because of the deep connections with the earth and wildlife that it promotes.

CD Sets

Seeing Through Native Eyes by Jon Young.
Nine hours of powerful storytelling offering insight into Wilderness Awareness, Tracking, Wandering, Community and Ecology, Survival, and the Language of the Birds. 8 CDs.

Advanced Bird Language – Reading the Concentric Rings of Nature
by Jon Young.
The universal language of nature is broadcast through sound, motion, and intent. Learn how to decipher the language of the birds, the sentinels of the forest, and step into a deeper realm of experience in nature. 8 CDs.

DVDs

The Sacred Hunt series, winner of 12 awards, produced by Randall L. Eaton, music by Ted Nugent, wildlife filming by Marty Stouffer. The Sacred Hunt (I): Hunting as a Sacred Path; The Sacred Hunt II: Rite of Passage; and, Respect and Responsibility: The Truth About Kids Who Hunt. Over 180 rave reviews From the *New York Post* to the *SF Examiner.*

To order, contact

OWLink Media

210 SE Cedar Hill Lane
Shelton, Washington 98584
www.owlinkmedia.com